Arctic Passage

Arctic

Passage

The Turbulent History of the Land and People of the Bering Sea 1697-1975

William R. Hunt

909.09

Charles Scribner's Sons
New York

Library of Congress Cataloging in Publication Data
Hunt, William R
  Arctic passage.
  Bibliography: p.
  Includes index.
  1. Bering Sea region—History. 2. Bering land
bridge. I. Title.
F951.H84   909'.09'6451   75-22370
ISBN 0-684-14466-2

Printed in the United States of America

To my parents

ACKNOWLEDGMENTS

This book grew out of the preparation for a course in North Pacific history which I offer at the University of Alaska. Discussions with students have kept my interest high over the years and a colleague, Phil Johnson, an engineer of broad scope, initially alerted me to the persistence of the human traffic between both shores of the Bering Strait. Contacts with marine scientists of the University of Alaska have been most stimulating and led to the fascinating personal experience of a Bering Sea winter cruise on the U.S. Coast Guard icebreaker *Northwind.* My thanks to the Coast Guard and to Marine Institute Director Dr. Donald W. Hood and to Dr. Peter McRoy.

Archivists and librarians of the Elmer E. Rasmuson Library of the University of Alaska, the Scott Polar Research Institute Library, and the Stefansson Collection of the Baker Library, Dartmouth College, have given me immeasurable assistance over the years and I am extremely grateful to them. Doris Nichols did a great deal of the typing of this manuscript with calmness and good humor, and I am also deeply appreciative of the help given by Margret Anderson, May Dollarhide, Joanne Floretta, Mary Hayes, Pat Little, Jeanne Rodey, and Judy

Stephenson. Students Jeanne Ostnes and John Halterman have also given valuable aid.

I have been fortunate in finding experts to read the manuscript: Dr. Michael Krauss and Dr. Claus-M. Naske of the University of Alaska went over the entire book and Dr. Peter Cornwall, also a colleague, corrected my chapter on World War II; Dr. John Bockstoce, curator of ethnology of the Whaling Museum of New Bedford, and Dr. Terence Armstrong of the Scott Polar Research Institute in Cambridge, brought their considerable knowledge to a reading of the text.

William Barr allowed me to read his translation of the Starokadom-skiy memoir and I am pleased to acknowledge my use of it.

The story of the Hudson's Bay Company's operation in Kamchatka is based in part on material from the company's archives and is published by permission of the Hudson's Bay Company.

As always, I owe much to my wife.

Finally, my thanks to Constance Schrader, a fine editor and thoughtful person.

CONTENTS

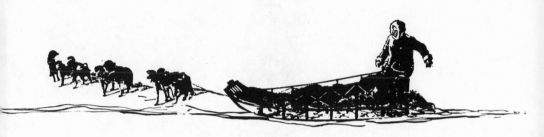

ILLUSTRATIONS

PREFACE

For thousands of years the continents of Asia and North America were united.[1] The first Americans walked through grass where the restless waters of the Bering Sea now form a stormy barrier, fog-bound and turbulent in summer and strewn with ice in winter. At some point in time after Asian peoples wandered from East Cape to what we now call the Seward Peninsula, the continents were severed and the land bridge disappeared. This happened over 10,000 years ago, and the waters rose to their present levels some 4,500 years ago. The severance of the land bridge remains one of nature's great mysteries.

The Asians who migrated across the land bridge were the ancestors of the American Indians. The time sequence is confusing and some conflicting archaeological evidence indicates man's presence in the Americas long prior to the believed migration period. There could, of course, have been other migrations at various times by several routes. However, there are remarkable linguistic connections between the peoples of the North and the American Southwest. Indians of the interior of Alaska speak Athabascan, a language which is closely related to that of the Navahos.

Scientists and other scholars will strive to learn more about the land bridge and the early migrations of peoples and animals. They will discover with more certainty whether the severance of the bridge was the result of a long, cataclysmic upheaval or of a continental drift, rather than the result of a submergence due to melting glacier ice. We do know that

the restless quest for food and man's enduring curiosity first brought him across the land bridge. The number of migrating people may not have been great—perhaps as few as 400 persons would have been enough to account for the sixteenth-century population of the Americas.

This is the story to be told. It opens with the migrants; then there is a gap in our certain knowledge of what occurred over thousands of years, until the modern era brings about a sudden lifting of the veil of obscurity. Once again, late in the seventeenth century, eager and hungry men traveled from west to east and marched with dramatic impact into the lives of an aboriginal maritime people. It is a story of a raw frontier and of cultural clashes—familiar and paralleling other frontier experiences in some respects; strange and foreign in other ways.

The Bering Sea frontier has not been an historical backwater, though its human drama has been little chronicled. Man's knowledge of the world's less traveled regions is subject to the degree of literary exposure these regions have had. Historians have not been particularly attentive to northern realms, but their silence is hardly a measure of historic vitality. Once Confucian scholars marveled that the brief, barbaric civilization developed by sixteenth-century Spanish and Portuguese adventurers could support such arrogance in its overseas representatives. Americans wince when their European cousins demean the New World's "short history." Similarly, western North Americans are dismayed at the obtuseness of the New Yorker, whose estimate of the vast region west of

the Mississippi River fixes on gun-slinging bad men and Indian wars.

What then should determine our appraisal of historical importance? In the eighteenth century, Kamchatka and Alaska were better known and much more the object of international attention than was California. Should wealth be the criterion? If so, it could be argued that few regions the size of the Bering Sea frontier have so richly abounded in the products men value. And what of the fascinating people who have coursed the waters of this region and populated its shores: the Kamchadals and Aleuts who stood in the way of the Russian advances; the fabulous exile, Count Benyowsky; the scientists Georg Steller and William Healy Dall; the hearty whalemen, sealers, and daring mariners of the American-Siberian trade; Tex Rickard of Nome's Northern Saloon who—with Jack "Doc" Kearns, Wilson Mizner, and Wyatt Earp—introduced boxing on the Bering Sea; Sheldon Jackson, who linked Siberia and Alaska by reindeer; George Kennan, and the other men of the Western Union Telegraph Expedition, who tried to tie the continents together with wire; the grim avenger, Captain James Waddell, of the Confederate Navy, who destroyed the Yankee whaling fleet; the mixed bag of English, Russian, and American sailors and adventurers—Captain James Cook, Otto von Kotzebue, and L. A. Zagoskin. These and others were Bering Sea pioneers. Their stories open a window on this most unique, and in many ways, mysterious region of the world.

CHRONOLOGY

26,000–	
8,000 B.C.	The land bridge forms.
8,600 B.C.	Migrations of the first Americans.
8,000–	
2,500 B.C.	The land bridge closes.
1697	Conquest of Kamchatka.
1725–1741	Expeditions of Vitus Bering.
1778–1779	James Cook's explorations of the Bering Sea.
1799	Russian American Company organized.
1805	First conservation of mammal resources.
1845	Yankee whalers begin hunting in the Bering Sea.
1854–1855	Crimean War in Kamchatka.
1865	Civil War and the *Shenandoah* cruise.
1865–1867	Western Union Telegraph Expedition.
1867	Purchase of Alaska.
1870	Pribilof Island lease granted to the Alaska Commercial Company.
1875	Russian-Japanese agreement on fisheries.
1879	Northeast Passage navigated by A. E. Nordenskiöld.
1892	Siberian reindeer taken to Alaska.
1898	Gold discovery at Cape Nome.
1898	First gold prospecting in Siberia.
1886–1911	Fur-seal controversy.
1900–1934	Nome to Siberia trade.
1907	Northwest Passage navigated by Roald Amundsen.
1922	Soviets gain control of Kamchatka and northeast Siberia.
1928	Schools established in northeast Siberia.
1930	Japanese begin fishing in Bristol Bay.
1941–1945	Ferrying Lend-Lease planes from Alaska to Siberia.
1942–1943	Aleutian Campaign of World War II.
1950	Building of DEW Line stations.
1959	Alaska becomes a state.
1970	First commercial air flight from Alaska to Siberia.
1973	Eskimos from Siberia and Alaska meet on the sea ice of the Bering Strait.

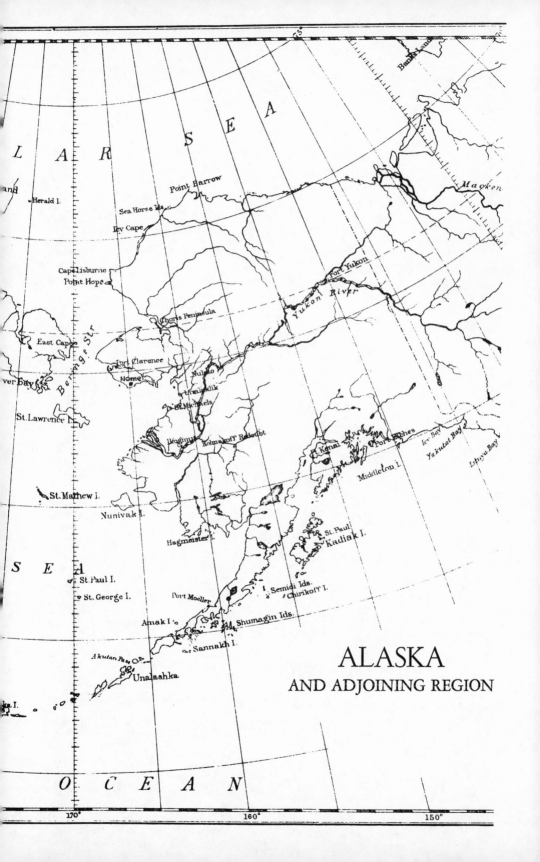

ALASKA
AND ADJOINING REGION

Arctic
Passage

1 — CONQUEST AND EXPLORATION

"If you could enjoy these advantages at home, what made you take so much trouble to come to us? You seem to want several things which we have; we, on the contrary, are satisfied with what we possess, and never come to you to seek anything!" [1] This reaction of the native peoples of southern Kamchatka to the Russian traders who invaded their lands was reported by Sven Waxell of the second Kamchatka expedition. He witnessed the wonder of an aboriginal nation about the marvelous civilization whose benefits were to be bestowed upon them. Other races in America, Africa, Asia, and Oceania shared the same doubts when the expansionist nations of the West pushed into their domains in the eighteenth century.

The question, of course, included the answer. The "several things which we have" brought the Russians to their Pacific frontier, as well as British and American adventurers to the Pacific Ocean frontier of North America. In Asia and America the lure was fur wealth—a lure that culminated in conquest, exploitation, and subjection. Western nations spoke of an "opening" of frontiers, a true expression of an egocentric point of view. Equally, the movement was a "closing," an irrevocable disruption, a destruction of technologically less powerful people and their traditions. Waxell's summation of the impact of Russian ways on the Kamchadals could be applied as well to American natives. "They showed themselves obsequious to the domineering, stubborn and contemptuous to any who sought to deal with them gently, and remarkably brave and obstinate in the stubborn resistance they put up with their primitive weapons." [2]

The Russian subjection of Siberian natives did not begin with the

I

work of the two Kamchatka expeditions headed by Vitus Bering, though these expeditions accelerated the process. In 1581 the Cossack Ermak led his followers across the Urals for their first plunders in the vast eastern territories. Gradually, over the next 100 years, the Cossacks pushed on to exploit the fur riches and pacify territory for the Moscovite Empire. Southeastern advances along the Amur River were checked by the powerful Manchu forces of China, but there was no concerted resistance north of the Amur. Following the great rivers, the Ob, Irtysh, Yenisei, and Lena, the Cossacks subdued the primitive natives who stood in their way. Tribute in furs was exacted mercilessly. To resist was to be decimated. Advances to the far northeast were slowed by the lack of easy river access and the forbidding climate. The Kamchatka Peninsula was not explored until 1696. A year later, Cossack Vladimir Atlasov led a party of 100 soldiers, conveyed by reindeer, to Kamchatka's east coast, where the Russians encountered Kamchadals for the first time. Soon after this, fur traders established themselves in Kamchatka to plunder and oppress the natives until they were driven to a desperate resistance. In 1731 the natives rose against their oppressors, but their rebellion was savagely crushed within a year.

It was part of the assignment of the second Kamchatka expedition, officially called the Great Northern Expedition, to compile information on the people and resources of northeastern Asia. Much of this work was done by Georg Steller prior to his 1741 voyage with Bering to America, and by a young Russian scientist, Stepan Petrovich Krasheninnikov. Krasheninnikov, only twenty-five years old in 1737 when he arrived in Kamchatka, did the major portion of the investigation and, with the help of Steller's notes, produced his study, *Explorations of Kamchatka*, which was published by the Russian Academy of Sciences in 1755. This book has long been the classic source on the Kamchadals of southern Kamchatka and, to a lesser extent, on the Koriak and Chukchi peoples inhabiting the regions farther north. In the *Explorations of Kamchatka* we get an invaluable picture of the recently subjugated peoples of the Bering Sea frontier and, indirectly, an insight into the attitudes of their Russian overlords toward the region and its inhabitants.

Krasheninnikov was not involved in the most exciting assignment of the expedition, the attempt to discover America from the west. His task was to provide a careful assessment of Kamchatka upon which the government could base its developmental policies. His temperament was well suited to the task. He was disposed to report the sober truth as he saw it, without exaggeration or inclinations to optimistic promotion. In weighing the advantages and disadvantages of Kamchatka, his report was balanced and careful. "The country has neither grain nor livestock. It is subject to frequent earthquakes, floods and storms. The only diversions are to gaze on towering mountains whose summits are eternally covered with snow, or, if one lives along the sea, to listen to the crashing of the waves and observe the different species of sea animals." [3] Considering this, Krasheninnikov commented, "it would seem more appropriate for this country to be inhabited by wild animals than by human beings." [4] On the other hand, pure air, healthy water, the absence of diseases, a climate neither excessively hot or cold, make the country "no less fit to be lived in than other countries which may have an abundance of other things, but are exposed to all these ills and dangers." [5]

Although Kamchatka might be "fit to be lived in," it did not attract large numbers of European Russians. A small number of colonists from other parts of Siberia were settled there among the natives, soldiers, and government officials, and plans were laid for a self-supporting agricultural economy. But attempts to achieve such an economy were sporadic and largely unsuccessful. Economic development remained a vision of government planners. Yet the region did provide riches for a few Russians who reaped profits from its most obvious resources—its people and its fur-bearing animals. Both were exploited shamelessly by mercenary interests. In time, the Kamchadals lost their identity as a distinct people, while the relentless hunting of sables, foxes, and other fur-bearing animals drastically reduced their numbers. Only the discovery of new fur resources to the west saved the land animals of Kamchatka from a total extermination.

The Kamchadals were a free, independent people before the Russians conquered them. Like that of their Eskimo neighbors in Alaska their social organization was loose and unstratified. No rulers or chiefs were recognized, though men esteemed for their wisdom and experience were highly regarded.

Russians could appreciate some of the skills exhibited by natives—hunting and dog-sled driving in particular—but generally considered them barbaric and contemptible. "They are filthy and disgusting," wrote Krasheninnikov, "they never wash their hands or faces, nor do they cut their fingernails, they eat from the same bowls as their dogs and never wash them. They all reek of fish and smell like eider ducks." [6] Different standards of personal hygiene have always formed a barrier between peoples, though many Siberian travelers observed little distinction between Cossack and native habits of cleanliness.

Kamchatka's great wealth was in the numbers of fur-bearing animals to be found there. The dense, glossy pelts of foxes were esteemed in the fur trade and the sables, because of their size and beauty, were considered superior to those hunted elsewhere in Siberia. These animals as well as hares, marmots, ermines, bears, wolverines, and weasels were caught in traps, poisoned, or shot with a bow and arrow. Kamchadals were delighted when Cossacks offered a single knife in exchange for eight sable pelts and a hatchet for eighteen skins. "It is quite true," Krasheninnikov reported, "that when Kamchatka was first conquered, there were some agents who made as much as thirty-thousand roubles in one year." [7]

All the natives of Kamchatka and northeastern Siberia, except for the Koriak reindeer herdsmen of the interior, used dogs for transport during the winter. Besides hauling sleds, dogs assisted in the hunt of mountain sheep and other land animals, and their skins provided a wide variety of clothing. Food for the dogs was easily obtained, consisting, primarily, of the salmon which abounded in Kamchatka's rivers. Great quantities of fish were taken in the summer and dried for winter use as dog food.

Marine mammals were also hunted. Seals were taken off the coast in winter and from the rivers and estuaries in summer. Natives clubbed sleeping seals on land and harpooned them in the water. Seal skins yielded material for boots and clothing, their oil provided lighting and heat for native dwellings; their flesh and blubber were important sources of food and were sometimes preserved for later use by smoking. Other mammals could only be taken at sea. These included the sea lion, fur seal, sea otter, whale, and, in northern waters, the walrus. All these mammals contributed to the native economy to varying degrees. The Chukchi's primary food source was the whale, which they hunted in the European manner, harpooning the beasts at sea from large boats and towing the whales ashore for butchering. Kamchadals, on the other hand, did not usually venture out to sea to hunt whales, but made good use of any that washed ashore.

In Siberia, as in Alaska, Russians paid only scant attention to native ceremonies and beliefs. Christians could only dismiss native beliefs as

Queen of Siberian Eskimos, Whalen, Siberia.
University of Alaska Archives, Charles Bunnell Collection

gross superstitions and deplore their barbarity. Most Russians assumed that Bering Sea natives did not believe in God and had difficulty understanding the aboriginals' conceptions of the supernatural. Krasheninnikov, however, conceded that the Kamchadals believed in God, but found their idea of God and notions of good and evil very strange. His assessment of the native character was not commendatory. "Their pleasure consists of idleness and of the satisfaction of their natural desires. They arouse their lust with songs, dances and love tales which they are accustomed to relate. Boredom, responsibilities, troubles, are considered the greatest misfortunes which can befall them; and to guard against these, there is nothing they will not do, even sometimes at the risk of their lives. Their guiding principle is that it is better to die than not to live in comfort, or to be unable to satisfy their desires. Thus they used to have recourse to suicide as a last resort to find happiness." [8]

It is hard to determine the basis on which the young Russian reached such curious conclusions. He does not illustrate the great fear of boredom nor the abhorrence of discomfort he seemed to have discovered, and one suspects that such tendencies might have been more manifest among the idle nobles of eighteenth-century St. Petersburg than the Kamchadals. As for the natives' suicidal propensities, there is evidence that this was a result of Russian oppression rather than an ingrained cultural trait. The only instances Krasheninnikov cites were the aftermath of battles with Cossacks when, after realizing that further resistance would be futile, Kamchadals hurled themselves into the midst of the enemy "with weapons in . . . hands so as not to die without avenging" themselves.[9] As late as 1740, Kamchadal warriors, after a futile rebellion, killed all their women and threw themselves into the sea from a cliff where they had taken refuge. Krasheninnikov himself relates that suicide "became so common among them when they were conquered by the Russians, that the Court sent orders from Moscow to put a halt to it." [10] No one seems to have considered that the Kamchadals might have had good and rational reasons for preferring suicide to falling into the hands of victorious Cossacks heated by battle.

Other judgments of Kamchadals reached by Krasheninnikov were equally derogatory. "They have no knowledge either of riches, of honor, nor of glory; consequently they know neither greed, ambition nor pride; all their desires are aimed to living in an abundance of everything they want, satisfying their passions, their hatred, and their vengeance." [11]

According to the curious reasoning of the young Russian, the ignorance of the Kamchadals caused them to avoid some vices and indulge in others. Krasheninnikov's conclusions were never as clear as his prejudices. The more closely one examines such statements, the more confusing they become. Using the same depictions of character traits, a sympathetic observer might have presented the motives in quite a favorable light, though Krasheninnikov cannot be condemned for reflecting the attitudes of his time.

Krasheninnikov found the Kamchadals extremely boorish. "They never doff their hats nor bow to anyone. They are so stupid in their discourse that only in their power of speech do they differ from animals." [12] Their religion mystified the Russian scientist: "They believe that the earth, sky, air, water, land, mountains and forests are inhabited by spirits whom they fear and honor more than their god." Sacrifices were made to these spirits and idols were kept in their dwellings, "and rather than fearing their god, they curse him for all their misfortunes." [13]

Krasheninnikov's notes on native customs are extensive, valuable records which seem to have gained much by his use of Steller's work. Steller had a great curiosity concerning native beliefs and he had the patience to satisfy it by means of extensive questioning. When the German scientist inquired about the Kamchadals' belief in a supreme being he did not depend upon a handful of informants, but put the same question to more than a hundred Kamchadals. Together, both men contributed to a monumental and timely work, the record of a people whose culture was soon to be overwhelmed. A few years later it would have been impossible to compile such a thorough description of the doomed nation. In 1741 the first Russian priests were sent out to convert the heathen and stamp out what remained of their traditional beliefs. What the Cossacks had begun with firearms was completed by the churchmen.

The experience of the Russians with the natives of northeastern Siberia, and particularly those of Kamchatka, set a pattern for the relationships of the Europeans with American natives of the Bering Sea. Every stage of the impact on the American natives was foreshadowed by the colonization of Kamchatka. It was as if a blueprint for American expansion had been laid down on the basis of the earlier experience. Actually, of course, developments on the frontier had little to do with planning. Declarations of fiscal and humanitarian policies for Siberia and

Alaska were issued from St. Petersburg often enough, but these were not realistically implemented or enforced. In the absence of firm control, initiative was left to opportunists who acted to fulfill their immediate needs. Ruthless exploitation, slavery, and genocide were the results of a lust for quick profits which could not be checked by a vacillating, largely indifferent government. Helpless peoples and the immense marine resources of the Bering Sea were wasted over decades of bloody, greedy, and mindless efforts launched from Kamchatka. The Bering Sea frontier was thrown wide open to lawlessness in the eighteenth century, and became tradition in the form of a strong and continuous force.

The scientists who observed the spreading Russian influence in Kamchatka had come as members of the most ambitious expedition ever launched by a western nation up to that time. Peter the Great, a fierce titan, and something of a genius, who had forced the Russians to look to the West and at modernity, determined that the geographic mysteries of his eastern realm had to be solved. According to legend, Peter had been embarrassed on his European travels when geographers queried him about the extent of northeastern Siberia. Some map makers indicated that Siberia and North America were connected, while others showed a severance. But for some careless record keeping by seventeenth-century officials, Peter could have demonstrated the true geographic situation without difficulty because a successful circumnavigation of East Cape (now Cape Dezhnev) had been made in 1648 and, strangely enough, had then been forgotten. Semen Ivanof Dezhnev voyaged from the mouth of the Kolyma River to the Anadyr River to accomplish one of the more outstanding geographic discoveries of the century; yet because there was no follow-up of his findings, his achievements were not brought to lasting notice until a century later.[14] Thus, in 1725 Peter appointed Vitus Bering, a Dane with a distinguished record in the Russian navy, as commander of the expedition. Just five weeks before the czar died, he issued instructions to Bering:

1. You are to construct at Kamchatka one or two boats with decks.
2. You are to proceed in these along the coast which extends to the north and which seems, in all probability (since we do not know where it ends), to be part of America.
3. With this in view you are to try to find where it is joined to America, and to reach some city in European possession, and to inquire what it is

called, and to make note of it, and to secure exact information and to mark this on a map and then to return home.[15]

Mark this on a map and then return home! Simple instructions indeed, but the task to be accomplished was a prodigious one. Transport was the major problem. There were no roads in eastern Siberia, yet men, provisions, and equipment for this major venture had to be taken to Kamchatka, where the discovery ships were then to be constructed. Hundreds of men and animals were to wear themselves out accomplishing this awesome task, but Peter's visionary scheme had to be carried through. Never mind the cost and the years of effort: the work must be done. There could be practical benefits too. Peter was aware of all the British and Dutch voyages in quest of a Northern Passage from the Atlantic to the Pacific Oceans. Perhaps the Russians could be successful in finding the passage from the Pacific Ocean side. This would be a great triumph. Great glory and possibly the domination of an important trade route would be the results of such a discovery.

The initial party of the first Kamchatka expedition left St. Petersburg in late January 1725. Several minor officers and technicians were selected on the way to the Siberian coast, including a surgeon, a geodesist, a quartermaster, four carpenters and three mechanics to build ships and boats, a priest, navigator, shipmaster, and clerk, plus soldiers and sailors. The men traveled across the Central Siberian Plains, floated down the Ob, Ketya, Yenisei, Tunguska, and Ilim Rivers and wintered in Ilimsk, about halfway across the great Asian continent. They built fourteen boats and eighteen barges for cargo and equipment and, in the following month of May, after many hardships, arrived in Yakutsk.

From Yakutsk they traveled in three companies, each of the principal officers heading the detachments, and arrived in Okhotsk in October. An early winter caused the death of many of the 200 horses, and so much suffering existed among the men that a mutinous spirit developed. With winter approaching, it was vitally important to build storage houses and living quarters as quickly as possible. Men deserted when they were not paid and some refused to search for the late-arriving party under Martin Spanberg, one of Bering's lieutenants. This company of Spanberg had over 200 men and much of the essential equipment for the expedition. The early winter had come upon them so swiftly that their boats froze fast in one of the rivers. They had to construct one hundred sleds to pull the cargo on to the village of Okhotsk.

Months of anxious effort and adversity passed. It was a constant struggle to maintain progress. But Bering and his officers kept the work going and the men in line. Finally on April 4, 1728, the keel of the new boat was laid—the ship was to be sixty feet long with a beam of twenty feet—and on June 8, it was christened the *St. Gabriel*. Sealing tar had to be manufactured and this caused a month's delay before the *St. Gabriel*, with its forty-four officers and crew, was ready to sail into the unknown. Bering's men had done their work well.

Once at sea, Bering was in a more familiar element. He voyaged north cautiously in the fog-bound waters, making a wary reach toward the top of the world, vigilant, prudent, plodding. Land was kept in sight almost the entire voyage, since the primary objective of the exploration was to ascertain if the continents were connected.

Bering stopped for fresh water at a bay he named Transfiguration. Twenty-two barrels of water were brought on board. Huts were seen but no people. The next morning eight Chukchi native men in a small boat approached the *St. Gabriel*, now out to sea. One of the natives was finally persuaded to go aboard. He told Bering through an interpreter "that there was an island in the sea on which live some of our people, but I know of no other islands or lands." [16] Several days later the *St. Gabriel* came upon the large island which Bering named St. Lawrence. Huts were seen here, too, but again no people, at least none who allowed themselves to be seen.

Bering reached latitude sixty-five degrees, thirty minutes, passed the narrow strait named for him, and called his officers for a decision. The question was whether to proceed farther north or to return, satisfied that the *St. Gabriel* "had reached and passed the most easterly point of Chukchi land." [17]

Spanberg, the second officer on this expedition, suggested that "after we have gone on the course we are on until the sixteenth of this month, and if by that time we are not able to reach sixty-six degrees, we should then in God's name, turn about and betimes seek shelter and harbor on the Kamchatka River whence we came, in order to save men and boat." [18]

Lieutenant Alexsei Chirikov was more daring and suggested,

As we have no positive information as to the degree north latitude
Europeans have ever reached in the Arctic Ocean on the Asiatic side, we

cannot know with certainty whether America is really separated from Asia unless we touch at the mouth of the Koluima, or at least the ice, because it is well known that there is always drift ice in the Arctic Ocean. Therefore, it seems to me that according to your instructions we ought to sail without questioning—unless we are hindered by ice, or the coast turns to the west—But should the land continue still farther to the north, it would be necessary on the twenty-fifth of this month to look for winter quarters in this neighborhood.[19]

Bering listened to Spanberg. On the sixteenth of August the order was given to turn back. The *St. Gabriel* had reached latitude sixty-seven degrees, eighteen minutes, longitude one hundred ninety-three degrees, seven minutes east from Greenwich—well beyond the point by which he could determine that Asia was not connected with America, if visibility had been clearer. On the following morning, Bering discovered and named the Diomede Islands and would then have been the first to see mainland America only a short distance away. But the weather was foggy. The day of this discovery would come four years later, in 1732, when assistant navigator I. Fedorov and geodesist M. Gvozdez took the *St. Gabriel* north and discovered the American coast opposite Cape Chukotsk. The Russians did not land, and thus did not gain full credit for determining that North America lay just across the Bering Strait from Siberia.

In 1729 Bering voyaged into the Bering Sea once more but made no notable discoveries. In July he set out across Siberia for St. Petersburg, arriving in the Russian capital on March 1, 1730. He gave Empress Catherine the following report:

> On the fifteenth of August we came to latitude sixty-seven degrees, eighteen minutes, and I concluded that according to all indications the instruction of the emperor of glorious and immortal memory had been carried out. I based my conclusion on the fact that there was no more land to the north, nor did any land join the Chukchi or East Capes, and so I turned back. Had I gone farther and met with head winds it would have been impossible to return that summer; and to winter in these regions was out of the question, because there are no forests, and the people are not under Russian jurisdiction but do as they please.[20]

Bering was criticized for not conducting his first expedition in a more scientific way. Some argued that he should have listened to Chirikov's advice instead of Spanberg's, because by the sixteenth of August he did not really demonstrate that the two continents were separated. He still had at least forty more days of ice-free navigation in those northern waters. He should have sailed onward until sighting ice before turning back. He was at fault for not venturing to the full limits of continued safe exploration. This criticism was not unreasonable; yet Bering's achievements were considerable when one bears in mind the difficulties involved. Launching a discovery ship in distant Siberia and opening the region to development were not mean accomplishments. Bering had then successfully navigated an unknown sea, passed into the Bering Strait, discovered the Diomedes and St. Lawrence Island, ascertained the southern tip of Kamchatka Peninsula, and charted portions of the Bering Sea for the first time.

In St. Petersburg Bering submitted several recommendations to the senate. He called for a voyage of investigation to America and for the opening of trade between the two continents. He thought that it would be advantageous for the empire to establish a sea route from Kamchatka to Japan and thereby open another trade route. He suggested, too, a charting of the northern regions of Siberia from the Ob to the Yenisei Rivers and from there to the Lena River. Bering's suggestions were enthusiastically received. Thanks to the growing prominence of the Academy of Science, Bering would carry scientists with him. The first scientific investigations of eastern Siberia and northwestern America would be the result of Bering's second expedition, officially known as the Great Northern Expedition.

The three-part exploratory program commissioned by the Russian Senate began in early 1733. Several unsatisfactory attempts under the command of various lieutenants were made to survey and map the Arctic coast of Siberia as the first part of the project. Spanberg, who was second in command under Bering on the first Kamchatka expedition, com-manded the second part responsible for charting the Kurile Islands. Spanberg made three voyages to the Kuriles, in the course of which he surveyed these stepping-stone islands to the rich kingdom of Japan. During all this time, Bering, as commander-in-chief of the entire program of five hundred and forty-six men, received increasing criticism from the senate because his progress was considered slow. Bering offered many excuses but was castigated for alleged neglect. At one point, to prod him a bit, his supplementary pay was stopped.

Under clouds of distrust and the questioning of his competence, Bering set sail on the Okhotsk Sea in 1741 for his second expedition in search of land east of Kamchatka—the third part of the senate commission. Bering commanded the *St. Peter* while Chirikov captained the *St. Paul*. Two other smaller cargo ships collided and sank before they could reach the eastern side of the Kamchatka Peninsula. The cargoes were lost—the first ominous disaster of the voyage. Two years' supply of food and materials were reduced to five months' rations.

The second disaster was one of an ill decision. At Avacha Bay on the southeast side of Kamchatka, the officers plotted their course in relation to Joseph Delisle's map, specially drawn for Bering's expedition, ignoring the 1732 sighting of the American land mass on Bering Strait by Fedorov and Gvozdez. The fateful decision was made to steer, not due east from the peninsula, but southeast in search of Gama Land, a mythical land mass which many map makers had placed in the North Pacific. In sailing southeast in search of the mythical Gama Land, the ships moved well south of the Aleutian chain and the Alaskan Peninsula before they changed course for the northeast. Precious days of the short northern summer were wasted.

Louis Delisle de la Croyère, assigned to the expedition as astronomer, was the half-brother of Joseph Delisle. Joseph was the younger brother of Guillaume Delisle, the most distinguished map maker of the early eighteenth century. Once again, the persuasion of authority overwhelmed good sense. Delisle urgently recommended the search for Gama Land even though the navigators wanted to steer east: "I am confident that the lands seen by Juan de Gama should be where they are seen on the map," Delisle once stated positively to the senate.[21] No doubt Croyère maintained the identical position on board, especially with his half-brother's map spread magnificently across Bering's table. Delisle further maintained that "the shores seen by Gama, which I have located opposite Kamchatka, are perhaps a part of a large coast contiguous to America, joining it north of California at the entrance discovered by d'Aguillar." [22] He suggested that land could be reached within, at most, 600 leagues by using either eastern or northeastern routes.

Lieutenant Sven Waxell, a member of the discussion which set the course, wrote later: "On the basis of the new information given by this map we agreed that we ought to touch at Juan de Gama's Land." [23] Waxell wrote further of the "unfounded and fake map." [24] But it was too late. He learned how false it was only after the voyage.

Chirikov felt that the decision was made in accordance with instructions of the senate to search for the islands east of Kamchatka. Gama Land was generally understood as an island southeast of the peninsula. This, coupled with the fact that the Aleutian Islands were entirely unknown and were not recorded on any map, implied that Gama Land was the only island in that area.

On May 4, 1741, it was decided to sail southeast by east to latitude forty-six degrees north, unless land was found before. Both ships sailed over the waters where Gama Land was supposed to be, then altered their courses when it became obvious that they had been duped by fantastic cartography. Soon fog made it impossible for the two ships to remain in contact. Valuable time was wasted as the two captains groped for each other before each abandoned the effort and sailed alone to the east.

Chirikov was the first to see signs of land in the air and on the water. Seals, sea gulls, and driftwood appeared and on the 15th of July he sighted land in latitude fifty-five, approximately at the lower tip of the Alexander Archipelago, near the present panhandle or southeastern region of Alaska. Rain, fog, and rocky shores prevented Chirikov from sending out a successful landing party. Finally, two days after sighting the coast, the young mate, Abram Dementief, led ten armed sailors in a longboat into a bay in search of fresh water. They did not return that night. A search party was sent in great anxiety. The following morning when two boats approached the *St. Paul*, Chirikov ordered the crew to prepare to get underway. Only when the boats came closer did he realize the men were natives and that Dementief and the others had been seized and probably murdered.

He cruised about the area, reluctant to leave but knowing the choice was inevitable. No trace of the lost sailors was seen. A council of officers agreed that resources and weather conditions made it impossible to spend further time in search of the crew members and that the *St. Paul* should continue its voyage back to Kamchatka. The *St. Paul* sailed southwest through the foggy days of August. Land at the top of the Kenai Peninsula was sighted on the first day of the month, then left behind as the ship coursed southward down into the middle of the Gulf of Alaska to about the fifty-third parallel. After a month of Pacific squalls and foggy skies, Chirikov spotted Unalaska of the Fox Islands. Later, toward the middle of September, the fog made navigation difficult. After anchoring one night in the fog, Chirikov found the next morning that he was in a huge bay of a good-sized island, probably Atka Island far out in the Aleutians. The terrain was volcanic, mountainous, apparently uninhabitable. But while waiting for the right wind, the Russians were approached by seven natives in seven kayaks and given fresh water in seal bladders. But the natives would not go aboard ship. Chirikov described them as muscular men resembling the Tartars in features, wearing no beards, but sporting multicolored hats of thin boards and feathers of birds, some with bone carvings attached to their headdress.

Chirikov continued a zigzag course setting north and south to test the existence of land. The incessant fog prevented accurate position taking. The captain inferred that since he came to land when he sailed north, and only water when he turned south, that the land to the north must be the coastline of America. It was, in actuality, the chain of the Aleutian Islands.

The last land Chirikov saw of the new world was the island of Attu, the last segment of the Aleutian chain. During all this time the strength of the crew was fast diminishing. They could not repair the ragged sails that flapped above them. Constant exposure to harsh wind, rain, and snow tore the canvas to pieces. Excessive moisture, cold, thirst, and hunger depleted the physical resources of every man aboard.

But even more serious was the dreaded disease of scurvy which now ravaged the sailors. It weakened the capillaries with resultant hemorrhages into the tissues, caused the bleeding of gums, and loosened the teeth. Anemia and gradual general debility often followed.

On the 21st of September, Chirikov was restricted to his berth as a result of scurvy. One by one the men died. First a sailor, then a lieutenant, the ship's constable, a midshipman. Finally, the astronomer of the mission, Croyère, died on October 8, the very day the *St. Paul* reached Avacha Bay, Kamchatka. Of the nearly eighty men who were aboard the *St. Paul* when it left Avacha Bay five months earlier, twenty-one were lost.

Meanwhile, things were even worse for the men of the *St. Peter*. Their voyage was a disaster; yet it had its glories, because one of the men aboard was a keen-eyed scientist, Georg Wilhelm Steller.

2 — FIRST SCIENTIST
OF THE BERING SEA

Few occasions in history have presented a scientist with the opportunities given to the young Bavarian Georg Wilhelm Steller, who was appointed to the second Kamchatka expedition. His were the first trained eyes to view a vast region hitherto veiled to Western knowledge. He was the first scientist to describe the teeming mammal life of the Bering Sea, the first to observe the customs of the aboriginal peoples of the Aleutian Islands and the Alaskan coast, and the first to examine the flora and fauna of Alaska's islands and mainland. It was a prodigious chance which the youthful German did not misuse, despite the frustrations and disasters of the Bering voyage and his own fiery impatience and rude arrogance. At every opportunity he classified scores of unknown plants. He gave us the only full description of the now extinct giant manatee, the sea cow, and he made careful notes on northern seals, the sea otter, various birds, foxes, and other animals. Incredibly, for all his accomplishments, his actual time on Alaska soil was confined to a mere ten-hour period, though he had months to investigate Bering Island where so many of his shipmates breathed their last.

For all the praise we might give Steller in retrospect, he returned from the voyage a disappointed man—though, characteristically, he blamed others for failing to support his activities. "I reappear with few useful discoveries, through no fault of mine but because the Captain Commander kept his promise so poorly that he only let me see the American mainland from a distance and was finally persuaded at last to put me ashore on three islands, though only for a few hours, without any assistance, like a malefactor, and with great reluctance and many sarcastic remarks not encouraging to my honest zeal." [1] Not unjustly, Steller felt that the expedition should have been prepared for a wintering in Alaska or the islands so that a second summer's season could have been devoted to scientific work. Though he blamed Bering's resentment at having had to spend so much time in Siberia for the quick departure, the reason—as he made clear elsewhere in the diary—was due to a lack of provisions necessary to wintering.

Squabbling among explorers was not an uncommon occurrence, particularly on expeditions haunted by failure. The Great Northern Expedition suffered from more than its share of the hardships, frustrations, and abrasive personal differences—factors that led to bitter divisions of opinion, acrimony, and recriminations. A firm leader who clearly delineates the roles of his subordinates and acts forcibly to restrain their rivalries is essential to a harmonious voyage. Unfortunately, Vitus Bering lacked the necessary decisiveness. As a result, the relations between Georg Steller and the Russian naval officers hindered and clouded the endeavors of the expedition. Steller acted as ship physician as well as the expedition scientist and did not command the respect of the officers in either position. Undoubtedly much of the blame must be attributed to Steller himself. Judging from his own diary of the expedition he was overbearing, arrogant, and supremely contemptuous of his fellows. The officers responded to his lofty disdain for their knowledge and capabilities by thwarting his efforts, mocking his judgment, and ignoring his advice. While treating the scientist kindly, Bering did nothing to settle the growing disagreeableness. The commander was too worn out himself to restrain either Steller or his officers. Steller was overly sensitive and a man of colossal ego, yet clearly talented, capable, and deserving of recognition. But it seemed to him, whether true or not, that "no proposal of mine, not even the most insignificant, was considered worthy of being accepted, because those in command were too much imbued with their own wisdom, until the disastrous end and a just dispensation exposed their unfortunately too naked vanity." [2]

Steller's poor relations with the Russian officers began before the voyage commenced. He quarreled with them in Siberia just as he had quarreled with his fellow German scientists and government officials. The cause of his ire was usually the same: colleagues did not show him enough respect, i.e. they neither consulted him duly nor followed his advice when he tendered it. Steller was not a reticent man and considered it quite proper to send reports containing his complaints about colleagues on to St. Petersburg, a habit that earned him the hate and distrust of all. He also offered advice to the senate in St. Petersburg on matters of commerce, agriculture, navigation, and military strategy, while the church officials of the Synod heard from him on the education and conversion of the Siberian natives. Steller's advice was generally good but was unheeded because of the form of presentation and his lack of authority.

Once on shipboard, the expedition officers had the opportunity to put the unpleasant young German in his place. Frequently enough he was reminded that he was not a seaman, hence could not really understand a particular problem. Nothing was more sure to arouse Steller's ire, and he could not tolerate "the brazen and very vulgar snubs by the officers, who coarsely and sneeringly rejected all well-founded, timely admonishings and propositions." [3] Steller censured the officers' arrogance and thought he knew its origin: "It should be stated here that during the 10 years in Siberia, when every one lived as he pleased and demanded and received so much homage from the ignorant mob as suited his notions, the greater number of our officers completely forgot themselves and, through habit, fell into the delusion of being infallible." [4]

Steller was not always right. When Bering finally abandoned the search for Gama Land or Company Land, said to lie southeast of Kamchatka, and altered his course to the north, the scientist was incensed because his sightings of seaweed, gulls, and ducks convinced him that land was near. His advice to maintain their course was rejected. "They commenced to ridicule sneeringly and to leave unheeded every opinion offered by anybody not a seaman, as if, with the rules of navigation, they had also acquired all other science and logic." [5] As always, Steller was certain: "At the time when a single day—so many of which were afterward spent in vain—might have been decisive for the whole enterprise, the course was suddenly changed to north." [6] Steller was more nearly right in arguing, before the voyage began, that land would be readily discovered by a northeastern course, though the land would have been the Aleutian Islands rather than the American mainland he anticipated.

The mainland of Alaska was first sighted on July 15, 1741, by Steller, as Mount St. Elias and other peaks of the coastal range of Alaska loomed up out of the sea. Steller's announcement "was regarded as one of my peculiarities" until clearer visibility made the discovery certain.[7] The sight of land, after a tedious, six-week voyage, was happily greeted by the *St. Peter*'s crew; yet Steller observed that Bering seemed indifferent, and "in the presence of all he even shrugged his shoulder while looking at the land." [8] Bering expressed his foreboding to Steller and the surveyor Frederic Plenisner, but did not wish to alarm the others. "We think now we have accomplished everything, and many go about greatly inflated," said Bering, "but they do not consider where we have reached land, how far we are from home, and what may yet happen." [9] Bering feared that trade winds might prevent their return. "We do not know this country: nor are we provided with supplies for a wintering." [10]

The first American land encountered was Kayak Island, lying a few miles off the mainland midway along the great arc of the Gulf of Alaska. Drawing closer to the island, Steller and his companions viewed "with the greatest pleasure" the beautiful forests of the island and its flat, sandy beaches.[11] It was a moment of triumph that all enjoyed as the ship was tacked to approach the island. But it was also a time of anxiety for Steller. How much time would he be given? He feared the worst when Bering did not call a meeting for a "harmonious consideration of what ought to be done." [12] The only discussion concerned the need for fresh water, which moved Steller to bark at his companions, "I could not help saying that we had come only for the purpose of bringing American water to Asia." [13] Poor Steller—and poor shipmates.

Steller was naturally burning to land with the watering party, but Bering refused permission on the grounds of possible danger. In blind anger the scientist threatened to report this denial to authorities in St. Petersburg; he pleaded and swore until Bering relented. Bering appears to have been a patient and forbearing man, not given to pettiness, but Steller's abrasive assertiveness must sometimes have been too much for him. As Steller left the ship Bering ordered a flourish from the ship's trumpeters, a mockery which the scientist accepted "in the spirit in which it was ordered." [14] Thus, on a note of discord and ridicule, the scientific investigation of northwestern America began.

Once ashore, Steller searched for signs of human habitation. He found a hollowed log that revealed evidence of its use for cooking just hours previously and bones of caribou that had been consumed. Soon he discovered a cave containing utensils, provisions, and arrows. Steller then ascended a steep hill from which he could see smoke in the distance.

Eager at the prospect of encountering the island's inhabitants, he hurried back to the shore and requested the use of a ship boat that he might seek out the natives. While waiting for his message to be conveyed to the ship, Steller did not waste a moment. Tired as he was after his overland scramble, he examined the novel plant life near the beach. From the ship, Bering sent word that there was no time for Steller's proposed excursion. Steller received "the patriotic and courteous reply that I should betake myself on board quickly as they would leave me ashore without waiting for me." [15]

At this point it is easy to sympathize with Steller as his hopes of examining an unknown part of the world were dashed. Yet Bering's indifference to scientific achievement is also understandable. He had fulfilled his mission of discovery—now he had other concerns. Water was an absolute necessity, and the world could wait for the unfolding of the natural glories of Alaska. A commander's first responsibility is to the safety of his men, and Bering had good reason to fear delay. Steller was unable to appreciate Bering's apprehension and moralized that the expedition would be punished for its failure to reach its goals by the withdrawal of divine favors. "It is probable that . . . we all saw Russia for the last time." [16] Despite the order to return to the ship, Steller remained ashore until sunset, sending off a Cossack to shoot bird specimens and tramping the island himself to make collections of flora and observations.

Toma Lepekhin, the Cossack hunter assigned to help Steller, brought the naturalist a most interesting catch, a colorful bird that Steller recognized as an American species of blue jay. This *Cyanocitla stelleri* or Steller's Jay as it came to be called, proved to Steller "that we were really in America." [17] Ravens and magpies were abundant and familiar to Steller, but he noted ten other strange birds, "distinguished . . . by their particularly bright coloring." [18] Other additions to Steller's bag of natural novelties included the salmonberry, a fruit found throughout Alaska and the Pacific Northwest.

Steller recommended that some Russian gifts be left in the cave he had discovered, in return for the articles he had removed. Although his suggestion was followed, his colleagues did not leave knives, as the naturalist advised, but an iron kettle, silk, a Chinese pipe, and tobacco, and in the process, they gathered more of the Indian articles from the cave. Steller feared that the Indians would eat the tobacco and might "conclude that we had intended to poison them," since they did not know the use of the plant.[19] Steller's unthinking companions invariably refused to follow his counsel to the letter. But these transgressions hardly compared with Bering's decision to depart at once. "The time here spent in investigation bears an arithmetical ratio to the time used in fitting out: ten years the preparations for this great undertaking lasted, and ten hours were devoted to the work itself." [20]

The *St. Peter* left Kayak Island on July 21, making slow progress to the west. In an effort to advance, Bering ordered a constant tacking from south to north and back again, but steady winds defeated these labors. On August 27, land was observed to the north and Bering decided to try to land and replenish the *St. Peter*'s water supplies. A landing was made on August 30. Steller was one of those permitted to go ashore on Nagai Island, one of the Shumagin Islands lying southeast of the tip of the Alaska Peninsula. Sailing Master Khitrov commanded a boat party to search for natives while Steller joined the water party. Steller grumbled at his exclusion from Khitrov's party which he attributed to a conspiracy to reserve the honor of the first discovery of Americans for the naval officers, but he was nevertheless happy to get ashore. Of all the officers, Steller hated Khitrov most.

The sailors of the watering party began at once to fill their casks with the nearest water at hand, from stagnant puddles lying close to the beach. Steller remonstrated with them and pointed out fresh springs that he discovered a short distance inland, but the stubborn sailors ignored the naturalist. If there was any occasion on which Steller should have been heeded, this was it. But even his authority as ship's physician had been diminished by his cantankerous manner. The sailors were short and sharp: "Why, what is the matter with this water? The water is good, fill up with it!" [21] Their obstinacy was to prove fatal to the expedition. Much of the subsequent suffering of its members was to follow from their ignorant and foolhardy provisioning of alkaline water, and the one time when Steller should have made a vigorous stand, he declined to do so. "As I was already accustomed to such treatment I paid no more attention to it and began to reconnoiter the land." [22]

Like the nearby Aleutian Islands, Nagai Island was treeless, except for willows never exceeding five feet in height. There were many berries, mosses, and plants, however, and Steller gathered a number of antiscorbutic herbs with which he hoped to cure Bering's scurvy. Several other seamen showed signs of scurvy. Steller called for a party of sailors to gather plants, but the naval officers found no merit in his suggestions. "Later, however, there were regrets enough, and when we had scarcely more than four able-bodied men left on the vessel, I was tearfully begged to help and assist." [23] Black and red foxes were seen as well as clouds of birds, including swans, pelicans, auks, ducks, snipes, gulls, sandpipers, puffins, sea parrots, and pigeons. No effort was made to hunt either birds or eggs to improve the crew's diet; yet the peril to the crew was made clear enough when one sailor, after whom the Shumagin Islands were named, died and was buried ashore. Even Steller did not propose the advantage of hunting birds, though he did make a final effort to do something about the water supply. "However, when I saw my opinion concerning the water again spurned and coarsely contradicted and had to hear myself, like a surgeon's apprentice . . . ordered to gather herbs . . . work . . . not considered worth the labor of a few sailors, I repented of my good intentions and resolved that in the future I would only look after the preservation of my own self without wasting another word." [24] Steller can hardly be blamed for his resentment. The barrier between himself and the Russian officers was by this time insurmountable, and Bering was too sick to intervene.

On September 4, while the *St. Peter* was attempting to continue its western course against a persistent wind, the Russians encountered their first Americans. Two natives in kayaks paddled toward the ship, shouting as they came. No one on board the *St. Peter* could understand what the natives were saying, but the Americans gestured toward the land, pointed to their mouths and scooped up sea water with their hands to indicate an offering of refreshment to the Russians. The Russians tied two Chinese tobacco pipes and some glass beads to a piece of board and launched it toward the closest kayak. In turn, one of the Aleuts tied a dead falcon to a stick and passed it to a Koriak aboard the *St. Peter*. Apparently the Aleut wanted the Russians to place other gifts between the bird's claws and return the falcon on the stick, but instead, the Koriak tried to pull the Aleut closer and, in alarm, the Americans released the stick.

A boat was lowered from the *St. Peter* for a shore party. Steller, Waxell, the Koriak interpreter, and several seamen rowed to the beach. A landing on the rocky shore was impossible; so three of the boat party undressed and waded ashore to be greeted by friendly Aleuts—natives of the Aleutian Islands—who presented a piece of whale blubber. One

Aleut was bold enough to paddle out to the *St. Peter* and was given a cup of brandy which he downed, then hurriedly spat out. Brandy not being well received, the Russians offered their second most prized delicacy, a lighted pipe. This, too, was rejected.

On the beach the Aleuts were quite taken with the Koriak interpreter, presumably because his features resembled their own. As the Russians prepared to return to the *St. Peter* some of the Americans held on to the Koriak, and others tried to haul the boat ashore. This confrontation between Americans and Russians was a classic case of mutual distrust and misunderstanding and was resolved by the classic method—a show of superior force. Three of the boat crew fired their muskets over the heads of the Aleuts, who swiftly released Koriak and boat and threw themselves on the ground. The Russians dashed to the boat. The first test of strength was concluded. All the elements of the future subjection of the Americans by their eastern neighbors had passed in review. Tobacco and liquor had made their initial appearance. The first echoes of the firearms soon to enslave a free people resounded from the hills. Both peoples were disappointed and frustrated by the events: the Russians because "we had not been able to observe what we had intended but on the other hand had met what we had not expected"; the Aleuts because, apparently, their intentions had been misunderstood.[25] The Russians laughed at the Aleuts' consternation as they picked themselves up "and waved their hands to us to be off quickly as they did not want us any longer." [26] These laughs of derision and the futile waving of the Aleuts were significant characterizations of the respective assertions of the two peoples. History was to demonstrate that the Aleuts were no match for the aggressive Russians. Yet waving the Russians away would not banish them. This first contact was a prelude and a brief but prophetic introduction to the subsequent bloody incidents that were to occur in the conquest of the Bering Sea.

Steller, accustomed to moralizing on his own endeavors and those of his companions, did not indulge in any reflections on the future of the Aleuts, though he made a close observation of their physical appearance. "They are of medium stature, strong and stocky, yet fairly well proportioned, and with very fleshy arms and legs. The hair of the head is glossy black and hangs straight down all around the head. The face is brownish, a little flat and concave. The nose is also flattened, though not particularly broad or large. The eyes are as black as coals, the lips prominent and turned up. In addition they have short necks, broad shoulders, and their body is plump though not big-bellied." [27]

The Aleuts wore what Steller guessed to be "whale-gut shirts with sleeves, very neatly sewed together, which reach to the calf of the leg." [28] Some had skin boots and trousers and carried iron knives. Steller speculated on the probability that the Americans knew the craft of metalworking. He also described the Aleut kayak, noting its resemblance to those of Greenland Eskimos. "The American boats are about two fathoms long, two feet high, and two feet wide on the deck, pointed towards the nose but truncate and smooth in the rear." [29] The boats had a frame construction covered with skins and a manhole which could be made watertight. To this circular hole was attached a strip of material which could be "tightened or loosened like a purse. When the American has sat down in his boat and stretched his legs under the deck, he draws this hem together around his body and fastens it with a bowknot in order to prevent any water from getting in." [30]

Steller did not believe that the Aleuts made their homes on the islands. He had not yet observed any of their dwellings and assumed that they only visited the wind-swept islands on hunting forays from the mainland. He also speculated on the origins of the Americans, noting their physical similarities to Siberian peoples, which suggested an Asiatic relationship.

Storms threatened the *St. Peter* throughout September and most of the crew suffered from scurvy. Despite such dire circumstances Steller was composed enough to comment acidulously on the behavior of his shipmates. "There was much praying, to be sure, but the curses piled up during ten years in Siberia prevented any response." [31] In the storm it was impossible to cook, and the suffering men were reduced to gnawing half-burned biscuits, and even this spartan fare was in short supply. On October 2 the storm abated, but only for a few hours before a southeastern gale struck them "so that the minds of all again became as shaky as were their teeth already from the scurvy." [32]

On November 4 land was sighted once more and this time the navigators were sure that they had reached Kamchatka. "It is impossible to describe how great and extraordinary was the joy of everybody at the sight. The half-dead crawled up to see it, and all thanked God heartily for this great mercy." [33] Bering, now dying from scurvy, was also aroused by the false expectation that their long voyage was nearing its termination.

He assured his men that their terrible misery was ended and called for the dispensation of what little brandy remained in the stores. The navigators congratulated themselves and pondered over charts that seemed to confirm their theories. In fact, the land sighted was not Kamchatka but Copper Island, a small island just east of Bering Island.

Lieutenant Waxell and Master Khitrov urged Bering to approve an immediate landing because of the physical debility of the crew and the condition of the ship. Bering wanted to find Avacha Bay on which Petropavlovsk was situated before landing, but the others insisted that the nearest harbor be sought. Khitrov called on the crew to support his conjectures and assured them that, "if this were not Kamchatka, he would let his head be cut off." [34] Bering called upon sailor Dimitri Ovtsin—a naval lieutenant before some misdeed in Siberia brought his demotion—for his opinion. Ovtsin concurred with Bering's view and was promptly driven from the officers' meeting, according to Steller, with cries of "get out, shut up, scoundrel, rascal." [35] Steller was asked his opinion but refused to express it on the grounds that it would be unacceptable unless it conformed to the officers' convictions, but he did agree to submit a written testimony to the miserable condition of the crew. The Russian officers, despite their wretched condition, wanted to be sure that they had evidence supporting their decision in the event of a government inquiry.

Finally it was agreed that they would land. On November 6 the *St. Peter* sailed into Komandor Bay of Bering Island. Before the ship passed the sandbar and rocky reefs of the outer harbor, a heavy surf threatened to pound the ship to pieces and panic reigned. "Oh, God! It is all over with us!" screamed the sailors, "Oh, God, our ship! A disaster has befallen our ship!" [36] Several of the superstitious sailors seized the bodies of two men, who had died earlier and were being held for a land burial, and threw them into the sea, apparently in the belief that the dead men were responsible for the threatening surf. Once the *St. Peter* passed the sandbar, it was again in placid waters and was safely anchored.

3 — DEATH AND LIFE
ON BERING ISLAND

The expedition members who had strength enough set about providing some shelter against the wind and snow flurries that swept the beach. Winter was fast approaching, and there was an immediate need to improvise some protection for Bering and the other seriously ill men who were carried ashore. The men instinctively constructed shelters which resembled the Aleut dwellings traditionally built in the same latitudes—pits hollowed out of the sand, roofed with canvas sails and other material from the *St. Peter*. Succor did not come soon enough for some of the seamen. Several expired soon after they were conveyed ashore—the death toll was mounting.

Blue foxes, at first observed joyfully by the mariners as a potential food supply, soon proved to be a great nuisance. The animals, unawed by the presence of men, darted about the camp, thick as flies, stealing any food left unguarded and terrorizing men too weak to drive them off. In one day, Steller and Plenisner killed sixty of the audacious beasts, felling some with axes and stabbing others with knives, using their carcasses as a temporary shelter wall. Each day the slaughter continued, until heaps of carcasses were strewn about the camp site, and still the foxes came, blind to their destruction in their mad quest for food. The bodies of the dead seamen were horribly mutilated before the surviving seamen could summon up enough energy to bury them in the sand. Even then, the rapacious foxes desecrated the shallow graves, digging the bodies from the earth and carrying away bloody limbs. Foxes also marauded the equipment and stores which the Russians were gradually bringing ashore from the *St. Peter*. They scattered the provisions, carried off clothing, tools, and anything else that was not secured. Steller recalled the greed of the Russians for the furs of Kamchatka foxes during the preparation for the voyage and wondered whether they were being chastised for it by the scourge of the Bering Island animals. Half crazed by the persistence of the thieving beasts, the Russians tortured and maimed as many foxes as they killed, gouging out eyes, slicing off ears and tails, half skinning some and half roasting others in their camp fires. Neither torture nor wholesale butchering helped. The foxes infested the camp in increasing numbers and with unchecked audacity.

On November 14, a week after the initial landing, Steller and other hunters clubbed to death four sea otters, the first ones killed on Bering Island. From their Kamchatka experiences the Russians were familiar with the sea otter and knew the value of its pelt in the Chinese trade. But the precious skins meant nothing to them now; they stewed up the best parts of the otter flesh to make a dish more palatable than that from the despised foxes and left the pelts to be devoured by the camp robbers.

In the wake of the Bering expedition, better-fed Russians were to visit Bering Island and the Aleutians for the primary purpose of hunting sea otters. The discovery of the sea otters in November 1741 initiated the conquest of the Bering Sea, the exploitation of its resources and people. For the succeeding century, the quest of the sea otter was to underlie every event that took place.

On December 8, Commander Bering's long suffering came to an end. For days he had lain half buried in the sand that had drifted into his wretched hut, protesting any efforts to clear it away. "The deeper in the ground I lie," he told Waxell, "the warmer I am; the part of my body that lies above ground suffers from the cold." [1] Bering's body was dug from the sand, tied to a plank, and thrust down into the ground, after which the burial service was read over his remains.

Throughout December other deaths followed that of Bering's; a total of thirty men expired in November and December. "Our plight was so wretched," wrote Waxell, "that the dead had to lie for a considerable time among the living, for there was none able to drag the corpses away, nor were those who still lived capable of moving away from the dead." [2] For days a dead man shared the hut in which Waxell and Khitrov lay, until the only able-bodied men left took time from hunting and other tasks to undertake burial. Weak as he was, Waxell offered some direction. Neither then nor later, when he had recovered his health, did he attempt to drive the men. That was not an acceptable way of exerting one's power and authority. "Severity would have been quite pointless." [3] Discussions on courses of action were participated in by all; the distinction between officers and seamen was erased by the circumstances.

Waxell was cheered when the sick seamen felt well enough to sit up for card games; their play helped them pass the time and overcome the melancholy that was as deadly as scurvy. All did not share his lenient view. "There were, though, certain members of our company who criticized my attitude on this point and told me to my face that I was not discharging my duties in accordance with the regulations." [4] These illiberal complaints did not originate with severe, regulation-minded Russian officers, but with the expedition's most notable civilian, Georg Steller.

"The sickness," wrote Steller, "had scarcely subsided, when a new and worse epidemic appeared, I mean the wretched gambling with cards." [5] In lurid terms he described the men's obsession with gambling, their constant conversation over gains and losses, a general debauchery that resulted in theft, hatred, quarrels, strife, and the wasteful killing of sea otters for their pelts. On this last result, Steller did have a point, if it was true that otters became scarce because their furs were used as gaming stakes. Yet it does seem that the naturalist overstated his case—whether out of concern for a dwindling food supply, his abhorrence of a mindless animal slaughter, or because of a revulsion at a recreation with which he had no sympathy.

While lacking the sunny bliss of the palm-studded islands of the South Pacific Ocean, Bering Island was not an entirely unfortunate place to wash up upon. Though unpromising in its rock-girded appearance, the island was not by any means infertile and desolate. Sea and land birds nested there in prodigious numbers. Foxes abounded all over the island, and its shores were the refuge of teeming herds of seals, sea lions, sea cows, and sea otters. With the Pribilof Islands of St. Paul and St. George far to the east on the Bering Sea, the Commander Islands constituted the world's major breeding rookeries of the fur seal.

Hunters had no difficulty finding plump ptarmigans, foxes, seals, and sea otters; and Steller busied himself gathering antiscorbutic herbs. By this time Lieutenant Waxell, one of the iron men of the expedition, was suffering from scurvy and was nursed by Steller. Steller was one of a handful of men who remained in good health—a blessing for the less fortunate. He had strength enough to turn his energies to the care of the sick, forgetting, for a time at least, the actual and imagined insults suffered on the voyage. For the first time, the young naturalist's word had weight; no one interfered with his supervision of the scurvy victims.

For once Steller would have the leisure to make a close investigation of a newly discovered land, and the island seemed to offer more natural curiosities than had been noted on the two previous landings of the voyage. While on Bering Island, Steller did his most important work—dissecting and describing the sea cow—a scientific task which would assure his fame for all time.

Steller also devoted much attention to the bird life of Bering Island, much of which was familiar. One bird, however, followed the sea cow's road to extinction and was long known only through Steller's description. This was a large cormorant, unable to fly, hence a prime target for food hunters. This bird, which weighed 12 to 14 pounds, was seen by only one naturalist, Steller, and disappeared about 1850. Other birds he was the first to discover were Steller's Jay, Steller's Eider, the rare Steller's Eagle, and Steller's White Raven.

Steller's botanical work was of equal distinction to his observations of marine life, birds, and land animals. He classified scores of unknown plants for the first time.

Through the winter the castaways subsisted on birds and various mammals, and in May the hunters brought in the first of the sea cows that fulfilled all the needs of the expedition. The first was a 4-ton monster with enough meat to feed the men for two weeks. Its rich, red flesh tasted like excellent beef, and its snow white, almond-flavored fat was "of such exceptionally good flavor and nourishment that we drank it by the cupful without experiencing the slightest nausea." [6] Steller's enthusiasm for the sea cow's potential was unbounded. "These animals are found at all seasons of the year everywhere around the island in the greatest numbers, so that the whole population of the eastern coast of Kamchatka would always be able to keep itself more than abundantly supplied from them with fat and meat." [7] Truly, Steller's sea cow, as it came to be called, was a marvelous beast; yet the naturalist's prediction for its future was based on a false estimate of its numbers. It is probable that the sole grounds of the mammal were the coasts of the Commander Islands.

In the spring it was decided to build a small ship from the remains of the *St. Peter*. Dismantling the stoutly built *St. Peter* occupied all of April, and on May 6, the keel of the new ship was laid. All three of the *St. Peter*'s carpenters had died earlier. However, by good luck, one survivor of the voyage, a Siberian Cossack, had some shipbuilding experience and supervised the construction. Twenty men constituted the building party. The others were responsible for providing food for all. In July, the ship was completed, and provisions—mostly sea cow meat and water—were laid aboard. On August 10, the launching of the new *St. Peter* took place, and three days later the survivors were ready for the sea.

Severe restrictions had to be imposed on individual baggage because of the limitation of space. Space had to be reserved for the valuable sea otter pelts which, as Waxell pointed out, were the spoils that repaid the men somewhat for their sufferings. Proceeds from the otters were divided, apparently according to rank. Steller received 80 skins of the 900 which were carried back, but he was outraged by his weight allotment of 360 pounds. He had to abandon what we recognize today as the single most precious trophy of the expedition—the stuffed skin of a young sea cow, as well as a sea cow skeleton and specimens of the sea otter, fur seal, and sea lion. Plant seeds, a pair of the sea cow's horny palatal plates, field notes, and personal items accounted for the 360 pounds he was allowed. Waxell's weight allowance was twice that of Steller's, but others' allowances must have been much less, since the total weight allowed the forty-six men was only $3\frac{1}{2}$ tons. Steller stormed and raged, but to no avail.

Crowded aboard, the men took a last look at their abandoned camp. New occupiers had already taken over. "We watched the foxes on shore ransacking our dwellings with the greatest glee and activity and sharing among themselves what was left of fat and meat." [8] Their passage to Petropavlovsk, the port they had left fifteen months earlier, took just two weeks. At long last the first American expedition had ended. Steller survived the voyage but died in Siberia shortly after reaching the mainland. Considering the limited landfalls of the expedition, Steller had gathered a comprehensive picture of the natural life of the Bering Sea. And despite his own reservations regarding his work, Steller deserves his high rating among the world's pioneer scientists.

THE WEALTH OF THE SEA

Georg Wilhelm Steller's hard-won fame rests on the accurate descriptions of the sea cow and other marine mammals which were published in his *De Bestiis Marinis*. His dissection of a female sea cow in July 1742 can easily be considered one of the high points of Pacific Ocean scientific activity. This great northern manatee is known only through Steller's notes and the few skeletons collected years later. For 100 years, the sea cow has been extinct. A living specimen was last seen in 1768, a mere 27 years after its discovery by the Bering expedition.

Steller observed these mammals along the entire shore of the island, where they fed on seaweed near the mouths of streams. The sea cow's appetite was huge. When not mating or caring for their young, they were continuously occupied in feeding along the sea edge, usually with half their body above the surface. June was the mating season and a strict ritual ensued. "The female flees slowly before the male with continual turns about, but the male pursues her without cessation. When, however, the female is finally weary of this mock coyness she turns on her back and the male completes the mating in the human manner." [9] In mating, the males penetrated their mates with a six-foot-long penis of corresponding thickness.

Sea cows were unafraid of people and allowed their approach without showing any sign of alarm. Prior to the landing of the Bering party, they had never known an enemy, but, unfortunately for their survival, their bulk and shore-feeding habits were to make them a helpless prey. The Russians found the flesh of seals strong and coarse and liked that of the sea otter even less, but the sea cow's meat tasted like the finest beef, and its fat was equally succulent. Until harried out of existence, the beast was to provide the most favored sustenance of the Bering Sea fur traders.

The huge mammal had instincts that seemed almost human. Although unwary in its own defense, the manatee tried to protect its kind from the butchering hunters. When the Bering men harpooned a sea cow and towed it to the beach, other animals formed a circle about the victim as if to prevent its sacrifice. "Some attempted to upset the yawl; others laid themselves over the rope or tried to pull the harpoon out of [his] body, in which they succeeded several times." [10] In astonishment, the Russians observed "that a male came two days in succession to its female which was lying dead on the beach, as if it would inform himself about her condition." [11] For all this sensitivity, the sea cows were otherwise obtuse. Regardless of the slaughtering that went on among the herd, they never shifted location to escape the bloody executions.

As a scientist, Steller's chief resources were his own intelligence and energy. While men like Johann Georg Gmelin and Louis Delisle de la Croyère traveled with servants, provisioned with European foods and wines, Steller traveled light—eating native foods for convenience and scientific interest. Typically, Steller tackled the problem of the dissection and description of the sea cow with dedication and energy. Handling the huge manatee was extremely difficult. In shape, the sea cow resembled a seal, though it had a large fluke like a whale. The largest sea cows were 35 feet long and 20 feet in girth.

The sea cow which Steller dissected weighed 8,000 pounds. The heart alone weighed 36¼ pounds and the stomach was 6 feet long, 5 feet wide, and so stuffed with food and seaweed that four strong men using a rope could scarcely move the animal from its place and only with great effort were able to drag it out of the sea. Rain and cold impeded Steller's efforts, while Arctic foxes were tearing at the mammal's flesh and carrying off Steller's paper, books, and inkstand.

This unpleasant work could not be performed without considerable manpower. Steller recruited seamen and paid them in tobacco. Fortunately Steller was a nonsmoker. Not unexpectedly, the seamen's work did not meet Steller's standards; yet, at the time, he expressed satisfaction that they did not desert him altogether in this gigantic task.

Steller complained often of a lack of assistance, but he seemed to have received a great deal of help from Plenisner, who made the six sea cow drawings that enhanced *De Bestiis Marinis*, and from other members of the surgical staff, as well as the Cossack, Lepekhin.

Steller's description of the sea otters on Bering Island was the first comprehensive report on the mammals to be published. The stranded Russian mariners appreciated the value of the pelts enough to tan them carefully, but they also depended upon them for a food supply.

Steller noted that the sea otter had been confused by Russians in Kamchatka with the beaver, because its fur more closely resembled the beaver than that of the familiar, smaller, river otter. Indisputably, argued Steller, the sea otter was an American sea animal which only occasionally found its way to the coast of Kamchatka. A full-grown prime skin is 5 feet long, and 24–30 inches wide, covered with a fine fur, the hairs of which are ¾ inch in length. Its jet black, glossy surface revealed a silver tinge when ruffled, and the presence of scattered white hairs enhanced its beauty. Unlike other marine mammals, the sea otter does not depend upon a thick blubber layer under the skin to maintain its body temperature in the frigid waters of its habitat. Instead it relies upon the insulation of air trapped in its hair; consequently the mammal is constantly preening and grooming its hair. Steller was unaware of this and other findings of modern biologists that have made the uniqueness of the sea otter even more clear. Of all its singularities, none is more amazing than its use of a tool to aid feeding. As it floats on its back, the otter breaks clams, crabs, and other crustaceans held in its front paws against a stone resting on its chest. Otter spend most of their existence on their backs feeding, preening, and sleeping. Females carry and suckle their offspring and copulate in this position. Despite its apparently leisurely habits the otter's appetite is ravenous. Each day it requires a quantity of crustaceans and fish equaling $\frac{1}{4}$ of its total body weight of up to 80 pounds.

The Aleuts of the Aleutian Islands were skilled hunters of the sea otter long before the Russians enslaved them to that purpose. They hunted at sea from their swift kayaks, using a spearlike weapon which was thrown from the cramped sitting position of the boatman. Hunting from such a platform was a difficult exercise even in the calmest seas. A keen eye and strong, steady throwing arm were essential to accuracy. Sea otters did not present a large target above the surface, and it required a consummate skill to strike them in the water. Once hit, the otter could offer little resistance. It could dive beneath the surface for a time, but if the spear had deeply penetrated its body, this evasion only exhausted and weakened the animal. Before long the otter had to return to the surface to breathe and die as its life's blood poured from the wound. As life ebbed away, the Aleut hunter guided his craft close and lifted his prey from the water.

"The sea otter is the mildest of all marine animals. It never makes any resistance to hunters, and only saves itself by running away if it can." [12] Thus Stepan Krasheninnikov in his report on Kamchatka reported of the most important resource of the Bering Sea. Natives of Kamchatka hunted the sea otter off the island's shores by spreading nets among the kelp beds where otters fed, by harpooning the mammals at sea from their small boats, and sometimes by catching them on ice floes that grounded near the coast. Kamchadals did not prize the sea otter pelt as highly as that of foxes and sables, but the Cossacks who traded for them knew better. In the Chinese fur market—upon which Russian expansion to eastern Siberia and Alaska was based—the sea otter pelt was supreme, commanding a very high price on the Chinese frontier. All too few otter furs were taken by the Kamchadals, and the Cossacks longed for more of the scarce pelts.

Consequently, the return of Waxell, Steller, and the other survivors of the Bering Expedition with bundles of sea otter pelts and reports of their abundance on Bering Island created a sensation. Russian traders swiftly responded to the possibilities of reaping fabulous wealth from the Bering Sea and organized expeditions to set out for the newly discovered islands. No longer was the Bering Sea a region interesting only to the geographer and scientist; now it attracted the entrepreneur—the course of Russia's eastern expansion quickened. But for the sea otter there would not have been a frantic effort to follow up the discoveries of the second Kamchatka expedition. In time there would have been little reason for the commercial initiative of Siberian merchants. All was changed by the presence of "the mildest of all sea animals," and within a few years, the quest of its glossy fur led to the enslavement of the Aleuts, and to the virtual extinction of the Bering Sea otters.

4 — THE ALEUTS AND
THE *PROMYSHLENNIKS*

The Aleuts were the first Americans to feel the impact of the Russian expansion. No one bothered to compile a precise census of the Aleut population, but their numbers were considerable, perhaps 20,000 to 25,000 persons, making the islands the most densely populated region in Alaska at that time. Despite their wind-swept barrenness, their rains and fog, the Aleutian Islands were well capable of supporting human life because of the wealth of the surrounding seas in fish and mammals. A rigorous climate certainly restricted the productive qualities of the land, but the barrenness was more than compensated for by the teeming life of the Bering Sea and North Pacific.

The *promyshlenniks,* as the Russian traders were termed, did not encounter the Aleuts with any fixed notions in mind; nor were they guided by governmental policies.[1] They responded to the presence of the aboriginals in the same manner as to the natives of Kamchatka. Aleutian natives, however benighted, were subjects of the czar and should peacefully support the fur quest of their betters. Russian needs were simple. They wanted the assistance of the skilled Aleut hunters in reaping the harvest of sea otter and, as a solace for their long separation from their homes, they desired the comforts of sexual companionship with Aleut women. In the satisfaction of these clear needs they would brook no interference. Resistance to either demand was savagely punished where the Russians were strong in number. Native peoples of Siberia—Kamchadals and others—had been handled in the same fashion and, in fact, Kamchadal hunters accompanied the Russians to the

Aleutians and assisted their enterprise in the newly discovered hunting grounds.

Exploitation of the sea otter in the Aleutians was a logical extension of Russian enthusiasm for furs when the sables of Siberia began to diminish and lose favor as a trade market item. Centuries of unchecked trapping exterminated the sable in some Siberian regions and brought the valuable animals almost to the point of extinction in other regions. Like the sable in Siberia, the sea otter in Russian America provided the foundation of conquest.

Sable furs were a mainstay of the revenue of the Russian government from the twelfth century on. The government at Novgorod and later Moscow established an annual tribute in furs from natives in the seventeenth century which was equivalent to an average of five or seven sables per man. But the eighteenth-century explorations, and especially reports of plentiful sea otters from the survivors of the second Bering expedition, changed the Russian fur trade drastically. Sable was a land animal, easily tracked in the winter snow when its fur was longest. Russians had hunted the sable for centuries and had mastered its habits and instincts. But the sea otter was a water animal, more elusive than the landlocked sable, and far more difficult to hunt. Russian hunters had absolutely no contact with this hitherto unknown animal and knew of no way to predict its habits and instincts. Furthermore, the Russian himself was a landlubber. He took to the sea with stiff legs and a queasy stomach. He was unfamiliar with the problems of uncharted waters and uncertain about ships. He accumulated lands from the Urals to the Pacific Ocean in about fifty years, but he took a century to go the shorter distance from the port of Okhotsk to Alaska.

The rich short-haired pelts of the sea otter were unsatisfactory for winter dress, but their novelty provided a base for a highly profitable trade market. The Chinese, especially the royalty, were insatiable buyers of sea otter skins, used mostly for trim on princely garments. China was the leading foreign trade market for Russia during the 1700s, and furs eventually constituted nearly 100 percent of Russian-Chinese trade. By the middle of the eighteenth century, a sea otter skin sold in Chinese markets brought seven to eight times the price in Kamchatka. A Chinese trader often paid thirty rubles for a sea otter pelt. In turn, a fox pelt equaled one sable skin, and two sable skins were worth one of the sea otter.

Sea otters were plentiful in the North Pacific, but their value was their doom. The hunters took them from the sea as if they were fish who spawned huge schools of offspring. In fact, the sea otter only produced one offspring a year. Not many years passed before the unchecked, uncontrolled hunt of the sea otter resulted in a sudden decrease in their numbers, almost to the point of complete extinction of the species.

Russian hunters were far better with a deadfall trap than with a sail and rudder. Few knew anything about navigation. Maps of the known seas were virtually ignored or at least unused by the captains of these hunting ships. The small ships themselves were quickly built of green timber and tar. Boats went out to hunt sea cows for their meat, and seals and sea lions for skins in winter. In the summer, voyages were made along the rocky shores of the Aleutian Islands in search of sea otters. Hunters quickly learned that the native Aleut was indispensable to his success. It was the Aleut, not the Russian, who could kill or wound a sea otter from over 100 feet away. The Aleut had hunted the sea otter for generations before the Russian had ever heard of it. And it was the Aleut who could successfully manipulate his small skin boat in pursuing the sea otter.

Some voyages lasted up to six years. Two years was the normal venture. But whatever the time, owners of the ships and sponsors of the voyages demanded that the ship return with at least twice the cost of building and outfitting the ship—a cost of from ten to thirty thousand rubles. Without this return profit, the sailors and captains were automatically considered indebted to the owners.

The *promyshlenniks,* the fur traders, were simple men and generally uneducated. They were totally committed to the success of their only calling—the collection of pelts from sable, ermine, fox, beaver, marten, wolf, and now sea otter. They were an unleashed group of adventurers—rugged, courageous, fearless, wildly independent in their search for skins. They retained no official connection with the government. Only the independent merchant and sponsor were recognized as authorities, but not once the hunters were out to sea and beyond watchful eyes. Out on the high seas and among the peoples of the Aleutians, the *promyshlenniks* could express their self-image of superiority without restraint of any kind. They were on their own. Stories of their deeds and misdeeds often reached governmental ears, but lack of confirmation and witnesses resulted in few recriminations and restrictions.

No fewer than thirty-five voyages were made by private Russian traders into the Bering Sea during the twenty years following the Great Northern Expedition. The lives of the Aleuts were hard because of these voyages and the men on them.

Atrocities began in the winter of 1745. An explosion of deadly firearms against a people who had only stone-tipped spears and walrus-bone knives began the crude intrusions of the old world into the new. On Attu Island of the Near Islands, at the extreme tip of the Aleutian chain, the first native was injured by a bullet. Two days later on Attu Island ten armed men, under Alexei Beliaief, went to explore their landfall. Before long the men encountered a settlement of Aleuts. The men, hungry for women after a long, arduous voyage, and unaccustomed to exercising civilized restraint, provoked an argument that ended in the outright killing of fifteen male natives. No other substantial reason, other than securing the women, was recorded for the killing. Additional gunpowder and bullets were rushed to the scene from the ship in support of the murderers. For nearly an entire year the peoples of Attu were ruthlessly harassed by the Russians at first welcomed to the island.

The years passed and the violence between the Aleuts and Russians continued. The isolation of the scene lent itself to lawless and unbridled actions. There was no effective government authority and might meant right.

In 1762 a conflict occurred which marked the turning point of Aleut-Russian relations. *Promyshlenniks* patrolled the waters of the Alaska Peninsula for food and furs and landed on one of the islands. Their uncivilized attitudes and actions toward the natives were habitual now, ingrained into their already rough personalities. Suddenly, a group of well-organized natives attacked and killed two Russians and injured three others. Another group almost simultaneously attacked the Russian base camp, killed four more Russians, and wounded four others. The makeshift shelters were burned to the ground. The Aleuts were clearly taking the initiative this time. Later in spring, two more intruders from the east were killed about three and a half miles inland from where their ship was anchored. This time the Russians killed seven native hostages in retaliation. In return for this, the Aleuts attacked the Russian camp but were unsuccessful. Offensive actions by the natives put the Russians in temporary retreat. They repaired their ship and returned home with their rich cargo of 900 sea otter pelts and 350 fox skins.

Even in their retreat they continued their outrages. Twenty-five young native girls were kidnapped from their home island and given the task of gathering wild berries and roots for the crew. The ship eventually reached the coast of Kamchatka where fourteen of the twenty-five girls and six Russians went ashore. Two girls immediately escaped into the hills. One was killed by the men. On the small-boat trip back to the ship the remaining eleven girls drowned themselves either in shame or despair. To protect themselves, the Russians threw all the remaining natives overboard to drown.

Authorities in St. Petersburg were aware of the atrocities committed by the unrestrained fur hunters. But authorities were a quarter of the world distant in the transportation and communication systems of the eighteenth century. Efforts at checking the lawlessness which represented the Russian nation to the people of the new world would come later in the formation of privileged trading companies. But during the decades of totally free traffic and totally free enterprise, authorities could only issue stern warnings against the *promyshlenniks*.

One such warning read in part:

> As it appears from reports forwarded by Colonel Plenisner, who was charged with the investigation and final settlement of the affairs of the Bechevin Company, that that company during their voyage to and from the Aleutian Islands on a hunting and trading expedition committed indescribable outrages and abuse on the inhabitants, and even were guilty of murder, inciting the natives to bloody reprisals, it is hereby enjoined upon the company about to sail, and especially upon the master, Ismailov, and the perevodchik, Lukanin, to see that no such barbarities, plunder and ravaging of women are committed under any circumstances.[2]

Such warnings were respected until anchor was pulled.

Word that the native people of the Aleutians had dared to take the initiative against the Russians spread among the fur hunters and eventually led to the final domination of the natives. A leader named Solovief heard of the death of his fellow Russian hunters at the hands of the Aleuts the preceding year and set out to teach the natives their place once and for all. He first put his own camp and men in order and discipline. Without strict adherence to the rules he set, there could be no success in revenging his people.

The natives attacked Solovief and his men and were driven back with heavy losses. One hundred Aleuts were killed; their boats were smashed. Then Solovief joined forces with several other companies of *promyshlenniks* until a substantial, though ragtag, force of arms and men resembled a small army. A blood-thirsty scourge of the islands ensued. Isolated settlements were destroyed and burned to ashes. Families were routed and killed. Tools, boats, and food were ruined. Elimination, not subjugation, of the native became the primary goal of the attacks.

Finally, Solovief led his forces to a fortified Aleut village of 300 and proceeded to attack the natives in full strength. Bows and arrows were no defense against the firearms of the Russians. No doubt about the outcome existed, even among the natives. The Russians filled bladders with gunpowder and blew up the log foundations of the village walls and houses. The natives had no chance and were quickly routed and slaughtered by the *promyshlenniks*. Perhaps as many as 3,000 Aleuts were killed during all the Solovief scourges. The exact number of deaths cannot be known, but the unrelenting savagery of the traders was clear. Solovief once experimented with the power of his musket by tying twelve natives together, one behind the other. He fired the rifle at point-blank range to learn that the bullet stopped with the ninth man. The Aleuts never attacked the fur hunters again.

The crude reign of Solovief in 1766 ended the free life of the Aleut people. No longer could the native people live in their own land without paying tribute in money, skins, work, and lives to the strangers from across the sea. Their skill as hunters was exploited beyond reasonable compensation.

It is not known with certainty when the Aleuts first migrated to the wind-swept islands extending from the Alaska Peninsula westward for over 1,000 miles. Archaeological evidence suggests that their ancestors, as those of other North American aboriginals, originated in Asia, but that they did not settle on the islands initially. Presumably, they crossed the Bering Sea land bridge, then moved south along the Alaska coast and eventually west to inhabit the chain of islands. That the Aleuts and Eskimos had common ancestors seems clear; yet in the several thousand years of adapting to their maritime environment they developed a singular culture which diverged from that of mainland Eskimos. Differences in language and customs evolved which stamped the Aleut culture as a highly distinctive one. These people flourished on their volcanic islands by adapting their life pattern to the dictates of the sea. Of all the people of northern Asia and North America, none has developed so predominant a maritime culture as the Aleuts. The land resources of the Aleutians are slender compared with those of the surrounding waters—fantastically rich in fish and mammals—thus the island people related more closely to the sea. In poetic truth, the Aleut once spoke of "my brother, the sea otter."

Yet the Aleuts lived on the land and drew some sustenance from it. Berries and herbs as well as a variety of birds and their eggs complemented their diet. Foxes and other small land animals were eaten, but these were not nearly as important a resource as the marine mammals. Certain deities were associated with the things of the land, while others belonged to the sea and its creatures. These two realms were kept separate. If, for example, a hunter wanted to lighten the rock-ballast in his kayak, he carried the rocks ashore. He would not dare anger the sea gods by throwing the rocks into the water. Conversely, the bones of the first sea mammal taken in a hunt could not be left on the land but had to be returned to the sea. Land and sea spirits alike assisted the Aleuts' sea hunting and were propitiated by colorful ceremonies enlivened by music and dancing. Other spirits protected individuals as well. Dead relatives and one's animal protector, having beneficial powers, lent special meaning to carvings and designs on amulets and wooden headgear. Evil spirits caused sickness and death. By raising supernatural power against these, cures could be effected by shamans, gifted individuals who knew how to deal with evil. Shamans crafted the sacred masks which were a feature of various rituals.

Such Aleut beliefs and ceremonies resembled those of mainland Eskimos, but there were differences. Aleuts did not fear the dead. Eskimos did so, and swiftly disposed of the bodies of deceased relatives, while the Aleuts postponed the departure of the dead from the living by periods of mourning marked by various rituals. Wailing, drum beating, and processions occupied the mourners until the bodies of the deceased were disposed of. Although the bodies of people of low status—slaves, and sometimes women and children—were cremated, others were buried in the ground or in caves, accompanied by objects which served as suitable offerings. Mummification was also practiced. Bodies were sometimes prepared by replacing the viscera with grass. The dead were dressed in their best parkas, wrapped in woven grass nets, and placed in sitting position in dry caves. All the articles associated with their living pursuits were left with the dead—the baby's cradle, the woman's sewing and cooking utensils, the hunter's kayak and weapons. In the spirit world the mummified dead would have what was necessary to carry on. These mummies have been well preserved despite the foggy, rainy climate of the islands because they were placed in carefully selected, warm, dry caves of volcanic hills. Once buried, the mummies were strictly left alone. To molest them would cause death.

In justice to the Russian interlopers, it should be noted that warfare and aggression was no novelty among the Aleuts. Warriors raided the villages of other islands to carry off women and booty. Captured warriors were enslaved, and relentless blood feuds were carried on by relatives of anyone injured by the inhabitant of another village. As in other societies, a great warrior was an honored man among his people.

Social organization of the Aleuts was somewhat stricter than that of the Eskimos. Elders and chiefs had some authority over commoners and slaves. They were something more than respected advisers; yet they probably did not exercise tyrannical powers. The principal pursuits of village people, hunting and warfare, were not conducted on so corporate a basis as to require highly centralized control; thus individual initiative was respected.

Families lived together in individual dwellings and, like the Eskimos, shared a community meeting center, the *kashim*. Wives were commonly purchased, and a man was entitled to as many women as he could support. It was also possible for a single woman to be shared by several men. As with the Eskimos there were circumstances in which a husband might invite another man to enjoy sexual relations with his wife. This was not a custom of meaningless occurrence but was a means of imposing or satisfying an obligation. Europeans misunderstood such practices and assumed that husbands were merely offering conventional hospitality in such cases. When the ships of Captain James Cook called at Unalaska, the English tars "pigged very lovingly together" with Aleut women and marveled at the patience of a husband while "we engrafted Antlers on his head." [3] What the English experienced actually had nothing to do with an Aleut tradition. They were participating in the transplanted Western custom of prostitution. The sailors paid in tobacco for favors received.

The Russians considered the Aleuts a barbarous and ignorant

people. The native custom of tattooing their bodies and faces was to them a disagreeable practice, but one they were familiar with, since Siberian natives also tattooed themselves. But even more disagreeable was the Aleut manner of wearing ornaments in the nose and lower lip. Men and women alike perforated the cartilage of the nose for the insertion of bone rods, rings of feathers, or dangling glass beads. Similarly, Aleuts perforated the corners of their lower lips and inserted bone pegs from the inside of their mouth. These pegs projected outward from ½ inch to 2 inches. "They can draw them in with their tongues but cannot remove them, because the entrance of air makes their teeth ache," noted Peter Simon Pallas, a German naturalist of the St. Petersburg Academy of Sciences, who compiled information received from the *promyshlenniks* on the new Russian subjects.[4]

The Russians found Aleut clothing remarkable. Both sexes wore long-sleeved skin shirts which extended to the calf of the leg. Sometimes these were made of bird skins taken from horned puffins. The feathered side was worn next to the skin. The outer side was treated with fish fat, colored red, and decorated at the seams with fringes of thin, slit hide. "In addition," repeated Pallas, "they have rain clothes, consisting entirely of strips of dried intestines of sea animals, neatly cut to fit each other. These are highly prized because of the great labor they cost." [5] Their outfit was completed by caps made of bird skins, decorated with walrus whiskers, beads, and bone carvings and complemented by a painted wooden screen "projecting above the eyes like a duck's bill." [6] The Russians thought the clothing bizarre and inadequate, but actually it was well suited to the rainy, mild climate of the islands—mild, that is, compared to the frosty Asian and American continental lands adjacent to the Bering Sea.

Aleut housing was more familiar to the Russians. Like the Koriaks and Eskimos of Siberia the dwellings were partially underground. An oval space was hollowed out of the ground and lined with mats. Driftwood or whale ribs were raised to support and provide a framework for a sod roof in which a hole was left to provide entry. Often these dwellings were large enough to accommodate several families in separate compartments. To Russian eyes these were wretched, primitive holes. They were, in fact, snug, adequate, and easily warmed by the seal-oil-burning lanterns which provided lighting and heat alike. The Russians were appalled by the stuffiness of the huts and the rancid pungency of seal oil, urine, and body odor. Yet such housing made clever use of the limited materials at hand and provided easily erected shelters which protected against winter winds and rain.

The Aleuts hunted with bow and flint-headed arrows, or with spears or lances tipped with stone or bone points. Iron-tipped weapons were rare before Russian trade made metal commonplace, though there were some fashioned from metal ship fittings that occasionally washed ashore. The primitive weapons were effective enough in the skilled hands of hunters whose sustenance depended more upon knowledge and endurance than sophisticated implements.

As a maritime people, the Aleuts had evolved superior seagoing vessels. Their kayaks—one-man boats constructed of tanned walrus hides stretched over a light wooden frame—have always commanded the admiration of Westerners. The Aleuts propelled these swift and steady craft with a single two-bladed paddle into the most treacherous waters of the world. For all their apparent fragility, the kayaks served the natives' purpose for sea-mammal hunting magnificently. Larger vessels, umiaks, were used to carry families or groups of hunters. These were also constructed of wood and walrus hide, but unlike the kayak, whose deck was enclosed except for the hole in which the boatman sat, umiaks were open above the hull. The kayak was long and narrow, about 15 feet long with an 18-inch beam, while the umiak was longer and much broader in beam.

Kayaks are among the fastest of man-propelled vessels. Smooth lines and light construction enabled the oarsman to maintain a pace that easily outdistanced Western sailing ships or the canoes of the Northwest coast Indians. Captain James Cook was amazed to find that kayaks had no trouble keeping pace with his *Resolution* while it was under full sail and doing seven knots in a good wind. Long voyages were not uncommon. The Aleuts sometimes undertook voyages from Kodiak Island to Sitka in the early nineteenth century, although coasting and short, island-to-island hops were more customary.

"In their persons we should reckon them extremely nasty. They eat the vermin with which their bodies are covered, and swallow the mucus from the nose," Peter Simon Pallas wrote of the Aleuts.[7] "Having washed themselves, according to custom, first with wine, and then with water, they suck their hands dry. When they are sick, they lie three or four days without food; and if bleeding is necessary, they open a vein with lancets made of flint, and suck the blood."[8] The Russians might have been forgiven if they had ignored the Aleuts, leaving them to their squalor and harsh lives; but unfortunately for the islanders, the *promyshlenniks* did nothing of the kind. Though the Aleut standards of personal hygiene occasioned scorn, the people were implements in the accession of wealth for the bold Russian adventurers. The Bering Sea was a treasure trove for those who commanded its resources, and the natives possessed the talents necessary for its exploitation. Willingly, if they were agreeable, and forcibly, if they resisted, the Aleuts had to lend their endeavors to the fur traders. Chinese fur buyers did not value the rich, dark pelt of the beautiful sea otter less because it was gathered by untidy people—and the *promyshlenniks* were not going to risk the turbulent waters of the otters' haunts when others could be compelled to do the hunting for them. "Bring in those pelts," commanded the Russians, and the Aleut men complied. How could they do otherwise when their women and children remained as hostages in Russian custody as insurance against rebellion? After a successful venture, a hunter could usually reclaim his family intact—though his wife and daughters might be a little worse for the wear. Of course the ultimate effect of the horrors inflicted upon the Aleuts, who were helpless against an aggression backed by firearms, was disastrous.

Their numbers were greatly reduced by the violence of the invaders. As a people they were debilitated and reduced to the status of slaves—slaves whose obeisance to their lords did not prevent them from rendering useful services. The Aleuts became a very well-traveled people as they assisted in the decimation of the sea otters of the Bering Sea and North Pacific. Hunters were forced to abandon their families as the Russian commercial network shifted to fresh grounds. It is highly improbable that any of the islanders were ever returned to Unalaska, Adak, or Amchitka, once they were torn away to hunt the waters of Cook Inlet and Prince William Sound, far to the south of their homes. And this was much less likely as the hunt shifted even farther to the south—to the waters of southeastern Alaska, to the shores of British Columbia, and eventually, as far as the coast of California.

The story of the Russian impressment of the sturdy Aleuts is not a pleasant one, yet its advantages to the conquerors did not always inspire horror in neutral observers. There is a lesson to be gained from the expressions of grudging admiration for such a complete subjugation of a hapless people. If, one hundred years after the Aleuts were first harnessed, a distinguished American scientist could view the atrocity in a favorable light, could there have been much hope for a more enlightened treatment of Alaska's natives under United States rule? In the early days of conquest, the Russian fur traders were inhumane, ignorant, and relatively unrestrained by the supervision of a benevolent government; yet some benefits ensued, according to the considered conclusion of William Healy Dall, the American scientist who took part in the Western Union Telegraph Expedition to Alaska in 1865–67. "It would seem brutal to advise force as a civilizer," Dall wrote of the Alaskan Indians, "but the Aleuts, who were thoroughly crushed and subjugated . . . are today the only large body of aboriginals in America who give any promise of ultimate civilization." [9] Dall had not seen many Aleuts in his travels. Indeed, there were not many to be seen; but like other Americans, he respected the exercise of stern authority by white men over natives. Dall's observations of Yukon Indians were the occasion of his historical comments, and although he had found the interior peoples peaceful, he noted that there had been incidents of violence against whites. The 1855 massacre of the Russian traders at Nulato on the Yukon River was the particular event Dall had in mind, and he heartily applauded the Russian retribution, also a massacre: "The result was wonderful. From that day to this not a native on the lower Yukon has lifted his hand against the whites. The bloody lesson was not thrown away. The strong hand, which alone commands the respect of savages, was worth a thousand missionaries." [10]

By most commentators, Russian and non-Russian alike, the Aleut story has not been viewed in the benign manner of William Dall. The forcible debasement of the natives has generally been condemned for the inhuman outrage which it clearly was; though, in fairness, the *promyshlenniks* should not be seen as unique. Brutality and oppression of weaker peoples has characterized all expansion during the course of human history. It is to the credit of the Russian government that it prohibited and severely criticized ill treatment of the natives, though ameliorating action lagged far behind the abuses.

The plight of the Aleuts under the disastrous rule of the Russian traders was not entirely ignored in St. Petersburg, though reporters of the situation did not place the blame directly on the *promyshlenniks*. In 1768–69 a naval expedition under Captain Krenitsin and Lieutenant Levashev was sent to chart the islands in which the traders were already well established. The navy men had an opportunity to observe the Aleuts but witnessed no Russian atrocities. By this time the Aleuts had been pacified. They were well broken to the Russian yoke—defeated, submissive, and rapidly declining in numbers.

Some of the islands were still well populated. Unalaska Island natives had sixteen villages and about 1,000 people, but the naval officers learned that "it was formerly much more populous." [11] Traders explained the population loss as due to the natives' disputes with Russians and to a general famine that occurred in 1762, "but most of all from a change in their way of life." [12] What had occurred seemed plausible to the Russians, and it certainly was not their fault. "No longer contented with their original simplicity, they [the Aleuts] long for Russian luxuries: in order therefore to obtain a few delicacies, which are presently consumed, they dedicate the greatest part of their time to hunting, for the purpose of procuring furs for the Russians." [13] Who could reproach the Russian fur traders? Certainly not Captain Krenitsin, nor the St. Petersburg Academy of Sciences to whom his reports were conveyed. Plainly, the greed of the Aleuts for "Russian luxuries" had regretfully disrupted the native pattern of life. "They neglect to lay up a provision of fish and roots; and suffer their children frequently to die of hunger." [14] How easy it was to explain away the disturbing consequences of commercial expansion by fixing the blame on the natives' lack of foresight. This rationale for the genocide of Bering Sea peoples was to be relied upon again and again. A century later, solemn reports recounting starvation and disaster in the wake of the American whaling fleet were to echo the same theme of neglectful natives, although some Americans did recognize the underlying causes of the famine.

But Russian officials were not entirely taken in by the traders' version of their relation with the Aleuts. In the same report which lays the decline in native population to the native insistence on hunting fur for the Russians to the detriment of their families, Captain Krenitsin noted the practice of imposing a tax on the Aleuts, to be paid in furs. Further, Krenitsin discovered that wintering Russian traders followed a standard practice of coercion: the traders "then endeavour to procure, either by persuasion or force, the children of the inhabitants, particularly of the Tookoos (leaders), as hostages." [15] Once the hostages were secured, the traders "deliver to the inhabitants fox-traps, and also skins for their boats, for which they give them quittances." [16] For the rest of the furs, the

Russians offered some of their "delicacies" which the Aleuts were supposed to crave so strongly that they starved their children: beads, fake pearls, goat's wool, copper kettles, and hatchets. In the spring, Krenitsin further reported, the traders deliver up their hostages and recover their traps. The Aleuts could not understand the tax imposed upon them. They could appreciate the transaction insofar as the well-armed traders compelled them to surrender a certain number of furs without recompense, but what puzzled them was the Russians' insistence that the tribute was then passed on to a distant ruler. Another enigma was the Russians' claim to represent a much greater number of people residing elsewhere "for in their own country all the men of the island go out together." [17] The presence of Siberian natives, Kamchadals and Koriaks, who accompanied the Russians was some comfort to the Aleuts, who "love to associate with people whose manner of life resembles their own." [18] But the Russian tyranny, perplexing as it seemed in some details, was real enough; Krenitsin was told that the traders "dare not hunt alone, nor in small numbers, on account of the hatred of the natives." [19]

The czar had reason to be somewhat concerned over his new Aleut subjects, but there were other problems on the Bering Sea frontier as well. It did not speak well of government administration of distant areas like Kamchatka if order could not be maintained, if convicts could destroy their keepers and escape with impunity. And the situation was aggravated when such affairs became common knowledge in Europe and pointed up the weakness of the czar's frontier. The Benyowsky escapade drew the attention of Europe to this frontier for the first time, and it is this that makes the incident important.

5 — DREAMS OF AN EMPIRE

No more amazing adventures have ever been recorded of the Bering Sea frontier than those of Mauritius August Count De Benyowsky who has written an account of them in his autobiographical *Memoirs and Travels.* Benyowsky was a Polish nobleman who had served with some distinction against the czar's army. While bearing arms in this revolt against the czar he was captured and sent as a prisoner to Bolcheretsk, on the west coast of the Kamchatka Peninsula. After encountering many adventures along the way, he arrived at his place of exile in 1770 and entered the governor's household as a teacher of foreign languages and music to the governor's daughter. Shortly before he became a part of the governor's household, he met a group of exiles who had formed a secret society. Their goal was to escape from Siberia. The society had an international membership, including Russians, Poles, and Swedes. An elected council of eight members made the plans, keeping their decisions from the membership at large. Strangely enough, Benyowsky was asked to head the society on his second day in town. Whether this was a recognition of his nobility or of his charisma is not clear. Membership was expanded to include free merchants, and even government officials who wished to join the revolt. All members uttered solemn oaths of secrecy, and those of the Russian faith were required to go to confession and take the Sacrament to corroborate their oaths. Winter was not the time for action; preparations were made for an escape in the spring.

Meanwhile, Benyowsky had become involved in a romantic relationship with the governor's daughter, Aphanasia. What young woman—denied the amusements enjoyed by other young people of her class and condemned to rude surroundings and the company of semibarbaric people—could fail to fall in love with the handsome count? Perhaps the count was susceptible as well; he was only twenty-six at the time. At any rate, Benyowsky neglected to tell Aphanasia about his wife. Little did Aphanasia dream, in her newfound joy, that fate would rob her of both lover and fond father.

Romance as well as conspiracy became complicated when a merchant, who had lost heavily to Benyowsky at chess, tried to poison him and other secret society leaders. Benyowsky accused the merchant before the governor. The would-be murderer, in turn, revealed the escape conspiracy without making any impression upon the governor who sentenced the culprit to death. Seizing the occasion, Aphanasia begged her father and his senior officials to obtain the abolition of the count's sentence of exile and secure him government employment. Benyowsky tells us that the young woman proclaimed "her sincere desire of seeing me happy, and of partaking in my happiness." [1] This was too much for the poor governor, who flew into a rage and heaped invective on the count. His colleagues eventually calmed him and, in an abrupt about-face, he decided to discharge Benyowsky's sentence on the theory that the poisoning attempt was a conspiracy against the government—hence its revelation merited a pardon.

When Benyowsky's comrades heard of his good fortune, they reacted decisively. At a meeting of the secret society, he was invited to drink a goblet of poison for his supposed treachery to the cause. Fortunately, his eloquence carried the day; his explanation of events assuaged the fears of the conspirators. "After having ended my discourse . . . consternation and joy was on every countenance." [2] The count accepted the group's apologies and they fell to considering "how much my liberation would lend to insure the execution of our project." [3]

The exiles planned to seize a ship and escape by sea at the first opportunity. Secrecy was difficult to maintain. Word of the plot reached Aphanasia. Now Benyowsky's fiancée, she rushed to him with her discovery, wishing to bid him farewell before taking her own life: "she could not live after such an affront." [4] After this declaration, the deceived Aphanasia fainted. The count, "exceedingly alarmed and distressed," yet "did not fail to arrange a plan . . . during the interval of her insensibility." [5] Throwing himself at his fiancée's feet, Benyowsky declaimed at length on the sincerity of his love: "I have lived for you, and if you could read my heart I am sure I would have your pity, for the possession of your person has become as necessary to my existence as liberty itself." [6] Nor was the liberty offered by the governor enough, as it would not bring him his former wealth and rank. Much of his happiness depended upon his capacity to share "fortune and dignity" with Aphanasia.[7] After all, a successor to her father might very well reimpose the czar's sanctions—then where would they be? "Represent to yourself, my dearest friend, the affliction and despair that would overwhelm my soul when I beheld you a sharer in my pain and disgrace." [8]

Predictably, the young woman melted in response to this emotional defense. All that she still required was some explanation for his lack of confidence in her. Most assuredly she would follow him "to the furthest limits of the universe." [9] "I told her, therefore, that I was prevented only by the fear lest she should refuse my proposals, on account of her attachment to her parents." [10] His intention had always been to carry her off with him. All was well with the lovers again.

Soon after this scene, the governor discovered the escape plans and Aphanasia warned the count. In an attempt to place Benyowsky in custody and thwart the plot, the governor was killed by the conspirators. The Siberian officials seized four of the exiles and denied the rest the safety of the fort. Benyowsky and his men responded by rounding up the settlement's women and children, 1,000 in all, locking them in a church and threatening to burn the building if the garrison did not surrender. This did the trick. The garrison gave up, and the conspirators, led by Benyowsky, took charge. The exiles were set to work provisioning the Russian ship the St. Peter & Paul for a long voyage. Provisions and all the valuables available—furs, jewels, money—were loaded aboard.

Aphanasia begged an interview with the count. Once again she had word of his deception: someone had told her that Benyowsky already had a wife. The Polish nobleman admitted the truth of the matter. His confession had only been deferred until a proper match could be arranged for the young lady. But Aphanasia was as adaptable as her lover. Neither the murder of her father nor the count's dubious conduct put her off. She would join him disguised as a boy and simply be as a daughter to him. Marriage she renounced forever. With this heart-tugging affirmation, the young woman disappears from Benyowsky's narrative. Her fate is just one of many obscurities beclouding the adventurer's *Memoirs and Travels.*

Count Mauritius Benyowsky.
University of Alaska Archives

The escapees' ship was made ready. Benyowsky ordered the local priest to celebrate a divine service of thanksgiving; required his associates, ninety-six strong, to make a personal oath of fidelity to him; and made the townspeople agree to accept his word as law until the ship sailed. On the 12th of May all was ready. After hoisting the colors of the Confederation of Poland over the *St. Peter & Paul*, saluting the town and the occasion with a fusillade from the ship's twenty guns, the escapees put to sea.

The voyage of the *St. Peter & Paul* was truly amazing, especially as told by Benyowsky—whose account of the voyage is implausible in many ways. One would expect that men anxious to avoid the czar's wardens would not linger in the Bering Sea, nor would a daring attempt to sail a route never before accomplished seem a logical decision; yet, we are told the exiles insisted upon a Northeast Passage course via the Bering Strait and the Siberian Arctic to Europe. Their meandering course took them to the Bering Islands, then north to the Bering Strait, south to Kodiak Island, west again to the Aleutians, then south to the Kuriles before finally bringing them to Japan and Macao where the improbable voyage ended. Their timetable was fantastic: the voyage from the Chukchi Peninsula at sixty-six degrees north latitude to Kodiak, 1,000 miles away, occupied three days. The journey from Amchitka in the Aleutians to the Kurile Islands was a matter of two days.

Benyowsky was such a liar that one might be inclined to write off all his exploits as a tissue of prevarication but for the partial corroboration of other witnesses. A chance encounter in the Bering Sea brought the British explorer Captain James Cook together with one of Benyowsky's former shipmates in 1778. A Russian fur trader, Erasim Gregorioff Ismailov, exchanged geographical information with Cook when the great circumnavigator called at Unalaska. Ismailov also described his adventures with Benyowsky, though the English officers were somewhat confused by the story because of mutual language difficulty. According to Ismailov, the *St. Peter & Paul* sailed due south from Bolcheretsk to the Kuriles, Japan, and eventually to China. In time he got to France, then to St. Petersburg, and back to Kamchatka. Because Ismailov seemed to know nothing of French, the English found his story suspicious. Later, at Petropavlovsk, they met other former members of Benyowsky's crew and then understood the affair more clearly.

Ismailov and some of the other Russians were probably unwilling participants in the escape voyage.[11] Benyowsky mentions Ismailov's misconduct and conspiracies before the *St. Peter & Paul* sailed and again at sea. On Bering Island, Benyowsky's men petitioned to have Ismailov and others abandoned ashore and he "complied with this general request." [12] Ismailov's relating of the voyage to Japan and China merits greater weight than the count's, whose memory was, to state it mildly, capricious.

According to Benyowsky's story, the *St. Peter & Paul* sailed around the southern tip of the Kamchatka Peninsula, then made a passage northeast to Bering Island. On this island, some thirty years before, Vitus Bering had died after his discovery voyage to America. On Bering Island the count met a strange character who had a daring scheme. This was a gentleman named Ochotyn, originally from Saxony, who had been exiled to Siberia and found service on one of the Russian fur-trading vessels. On his third Aleutian voyage he and fifty other malcontents seized this ship and two other vessels and threw off the Russian yoke. Soon Ochotyn gathered 134 determined men under his command and undertook to create a Bering Sea empire of his own. Natives, impressed by Ochotyn's fair dealing, flocked to his standard. With their support the bold Saxon expected to be able to contend with any force the Russian traders might mount against him.

Ochotyn recognized a kindred soul in Benyowsky and suggested the two adventurers join forces. On the grounds of his interest in a speedy return to Europe, the count declined, but offered to try to enlist a European power in support of Ochotyn's cause. All this seemed to have been a whole cloth fabrication of a fictional character on Benyowsky's part—yet perhaps not entirely fictional.

Ochotyn's role must have tempted the count, since he was to execute a similar program—not in the cold, inhospitable Bering Sea with a shipload of impressed seamen and exiles longing for a return to Europe but in lush, tropical Madagascar.

Obviously North Pacific history would have been enriched if Benyowsky had become the Ochotyn he imagined, but it was not to be. Instead he raised a cross on Bering Island to commemorate "his happy deliverance from exile at Kamchatka," and then put to sea.[13]

Sailing north, the *St. Peter & Paul* almost met disaster in an encounter with drift ice. "The considerable masses of these ice drifts formed whole mountains around us, and threatened us with inevitable destruction." [14] Ice crashed against the vessel's sides and battered her about unmercifully; "the whole company were alarmed, even to stupefaction." [15] Next, the wind rose to frightening force, carrying away sprit-sail yard and fore-topmast. Against his better judgment the count had been persuaded by his men to attempt a passage to Europe by way of the Bering Strait and along the Arctic coast to the west. Now the men regretted this course and urged their leader to abandon the Northeast Passage attempt and turn southward. No amount of turmoil, no threatening ice nor lashing wind deterred Benyowsky when given such a natural occasion to lecture his confederates: "This occasion gave me ample matter to reproach them for the little confidence they had shown me. . . . I thought it necessary to represent to them the many unhappy consequences which would result from being exposed a second time to submit to their pleasure." [16] His tongue lashing was received humbly, since the "dreadful objects which had alarmed them . . . were still present around us, and gave every degree of efficacy to my discourse." [17] Without difficulty the entire company promised that in the future they would "leave me at liberty to do whatever I might think proper and advantageous." [18] After this affirmation of power, the commander could afford to be magnanimous—an extraordinary allowance of brandy was given all hands.

Ice navigation was a tricky enough job on a happy ship, but the count had to contend with mutiny after mutiny. Such outbursts were quelled with resolute strength tempered by an enviable Christian forebearance; though often urged to punish mutiny with death, he preferred the lash. By clever seamanship and stratagems, such as setting fires under each mast to keep the sails free of ice, he extracted the ship from the dangerous ice and voyaged far enough into Bering Strait to sight both Asian and American lands before turning south. Other navigators before him had ascertained the separation of the two continents, but presumably Benyowsky wanted to confirm their findings.

The *St. Peter & Paul* passed through the Aleutians and put in at Kodiak Island. There Mr. Ochotyn's men controlled the island and employed the natives as fur hunters. Before departing from the island, Benyowsky left a letter for Ochotyn which offered advice from one freebooter to another: Keep your men busy so they won't have time to plot; keep a party of native bodyguards near at hand for personal protection; go south and locate on islands with better climate. "Adieu, my friend, I wish you every prosperity, and you may depend upon my best exertions to cause some European power to accept your proposals." [19] Benyowsky's suggestion that Ochotyn relocate to the south undoubtedly came from the heart. It was precisely what he himself had in mind for his next adventure.

After departing Kodiak, the *St. Peter & Paul* voyaged south out of the region of our concern. Needless to say, Benyowsky enjoyed a number of adventures. He discovered an agreeable "Island of Liquor"; visited Japan; called at a South Pacific island where he was beseeched to stay permanently and was offered land and a lovely lady as inducements. The count promised the island folk that he would return—once rid of his mutinous riffraff—bringing with him "virtuous, good, and just men, to dwell upon this island, and to adopt the manners, usages, and laws of the inhabitants." [20] Formosa was the next call, and after a violent reception, Benyowsky's charm brought another offer from the nobility. If he would return with sufficient men and ships to drive all Chinese away, he would be awarded a province as his personal dominion.

By the time the count got back to Europe, empire building was in his blood. His estates in Europe—if indeed he owned any—did not have the allure of Pacific domains. Benyowsky traveled to Paris to solicit support for the establishment of a colony on Madagascar. While in Paris, he met a relative, Casimir Pulaski, who was preparing to travel to America and join the colonial army in its struggle against England. Benyowsky had a great idea. Tell the Americans that he would put Madagascar at their disposal! The island could be used as a base in the war with the British. What Benyowsky's military strategy was is impossible to fathom; but perhaps his tactics were more personal in nature and directed to ingratiating himself with the new republic.

At any rate, after the failure of his first venture on Madagascar, he voyaged to America and offered his services. Despite that Benyowsky "had the misfortune to fall into the hands of enemies" and was jailed by the British, the American officials seemed to have been somewhat suspicious of the Polish soldier of fortune.[21] He had been recommended by Benjamin Franklin and provided with a horse and money by General Horatio Gates, but Congress did not want his services. In December 1779, Benyowsky petitioned Congress, writing in Latin, of his "determined resolution" to sacrifice the remainder of his life in the United States." [22] Congress, though "having a grateful sense of his offer," found that "the circumstances of the army will not admit of his being employed." [23] Thus, instead of serving the American cause, Benyowsky turned to his Madagascar project once again. Our cultural heritage must be the poorer for the reluctance of Congress to give a post to the splendid Pole.

Benyowsky's published *Memoirs and Travels* end just after he won French support for the establishment of the Madagascar colony. Benyowsky spent three years on Madagascar but did not win his dream empire. After returning to France in disgrace, he found an English backer and returned to Madagascar to wrest by force the prize that had eluded him. French forces sent to the island cut short his career. He was executed as a pirate on May 23, 1786, perhaps lamenting that he did not confine his imperial ambitions to the Bering Sea.

Count Benyowsky's escape from Siberia had surprisingly far-reaching influences. When he returned to Europe in 1771, his exploits were the sensation of the moment. In Paris he titillated the salons with adventure stories of the North and South Pacific Oceans. At the time, France's relations with Russia were at a low point, and the Russian ambassador in Paris was gravely concerned about the impact of the Kamchatka escape. The count missed no occasion to describe the vulnerability of Russia's Pacific frontier, and the ease with which Kamchatka could be taken by a foreign power. Indeed, the easy escape of the exiles demonstrated convincingly the weakness of the Russian hold. Reports and rumors flew between Paris and St. Petersburg and from Kamchatka to the czar's capital. Word came that the French would give Benyowsky a frigate for the capture of Kamchatka, a rumor that gained currency when the count's promise to return and carry off Bolcheretsk residents to California was also reported to St. Petersburg. Something would have to be done, argued Russian officials, to shore up the empire's eastern defenses.

Some action followed. Soon after the Benyowsky affair the seat of Kamchatka's government was moved from Bolcheretsk to the fine harbor site of Petropavlovsk. Additionally, the new governor of the province founded a settlement on Urup—one of the Kurile Islands. But the Russians were not alone in their alarm over threats to their frontier interests. Spain, long a claimant of the entire North Pacific, grew more and more uneasy about Russian activity in the Bering Sea. Counter-measures against the Russian advances seemed an urgent necessity. Ships were dispatched north to Alaska from Mexico, and an overland expedition established a mission and garrison at Monterey on the coast of northern California. Suddenly the lands and waters of Siberia and Alaska were the focus of international attention. Now the status of the Bering Sea as a private fur preserve of a few hardy adventurers was radically altered; the region might well have become a stormy center of Russian-Spanish conflict.

Then fresh alarm both in St. Petersburg and Madrid. A third maritime power, little awed by the pretensions of a declining Spain or a weak maritime nation like Russia, showed its flag in northern seas. In 1778, ships of the British Royal Navy—the *Resolution* and the *Discovery*—commanded by the great Pacific explorer, Captain James Cook, appeared unannounced off the coast of northwestern America and northeastern Asia. The Royal Navy reigned supreme among the maritime forces of the world; its presence caused consternation indeed! What were the British intentions in the north? Now all Europe awaited events with marked agitation.

Geographic knowledge of the North Pacific took a giant bound forward with the work of master navigator, James Cook. He did not, however, undertake additional scientific work as on his first two circumnavigations when scientists were taken along. Cook had been instructed to watch for a Northwest Passage along the coast south of the Bering Sea and, if none was discovered, he was to sail through Bering Strait and attempt either the Northwest or Northeast Passages from there.

After his careful searching of Cook Inlet, the explorer reached the Aleutian Islands in June 1778, making a perilous passage between Unalaska and Ungala Islands. Aleuts paddled their kayaks out to the *Resolution* and the *Discovery*, boarded the vessels fearlessly, and did a little trading. The English could see that the Aleuts were accustomed to Europeans from their casual manner and the bits of Western clothing some of them wore. The English could not, however, read the Russian notes that the natives showed. These notes were actually receipts for taxes paid by the Aleuts which they probably offered to defer any further exaction of tribute from the white men.

Because of heavy fog and contrary winds, Cook remained in anchorage off Unalaska for several days and made several shore excursions. He was favorably impressed by the peaceful Aleuts—"very good looking people and decently clean." [24] Among some natives enjoying a repast of raw halibut, Cook observed a middle-aged woman "of such a mien as would at all times and in all places command respect." [25] His sailors liked the Aleuts too. "Their women might be called beautiful, to some we had seen in King Georges Sound," wrote one.[26] And there was a reason for the sailors' benevolent attitude: the women were "so kind, that we purchased their favors with a few leaves of tobacco, of which they make snuff—but the men chew." [27]

When the weather cleared, Cook sailed into the Bering Sea, crossed Bristol Bay, and made a landfall at Cape Newenham where Lieutenant Williamson was sent ashore. As was customary, "he took possession of the Country in His Majesty's name, [and] left on the hill a bottle in which was inscribed on a piece of paper, the ships' names, date, etc." [28] The two ships then sailed north, making slow progress for lack of wind, but taking advantage of the calm to cast out fishing lines. Great halibut weighing up to 100 pounds were taken and cods so numerous that Cook distributed salt for their preservation. The waters of Bristol Bay are one of the great fisheries of the world, and it was no task to provision the *Resolution* and the *Discovery*.

On July 21 the English ships were near St. Matthew Island when they encountered Eskimos for the first time. The Eskimos, apparently inhabitants of the Kuskokwim Bay region, approached the ships in their kayaks and offered furs. "They appeared to be wholly unacquainted with people like us, they knew not the use of tobacco, nor was any thing foreign seen about them, except a knife may be looked upon as such." [29] Russian traders had not yet developed an interest in the northwestern Alaskan mainland, thus the Eskimos had not been subjected to their rule. Their wariness, however, indicated that they knew something of the Russian-Aleut relationships. When they saw English boats, which had been sounding the coastal waters, approach, they abruptly ended the trading and paddled away in alarm.

Cook continued north, entering Bering Strait and landing on Sledge Island, a few miles off what is today Nome, Alaska. On July 6 he observed and named King Island in Bering Strait, and on the 10th crossed to the Siberian side of the strait and landed in St. Lawrence Bay near a Chukchi village. The Chukchi were more familiar with Europeans than were the American Eskimos. "As we drew near three of them came down towards the shore and were so polite as to take off their caps and make us a low bow: we returned the compliment but this did not inspire them with sufficient confidence to wait our landing, for the moment we put the boats ashore they retired." [30]

The English explorers were the first non-Russian white men to make contact with the Chukchi, and it was clear that the natives, though "polite" enough to bow, were not dominated by Russians in the Kamchadal or Aleut fashion. They allowed the English to distribute gifts but could not be induced to lay down their weapons, "which they held in constant readiness never once quitting them." [31] Chukchi caution and belligerence helped them preserve their independence from the Russians until recent times, though from the eighteenth century on, they were willing enough to trade.

According to the latest Russian map which Cook had in his possession—that published by Staehlin in 1760—the land of the Chukchi should have been the huge island called "Alaschka" that occupied a large portion of the Bering Sea on the map, but Cook correctly asserted it to be "the Country of the Tchuktschians explored by Behring in 1728." [32] At the time, Cook's comments on the erroneous map were reserved; he withheld judgment on it until he had made further observations. Later, after he knew the Bering Sea better, he wondered what induced Staehlin "to publish so erroneous a map in which many of these islands are jumbled in regular confusion, without the least regard to truth and yet he is pleased to call it a very accurate little map?" [33] Armchair cartographers who distorted geography were the bane of explorers, and Cook roundly damned "a map that the most illiterate of his illiterate sea-faring men would have been ashamed to put his name to." [34]

Sailing north once more, the English explorers made their first attempt to penetrate the Arctic Ocean ice pack. Had the sea been open, they would have voyaged eastward through the long-sought Northwest Passage. However, after passing through Bering Strait into the Chukchi Sea and passing Point Hope and Cape Lisburne, their western course was halted north of Icy Cape. Walrus, or sea horses as they were called, were seen everywhere on the pack ice, and both ships put out boats for a hunt. Nine of the huge mammals were taken. Many of the seamen found walrus flesh a welcome change in diet; others thought it disgusting but ate it because their commander did. Cook's sailors fervently believed that he led a charmed life and believed in following his example. It is remarkable that anyone could eat walrus in the manner in which it was prepared. "We towed it overboard for twelve hours then boil'd it for four hours and the next day cut it into stakes and fry'd it; and even then it was too rank both in smell and taste to make use of except with plenty of pepper and salt and these two articles were very scarce." [35]

Cook wrote an excellent description of the walrus.

> They lay in herds of many hundred upon the ice, huddling one over the other like swine, and roar or bray very loud, so that in the night or foggy weather they gave us notice of the ice long before we would see it. We never found the whole herd asleep, some were always on the watch, these, on the approach of the boat, would wake those next to them and these the others, so that the whole herd would be awake presently. But they were seldom in a hurry to get away till after they had been once fired at, then they would tumble one over the other into the sea in the utmost confusion, and if we did not at the first discharge, kill those we fired at out right we generally lost them tho' mortally wounded. They did not appear to us to be that dangerous animal, some authors have described, not even when attacked, they are rather more so in appearance than in reality. [36]

In late August, Cook gave up the effort to penetrate the ice pack, resolving to try again the next summer. On September 3 the ships anchored once more in St. Lawrence Bay, on the Asian side of Bering Strait, but the Chukchi showed no inclination to visit the English vessels. Continuing south, Cook crossed to the American side and entered Norton Sound. Landing parties were sent ashore near Cape Denbigh to get fresh water and spruce for the brewing of an antiscorbutic beer. Eskimos were again encountered. Natives in umiaks paddled out to the ships and performed some music for the visitors, which was found "agreeable." Some trading was done before the English sailed off.

Early in October, Cook reached the Aleutians once again. The ships anchored on the north side of Unalaska, and the carpenters set about replacing the ships' sheathing above the waterline. Cook kept other seamen busy picking berries and catching fish. Scurvy would never ravage the men of the *Resolution* and the *Discovery* if he could help it.

On October 8 Cook received from an Aleut a very singular present, a salmon-filled pie made with rye flour. Unmistakably this was European food, and letters delivered with the pie—though incomprehensible because they were in Russian—confirmed that there must be Russians in the neighborhood. Cook quickly decided to send a messenger to the

Russians and chose Corporal John Ledyard of the marines, "an intelligent man," to accompany the Aleuts and find the Russians.

John Ledyard, the only American serving with Cook, was the first of his countrymen to observe the Bering Sea and its peoples. Ledyard was only twenty-seven years old in 1778, but he had already led an adventurous life. Studies at Dartmouth College, which he attended in 1772–73, bored him; so he absented himself without leave to undertake a canoe voyage on the Connecticut River. After this, he served before the mast on a merchant ship's voyage to Africa and the West Indies. In Gibraltar he impulsively enlisted in the British army, but was rehired by his ship's captain before his military service commenced. Next he voyaged from New York to England, enlisted in the British army in 1774, deserted in 1776, joined the Royal Marines and met Captain Cook, who signed him on the *Resolution*. Ledyard's published account of his voyage on the *Resolution* alerted his fellow Yankees to the abundance of fur animals on the Northwest coast and the high value they had in the Chinese market. Soon after the Yankee traders established their long and profitable trading circuit from New England to the Northwest, Hawaii, and China, Ledyard was anxious to return to the Bering Sea and started off across Europe and Siberia.

Ledyard's travels on Unalaska to make contact with the Russians were reported fully in his book.

> The first day we proceeded about 15 miles into the interior part of the island without any remarkable occurrence until we approached a village just before night. This village consisted of about thirty huts, some of them large and spacious though not very high. The huts are composed of a kind of slight frame erected over a square hole sunk about 4 feet into the ground; the frame is covered at the bottom with turf and upwards it is thatched with coarse grass; the whole village was out to see us and men, women and children crowded about me. I was conducted by the young Chief who was my guide and seemed proud and assiduous to serve me into one of the largest huts. I was surprised at the behavior of the Indians, for though they were curious to see me, yet they did not express that extraordinary curiosity that would be expected had they never seen a European before, and I was glad to perceive it, as it was an evidence in favor of what I wished to find true, viz. that there were Europeans now among them.[37]

Shortly thereafter, three Russian traders decided to travel back to Cook's ships with Ledyard. Thus, curiously, an American introduced the Russians to the great British captain. Who could have predicted, at that early date, which of the three nations represented at the meeting would come to dominate the Bering Sea?

The three Russians whom Ledyard brought to Cook were friendly enough but unable to satisfy all his queries on Bering Sea geography. However, a couple of days later, another trader arrived who had much more information. This was Erasim Ismailov who had accompanied Count Benyowsky on his remarkable escape from Kamchatka in 1771. Ismailov told Cook about his voyage to Japan, China, and France; but, because he did not seem to know a single word of French, the English explorer had some doubts about the alleged voyage. Other accounts of the Benyowsky adventure indicate that Ismailov was put ashore on one of the Kurile Islands and returned to Kamchatka from there. This version of his voyage would account for his ignorance of French. Ismailov was able to fill Cook in on all the Russian discoveries made in the Bering Sea, providing details that complemented the explorer's findings. Apparently the Russians knew very little of the American mainland of the Bering Sea. Their landings had "always been repulsed by the Natives, whom they describe as a very treacherous people; they mentioned two or three Captains or chief men, that had been murdered by them and some of the Russians here shewed us wounds which they said they received there." [38] On a subsequent visit to the English, Ismailov provided Cook with manuscript charts of the region. This accurate information, when combined with the charts compiled by the English, made it possible to produce the first reliable maps of the North Pacific and Bering Sea. These results of shared knowledge were published in England and Russia in 1780. The dissemination of this geographic knowledge did not have to await the return of Cook's expedition, because Cook gave Ismailov charts and letters addressed to the British admiralty, which the Russian sent on via Kamchatka and St. Petersburg.

Cook spent ample time on Unalaska to observe the traders' operation. Russians shared a dwelling with Kamchadals and Aleuts and supervised the fur hunting. "The first and great object is the Sea Beaver or Otter; I never heard them enquire after any other Animal, not that they let other furs slip through their fingers when they can get them." [39] Cook did not know how long the Russians had been established on

Unalaska and the other Aleutian Islands, "but to judge from the great subjection the Natives are under, it must have been some time." [40] To Cook, the Aleuts seemed "the most peaceable inoffensive people I ever met with, and as to honesty they might serve as a pattern to the most civilized nation upon earth." [41] He assumed that the Aleuts' gentleness resulted from Russian subjection and the "severe examples" imposed upon them by their overlords, and he approved of it: "If this was done at first it was excusable since the most happy consequences have attended, and one sees now nothing but the greatest harmony subsisting between the two Nations." [42] Although the Aleuts seemed to enjoy their liberty and property unmolested, Cook guessed that they were actually tributaries to the Russians.

Greatest harmony also existed between the English sailors and the Aleuts as Captain Clerke, Cook's second-in-command, made clear: "The reception they gave at their Houses and their civility during the visit, was perfectly consistent with that happy and extensive benevolence which appears to have so general an influence upon all their actions." [43] Clerke was gratified that "to make our Entertainment as compleat as these good People could render it, the Ladies offer'd their services, and there was really not wanting strong temptation, for all were exceedingly clean and decent, and many of them handsome." [44] For such services the tars handed over a handful of tobacco to the best-looking women and a few leaves "for one of inferior Charms." [45] Cook, too, praised such "great civility to our people, the Women grant the last favour without the least scruple; young or old, married or single, I have been told, never hesitate a moment." [46]

Cook's men even enjoyed home visits. David Samwell, the *Discovery* surgeon, described one such visit when he and his shipmates climbed down the ladder entry to a half-buried Aleut dwelling to encounter the "potent stink of putrid fish." [47] This did not put off the seasoned veterans of Tahiti and Hawaii. "Having been used to many strange Scenes since we left England, we spent no time in staring about with vacant astonishment but immediately made love to the handsomest woman in Company, who in order to make us welcome refused us no Favour she could grant tho' her Husband or Father stood by." [48]

Samwell marveled that the chastity of the women seemed not to concern the Aleut men. He assumed that Aleuts customarily offered their wives as a gesture of hospitality; whereas traditionally among Aleuts, the acceptance of such a favor imposed obligations on the recipient which were not lightly undertaken. While the British were puzzled at the apparent indifference of native men to their pleasurable bouts, they were even more surprised at the forbearance of the Russian traders. Although the traders and tars did not share a spoken language, the British managed to discourse on a burning curiosity. Why, asked the sailors—presumably in the international sign language of obscenity—don't you enjoy the freely bestowed favors of the fair sex? The Russians responded with a gravity which must have been maintained at the expense of considerable will power: They would not couple with natives who were unbaptized. David Samwell, surgeon of the *Discovery*, did not greet this expression of reticence with laughter: "It would have appeared impossible to us notwithstanding their remonstrances had we not met with an instance of the like before." [49] Had not the "beautiful Nymphs" of Tahiti murmured that the Spaniards had denied themselves in similar fashion? The Tahitian women complained of this Spanish obstinacy to Samwell and his fellows: "We gave them every consolation in our power." [50] The British were more than willing to console the Aleut women. "We could never yet perceive the want of the Fingers of the Priest to work her forehead with the Sign of the Cross." [51] Later, when some of the veterans of Unalaska amours discovered themselves inflicted with venereal disease, they might have had second thoughts concerning the Russians' scruples.

On October 26, 1778, the English put to sea once more—bound for Hawaii and the fatal destiny awaiting the great commander there. Cook died in Hawaii, but his ships returned to the Bering Sea the next summer for another attempt at penetrating the Arctic Ocean ice.

Some of the officers Cook trained went on to have brilliant careers. A few returned to the North Pacific for further exploration—notably, George Vancouver. John Ledyard dreamed of journeying back, yet could not achieve his goal. Another of Cook's officers, Joseph Billings, returned a few years later and got to know the Chukchi better than anyone else had up to that time.

6 — THE IMPRESS OF CIVILIZATION

In 1785 the Russian government equipped a major expedition to explore and map the Bering Sea, the Aleutian Islands, and the Arctic coast of Siberia. Command was vested in an Englishman, Captain Joseph Billings, who had served under Captain James Cook on his third voyage to the Pacific Ocean. In the official circles of St. Petersburg there was a certain magic in the name of James Cook that reflected to the credit of anyone associated with his successful voyages. This association with Cook probably had a great influence on the selection of Billings, though the English mariner was to reveal little of the exploratory talent of his former commander. Geographical exploration was the principal purpose of the Billings expedition, but he was also ordered to look into the alleged mistreatment of Aleuts by the Russian fur traders. Billings' report on the Aleutian situation, and the published accounts of two other participants in the voyage, Martin Sauer, formerly one of Cook's men and now secretary to the expedition, and General Gawrila Sarytschew, a Russian naval officer, fully substantiated earlier records of the traders' tyranny.

As with the second Kamchatka expedition of Vitus Bering, Billings had to supervise the building of an exploration vessel on the Okhotsk Sea. Conditions had improved in eastern Siberia since Bering's time; Russian workers and some materials were more readily available, but it was still a major project. It required months of effort before the *Glory of Russia* was launched at Okhotsk. From there the ship was taken to Petropavlovsk in October 1787, where the expedition wintered. In the spring of 1788 the Billings expedition sailed for the Aleutian Islands.

Off Unalaska Island, the *Glory of Russia* met native kayaks. Martin

Sauer was much impressed by the agility and skill of the Aleut boatmen. The Aleuts guided their kayaks among breakers dashing against reefs and rocks with an extraordinary disdain for danger, awing their spectators by sharply overturning and revolving their trim vessels, "sporting about more like amphibious animals than human beings." [1] Their spectacular display of maritime acrobatics gave the Aleuts a command of the waters which reminded Sauer of Shakespeare's lines:

> He trod the water,
> Whose enmity he flung aside, and breathed
> The surge most swoln that met him. [2]

Sauer thought the kayaks of the Unalaskans superior to those of other Aleuts: "If perfect symmetry, smoothness, and proportion, constitute beauty, they are beautiful: to me they appeared so beyond any thing I ever beheld." [3] The skins of some of the vessels were as transparent as oiled papers, "through which you could trace every formation of the inside, and the manner of the natives' sitting in it." [4] Sauer painted a most agreeable picture of the boatmen, whose "first appearance struck me with amazement beyond expression." [5] In his "light dress, painted and plumed bonnet, . . . with perfect ease and activity," the Aleut boatman was an elegant figure. [6] While ashore, the natives wore boots, fashioned out of sea lion hide in addition to their bird-skin parkas. They also wore skin trousers on land, but the men discarded both boots and trousers when they took to their kayaks.

Once ashore, on a tiny island near Unalaska, Sauer had a better chance to observe the natives. The Englishman did not find the Aleuts repellent, despite their tattoos and the wearing of nose and lip ornaments. "They are very clean in their persons . . . the women are chubby, rather pretty, and very kind." [7] When native women were praised as being "kind" it was usually because they indulged the sexual appetites of visitors, but Sauer did not give any details.

Sauer watched Aleut women dance, wearing masks that seemed to have some religious significance, to the rhythm provided by a drumlike instrument. The Englishman inquired into the significance of the ceremony but could get no explanations because of the destructive zeal of one of his companions, an "illiterate and more savage priest, who, upon hearing that some of our gentlemen had seen a cave in their walks, where many carved masks were deposited, went and burnt them all. The priest also threatened the Aleuts for worshipping idols and forced many to be christened by him." [8] Such evangelical aggression must have been disturbing to the wondering Aleuts, among whom Russian Orthodox missions had not yet been introduced. They obviously had not fathomed the hasty abjurations of the clergyman to renounce the devil and all his works. It appeared to Sauer that the natives "regarded this as an insult: be that as it may, however, they were not pleased, but had not power to resent." [9]

Russian priests, however arrogant and intolerant, were accustomed to having their way on the Siberian frontier. On the overland journey from Yakutsk to Okhotsk, the same priest accused two Tartar guides—wrongfully as it turned out—of stealing some of his property and had them tied to a tree and flogged. When the Tartars' innocence was confirmed, the priest airily dismissed their punishment, asserting that as they had not been Christians, no harm had been done.

Twelve Russian traders occupied Unalaska Island at the time of Sauer's visit. They had been there for eight years and were preparing to return to Okhotsk with the furs that had been secured. "These people lord it over the inhabitants with more despotism than generally falls to the lot of princes," commented Sauer, "keeping the islanders in a state of abject slavery; sending parties of them out on the chase . . . selecting such women as they like best, and as many as they choose." [10] Despite their long term of service in the Aleutians, the traders were not anxious to return to Siberia "for, by changing of places, they change situations, and become themselves as much the slaves of power, as the poor natives are to them." [11]

Once the Aleuts understood that Billings' men were not traders and indeed had been charged with the investigation of the traders' aggressions, they expressed their grievances. General Sarytschew, who took their testimony, assured them "that their oppressors would be severely punished for their conduct." [12] Sarytschew "used every exertion to convince them that our august empress wished for nothing so much as their happiness, having strictly prohibited every disorderly proceeding." [13] If the Aleuts gained any satisfaction from such assurances, it must have been short-lived. For all its benevolent intent, the Russian government had no effective means of policing the traders. The

Eskimo umiak with sail.
University of Alaska Archives, Lomen Family Collection

establishment of a consolidated trading company which could be supervised to some extent was still years in the future.

Off Unalaska, the crew of the *Glory of Russia* encountered a hunting party at sea. There were five kayaks and a three-seated vessel searching for sea lions and seals under the direction of one Russian. Several of the Aleuts were hoisted aboard the *Glory of Russia* and begged to be taken along, but Billings could do nothing for them. "The Aleuts left us with reluctance," related Sauer, "and complained bitterly of the treatment that they met with, and of being compelled to serve for years without receiving any recompense." [14]

Billings next sailed to Kodiak Island, south of the Aleutians, where the Russians maintained a large post. Kodiak was the domain of Grigori Shelikov, styled "The Russian Columbus" by some admiring historians. Shelikov certainly had talents, but they were more in politics than in geographic discovery. For years he had lobbied for a trading monopoly, a privilege that was granted in 1799 just after his death. But in 1790 when Billings called at Kodiak, Shelikov's company was just one of many competing in the Bering Sea and in Alaskan fur commerce. Although the Russians held 200 women as hostages for the good behavior of the hunters, harmony seemed to prevail. Shelikov's manager did not permit mistreatment of the Eskimo inhabitants and allowed the hostages to visit their relatives in rotation. Sauer was favorably impressed with such liberality and with the Russian system of provisioning. Some of the native men were released from their fur-hunting duties to insure the supply of winter provisions. Even more noteworthy was a school on Kodiak, run by the traders, in which young Eskimos were taught to read and write Russian. One of the traders took advantage of the presence of a priest to marry a native, the mother of several of his children.

Leaving Kodiak, Billings passed through the Aleutian chain once more and sailed north to the Bering Strait. Once beyond the Pribilof Islands, the expedition did not encounter any Russian traders; their activities were confined to the Aleutians, Commander Islands, Pribilof Islands, and the Kodiak region. Billings exchanged gifts with the Eskimos who inhabited St. Lawrence Island and the adjacent Bering Strait coast—people who were fortunate in being little affected by Russian commerce. These meetings were friendly and passed without any unpleasant incidents.

Billings then crossed to the Asian side of the Bering Strait and called at a Chukchi village. The Chukchi peoples' remoteness from the Russian centers of southern Kamchatka and their warlike qualities protected them from the subjection imposed on Kamchadals and Aleuts. Chukchi traded with American Eskimos and passed items of Russian manufacture in a trading network that extended as far east as the Mackenzie River of Canada. Trade did not produce amity, however, and the Chukchi and American Eskimos were often bitter foes. One of the trade offerings of the Chukchi to Billings' men was the favors of women—not Chukchi women, but American slaves captured by raiding parties.

By the time Billings landed among the Chukchi to commence an overland exploration, he had accumulated enough information on the Russian traders to constitute a damning report:

> I have been . . . an eye-witness of the abject state of slavery in which these unfortunate islanders live under the Promyshlenicks (hunters) . . . These people employ all the men of Oomlashka and Sithanak in the chase, taking the fruits of their labour to themselves, and not even allowing the natives necessary clothing . . . upon the arrival of their vessel at any place where they propose making a stay, they haul her on shore; immediately send the natives out on the chase, even to the furthest of Shumagin's islands; and then take by force the youngest and most handsome of the women for their companions.[15]

Billings also referred to the squabbling among competing traders: "If another vessel arrives, they unite their companies, or else the stronger party takes the natives from the weaker. They inflict on the natives what punishments they please, and are never at a loss to invent a cause." [16]

Sauer summarized Billings' report in his published narrative and also appended the impressions of another Russian officer who related that the traders robbed the Aleuts of their furs, "and, if the least opposition was made, they were silenced by the muskets of the hunters. Wives are taken from their husbands, and daughters from their mothers; indeed the barbarity of their subduers to the crown of Russia is not to be described." [17]

THE FRENCH IN THE NORTH PACIFIC

The French government was not slow in making its own investigation of the fur riches of the North Pacific reported by James Cook. An expedition under Jean La Pérouse was ordered to round off its exploration of the Pacific Ocean by voyaging to the Northwest coast and the Bering Sea to examine the potential for French commerce. In 1786 La Pérouse traded with Indians of Lituya Bay—on the Gulf of Alaska just north of the southeastern archipelago—acquired 1,000 poor-quality sea otter skins and assessed the competition for this lucrative yield. He doubted that French merchants could compete with Spaniards on the California coast or with the Russians in Alaska, but thought there was a potential for trade in the region south of Alaska and north of the Spanish colonies. La Pérouse's work was hampered by disaster. In July a squall caught two of La Pérouse's survey parties in Lituya Bay, sweeping twenty-one officers and men to their deaths—a catastrophe that foreshadowed the loss of the entire expedition which was to occur later in the South Pacific. After this misfortune La Pérouse sailed south, planning to return the next year to explore the Bering Sea.

During the same season, the English trader John Meares, who was to help precipitate the Nootka Sound fracas between England and Spain, also ventured into the Bering Sea. Meares' *Nootka*, which had been fitted out in Malacca for Northwest coast trading, passed through the Aleutians in the fog in a venturesome northern voyage and landed on Unalaska early in August. Russian traders entertained Meares hospitably, but the Englishman was not impressed by the Bering Sea outpost. Much richer pickings, he figured, were to be had in southern waters of the Northwest coast, where the Russian influence was slight. It was obvious to Meares that the sea otter had been overhunted in the Bering Sea, and he saw no reason to linger there. The same conclusion was reached by other traders, British and American, who were venturing into the North Pacific. None was interested in any marine mammal except the sea otter.

In September 1787 La Pérouse reached the Bering Sea with two frigates and made for Petropavlovsk. Before setting out for the South Pacific, he solicited the aid of Kamchatka's officials for a member of the expedition, Barthelemy de Lesseps. Lesseps, a young man who served La Pérouse as a Russian interpreter, was to carry expedition reports overland across Siberia to France. But for this arrangement, all the La Pérouse records would have been lost to posterity.

Lesseps was one of the few foreigners to travel in Kamchatka in the eighteenth century who spoke Russian, and he was able to gather a good deal of information traveling the length of the peninsula on his way to the west. He learned of the agreement made the year before between Shelikov and a Captain Peters, an English trader from Macao. Peters had proposed to take the furs Shelikov had gathered on Kodiak and the Aleutians to China and return to Petropavlovsk with provisions for the Russian trader. Shelikov had to travel to St. Petersburg for permission to enlist Peters' services and apparently succeeded in getting it. But the contract was forestalled. Peters' ship was wrecked off Copper Island on its return from the Northwest coast to Kamchatka. The only two survivors, a Portuguese and a Bengal, wintered on the island, and in the spring they were rescued by Russians and taken to Kamchatka.

In Bolcheretsk, Lesseps found that Frenchmen did not enjoy a good reputation. Siberians indentified the French with the notorious Count Benyowsky. Lesseps labored to convince his hosts that Benyowsky was actually a Hungarian or Pole. Memories of Benyowsky's escape and the atrocities he committed were very fresh. "This slave called himself a Frenchman, and acted like a true vandal," Lesseps thought.[18] The Russian version of Benyowksy's adventures differed somewhat from the famed exile's own account. In the Polish troubles of 1769, Benyowsky's "medley troop of foreigners, or rather robbers . . . ransacked the country, massacring every one they met." [19] Quite properly the Russians did not treat him leniently after taking him prisoner. "Banished to Siberia, and afterwards to Kamchatka, his fiery and vindictive genius accompanied him. Escaping from the mountains of snow, under which the Russians supposed him to be buried, he suddenly made his appearance at Bolcheretsk with a troop of exiles, to whom he had imparted a spark of his own audacity." [20] He surprised the garrison, killed the governor, and compelled all to submit to his will. Kamchadals had to supply him with provisions, and "not content with the sacrifices obtained, he gave up their habitations to the unbridled licentiousness of his banditti, to whom he set an example of villainy and ferocity." [21] The young Frenchman assured his Russian friends that Benyowsky did not represent the higher type of Western European civilization, but it was hard to soften the impressions left by the daring adventurer. "This suppositious Frenchman was the only one they had yet seen in the peninsula; and from such a specimen of our nation, they certainly could not love, and had sufficient reason to fear us." [22]

Benyowsky's exploits seemed as savage to Lesseps as they did to the

Siberians, but the young explorer saw evidence of Russian inhumanity as well, particularly in the treatment of the Kamchadals. The natives were mild, honest, and hospitable, but easily deceived. Russian traders and Cossacks traded with natives to enrich themselves. "Their industry is a continual knavishness, it is solely employed in cheating the poor Kamchadals, whose credulity and insuperable propensity to drunkenness, leave them entirely at the mercy of these dangerous plunderers." [23] Although the Kamchadals, "have not yet bartered their rude virtues for the polished vices of the Europeans sent to civilize them," Lesseps was not hopeful for their future.[24] The Russian government did try to select officials of a stamp superior to the villainous Cossacks and merchants in the hope of securing just treatment for natives, but they could not counter the predations of the greedy exploiters. Desire for gain and licentious conduct proved stronger than the zeal for reform. Like other visitors, Lesseps observed that Christianity had not taken deep root among the natives. The clergy were ignorant and lightly supervised; some imposed heavy levies on natives for the administration of their services.

Of the three major native races of the Bering seaboard—Kamchadals, Koriaks, and Chukchi—Lesseps liked the Koriaks the least. Their manners were a mixture of duplicity and mistrust. They were "suspicious, cruel, incapable either of benevolence or spirit" and "robbers by nature; they have all the vices of the northern nations of Asia, without the virtues" and performed no service without demanding compensation.[25]

Presumably it was the last tendency which soured Lesseps on the Koriaks among whom he traveled; yet he also seemed to be influenced by the Russians' view of the benevolence of their rule. He censured the Koriaks for their resistance to the Russians and their continued insurrections. At the time of his travels, the Kamchadals had already abandoned their resistance, while the Koriaks were still capable of worrying their conquerors. Lesseps saw no virtue in the natives' tenacity, nor honor in the custom—once practiced by Kamchadals earlier—of choosing suicide over flight or surrender after a battle. Commercial intercourse with the Russians had not made them more civilized, but only greedy for wealth and plunder. "They seem to feel a repugnance to civilization, and to consider their own manners and customs as absolutely perfect." [26]

Although Lesseps did not travel through Chukchi country, he met a party of Chukchi who had traveled south from the Anadyr region to trade with the Russians at Gizhiga. By this time the Russians had given up their attempt to conquer the Chukchi, who had proved too pugnacious for their taste. These traveling Chukchi were anything but hostile. Nothing would please them more than the reestablishment of a Russian fort on the Anadyr River. Their militancy had been an error which they were anxious to repair by assisting Russian settlers who might be willing to come to Chukchi territory. Lesseps was quite taken by these solemn assurances, but the Russians did not seem impressed by the Chukchi offer. By traveling all the way to Gizhiga on the Okhotsk Sea, the Chukchi certainly demonstrated an interest in the Russian trade, but both peoples seemed to have preferred a more neutral ground for a major commercial contract. The place chosen, at some point around 1780–90, was west of the Chukchi region, not far distant from the Arctic Ocean, near the mouth of the Kolyma River. The annual trade fair there was well established by 1821, when Captain John Dundas Cochrane, the eccentric British traveler, observed the proceedings.

According to Lesseps, who did not indicate whether his information came from the Chukchi or the Russians, the Koriaks had been responsible for Chukchi clashes with Russians. The perfidious Koriaks inflamed the Chukchi "either by false reports, or by inciting them to attack such parties of Russians whom they could not, or dared not, attack themselves." [27] By such artful tactics, the Koriaks induced the Chukchi to "the many acts of cruelty with which the Tchoukchis have been reproached, but which form no part of their character." [28]

Possibly Lesseps might have had to reassess his views of the Chukchi character had he actually traveled in their country. His adverse response to the Koriaks derived from their unbending and hostile spirit—qualities manifested by the Chukchi with a sustained vigor which kept them free of the Russian yoke long after the Kamchadals and Koriaks had submitted.

THE RUSSIAN AMERICAN COMPANY

James Cook's voyage into the North Pacific and Arctic Oceans was momentous for several reasons. His careful navigation had dispelled the myth of the existence of a Northwest Passage entry anywhere on the American coast south of Bering Strait. His exchange of geographic information made possible the preparation of the first accurate maps of the North Pacific. In 1780 the Russians and the English published the cartographic results of their combined efforts in discovery. But the greatest impact of Cook's third circumnavigation followed upon the news of the reception given for the English seamen at Canton, China, on their return voyage. Somewhat casually, Cook's men had acquired furs from Northwest coast natives at various places and were astounded at the prices offered for them by Canton merchants.

News of the great fur wealth of the Northwest coast excited English and American shipping interests. Within a few years of Cook's voyage, traders from old England and New England established a valuable trade along the coast, a trade which stimulated the westward expansion in North America. Naturally the intrusion of the traders into the North Pacific was viewed with alarm by both Spain and Russia. Spain tried to enforce her ancient claims to the region by seizing ships of English traders at Nootka Sound, British Columbia. For a time war between the two European powers seemed imminent, but Spain backed off, finally relinquishing its long-held claims to sovereignty over the Northwest coast.

Russian claims were stronger than those of Spain. By right of discovery and colonization, Russia's claims to Alaska could hardly be questioned. Yet the encroachments of the maritime traders were, for the most part, south of the Russian trading empire; along the coasts of what is now Canada, Washington, and Oregon. As important as these activities were for the development of the Pacific Northwest, they lie outside our consideration of Bering Sea history.

Russia reacted to the increased maritime activity in the North Pacific by granting a trade monopoly to a single fur-trading firm. There were other sound reasons for taking this action. For years the czar's government had heard complaints from rival merchants, each blaming others for various skulduggeries, including armed attacks on trading stations in the Aleutians and elsewhere. Also, the efforts of the Russian government to protect the rights of natives had not been effective. Reports of atrocities against natives by rapacious *promyshlenniks* were received regularly, despite the stern warnings issued from St. Petersburg. Then there was the question of providing for the souls of the natives. The clergy urged the czar to allow missionaries to go out to the Bering

Sea frontier. But before the great work of salvation could be undertaken, order would have to be maintained.

Thus it was that a company formed by Grigori Shelikov was given exclusive trading rights in 1799—a privilege that the merchant had long lobbied for but, as he died in 1796, did not live to see. Shelikov was a great organizer and never allowed truth to stand in the way of his ambitions.[29] In 1784 Shelikov had established a post on Kodiak Island and from there supervised the hunting done by Aleuts in the Bering Sea, Cook Inlet, and eventually, Prince William Sound. When the company received its monopolistic charter in 1799, Kodiak became the headquarters of the reorganized Russian American Company. It was this company which was to control the commercial destinies of the northern frontier until Alaska was purchased by the United States.

Shelikov wrote an account of his 1783–84 voyage to Bering Island, the Aleutians, and Kodiak in which he matter-of-factly described how he dealt with the natives. At Unalaska Island he took a dozen Aleuts, "who voluntarily came and offered me their services," aboard his ship and sailed through the Aleutian chain to Kodiak Island.[30] The Eskimos there did not welcome the Russians, although they were told "that they might safely receive us as friends." [31] Rather forcibly the Kodiak Eskimos insisted that the Russians retire from their coasts and threatened to kill the encroachers. Shelikov took umbrage at this unkindly greeting and informed them "that they might as well lay aside their insolence, and rather enter into a friendly traffic with us." [32] Of course, the Kodiak Eskimos knew from the experiences of their neighbors just what the "friendly traffic" would mean, and were determined to avoid enslavement. Shelikov offered gifts and assurances: "We, on our parts, were come, not for engaging in quarrels and hostilities, but to gain their affection in friendly intercourse." [33] Yet the Aleuts continued in their "perverse and obstinate behavior," and there could be only one resolution.[34] In several pitched battles in which the Russians had the advantage of five cannons, the natives suffered heavy losses. From the survivors, Shelikov retained 400 natives as prisoners and equipped them for sea otter hunting. "They proved constantly faithful allies," and their fidelity was assured by the fact that Shelikov kept twenty of their children as hostages.[35]

Unlike some traders, Shelikov paid the native hunters for their services. He was out to dominate the trade and realized that abusive treatment of his labor force would be detrimental. His trading rivals were outraged by his successes and his false claim to have discovered Kodiak Island. They, too, were trying to get exclusive trading privileges, but Shelikov was too wily for them. Russian churchmen supported Shelikov's company because he offered to support missionaries in the island settlements. This supposed sympathy for the cause of Christian endeavor was probably more of a stratagem than an expression of a genuine commitment.

In 1791 Shelikov had had the good judgment to hire Alexander Baranov as the manager of his Kodiak station. Baranov was a fabulous character—energetic, intelligent, and imaginative. He was made governor of Russian America in 1799 and dominated events in the North until his retirement in 1819. Baranov, like Nicolai Rezanov, who succeeded Shelikov as director of the company in 1796, had a clear vision of the place Russia should occupy in the North Pacific. Things did not work out according to their imperial designs, but it was not for lack of effort.

The chief problem of the colonies was that of supplying provisions. Rezanov and Baranov made several moves to overcome this difficulty. Their most ambitious project was to establish an agricultural settlement at Fort Ross, California. The hope was that the land farmed there could provide foodstuffs for the Alaskan colonies, but poor selection of land and poorer farming methods doomed the project to failure. Fort Ross was eventually sold to an American in 1841.

Even at the time of the acquisition of Fort Ross, greater Russian horizons were envisioned by the two Russians. The idea of controlling the North Pacific and possibly the entire Pacific Ocean was a natural consequence of holding a northern Californian colony, in addition to holding the Hawaiian Islands located so strategically in the middle of the great Pacific. Only indirectly does the history of Hawaii relate to the history of the North Pacific. But this resulted only from the thwarting of the plans of Rezanov and Baranov. Had their designs been successful, the North Pacific would indeed still be a Russian lake.

In 1815 a ship of the Russian American Company was shipwrecked on the Hawaiian Island of Kauai. Like all the other islands at that time, Kauai was controlled by a native king. Baranov saw this shipwreck as an opportunity by which Russia could gain some influence over the islands. He immediately sent Dr. Georg A. Scheffer, a shadowy German physician, as an envoy to deal for the Russian American Company in Hawaii. Scheffer was instructed to establish regular trade agreements with the Hawaiians. At first he was quite successful with King Kamehameha, claimant to the entire island chain, although at the time unable to maintain his claim.

But European and American traders became alarmed and warned King Kamehameha of Russian skulduggery when Scheffer began to acquire plantation land for provisions for the Russian American colonies. In actuality, Russian designs on Hawaiian independence were no more threatening to it than those of other foreigners, but the Europeans and Americans were able to arouse suspicion in the king and thus protect their own interests.

Scheffer then instigated a rash counterattack. He convinced himself that King Tomari of Kauai stood a good chance of overthrowing King Kamehameha. With Russian help, Tomari would assume dominance of the entire island group. If it had been successful, Scheffer's coup would have established the Russians in a most favorable position to carry out Baranov's economic and political goals.

As it developed, the adventure became a farce. The Russian flag rose over Kauai—but only briefly. Instead of responding to Scheffer's request for an armed ship and 500 soldiers, Baranov repudiated his agent. As the bubble burst, Scheffer ran for his life and his promises of armed support for Tomari were revealed as illusions.

Because of the resulting geographic and scientific discoveries, another attempt at Russian hegemony of the Pacific succeeded in reflecting considerable credit on the czar. The tremendous maritime effort of the Russians in the first half of the nineteenth century established Russia as a first-class maritime power and a solid rival to England and the lesser maritime nations. From 1803 to 1840, thirty-six voyages to the Pacific Ocean were undertaken by Russian warships. Many of these ships, after leaving their Baltic ports of origin, made the long voyage to Sitka and Petropavlovsk. If the voyages did not establish the fact that servicing Russian America by sea routes was more economical than by the Siberian routes, they certainly added to the knowledge of the world. Navigators like Captain A. J. Krusenstern performed honorably and successfully in the tradition of James Cook, the greatest Pacific navigator of them all.

Often the Russian ships carried a naturalist who was able to gather collections and make observations. G. H. Langsdorff accompanied Krusenstern on his circumnavigation, while the naturalist-novelist Adalbert von Chamisso served with Otto von Kotzebue during his attempt to probe the Arctic coast of Alaska.

Still another aspect of Russia's ambitious Pacific policy was the hope of opening commercial negotiations with Japan. As early as 1778 Russian ships were sent to Japan for this purpose, but the Japanese refused to have anything to do with the foreigners. Another attempt was made in 1792, then again by Krusenstern on his 1803–7 voyage, but all the Russians received for their efforts was humiliation. Finally, Russia gave up on Japan. However, they did continue to sponsor circumnavigations. The most notable, from a scientific point of view, was that commanded by Captain T. Litke (1826–29) who made significant astronomical and oceanographic observations, as well as discovering islands in the Caroline Archipelago.

But it was the forest-surrounded community of Sitka that the inspired Baranov brought to the forefront of Russian Pacific interest in the nineteenth century. Long before there were any other towns on the Pacific coast, except the few sleepy Spanish missions in California, Sitka was a thriving industrial settlement. It became the capital and chief trading center of Russian America in 1799, when the headquarters of the Russian American Company was moved from Kodiak Island to the more favorable site in the Alexander Archipelago. Here, at his "Paris of the Pacific," Baranov received traders from all the maritime nations.

The Russians and their Aleut hunters were intruders on Sitka Sound, since the area had long been occupied by the proud Tlingits, one of the most highly cultured native peoples in America. The Tlingits gloried not in war but in beauty, as their art and handicraft showed. They had an exquisite skill in transforming natural materials into objects of utility, grace, and significance.

But in 1802 the Tlingits were pushed beyond their point of endurance by the arrogant Russians and reacted with determination and tactical skill to drive the Europeans away. Tlingit warriors burned the Russian stockade and made captives of the survivors after a short, fierce battle. They awaited the return of Baranov with a reinforced party. Two years later the Russians were back with the support of a considerable fleet. Tlingit Chief Katlian led a vigorous defense; but with the *Neva*, commanded by Captain Lisiansky, shelling the Indian stockade with cannons at short range, the Tlingits abandoned the fortress. They left behind many dead warriors and a number of their children who were sacrificed to expedite the flight. The conflict quickly ended, as it always did wherever Western technology and aggression confronted native Americans. Sitka continued its development as the Pacific coast center of trade, shipbuilding, and metalwork.

At the same time, Baranov continued to enlarge the economic and political power of the Russian American Company. Basically, the company was a commercial fur-trading enterprise, owing its legal existence to a twenty-year charter granted by the Russian government. Exclusive trade rights were given under the charter, which was renewed in 1821 and again in 1844. The company was effectively the only government wielding political, economic, and military control over its vast monopoly.

No courts existed in the colonies, but the charter provided that in serious cases the accused be sent to the nearest Russian authorities in Siberia. Lesser matters were to be determined by the governor of the Russian American colonies, or in some cases, referred to a special commission. Authority of the governor over the people, whether Russian, Creole, or native, was virtually absolute.

Russian employees contracted to work for the company for a seven-year term, although the term could be renewed for another seven years, merely upon the request of the company. Those owing money to the company could be held until their debts were paid. Employees were "subjects" as long as the governor was the representative of the czar, with unchallenged control over them.

Theoretically, under the charter the natives had the right to complain to the governing board in St. Petersburg about abuses of local authorities. Needless to say, the right of appeal was an illusory one when appeal had to be made from great distances by those whose petition could only pass through company channels.

Native chieftains became company subordinates and helped maintain political and social control over the natives for the benefit of the company. On the other hand, Russian and Creole employees did not even have the natives' right of appeal to the company governing board. Presumably, it was felt that government authorities at Okhotsk could look after their rights; yet it was illegal to transmit complaints by a third person. This left a complainant in the awkward position of requiring permission to secure passage on a company ship in order to appeal to governmental authorities about unauthorized company procedures and practices.

The charter required management to report directly to the czar everything relating to its affairs. As time went on, Russian governmental control was further extended by appointment of naval officers in the colonial administration and by establishment of a permanent council that consisted primarily of government officials. Thus the Russian American Company could not be compared with such commercial entities as the Hudson's Bay Company of England. But whatever changes there were in the relationship of the company to the government, conditions did not change for the inhabitants of Alaska. They remained under the absolute authority of the governor who, at the beginning of the nineteenth century, was the vibrant Alexander Baranov.

Baranov reigned and received in grand style. He thirsted for news and for trade goods that he could acquire from foreign ships. The Baranov manner of entertainment was legendary. He had an unquenchable thirst for vodka, rum, or whatever was available and delighted in staging informal drinking contests with his visitors, who were never allowed to abstain. These prodigious affairs were carried to the ultimate when the guests had slipped beneath the table and Alexander Baranov, governor of the Russian American Company, could reel triumphantly off to bed.

Baranov's drive and purposefulness deserve full credit. If any single person made the commercial venture successful in the remote North Pacific, it was Baranov. Not only did he pacify and humble the natives and carry on a prosperous trade; but he, as much as anyone, created a Western civilization—for good or bad—in North America.

REZANOV AND CONSERVATION

In 1805 the first fur-mammal conservation measures to be introduced in Russian America were laid down by Nikolai Petrovich Rezanov. Rezanov was a Russian nobleman who had married Shelikov's youngest daughter, become imbued with his father-in-law's vision of the potential of Russia's Pacific provinces, and had been instrumental in securing the first charter of the Russian American Company. Now Shelikov was dead and Rezanov headed the enterprise, while Baranov remained as colonial governor.

Rezanov had been dispatched by the czar to open trade negotiations with Japan prior to making his first inspection of the American colonies. His frustrations with the Japanese mission were extreme. In October 1804 he reached Nagasaki where he remained for months, trying to negotiate with officials. The Japanese had no intention of extending their Western trade, which for 300 years had been restricted to a small exchange with the Dutch. But they wasted much time before making their position clear. In April 1805, Rezanov had two ceremonial interviews with an emissary of the Japanese emperor at which his hopes were dashed: Russian ships were forbidden to enter Japanese ports, and the gifts and message sent by the czar were summarily refused. Fifty years were to pass before Russian warships would follow those of the United States into Japanese ports to force the Japanese to open commercial relations.

In disgust, Rezanov left Japan for Kamchatka, later sailing from Petropavlovsk for Alaska, calling at the Pribilof Islands in June. Two years before Rezanov's visit, Baranov had dispatched a ship from the Aleutians to collect the fur-seal pelts that had been gathered there, but for years, little attention had been paid to the seal islands. Baranov had his hands full with the expansion of hunting activities in southeastern Alaska and farther south, where the sea otter was still king. Pribilof fur seals still ranked far below the otter as a market commodity, and there had been little supervision of the Russian overseers and Aleut hunters on St. Paul and St. George.

Few Russian subjects had the privilege of sending dispatches directly to the czar; but as Rezanov's standing at court was very high indeed, he was granted the right. His first letter from Alaska concerned the Pribilofs. "The multitude of seals in which St. Paul abounds is incredible; the shores are covered with them." [36] Rezanov was told that seal numbers had decreased 90 percent since the first days of Russian occupancy. "As over a million had already been killed, I gave orders to stop the slaughter at once, in order to prevent their total extermination." [37] Hunters were ordered to concentrate on collecting walrus tusks from the prolific herds of Walrus Island, near St. Paul, while the seals were left alone. "These islands would be an inexhaustible source of wealth were it not for the Bostonians, who undermine our trade with China in furs, of which they obtain large numbers on our American coast." [38] American commercial rivalry disturbed Rezanov. He was informed that fifteen to twenty ships made the long voyage from New England to the Northwest coast each year to gather Alaskan furs which they carried to Canton. Rezanov recommended the construction of a well-armed brig to police the North Pacific and Bering Sea.

As a solution to the colonial provisioning problem he suggested a trading agreement with the Spanish government, by which Alaska and Kamchatka could be supplied with food from the Philippines or Chile. Food provisioning had always been the weak link in the colonial economy. The costs of shipping provisions overland from Europe to the Pacific were detrimental to fur trade profits, particularly with the extension of the colonies and the growing scarcity of furs. Agricultural experiments in Kamchatka and Alaska had not solved the problem, and Baranov had come to depend upon Yankee traders for a substantial portion of his needs.

Baranov's first contact with a foreign trading vessel came in 1792, when the *Phoenix* of the British East India Co. appeared in Prince William Sound. English and American ships had initiated Northwest coast trading in the 1780s, following the return of James Cook's expedition to Europe, with reports of the fur wealth of the region. Baranov learned from Captain Hugh Moore and his American mate, Joseph O'Cain, of the successful coastal trading in furs as far south as California, and Baranov longed to have a ship like the *Phoenix*. In 1801, O'Cain met Baranov again, this time in Kodiak. O'Cain was the mate to Captain Ezekiel Hubbel on the *Enterprise* of New York, and part owner of the ship's cargo of molasses, rum, sugar, flour, tobacco, canvas, and firearms. Because of the Napoleonic Wars in Europe, Baranov had not received provisions from Siberia for several years and, out of necessity, traded O'Cain furs in exchange for the *Enterprise*'s cargo.

O'Cain returned to Kodiak in 1802, this time with a ship he commanded and named after himself. Again he had precious provisions which Baranov needed, but the Russian trader had neither cash nor furs to barter. Baranov wanted O'Cain's firearms, especially because his Sitka post had been captured by Indians, and he was determined to defeat the Tlingits and reassert his authority over southeastern Alaska. O'Cain provided the solution. If Baranov would give him Aleut hunters, he would carry them to California to hunt sea otters, then return them to Kodiak. O'Cain would pay in stores for the Aleuts' services and give Baranov a share of the fur gathered. The deal was made and it proved advantageous. O'Cain returned in March 1804 with the Aleuts, 1,000 pelts for the company's share, and an offer of a continuing arrangement.

Rezanov's tour of inspection included a visit to the company post on Unalaska, where he inquired into the conduct of the Russian traders. All the Aleut leaders assured Rezanov that the company agent "had been a father to them." [39] Rezanov assembled the entire native population to inform them of the czar's solicitude for their well-being and urged them to express any complaints without fear. No grievances were forthcoming; so Rezanov distributed medals to the chief agent and his interpreter and, in the presence of the natives, had a Russian trader from Atka Island punished for beating a native woman and her infant, and then had him sent off in irons on a ship bound for Siberia.

Georg Von Langsdorff, a German physician and naturalist who accompanied Rezanov, estimated that the population of Unalaska, and the other Fox Islands nearby, consisted of only 300 Aleuts—down from some 3,000 reported there in the 1780s. The Russian practice of recruiting Aleuts for hunting on the Pribilofs and along the Northwest coast accounted for the depopulation, the extent of which, the traders "appeared anxious to conceal." [40]

CAPTAIN COCHRANE OBSERVES SIBERIA

Like Corporal John Ledyard, the American adventurer who served under James Cook, Captain John Dundas Cochrane wanted to link Siberia and Alaska through his own pedestrian feats. In 1820 the Englishman set out to walk across European Russia and Siberia to the Bering Strait. From there he hoped to cross over to North America and push on across that continent, perhaps going along the Arctic coast and discovering the Northwest Passage along the way. Cochrane was quite an egotistical character, but his observations on Siberia and the Russian American Company were often shrewd.

The Russian government welcomed Cochrane's plans and even asked him how much money he would like to have for his expenses, but he refused to accept any. In actuality, he needed very little money. The government recommendations authorized him to use the well-organized post horse system in Siberia, and the hospitality of Russian peasants and natives along the way made food and lodging easy to come by.

Cochrane had overwhelming confidence. By his own admission, no one was his superior in physical perseverance and endurance. Yet Siberia offered more hardships to the traveler in severe weather, primitive standards of comfort, and vast distances than any other region of the world—except, perhaps, for remote parts of Central Asia, Africa, and Arabia.

In the first months of his journey, rough roads and mosquitoes plagued Cochrane. Veiling his face in a net, he preferred to walk whenever possible. As he pushed eastward, the weather turned colder but did not deter him. He was proud of his ability to withstand the cold. He walked the streets of Yakutsk in British woolens when the temperature was well below zero. "The natives felt surprised," he wrote, "pitied my apparent forlorn and hopeless situations, not seeming to consider that when the mind and body are in constant motion the elements have little effect on the person." [41]

Suspicion of John Ledyard's intentions prevented him from reaching eastern Siberia on his late eighteenth-century jaunt, but Cochrane, after being warned not to inquire into the affairs of the Russian American Company, was even given a Cossack escort throughout his Siberian journey.

Cochrane had planned to proceed directly to Kamchatka, but diverted his course when he heard that a Russian expedition headed by Ferdinand von Wrangel was exploring the coastline of eastern Siberia. The Englishman, ever longing to be an explorer, traveled to Wrangel's headquarters at the mouth of the Kolyma River. Cochrane wanted to join Wrangel's exploration party, but, as a foreigner, he was not permitted to do so. In lieu of this, Cochrane had advice to offer: "I was fortunate as to propose some things which appeased and proved of service to the expedition, and which were either adopted, or improved by the Baron." [42]

The two naval officers got on very well during the winter, and Cochrane was given suitable winter clothing and equipment—a parka (trimmed with sable and marten furs), skin trousers, a fur hat, warm boots, gloves, and a bear skin for bedding. Although the Englishman had been proud of his ability to withstand the cold in his woolens, he was pleased to be better clothed and was moved to quote the poet Matthew Prior:

> If any nation pass their destined days
> Beneath the neighb'ring sun's directer rays;
> If any suffer, on the Polish coast,

The rage of Arctos, and eternal frost;
May not the pleasure of Omnipotence,
To each of these some secret good dispense? [43]

The winter passed pleasantly. Cochrane borrowed reading material from Wrangel and joined the amusements of the natives. Feasts were celebrated by the natives with the cheer of copious amounts of liquor, games, and dances. Sliding down nearby icy hills was one diversion which Cochrane enjoyed, particularly when one or two young girls perched on his knees for the descent.

In March, Cochrane, supplied with dogs and sleds by Wrangel and guided by one of his officers, left the exploration base to pursue his hopes of continuing his journey to America. He had been told that the Chukchi of the Bering Sea traveled west each spring to attend a great trade fair at Ostrovnoe, on the Maley Anyui River, a tributary of the Kolyma 150 miles east of Nishney Kolymsk. This trade fair was an important center of the trans-Bering Strait commerce; it was the point at which the Chukchi passed on their furs, and those secured from Alaska's Eskimos, for items of Russian origin. Some of the Russian goods eventually reached American natives along a commercial network that extended as far east as Canada's Mackenzie River. If tobacco and other goods could be conveyed to America by the Chukchi, reasoned Cochrane, perhaps *he* could be, as well.

The Chukchi had not been conquered by the Russians nor had they accepted the blessings of Christianity; yet some of those who traveled to the trade fair accepted baptism there. The sacrament was not administered by a mere sprinkling of water. The new Christians had to strip to their trousers and be plunged three times in a large iron cauldron full of icy water. With the temperature at 35° F. below zero, baptism was a severe test of religious zeal; yet, Cochrane learned, some applied two or three times for the ceremony in order to gain the customary encouragement—a gift of tobacco.

A Russian official opened negotiations with the Chukchi on Cochrane's behalf. The Chukchi were told that the czar wished Cochrane to visit the two strange ships that had been reported in the Bering Strait and hoped that they would guide the traveler to the coast. Wily traders as they were, the Chukchi responded with the request that the czar provide 5,000 pounds of tobacco for their services: "He could be no great

Emperor who could not make so small a present, seeing that he could command the riches of all his people." [44] Each year the Chukchi traders were required to submit a tribute in furs to the czar for the privilege of trading at Ostrovnoe; so they had reason to believe that the czar possessed great riches. This exorbitant demand was probably not made seriously, because the Chukchi did not even believe that Cochrane was sent by the czar. Cochrane, they observed, could not speak either the language of the Russians or of the Chukchi; how would he be of use to the czar as an interpreter? At this penetration of his role, Cochrane confessed that he was just a poor traveler. But the Chukchi could see no point in helping him unless they received a reward. Thus the matter terminated. Cochrane would have to find other means of getting to the Bering Sea. Although Cochrane does not mention it in his account of the proceedings, one Chukchi leader offered him the means of reaching the Bering Sea at no cost. This disinterest in gain aroused the captain's suspicions; so he declined the risk of desertion or worse.

Despite his disappointment with the avarice of the Chukchi, Cochrane observed their trading activities over the seven-day duration of the fair with great admiration for their sagacity. "They have their own mode of calculating, and before the fair is commenced, they fix the price of their goods, to which they adhere more strictly than the Russians." [45] Tobacco was the chief item they desired in exchange for their reindeer skins, furs, and walrus tusks; and they were keen judges of its quality and weight. "The detection of the slightest fraud on the part of the Russians is sufficient to the Tchuktchi to cut the party short, and deal no more with him." [46]

A professed reluctance to trade was often expressed by the Chukchi in the course of negotiations. They asserted their need for tobacco was not pressing "as they could get it much cheaper in the Bay of St. Lawrence, from the ships which usually call there." [47] Of course this could hardly have been entirely accurate. Tobacco was the mainstay of the Chukchi's Alaskan trade, and they were themselves heavy consumers. The appearance of ships in the Bering Strait and Gulf of Anadyr was very rare indeed at that time. Ships of the Russian American Company did not trade there regularly, and the American whaling fleet had not yet commenced its Bering Sea operation. It may be that an American or English trader, engaged in the sea otter trade of the Northwest coast, had voyaged far enough north to encounter the Chukchi; but such an occurrence could not have been common. The Chukchi assertion was more prophetic than real. After mid-century they were to receive American trading ships with great frequency, but for some time, the Kolyma fair would remain the source of their western goods.

In 1842, the Russian American Company explorer L. A. Zagoskin complained that the Kolyma trade persistently hampered the company's American operation. Zagoskin's proposals for interfering with the Chukchi-American Eskimo traffic were never acted upon and the trade continued. It is not known when the Chukchi gave up their annual trek to Ostrovnoe, but the trade must have been affected by the proliferation of American ships during the whaling era and subsequently.

Cochrane had no doubt that the Chukchi actually had some chance to trade on the coast. "Whatever trade they may carry on with these vessels, the Tchuktchi appear to know the value of a more direct and first-hand trade; nor can this be doubtful, when the toils and dangers of their journey and the small profits are considered—at least, small when compared with the profits they sometimes receive from the few vessels which now and then visit their coast." [48] This trading opportunity, however infrequent, made the Chukchi tough bargainers. Even the generous distribution of vodka by the Russians did not induce the Chukchi to sell their most valuable furs cheap "and were nearly all taken back with them to their country." [49]

A member of Wrangel's expedition, Midshipman Matiuschkin, escorted Cochrane to the Chukchi fair; his account of the proceedings substantiates that of the Englishman. Matiuschkin's remarks on the Chukchi trade with Americans provide useful details on the Bering Sea exchange:

> The trade with the Americans is an exceedingly profitable one, both to the Russians and to the Tchuktches; the latter are in truth only carriers, as they buy the furs and other articles with the Russian tobacco, hardware, and beads; they give half a pood of tobacco to the Americans for furs, which they sell to the Russians for two pood of the same tobacco; thus their gain is 300 percent. The same two pood of tobacco may cost the Russian trader 160 roubles at the outside, and he sells the furs bought therewith for at least 260 roubles, a profit of 62 percent. The furs consist chiefly of black and silver grey fox, stone fox, lynx, wolverine, river-otter, beaver, and a species of marten unknown in Siberia, of remarkable beauty, and nearly

resembling the sable in the nature and colour of the fur. Besides these the Tchuktches bring from America bear-skins, thongs of walrus-skin, and a quantity of walrus-teeth. They add nothing of their own, except whalebone sledge-runners, a large quantity of clothing made by themselves from the skin of their rein-deer, and a kind of bag of seal-skin, in which they pack the American furs.[50]

According to Matiuschkin, the czar's government prohibited the trade of liquor; yet some was secretly carried in and offered to the Chukchi who eagerly parted with pelts worth 250 rubles for a couple of bottles of bad brandy worth only a few rubles at Irkutsk. While Matiuschkin estimated that the Russian traders made a profit of 62 percent on their tobacco, Cochrane guessed that it might run to 100–120 percent. Whatever the margin, there was no doubt about the Russians' eagerness.

Matiuschkin was familiar with the successful resistance of the Chukchi to the Russians and the commercial relationship that had developed. Prior to about 1780 the Chukchi had insisted that the trade fair be held at Anadyr because they were disinclined to venture into the Russian-dominated interior. Once persuaded of the peaceful intentions of the Russians and the greater profit they would gain by traveling to Ostrovnoe, they began to make the long journey each year. According to Matiuschkin and other sources, the Ostrovnoe fair had been established some forty years before his visit.

The most startling information provided by Cochrane referred to the presence of American natives at the fair:

> The other articles of fur come from a nation on the American continent, called the Kargaules; two of whom were at the fair. They bear more nearly the features of the Tchuktchi than those of the hideous-mouthed inhabitants of the islands in Behring's Straits, although with a browner or more dirty colour. The furs brought and sent by them consist of many thousands of black, brown, blue, red and white foxes, martens . . . some beavers, river otters, bears, wolves, sea-dogs, and sea-horse skins; a few articles of warm clothing, and some ornaments carved out of sea-horse teeth, representing the animals common among them.[51]

Matiuschkin did not mention the American natives in his very brief account of the fair; so there is no supporting evidence of Cochrane's statements. Certainly it is not inconceivable that American Eskimos could have traveled with the Chukchi; yet such participation would have threatened the Chukchi's position as middlemen. The most plausible explanation is that the Americans were slaves of the Chukchi, captured in battle, rather than independent traders at the last stage of a trans-Bering Strait venture. Other Western travelers to the Bering Sea had reported on the presence of captive American Eskimos in Chukchi villages, a fact which supports the slavery supposition. Nothing known of the tenacity of the Chukchi and their hostility to all their neighbors suggests that they would have permitted Americans to undercut their profitable trading role.

After the fair was over, Cochrane and Matiuschkin returned to Nishney Kolymsk. The English traveler's mission had been fruitless; yet he showed good judgment in not traveling with Chukchi. Cochrane knew the travails suffered by his countryman, Joseph Billings, who traveled in Chukchi country some years earlier. The Chukchi had given Billings a very hard time—despite the fact that he was in the czar's service, traveled with other Europeans, and paid his guides. Lacking each of these advantages, Cochrane would have been foolhardy to trust himself to the Chukchi.

Leaving Nishney Kolymsk, the indomitable Captain John Dundas Cochrane reached Okhotsk in June of 1821. He had started out for the 2,000-mile journey by dog sleds on March 27, accompanied by a Cossack and by a native escort. "The difficulties I have had to contend with surpass everything of the kind I have before seen, and required every exertion of mine to conquer." [52] Cochrane upheld his hopes of reaching the Bering Strait and crossing over to America. Once in America he planned to survey the Arctic coast. The course of the coast east of Kotzebue Sound was not known, and an exploration would have been useful work had Cochrane been able to undertake it; yet it is extremely unlikely that he would have had much success. His travels in northern and eastern Siberia had been, by his own account, arduous enough, though he had the full assistance of Russian authorities. In effect, he had the services of a small, well-equipped expedition. In Arctic Alaska he would have been entirely on his own and without the authority or resources to command the assistance of any Eskimos he might have encountered. In all probability he would soon have perished unless he had been fortunate enough to find Eskimos willing to shelter him. In short, his scheme was ridiculous. However, a man unpossessed of common sense does not attain a command in the Royal Navy; thus, in Okhotsk, the captain abandoned his American folly.

In Cochrane's own narrative of his decision, he ascribed his retreat to high principles. He was really an amazing character—tough, resourceful, and confident. This would be clear enough from the extent of his travels but is further supported by his own declarations. What made him change his mind in Okhotsk, he alleged, was not a realization of the futility of the American explorations—which, incidentally, were substantially carried out by John Franklin's expedition of 1825–27 by way of the Mackenzie River to the Arctic Ocean and westward along the coast—but his sensitivity to the endeavors of others. Cochrane had been told that a Russian naval expedition planned a voyage to the Bering Strait and Arctic Ocean: "I will not act against them; and, therefore, I cannot act at all. It would be madness and presumption in me, to attempt a task of the kind while an expedition is there. . . . Should that officer withdraw entirely, I will hereafter undertake the same journey, and may possibly do that by good fortune which even more zeal and talents cannot execute!" [53]

The officer whom Cochrane identified as heading the Russian expedition was a Captain Ivan Vasilev, who did not execute the explorations the Englishman had in mind, although he attempted to do so. If the Vasilev expedition was responsible for discouraging Cochrane, he certainly had not lost his zeal for exploration generally. He had only set out for Siberia after the admiralty had rejected his proposal to explore Africa's Niger River, and from Okhotsk he wrote to London announcing his availability and boasting of his competence. "I feel certain that one half the difficulties, and nearly all the dangers and exposures to which travelers, *in any climate,* are most commonly subjected, and of which they do so much complain, are the result of either their own physical incompetency, or want of prudential foresight." [54] He proclaimed his disdain for those who made much ado about nothing and who wrote "expensive quartos upon a subject which might be compressed into a duodecimo." [55] (Cochrane's own publication fell between these extremes —a two-volume octavo of nearly 700 pages in the second edition.) Once more he offered to set out for Africa if the venture would benefit mankind and be to his personal advantage. These sentiments were uttered in London upon Cochrane's return from Siberia, but they only echoed those he had made in Okhotsk. Clearly, Cochrane was still bitten by the African exploration bug. It is a curious parallel between the adventures of John Ledyard and Cochrane that the former set out on his fatal African explorations after returning from Siberia, while Cochrane's first and subsequent choice was a sponsored African expedition.

But to turn from the tricky morass of an adventurer's ego—that misty region always so rich in bombast, aspiration, and frustration—to more concrete matters. Because he made a thorough observation of the land and its people, it is profitable to examine Cochrane's further fortunes in Kamchatka. The Englishman left Okhotsk for Petropavlovsk on August 24, 1821, reaching Kamchatka after a two-week passage. There he found that Captain Vasilev's expedition had returned, after failing to get much beyond Icy Cape on the American Arctic coast. He heard that another Russian naval officer, Captain Otto von Kotzebue, would make another voyage to Kotzebue Sound—though with the primary purpose of protecting Russian commerce in that part of the world rather than discovering the Northwest Passage. Cochrane was keen on the Northwest Passage and thought that the success of William Parry's first voyage (1819–20) in making a deep penetration of the Arctic Ocean from the Atlantic side should have encouraged Vasilev to try again. In fact, for good and sound geographic and commercial reasons, the Russians lacked England's persistent enthusiasm for the long-sought Northwest Passage.

Cochrane had much to say about Kamchatka's natives. As evidence that natives behaved like "people but yesterday discovered," he cites their exchange of valuable furs for trifles or a glass of spirits.[56] A traveler of clearer judgment might have concluded that such bad bargaining resulted from demoralization after 120 years of oppression and too many glasses of spirits.

Of the benefits to the natives from the introduction of Christianity, Cochrane was dubious. Natives were Christians in name only; there seemed to be plenty of clergy in Kamchatka—twenty-six by his count—but little sign of learning and piety. Petropavlovsk's school offered no education to natives and little more to Russian children. It was governed by a priest and a regular schoolmaster; "but the one is a great rogue, and the other a greater sot." [57] Clerics maintained a great distinction between practice and precept and earned large revenues from the poor people, giving little in the way of moral or intellectual instruction in return. "I do not know how laborious the duty of a Russian priest may be in a large congregation, or whether it is the same as in a small one, but . . . in . . . Kamtchatka, they do not occupy themselves for the benefit of the public three hours in twenty-four, the remaining twenty-one are occupied in trading, hunting, fishing, etc." [58]

Another result of 120 years of Russian hegemony in Kamchatka comes to light in Cochrane's estimates of the population. If his estimates were reliable—and he traveled considerably over a year's time—they reveal a great decline of native peoples. The entire population, including 1,268 Russians, was only 4,574. Smallpox, venereal diseases, and the Russian "spirit of persecution" caused the depopulation, according to Cochrane.[59] This population estimate was close to that made some twenty years later by another Siberian traveler, George Simpson of the Hudson's Bay Company.

Cochrane met three English residents of Petropavlovsk. One, described only as a Cockney who had been exiled from Moscow for forgery, was well received everywhere and was one of the few exiles Cochrane encountered. Large settlements of exiles were apparently never established on the Bering Sea frontier, although most eighteenth- and nineteenth-century travelers met a few.

Petropavlovsk's harbor was full of bustle: eight ships, probably a record number, were anchored there. These included two foreign trading vessels—one a brig under Portuguese colors representing foreign merchants of Macao; the other an American ship with English officers and a *Kanaka* (Hawaiian) crew, bearing a gift of salt to the czar from Hawaii's king. The presence of both ships was significant. All the merchant shippers of the Pacific Ocean were cognizant of the Bering Sea commercial situation and hopeful of capitalizing on the weakness of Russia's maritime service. For sixty years Yankee traders, English merchants representing the East India Company or other mercantile interests, and other enterprising mariners had shown a keen, if sporadic, interest in the Bering Sea trade. It had long been common knowledge that the Russian American Company had trouble provisioning its Alaskan colonies, and that the inhabitants of eastern Siberia were receptive to goods carried by foreign vessels. A regular trade between Kamchatka and the Orient or Hawaii might have been a beneficial development for all parties—except, perhaps, for the Russian American Company, which resisted encroachments on its fur trade.

Despite the needs of Siberia and Alaska and the occasional recourse

Main Street, Petropavlovsk, Siberia, 1899.
University of Alaska Archives

to foreign shipping, Russian American Company officials feared for the company interests because of commercial rivals. As long as the company lasted, it looked upon the Bering Sea and adjacent Pacific regions as a corporate preserve—closed to foreign interlopers. Whether or not a more receptive stance would have improved the company's position is a moot point. Nor can it be determined whether the encouragement of various proposals offered by foreign merchants would, in fact, have proved lucrative enough to sustain regular traffic. Arguments in favor of liberal trading policies were made often enough, but a regular Siberian trade did not develop until mid-century, and this was ancillary to American whaling activities. A direct commercial intercourse between American Pacific ports and Siberia was even later in development, dependent as it was on the Alaskan gold rushes and the creation of population centers in California and the Pacific Northwest.

To Cochrane the trade policies of the Russian American Company made little sense. He believed that the company should contract with the government for the provisioning of flour for the Bering Sea and Sea of Okhotsk settlements and employ the shipping, thus relieved, in trade with the region's aboriginals. Profits could thereby be gained, and prices could be kept low. "But such is the pertinacity and jealousy of those composing that body, that they will do nothing even to benefit themselves, if it be also of benefit to others." [60] In consequence, the potential of a trade with Hawaii or other Asian or Pacific Ocean centers was ignored. The opportunity to develop a whale fishery was passed up. Thirty years later, after whalemen from New England demonstrated the value of the whale fisheries, the company finally determined to move into the field but found itself without the necessary ships and personnel. Because of the culpable neglect of the company, "the eastern frontiers of the Russian empire remain in their original barren, impoverished and savage state, instead of boasting a flourishing trade, carried on by a civilized, organized and friendly population." [61]

Agriculture was also neglected. Cochrane considered the climate and soil of Kamchatka to be as suitable to production as that of Canada and New England; yet little was accomplished. Only a small stock of cattle was maintained in Kamchatka: "A century would elapse before what can be termed herds of cattle could be seen wandering and feasting upon the almost unbounded pastures of the peninsula." [62] Cochrane had the impression that there had been more cattle fifty years earlier when the

Cook expedition had visited the region. In Siberia the Russian American Company did not have a monopoly, but it was the largest single enterprise and could have advantageously fostered all aspects of the economy.

While at Okhotsk, Cochrane discerned that the Amur River was the key to the economic prosperity of eastern Siberia and wondered that the Russians did not wrest it from Chinese hands. At mid-century, Russia did just that, and this move—like the later construction of the Trans-Siberian Railroad—left the Bering Sea as isolated as ever. The course of Siberia's economic expansion was rational if not inevitable. It left the Bering seaboard's interests to non-Russians—the freebooters, the small traders, the individuals content to gather crumbs in the backwater while the great push to the Pacific occurred far to the south.

Cochrane counted forty-two dwellings and fifteen public buildings in Petropavlovsk, most of which were "like the rest of the city, but emblems of misery and wretchedness." [63] Notwithstanding the personal happiness the captain was to find in the chief town of Kamchatka, he could not praise it. "I have never seen on the banks of the Frozen Sea so contemptible a place, hardly meriting the name of a village, much less that of a city; yet such is the place which has been eulogized from one end of the world to the other." [64] Some writers had apparently overpraised Petropavlovsk's amenities. "The erection of hospitals, of schools, of churches, and the diffusion of happiness and knowledge, have been extravagantly vaunted in magazines and reviews, in defiance of the most lamentable facts of a very opposite description." [65] Why bother with a governor in such a place? queried the Englishman, a civil commissary would be enough. Only the Koriaks were happy, because they retained some independence. "The Russians complain of being sent to such a vile place, utterly destitute of society; the Creoles of their being kept in a state of poverty; while the Kamtchatdales bitterly lament the association with either the one or the other." [66]

In his travels throughout the peninsula Cochrane found an abundance of natural wealth. Fur-bearing animals still existed in prodigious numbers; some 30,000 pelts, he estimated, were used by natives or exported. Dogs did all the work required of horses in England without calling for much maintenance. "They are fed as circumstances may dictate, being always left to shift for themselves from June to October." [67] Game birds, fish, venison, whales, and other marine animals contributed to the natives' larder. "Upon the whole, therefore, there are no people at whose disposition Providence has placed more of the necessaries of life, than the inhabitants of Kamtchatka." [68] Why then did they live "in that filthy and famished condition which formerly characterized them?" [69] Cochrane speculated that the population might have been too large for the available resources, but also censured aboriginal habits as severely as he criticized the Russian administration.

The natives seemed amiable and honest and were established in clean, comfortable Russian-style villages, which they left during the summer for their fishing camps. Winter clothing consisted of the traditional animal furs and skins, but by that time, Russian articles of dress were commonly worn in the summer. As to character "the Kamtchatdale is still the same lazy, drunken, servile animal as formerly." [70] It is not clear where Cochrane garnered the knowledge of the earlier ways of Siberia's natives. He probably relied more on what Russians told him than on the literature on the subject. Whatever his sources, he always expressed himself in the confident manner of an expert. In this tendency he was only a trifle more assured and arrogant than was common with travelers of his day. Cochrane's observations could be acute and sensible, or they could be incredibly naïve. He was surprised, for example, that people who had been oppressed and neglected for 120 years did not have all the orderly habits of other European societies. Cochrane appeared to believe that the example of Russian neglect and maladministration would somehow stimulate the natives to greater efforts.

In Petropavlovsk the good captain found happiness. A pretty native girl caught his roving eye. He was smitten and they married. After some time the couple traveled to England, but not to settle down. Cochrane soon set out for Venezuela, where his restless bones were finally stilled by a fatal fever.

7 — SCIENCE AND WAR

Europe was at peace in July of 1827 when Captain F. W. Beechey of Britain's Royal Navy sailed his *Blossom* into Avacha Bay, Kamchatka. The hospitable Russians were pleased to entertain the British officers as on the previous visit under Beechey in 1826. It enlivened the summer social season whenever a vessel called at Petropavlovsk. Entertainments as well as delicacies were exchanged. The Russians offered seal meat and the British presented a turtle from the South Pacific to their hosts. It did not take long to see the sights in Petropavlovsk. Of greatest interest to Beechey were the monuments to Captain James Cook's successor, Captain Charles Clerke, who took command after Cook was killed in Hawaii. Clerke fell ill on the last Bering Sea voyage and was buried in Petropavlovsk. Another monument honored the French explorer La Pérouse.

Maritime traffic was not heavy in northern waters at this time. Occasionally, ships of the czar's navy or the Russian American Company made an appearance, but few foreign ships ventured so far north. Beechey's purpose was exploration. He hoped to pass through the Bering Strait and meet John Franklin, who was exploring the Arctic coast from the Mackenzie River to the west.

Beechey enjoyed the entertainment offered to him at Petropavlovsk, but he was a conscientious officer who did not believe in wasting much time. Accordingly, he sent a barge out to make a meticulous survey of Avacha Bay on which the town was located. Under other circumstances, the Russians might have resented the surveying of one of their harbors by a foreign navy, but the Kamchatka officials took no notice of the work. After all, much of North Pacific geography had been revealed by the surveys of James Cook and other Royal Navy men, and the British published such charts for the use of all. Who could foresee any threat to Petropavlovsk in such a survey?

Captain Beechey was certainly not anticipating a naval campaign in the Bering Sea; yet he could not help sizing up the harbor with an eye to tactical potential. Like most foreign visitors to Russia's Bering Sea frontier, he noted the neglect of the principal settlement and its lack of defenses. At the time, this carelessness did not matter, "but should the North Pacific ever be the scene of active naval operations, Petropavlovsk must doubtlessly become of immense importance." [1] In the case of war, he noted, a few judiciously placed guns would effectively protect the harbor's entrance. Some years later, some of Beechey's compatriots were to discover this fact for themselves.

After departing from Avacha Bay, Beechey sailed to Seward Peninsula, Alaska, and charted the only good harbor on the Alaskan side of the Bering Sea. Port Clarence, which he named, never developed a sizable settlement despite its natural advantages. The rich gold diggings of the Seward Peninsula were too far distant to allow the Eskimo village to become a supply and transport center to the mines. Port Clarence was chosen as the crossing place of a Western Union telegraph line (1865–67). Later in the century it attracted the missionary Sheldon Jackson as the best possible place to situate the first reindeer herd, which he imported from Siberia.

Other scientific work accomplished by Beechey's men was quite extensive. Collections of botanical and zoological specimens from the South Pacific, North Pacific, and Arctic Oceans were described and illustrated in publications issued some years later. The *Blossom*, anchored off St. Lawrence Island, engaged in trade with the Eskimos. The British got some ivory and items of handicraft in return for glass beads and tobacco. Lieutenant George Peard of the *Blossom* was impressed by the trading methods of the Eskimos. "They behaved with the strictest honesty, and if the bargain was objected to by either party, immediately returned whatever had been thrown down into their boats for exchange." [2]

Some years later, Captain Henry Kellett (1845–51) made further charting and scientific efforts in the Bering Sea in the course of the Royal Navy's search for the missing John Franklin. Expedition naturalist Berthold Seemann was startled to notice the large numbers of Yankee whalers in the Bering Sea. In 1849–50, he saw more American ships there than the entire British whaling fleet numbered. On this cruise the British were met with hostility by the Eskimos of Kotzebue Sound and some blood was shed. But this was an isolated incident. Generally, explorers had no conflicts with peoples of the Bering Sea and Arctic Ocean.

Like Kellett of the H.M.S. *Herald*, William Hooper of the H.M.S. *Plover* made several attempts to seek out Franklin by penetrating the Arctic Ocean from the Bering Strait. He spent ten months among the Chukchi, a people he praised for their honesty and good nature. Hooper made valuable observations, which he later published, on the flora, fauna, and ethnology of the Chukchi Peninsula.

Although foreign scientists, particularly those of the Royal Navy, made some contributions to the scientific investigation of the Bering Sea in the eighteenth and first half of the nineteenth centuries, significant work was carried out by Russians. The accurate maps which resulted from Russian cooperation with James Cook have been mentioned, and there were other cartographic landmarks to follow, notably, Mikhail Tebenkov's *Atlas of the Northwest Shores of America*, the plates for which were engraved in Sitka. The Russians also conducted the most studies in other sciences, such as geology, zoology, and botany. In ethnographic and linguistic study, the most important contributions on the Aleuts and their language came from the great missionary, Ivan Veniaminov. In 1821, V. S. Khronchenko voyaged to the mainland of southwestern Alaska, north of the Aleutians. Virtually nothing had been known of this region prior to Khronchenko's journey. There had been a voyage to Bristol Bay in 1818 by Peter Korsakovskiy and he discovered Nunivak Island, but he did not even note the mouth of the great Yukon River. In fact, it was not until 1834 that the Russians explored the mighty waterway which is one of the greatest of North American rivers. This followed the establishment of Fort St. Michael, near the mouth of the Yukon, in 1833.

The most important explorations conducted by the Russians were those of L. A. Zagoskin, a naval officer in the Russian American Company service. Zagoskin voyaged to St. Michael in 1842 and prepared to travel to the interior from there. Trade development was the chief purpose of these journeys, but the explorers were also instructed to watch for a "lost colony" of Russians who had been reported at several locations over the years. The Seward Peninsula was one location considered possible; yet there is no clear evidence that such an early settlement of Europeans actually existed.

OTHER SCIENTIFIC WORK

Since the initial efforts of Georg Steller, a number of scientists representing several nations had made the Bering Sea the focus of their inquiries. After Steller, the most significant scientific work was carried out by William Healy Dall, who had originally gone to Alaska as a member of the Western Union Telegraph Expedition (1865–67). Dall stayed on after the termination of that project to do field work on the Aleutians and elsewhere in Alaska.

Dall, who was born in 1845, was a highly productive worker until his death in 1927. His chief interest was in mollusks, but a sampling of his publications indicates the wide range of his intellectual interests:

"Languages of the Tribes of the Extreme Northwest: The Aleutians and Adjacent Territories."

"List of the Birds of Alaska."

"On the Remains of Later Prehistoric Man Obtained from Caves in the Catherina Archipelago, Alaska Territory, and Especially from the Caves of the Aleutian Islands."

"Pacific Coast Pilot, Coast and Islands of Alaska."

"Pliocene and Pleistocene Fossils from the Arctic Coast of Alaska, and the Auriferous Beaches of Nome, Norton Sound, Alaska."

"Report on Coal and Lignite of Alaska."

The scientists of the Harriman Expedition (1899) produced a lucid, multivolume report on the geography, people, and resources of Alaska and described a portion of northeastern Siberia. Edward H. Harriman, the railroad mogul, planned this cruise as a pleasure jaunt for himself and his family, then generously decided to take along a number of scientists and artists. It has been suggested that Harriman was neither interested in recreation nor in science in arranging his expedition but was actually looking into the potential of a trans-Bering Strait railroad. There is no evidence that Harriman was so motivated, but it would be difficult for the famous railroad builder to visit any part of the world without raising suspicions that a rail scheme was on his mind, especially if he denied such interest.

As the *George W. Elder* cruised north, Harriman's scientists marveled at the scenic beauty of the Inside Passage and the huge glaciers of the Gulf of Alaska. They noted the distinct changes in natural features of lands to the north and west of Cook Inlet. For some 2,000 miles of cruising they had never been out of sight of magnificent spruce forests. Now as they passed Kodiak Island and made for the Aleutians, they would steam 2,000 miles without a glimpse of a tree. Not that they found the Bering Sea lands ugly. John Burroughs described the scene as the *Elder* sailed out of Dutch Harbor, where "high, rolling, green hills [were] cut squarely off by the sea, presenting cliffs seven or eight feet high of soft, reddish, crumbling rock . . . touched here and there on the face with the tenderest green. It was as if some green fluid had been poured off the rock faces and been caught upon every shelf and projection." [3] The color was deepest in all the wrinkles and folds on the slope and in the valley bottoms. "The effect was extremely strong and beautiful. The clouds rested low across the hills and formed a dense canopy over the vast, verdant cradle; under this canopy we looked along a soft green vista for miles back into the hills where patches of snow were visible." At another point, Burroughs noted a beautiful waterfall which had carved a trough or cradle down to within 100 feet of the sea. "Everywhere such a sweep of green skirts as these Alaska hills and mountains present, often trailing to the sea!" Burroughs grew ecstatic over the vista. "A thousand miles of this kind of scenery, passing slowly before one on a succession of summer days, make an impression not easily thrown off." [4] It is pleasant to record Burroughs' delighted impressions. So often the superlatives applied by voyagers to the Bering Sea run to the other extreme of natural description. All is seen to be "harsh," "stormy," "desolate," and "fogbound." With Burroughs we can experience a more pleasant aspect of the northern regions.

But large-scale, privately financed scientific ventures like the Harriman Expedition were rare. One notable exception was the Jesup North Pacific Expedition (1900–1) which resulted in a monumental study of the human culture of the region. This publication still leads contributions in the several fields it encompasses. Most of the scientific investigation was of smaller scale.

THE JESUP NORTH PACIFIC EXPEDITION

The Jesup North Pacific Expedition greatly increased the knowledge of the lands and peoples of the Bering Sea frontier. A number of scientists were commissioned by the American Museum of Natural History to do field observation and research in particular areas. Investigation was not confined to Siberia and Alaska, nor did it encompass all of the region. Studies were made of the peoples of British Columbia and other northwest Indian cultures as well. In particular, important gaps in the knowledge of Siberian culture were filled by the research conducted then.

Waldemar Jochelson, who was also a student of Aleut culture, observed the Koriaks of Kamchatka in 1900–1 and published the massive results of his work in 1905. Every aspect of the Koriak culture was described by Jochelson in careful detail, and he also wrote an excellent summary of the Russian contact with the natives from the seventeenth century to the time of his own sojourn in Kamchatka. Jochelson criticized the missionary efforts of the Russian Orthodox Church among the natives. Except for the distinguished work of Father Ivan Veniaminov and a few others, he felt that their record "cannot be considered honorable." The reason for the missionary failure seemed clear. "Up to the present time, the priests and monks sent to the far northwest are men of little education." [5] Thus, the scientist voiced the same complaint as Martin Sauer of the Billings Expedition 100 years earlier, who noted the arrogance of Siberian clergy.

The Koriaks had much to tell Jochelson of American whalers who had been visiting them each season for half a century. Why were the czar's men so inferior to the Americans, asked one native? The Koriaks appreciated American trade goods and had developed a great fondness for their liquor.

Jochelson learned that the whalers had, on occasion, mistreated the Koriaks. In the archives of the Gizhiga district, he found documents describing an 1856 robbery "by men of unknown nationality who arrived on ships." According to the records, the natives of the coastal village of Kamenskoye were off hunting seal when two ships anchored offshore. Only two Koriaks were in the village, and they fled as the whalemen launched their whaleboats and rowed ashore. Hiding near the village, the natives watched the seamen as "they carried out of the houses fox, reindeer-hide and fur garments." [6] This must have been an isolated occurrence because the Americans, on the whole, enjoyed a good reputation among Siberians. When the 1856 robbery was reported to St. Petersburg, there was some discussion of the merit of asking the United States government for an explanation, but the foreign affairs minister decided against it. The testimony of two Koriaks was not sufficient evidence, and it was not certain that the robbers were actually Americans.

Another member of the Jesup Expedition, W. Bogoras, studied the Chuckchi in 1900–1. He gathered much fascinating material on the Bering Sea peoples who were still not well known to the Russians at the time. The Chukchi also told him of the Bering Strait warfare of earlier times. Once, the boat of two Chukchi of Indian Point was driven ashore on St. Lawrence Island by a tempest. One of the unwelcome visitors was killed at once, his skull pierced by a sharp drill. The other, a shaman, was told that he would become a slave. Shamans were powerful "medicine men," and the enslaved Chukchi called to his walrus spirits for help. "A number of walrus came, and formed single file, so that he was able to walk on their heads. After he had stepped on a walrus, it would dive into the water and join the file in front." By this odd means, the shaman reached Indian Point safely, and there inspired the villagers to retaliate against the St. Lawrence Island Eskimos. The next summer, warriors from all the Chukchi villages gathered at Indian Point, then crossed the Bering Strait in their skin boats to land on St. Lawrence Island in a thick fog. The attacking force, crying like wolves to confuse the islanders, swiftly conquered their foes. All the island men were butchered. Some of "the women, from sheer fright strangled themselves." [7] Survivors were carried back to Indian Point after a victory feast of walrus meat.

Four years later, it was the turn of other villagers of St. Lawrence Island to take revenge on the Siberians. A raiding party attacked Indian Point at night. "They killed them simply by thrusting their spears through the skin walls of the sleeping rooms." Now the butchery was equal on both sides. The next year, the St. Lawrence Island Eskimos visited the Chukchi in peace, bearing gifts. Together, the neighbors sat down to a feast of reindeer, a meat which the Americans discovered to be very tasty. Harmony was restored.

No one can say with any certainty how often, in the intricate mosaic of the histories of Bering Sea peoples, bloody conflicts ensued. But the oral tradition describing warfare was still strong in the early years of this century, and there is no reason to doubt its veracity.

Bogoras reported that the maritime Chukchi were uninfluenced by the Russians but had learned much of modern ways from American traders and whaling men. Some had shipped on whalers and voyaged to the Arctic Ocean, to Nome, St. Michael, and even San Francisco. One native reproached Borogas: "The Americans on St. Lawrence Island teach the children; why do not you do the same here?" [8] Borogas had no answer to this appeal for education.

Like other visitors, Borogas learned of the suffering Americans had caused by their wasteful hunting of the walrus. Conditions had improved by 1900, however, because fewer whalers were active and it was no longer profitable to hunt walrus. One Siberian Eskimo told Borogas of the early contact with the whalemen: "When the Americans came to us, we had a talk with them, and we said: 'take the whales, but leave us our walrus. We also want something to eat. We shall give you all the walrus tusks.' And they consented." [9] Unfortunately, this "agreement" was all too frequently breached.

The Chukchi had a very strong taboo that made them hostile to whites who wished to settle among them for trading. Whites insisted on burning wood fires in the winter and this frightened off the seals and walrus. One Eskimo put it clearly to an American who wanted land for a store: "No—American man plenty fire, small air by and by, walrus, seals, come away. Indian Point men seek 'em, hunt 'em, no nothing. By and by die. No! American man trade 'em whiskey plenty, Indian Point men drink 'em, fight. No good. American man plenty s—— of b——." [10] How could the condition of things be better summarized?

FORT ST. MICHAEL

"The infliction sent them by Providence was great, but the blessing that resulted was likewise great, as all those who are left are Christians." [11] Such were the reflections of L. A. Zagoskin, a naval officer in the service of the Russian American Company, on the effect of the establishment of a Russian post on Norton Sound on the Eskimos. Smallpox had decimated the population, but the survivors had gained the benefits of Christianity. In the course of the most extensive explorations undertaken in interior Alaska during the Russian era, Zagoskin visited St. Michael in 1842. Fort St. Michael had been founded in 1833 and became an important trading station for the Bering Sea and Yukon River regions. St. Michael was not the first Russian trading station established on the mainland of Alaska's Bering Sea coast. In 1818 Fort Alexander had been built on Bristol Bay, at the mouth of the Nushagak River. In the 1820s and '30s several parties of explorers pushed into the interior from Fort Alexander to investigate the trading potential of the great basin of the Kuskokwim River. Eventually posts were established up-river. Thus it was by means of the two greatest rivers in Alaska, the Yukon and the Kuskokwim—both of which flow into the Bering Sea—that the fur trade in the interior was introduced. In the 1840s Fort St. Michael became a much more important trading center than Fort Alexander; yet the latter post remained in existence throughout the Russian period.

The first Russians at St. Michael found that the Eskimos were accustomed to the use of white men's goods. They used tobacco, iron, metal pots, knives, lances, and steel flints. Some of these things had reached the Eskimos through trade with Bristol Bay Eskimos, who received these goods from Russian traders at Fort Alexander. But this southern trade was secondary to a long established trading relationship with the Chukchi of the Bering Strait, who passed on Russian articles to the southern Bering Sea. The major language division among Eskimos of the Inupiaq and Yupik languages had its geographic boundary at the north coast of Norton Sound. Eskimos north of this line, including all those of the Arctic coast of North America, spoke Inupiaq; those of the southern or western division, from Norton Sound to Prince William Sound, spoke Yupik—yet a language division had not affected the ancient trade that had developed between native peoples of northeastern Asia and America. However, trade was somewhat disrupted by the building of Fort St. Michael. Zagoskin heard that Eskimos from Sledge Island in the Bering Strait, near the site of Nome, curtailed their voyages to southern Norton Sound in 1837 out of fear of the Russians. In that year, 200 Sledge Island Eskimos tried to drive the Russians away from Norton Sound, but the natives' attack on a party of Russian hunters was repelled, and they did not venture to attack the fort.

Fort St. Michael was built on a small island near the mainland. Its buildings—a house for the manager, a barracks, and storehouses—were surrounded by a wooden palisade. Six three-pound cannons, placed on two watchtowers, provided the chief defensive armament. The swampy island, 7½ miles long and 8 miles wide, was chosen for its proximity to the Yukon River mouth and its defensive position. Otherwise the site had little to recommend it. There was no harbor suitable for ships on the island, and it was not prolific in vegetation or wildlife. Because of the shallowness of the Bering Sea, due to the build-up of silt from the Yukon River, deep-draft vessels could not approach very near to the mainland.

Eskimos of Norton Sound hunted seals, the beluga or white whale, and fished for herring and salmon. On the mainland they killed caribou for food and fur-bearing animals for trading purposes. Birds, too, were plentiful and were hunted primarily for food. The climate was more rigorous than that of the Aleutian Islands. Freezing temperatures and snow prevailed from September through March, and offshore sea ice remained as late as May. Yet the Norton Sound winter was less severe than that of Kamchatka or the Arctic Ocean coast.

Zagoskin was first to describe the Eskimos of Norton Sound in the manner of detailed ethnographical investigation. He was favorably impressed with the independence and vigor of the stocky people and with their institutions. Chiefs were not recognized, though there were certain distinguished heads of families whose advice carried weight and who could, on occasion, impose their authority on individuals. "They have no fights or angry quarrels among themselves. There are no abusive words in their vocabulary. An insult is avenged by the death of the offender, or by the blood of his descendants of the families involved if they do not come to some sort of a peaceful agreement." [12]

That the natives seemed selfish and ungrateful to the Russians was the fault of the traders for not earning the natives' respect and for giving them presents on first contact "without regard for services rendered." The Eskimos concluded that the Russians did not value their own goods and raised the exchange prices of their furs accordingly. "They saw that the Russians did not find their native womenfolk unattractive, and they are not jealous by nature, they at once began to profit by this situation." Zagoskin admired Eskimo hospitality and the custom of sharing possessions for the common good. "They are a people who place the principle of helping their neighbors at the head of their moral code. They are not jealous, not acquisitive, not cruel." As to their intelligence, "we have no way of testing their intellectual ability by any educational system, but to do them justice, we must admit that they are shrewd, enterprising, sound of judgment, vigilant, and gifted with a fine memory." [13]

The Eskimos seemed receptive to the instruction they received in Christian beliefs. Zagoskin referred to the natives living near Fort St. Michael in 1842 as Christians. Their conversion must have been effected at the fort by a baptism ceremony officiated over by a trader. It was not until 1844 that a missionary priest took up residence at Fort St. Michael. It could be, however, that priests visited the post prior to that time. Ivan Veniaminov, the energetic, humanitarian, and scholarly priest, who had served the Aleuts on the Aleutian Islands from 1823 to 1838, made visitations to Nushagak in 1829 and 1832 before a resident priest was moved there. He or other priests might also have journeyed to Norton Sound before 1844.[14]

In the course of his extensive explorations of the Yukon and Kuskokwim river basins, Zagoskin directed his attention to the best means for organizing and consolidating the Russian trade network. He was expected to find a good way in which the aboriginal fur trade between Alaska and Siberia via the Bering Strait could be countered. He recommended that Russian traders buy every available fur gathered by natives of the Bering Sea coast and have on hand all the trade goods they desired. That the Russians at St. Michael were not dominating the trade was obvious by statistics Zagoskin cited: only 350–500 beavers, 100 river otters, and 150 fox skins were reaching St. Michael each year. However, some of the trade was drawn off by Russian traders on the Yukon River. The Nulato post, founded in 1838, was 550 miles upstream from the Yukon delta. This station, and others on the Kuskokwim River, brought in considerable quantities of furs from the Alaskan interior, but did not draw furs from northwestern Alaska or the Arctic coast.

Earlier efforts to move into the northern trade had proven abortive. In 1838, the company dispatched a party of Aleuts and Russian Creoles to the Bering Strait and Kotzebue Sound to trade along the Arctic coast of Alaska to the east, but the Eskimos proved too hostile and the traders had to retreat. No post was ever established on the Bering Sea north of St. Michael or on the Arctic coast; so the Russians could not effectively control the Bering Strait trade. It was part of Zagoskin's mission in 1842–44 to reach Kotzebue Sound from the interior, but he did not achieve this goal. His journey north and east of Norton Sound provided considerable information on natives and fur potential and, if followed up, could have led to Russian dominance of northwestern Alaska, but other interests took priority. This spared the Eskimos north and east of Norton Sound from a close contact with the Russians and left the Bering Strait trade in Chukchi hands.

The Russian American Company could not depend upon a large staff of skilled traders. Most of its personnel consisted of Creoles of mixed descent and of natives. Of the Russian members, men of education and capability were few. A station supervisor had to be literate in order to keep the company books; yet to take full advantage of opportunities of the vast country, something more was needed. "It is not my business to discuss the question as to whether literacy is desirable without culture," observed Zagoskin. "Here it is enough to record that the truly literate people to whom one could entrust the administration of the country . . . are very scarce in the colonies." Understandably, Zagoskin was dismayed by the ignorance of the Russian clerks and doubted their ability to exploit the country he and others had explored. He was also concerned about the spiritual welfare of the natives of Alaska. "The greatest possible care should be taken not to damage, by the introduction of new elements with the lives of natives, those basic virtues which control the lives of all peoples who are directed by the dictates of nature, by the Light of God." [15]

Truly literate people were scarce in Alaska, as Zagoskin observed, but the future of the colonies might have been very different if there had been a few thousand Russian peasants dwelling there—literate or not. Usually, there were 500–600 Russians living in Alaska. The high point was 823 persons in 1839. This failure to build up a population played a critical part in Russia's failure to hold Alaska.

THE CRIMEAN WAR IN KAMCHATKA

Captain Beechey of Britain's Royal Navy had been right in declaring the defensive strengths of Petropavlovsk. He had also been right to survey Avacha harbor in the interest of science and naval strategy. Although he could not have foreseen the events that were to precipitate a conflict between England and Russia, the two powers did collide some years following Beechey's call at Petropavlovsk.

The year was 1854 and the North Pacific campaign of the combined British and French fleets was incidental to the Crimean War, a conflict waged principally in the Black Sea. Western historians have paid little attention to the North Pacific venture of the Allies. Not only was it peripheral to the main war action; it was a crashing failure, a deep embarrassment to the Allied navies. No monuments loom in London or Paris to commemorate this assault on Russia's sparsely protected frontier.

At the outbreak of the Crimean War, the czar's Pacific forces consisted of a mere 1,000 soldiers, one seaworthy frigate, three corvettes, and a few unarmed merchant ships—this to defend a coast stretching from the Arctic to the Chinese frontier. But Russia did have a leader: General Nicholas N. Muravyev, the dynamo who from 1847 to 1861 won control of the Amur River, adding 400,000 square miles to the Russian empire, and was the first proponent of a Trans-Siberian railroad. As a minor diversion from his empire-building activities, he organized the defeat of the British and French forces on the Pacific coast.

On paper the Allies had all the advantages. Against virtually unguarded shores and a minuscule fleet, Rear Admiral David Price's British squadron at Callao, Peru, had six ships, mounting 300 guns and 3,000 men. The French squadron, also stationed at Callao, and under Price's command, consisted of six ships, 190 guns, and 2,000 men. Admiral Price was an aged veteran of the Napoleonic Wars, brought out of retirement after thirty years of military inactivity. His second-in-command, the French Rear Admiral Febvrier-Despointes, equalled Price in antiquity and ineptness.

In May 1854 Price received word of the outbreak of war. Without waiting for the assembly of both Allied squadrons, he decided to attack the Kamchatka Peninsula with the four British and two French ships then available in Callao. Whether any overall strategic reasoning motivated Price is not clear. Obviously he had a good opportunity to seize territory and booty in the North Pacific. Petropavlovsk, for all the value of its fine harbor, was hardly more than a backwater village. Except for the occasional Russian American Company ship there was little commercial activity. Some 200 houses, a church, barracks, a hospital, and a few stores—the chief of which were owned by Americans—constituted the principal Russian town on the Pacific. Sitka and other Alaskan settlements were exempted from an Allied invasion because of an agreement of neutrality between the Russian American Company and the Hudson's Bay Company. By this arrangement, approved by the Russian and English governments, the American possessions of both companies were inviolate. Since the Hudson's Bay Company had leased southeastern Alaska, the panhandle, for fur exploitation, it was a mutually satisfactory situation.

The Allied approach to the Bering Sea was anything but devious. No serious effort was made to disguise the squadron's destination, and, upon a stop in Hawaii, American traders got wind of the Allies' plans and passed them on to the Russians. Petropavlovsk's defenders thus had ample time to prepare a reception before the British and French ships, after a three months' cruise, made their appearance. Land batteries had been mounted on a sand spit before the inner harbor, and the forty-four-gun frigate *Aurora*, was anchored behind the spit. Unaccountably, Admiral Price gave the Russians an additional margin of time by waiting off the town two days before finally launching a bombardment. His ships mounted 236 guns to the defenders' 101, and his superiority in men was even greater. Once the Russian batteries were silenced, the Allies had only to land their troops to mop up the surviving Russians. Yet at the close of the first day's exchange, the Allies suffered more than their opponents. The aged Admiral Price, severely shaken by the result, shot himself in despair and died, after hours of lingering agony.

On the second day of the bombardment most of the Russian guns were put out of action, yet the Allies hesitated to follow up their success. Four days passed before the bombardment was recommenced to prepare the way for a landing party. The respite gave the Russians time to shore up their defenses. Upon the advice of three American deserters from whalers, the Allied command chose a landing place which brought them complete disaster. They failed to reconnoiter the landing area before 700 sailors and marines were put ashore. Instead of attacking the town full strength, the invading force struggled over difficult terrain, wasting time and energy, and was very effectively ambushed. Virtually the entire Russian garrison of 300 men poured their fire into the invaders who finally broke under the intense assault. Survivors dashed in panic for their ships, leaving 208 dead on the field. Russian resoluteness in defense of their soil was unaffected by the fact that they had never heard of the "Eastern Question" which precipitated the war. The first amphibian invasion effort on the Bering Sea was repelled; the badly demoralized Allies raised anchors and put to sea. Nothing more could be done before the winter freeze-up. The fleet steamed south to lick its wounds and gather reinforcements for another attempt the next year.

In April of 1855 the Allies returned with a greatly augmented fleet, thirteen ships in all. Surely now they could eradicate their previous debacle with a glorious victory—if it could be termed so in the face of such unequal forces. But the invaders were denied even such dubious honors. Muravyev had anticipated the Allies' return and chose not to squander manpower in defense of a Bering Sea outpost of no particular value to his enemies. Instead he ordered a concentration of his forces at the mouth of the Amur River. Petropavlovsk was to be left undefended.

On the arrival of the Allied ships off Petropavlovsk the Russians had not yet evacuated. Prompt action would have thwarted Muravyev's plans.

But the Allies, though under new commanders, displayed their former ineptitude. Instead of attacking, the fleet stood well off the peninsula while two ships were dispatched to guard the entrance to the bay. In a dense fog, the Russians' two small warships and four merchant vessels, carrying the soldiers and residents of Petropavlovsk, put to sea, cleanly escaping the very loose Allied blockade. Eventually the British and French landed to discover the Russians had given them the slip. Except for a few American traders and natives, the town was depopulated. This fog-shrouded escape was to be reenacted in another Bering Sea war, almost a century later, when American forces would storm Kiska Island in the Aleutians only to find that the Japanese garrison had vanished.

Even at mid-century, before Russia gave up its American colony, the stars and stripes fluttered over many a trading post. When the vengeful sailors of Britain and France landed, the American flag flew over the town. "I guess ye're rather late, Admiral," proclaimed the American trader who boarded the British flagship.[16] The traders saw no reason to leave; business would go on despite the Crimean War. To the credit of the Americans, they did not bite the hand that fed them, at least initially, but encouraged the admiral to seek the missing Russians to the north on the Anadyr River. To the equal credit of the Royal Navy this misinformation was disbelieved with equanimity. "It was not to be supposed," wrote one officer, "That he would repay [Russian] kindness with a betrayal of confidence; nor do I believe he was asked to do so." [17]

Traditions of Britain's Royal Navy demanded that some investigation be made of these fiascos. This practice, though painful for all concerned, undoubtedly had much to do with the maintenance of a superior service over the centuries. But for some reason—perhaps because public attention was fixed upon the startling unpreparedness and mismanagement of the principal military forces in the Black Sea—no government inquiry was made of the North Pacific campaign. No court martials, no exposures followed. The affair was hushed up. The mighty *London Times*, thundering away at the disastrous mishandling of the seige of Sevastopol, took no heed of the farcical operations of the Pacific fleet.

Farther south, the Allies fared no better. Because North Pacific charts did not show that Sakhalin was an island, a British fleet caught two Russian ships in a "bay" between the mainland and Sakhalin Island. Fog interfered with the pursuit; so the British waited for the fog to clear, sure that the enemy was bottled up. When the fog lifted, no Russians were to be seen. Although their prey had merely sailed around Sakhalin Island, the British assumed the Russians had passed through their blockade.

The Russian ships which had escaped Petropavlovsk were discovered by the Allies in De Castries Bay, on the Asian mainland opposite Sakhalin, but as the Russian strength was slightly superior, no attack was launched. Two distant, futile shots were fired by a British ship and reinforcements were awaited. As usual, the Russians had disappeared by the time a larger Allied squadron returned to the bay. The last North Pacific battle of the Crimean War also ended in an Allied repulse. An amphibious force assaulted Muravyev's Cossacks at the mouth of the Amur River but was defeated and driven off.

In June of 1856 news of the end of hostilities reached the Pacific, and the Allied fleets returned to their usual stations. Needless to say, Russia's capitulation owed nothing to the dismal record of the Allies' North Pacific fleet. Except for the capture of a few trading vessels and the acquisition of a store of furs taken from one of the undefended Kurile Islands, the fleet's achievements were nil.

But the war certainly affected the future of Russia's chief Bering Sea settlement, accelerating a decline already foreshadowed by the mid-century Russian annexation of the Amur region. Petropavlovsk's gallant garrison was not reestablished after the peace; nor were the government buildings, burned by the Allies in 1855—either in retaliation or by accident—replaced. Although the port remained a trading center, its population declined. A further setback occurred with the sale of Russian America to the United States in 1867. After that event, the few vessels calling at Petropavlovsk were more often foreign than Russian.

Kamchatka's stagnation contrasted with developments on the opposite Bering Sea shore. With the discovery of gold in the Seward Peninsula in 1898, the American North boomed. Nome, Alaska, with its thousands of miners, supplanted Petropavlovsk as the chief population center of the Bering Sea. But the Kamchatkans did not forget their moment of glory. Each year on September 4th they celebrated their victory over the British and French with gay festivities. A suitable monument was raised to commemorate those killed in the conflict, Allies as well as Russians.

In England the defeats did not go entirely unnoticed. Captain Bernard Whittingham, a member of the Royal Engineers, had been aboard one of the English frigates which allowed Russian ships to escape

De Castries Bay. In 1856 he published his *Notes on the Late Expedition against the Russian Settlements in Eastern Siberia*. Whittingham "attempted to bring out the different phases of an ill-directed expedition with candour, yet . . . could scarcely hope that the criticisms passed upon it would be deemed as respectful to the chief in command." [18]

In an appendix he referred to the 1854 invasion of Petropavlovsk as one which "however ill conducted or disorderly" should not have miscarried.[19] He pointed out the superiority of Allied arms and the advantages of having "exquisitely finished surveys" of Petropavlovsk and Avacha Bays.[20] Whittingham called on naval officers to explain why the defending batteries could not be silenced by a superior fire power. "Unhappily the un-English and unmanly policy of veiling ill successes, caused by the ignorance of the art of war on the part of chiefs, is rapidly gaining ground amongst us." [21] Bare, stiff dispatches from commanders were all too often, he averred, used to conceal mishaps caused by incompetence and extolled anything resembling a success.

In later years, visitors to Petropavlovsk invariably commented upon the war. Most Englishmen had no knowledge of the defeat prior to encountering the historical evidence—and this annoyed them. In 1866 Frederick Whymper, in Kamchatka with the Western Union Telegraph Expedition, noted that the 1855 Allied expedition "has been duly laid before the public, but it is not so generally known that our first attack, the previous year, was by no means a subject of congratulations for us . . . it has been kept uncommonly quiet." [22]

Similarly, in 1881, an English zoologist, F. H. H. Guillemard, viewed the war monument with some surprise and admitted his ignorance of the battle, "owing to the success with which the matter was hushed up." [23] With no surprise we learn that one of the ubiquitous American traders, Captain Hunter, was on hand to describe the campaign to Guillemard. According to Hunter's account, the Allies had split their landing force and some fatalities occurred when one invading party fired on the other. Guillemard wondered that an insignificant town could occasion a "defeat as humiliating as it was ridiculous," and observed that townspeople were still annoyed at the burnings of 1855.[24] During Guillemard's visit, the war monument—a twenty-five-foot obelisk sent from Europe and erected the previous year—was dedicated.

Despite the successful defense of the Russians, the Crimean War action highlighted the remoteness of their Alaskan colonies. But for the neutrality agreement between Britain and Russia, the thinly populated Russian American Company settlements would have been in danger of being savagely mauled. Muravyev's thin line of 1,000 Cossacks could not have been stretched across the North Pacific to aid Sitka, Kodiak, and other trading stations where the Russian American Company lacked the men, ships, and harbor fortifications necessary for effective defense. St. Petersburg officials, who favored a concentration of national effort on the newly acquired Asian territory and the relinquishment of Alaska, gained support for their views. Why continue to underwrite colonies, they argued, which were unprofitable and indefensible? What good was it to boast that the Bering Sea was a Russian lake? The Russian American Company was not able to exercise the commerical domination of the region, and its enterprise was unprofitable to the fatherland. Constant intrusions of Yankee whalers and traders were weakening Russia's precarious hold on her North Pacific empire. It was ironic that while the Russians were losing money in their far-flung Alaskan-Siberian fur enterprise, other entrepreneurs with a more specialized, closely focused operation were finding the North Pacific and Bering Sea to be extremely profitable. A tendency to write off the value of the northern seas prematurely has been characteristic of Bering Sea history. While the Russians fumbled and vacillated the Yankees moved in with a vengeance.

8 — INVASION OF YANKEE WHALEMEN

"**B**low-ows, thar she blows." The glad cry announcing the sighting of a whale was first heard in the North Pacific, south of the Alaska Peninsula, in 1835. It was Captain Barzillai Folger's *Granges* which first discovered the rich hunting ground, and the ship's return to New England with a full load of whale oil and whalebone alerted other whalemen to the commercial possibilities of the distant region. Other New England ships moved into northern waters, hunting on the Kodiak ground, south of the Aleutians, in the Sea of Japan, and the Okhotsk Sea. In 1845 the hunters moved into the Bering Sea, either by way of the Okhotsk Sea or by passing through the Aleutian Islands. Soon, up to 250 vessels were coursing the ice edge each summer, following the receding ice which the bowhead whale favored for his feeding ground. Some of the whalemen distinguished the Greenland right whale of the North Pacific from the bowhead of the Bering Sea, though both were of the same family. In the 1840s and 1850s the New England hunters killed bowheads by the thousands. The success of the new enterprise outraged the Russians, who resented the exploitation of waters they considered their own preserve. Officers of the Russian American Company protested to St. Petersburg, then made preparations to equip a Russian whaling fleet, but the outbreak of the Crimean War in the 1850s nipped the Russian effort in the bud. By this time, Bering Sea whales were becoming scarce, but a new hunting ground—even more distant and much more perilous—had been discovered. In 1848 the first American ship, the *Superior* of Sag Harbor, New York, passed through the Bering Strait to enter the Arctic Ocean and others followed.

THE WHALE

It was the bowhead or Greenland right whale which induced the hunters of New England into the Bering Sea, the Okhotsk Sea, and the Arctic Ocean. This giant beast is characterized by its ponderous head, making up one-third of its entire length of up to sixty-five feet.

The sheer bulk of the bowhead threatened the puny men who dared pursue it in their fragile boats. This bulky mammal owed its commercial value to its prodigious yield of oil, up to 275 barrels, and its *baleen* or bone which could weigh as much as 3,500 pounds. The baleen of the bowhead is attached to its jaw in long, finely fringed, transverse layers which project downward and outward. These flexible sections of bone, running to a fourteen-foot length in a large animal, lie flat, side by side along the upper jaw, and are actually an extension of the corrugation of the roof of the mouth. As many as 700 of the thin, tapering strips aid the feeding process of the otherwise toothless bowhead.

In feeding on the myriad quantities of small, red, shrimplike crustaceans that are found in great quantities in northern seas, the bowhead rushes forward with his huge jaws agape. Tremendous numbers of the crustaceans, called *brit*, are scooped into a mouth opening that can be as much as thirty feet; then the bowhead closes its jaws and expells the water, using its massive tongue, while the baleen retains the brit until it can be swallowed. The bowhead's tongue is a mass of spongy fat that contains one-tenth of the entire oil yield of the leviathan's body. After feeding on or near the surface of the water, the bowhead returns to the depths in the same dramatic fashion as the sperm whale and other whales, throwing its back out of the water, then upturning its tail in the air as it dives or *sounds* below the surface. The last sight one can have of a sounding bowhead is the flash of its twenty-five-foot-wide tail, or flukes, as the beast disappears.

But once seen, the bowhead can be expected to reappear on the surface for breathing at no great distance from its sounding. Although it seldom stays on the surface for more than two or three minutes, except when feeding, it usually stays below for only five to fifteen minutes. The bowhead's lung capacity, however, does permit it to remain below for over an hour if it is threatened on the surface. On resurfacing, the bowhead spouts seven to ten times, issuing the telltale sign of respiration, the clouds of moisture which can be observed over long distances by keen-eyed hunters.

When attacked, this marvelous mammal can dive to depths of 4,800 feet to elude pursuers, but the exertion is tiring and the animal returns to the surface with diminished strength. In the Bering Sea, however, the water is comparatively shallow and less of a refuge. If the ice edge is near, the bowhead sometimes dashes for the protection the ice offers. Once the whale is under the ice, the hunters are thwarted. Even if they have harpooned the bowhead, they must cut the line and allow it to escape. For all the wonders of its physiology, the whale is not generously equipped with defenses against its human enemies. Its best defense is an ability to hollow its back when it is under attack. This instinctive reaction leaves its blubber limp, and a harpoon is likely to rebound off the slackened flesh. The whale's great size and weight—a ton to a foot is a rule-of-thumb weight measure—reduces the number of its predators, but the same massive scale and the necessity for surface breathing make escape from hunters difficult. Aside from man, the whale's only hunter is the killer whale or *orca*—actually a member of the dolphin family. Large killer whales run to lengths of twenty-five feet. Slim and fast, these mammals hunt in packs and attack by seizing the underlips of the victim with powerful teeth, forcing the injured whale's mouth open and eventually causing it to drown. Killer whales then tear out the tongue, preferring it to the rest of the whale meat.

Another whale most commonly hunted by man in the Bering Sea and Arctic Ocean in the last century was the giant sperm whale. Unlike the bowhead, the sperm whale is gregarious and is generally encountered in pods or schools. The sperm whale was known in all the world's seas, while the bowhead existed only in far northern regions. In other ways the sperm's habits and physical characteristics vary greatly from the bowhead's. It feeds in very deep water where large squids form its diet. Instead of baleen-packed jaws, its mouth has sturdy teeth, weighing up to several pounds each. These teeth were harvested for their curiosity value, but the commercial interest in the sperm whale was in the oil alone.

Basically the whale-hunting methods employed by Americans in the Bering Sea were the same that had been followed for 200 years and more. Once on the hunting ground, a crow's nest was rigged on the main mast and a perpetual daytime watch was maintained. The whaleboats were fitted out and swung outboard on davits for quick launching. Most ships carried two boats on each side and two spare boats on skids over the main deck just forward of the poop deck. Boat equipment consisted of two tubs of strong hemp line, several toggle irons or harpoons, several hand lances, a bomb gun, hatchet, knife, spade, boat hook, and fresh water and emergency rations. All the equipment was carefully inspected. Whale hunters knew their business and appreciated its hazards. Everything had to be in excellent working order to reduce the chances of failure.

As soon as a whale was sighted, its position was noted and the boats were let down. Now the chase commenced. Depending upon the whim of the great beast as it sounded, reappeared, and sounded repeatedly, the boat crew might be in for hours of hard rowing before they could get close enough to begin their attack. When he judged the moment favorable the boat officer gave the signal and the harpoon was launched at its target. A fair hit would be immediately evident. Blood would pour from the wound as the mammoth beast lashed out at random with its flukes, then sounded, trailing the harpoon's hemp line which, hopefully, was firmly fixed to the boat. No one could calculate how long the fight might continue. After each sounding the whale was more exhausted; yet his awesome strength was capable of sustaining a struggle for hours, over which the hunters must time after time strain their weary muscles to bring the boat near the prey. Not too near, however, as there was the ever present danger of the small craft capsizing as the infuriated mammal thrashed the water. "A dead whale or a stove boat" was an old saying that expressed the constant menace. Frequently the fight was terminated by weakening the whale with lances repeatedly thrust into his bulky flesh or by firing a bomb gun, the projectile of which exploded within the whale's body. With this the whale was finished. No more the monarch of the seas, he was now a mound of bloody flesh, buoyant but still as life passed out of him.

Now the whale was securely fastened to the boat, or several boats if they were at hand, and towed to the ship. If other whales were present, the boats set out once more in pursuit, after lashing their first victim to the ship, but if no other prey were visible or bad weather threatened, the butchering commenced at once. All hands participated in the bloody, odiferous, hard labor that followed. The whale was attached to the ship by a chain passed through his spout hole and another secured to his flukes. A temporary platform was built over the side of the vessel from which the men could sever the head and strip off the blubber from the carcass. To sever the head, a man stood on the slippery mass of flesh and chopped through the spinal column with an axe—very risky work in heavy seas when sharks, attracted by the blood, might be swimming about nearby. Before the head was hauled up on the deck, pails were lowered to dip out the oil it contained. The head of a sperm whale yielded from fifteen to twenty barrels of oil. It was not necessary to cook out the oil, though it was heated before barreling, to prevent it from becoming rancid.

The cutters used sharp spades to strip the blubber from the whale's body. The carcass was revolved with the aid of the ship's windlass and a line surrounding the whale's body, and the blubber was easily pulled off in long strips about eight inches thick. Once the blubber and head were removed, the carcass was cut adrift and the rest of the work was performed on the deck of the ship. The bowhead's baleen was taken from its jaw, and was usually cleaned and packed in bundles on the voyage home. Baleen prices reached four to five dollars a pound in the peak years of Bering Sea whaling, and the product from one whale could net as much as $17,000. The quantity of oil dipped from the head or boiled out from blubber and tongue in the two brick-enclosed kettles aboard varied greatly depending upon the size of the individual whale. Some yielded as much as 130 barrels. The amount of bone and oil carried to New Bedford by the *Addison* after its cruise from 1856 to 1860, in which Mary Chipman Lawrence participated, was about average for the time: 27,187 pounds of baleen and 2,442 barrels of oil.[1] Profit from the voyage, of which the crew shared 35¾ percent, was a little over $50,000 after the outfitting costs of $27,654 were deducted from the total receipts.[2]

It took three days to try out a large whale on the Bering Sea grounds. Work was carried on around the clock. Men waded in whale blood and were besplattered with oil throughout the operation. The odor of the cooking blubber permeated the entire ship. Seamen got no relief from the smell when they were off duty; their food, clothes, and bunks reeked. Still the discomfort had its consolations. All the men depended upon shares in the profit for their income. If the kettles did not boil there was no gain for anyone. The stink of blood and oil meant money—and money alone brought whaling men to the Bering Sea.

THE WALRUS

When Bering Sea whalemen found the bowhead and sperm whales in short supply, they sometimes hunted walruses for their oil and tusks. Walrus could be harpooned while they were swimming, but more often they were killed with rifles while they congregated on ice floes or on the rocky breeding grounds found on several Bering Sea islands. Russian hunters decimated most of the Pribilof herds when their fur-seal yield of the islands diminished, and American whalemen hunted walrus intensively in other places. It has been estimated that 85,000 walruses were slaughtered between 1869 and 1874 to produce 50,000 barrels of oil, and perhaps a total of 200,000 were killed from 1860 to 1880.[3] The total Bering Sea catch of the last 100 years was in the range of two or three million.[4] Whalemen hunted walruses largely to kill the time between their entry into the Bering Sea ice pack in mid-June and the pack opening in July when the ships could sail east to Point Barrow.

It was not unusual for a single rifleman to kill a herd of 100 animals on an ice floe without changing his position. Noise did not disturb the lounging giants, though a shot that was not fatal would panic the herd. A wounded walrus alerted the others to danger and they would plunge into the safety of the water and be gone. It was necessary to pierce the brain at the back of the head to kill a victim instantly.

A full-grown bull can exceed 2,000 pounds. Walruses are virtually defenseless on land; their bulk and clumsiness present an easy target to firearms. Most adults average ten to fourteen feet in length and have a girth of around eight feet. Their small, rounded, whiskered heads mount ivory tusks up to two feet in length, having considerable value. San Francisco traders handled some 10,000 tusks annually in the 1890s, shipping most of them to Chinese markets.

In the water the walrus loses his ungainliness and is capable of stoving in a small boat. Bering Sea walrus are not notably ferocious but attacks on boats have been recorded. On the whole the walrus was a hapless victim of the hunters who scoured the coasts of Kamchatka and Alaska, invaded the island breeding grounds of the Bering Sea, and combed the shores of the American and Siberian Arctic. Unlike native hunters, white men took only the oil and ivory, wasting the flesh and hides. Fortunately for the preservation of the walrus and for the natives who subsisted on these animals, the decline of the Bering Sea whale fishery occurred before they were entirely wiped out. Today walrus can still be found in considerable numbers, and herds within the United States' jurisdiction may not be hunted by white men.

The walrus hunt was devastating and wasteful. Hunters were not concerned for the people who depended upon walrus hides and meat.

Captain Louis Lane's Eskimo crew after a walrus hunt.
University of Alaska Archives, Barrett Willoughby Collection

After the slaughter, hunters stripped the blubber from their catch and left the rest, save the tusks, on the ice. The blubber was carried to the ship and tried or boiled out in the same manner as the whale blubber. A kill of 500 walruses would yield about 300 barrels of oil. No romance here, no thrill of the hunt, just a wholesale slaughter of valuable animals.

Today it is estimated that the Bering-Chukchi Seas walrus population numbers 90,000 animals, some three-quarters of the world's total. Only two marine mammals—the whale and the elephant seal—are larger than the walrus, which can reach a weight of nearly two tons and a fourteen-foot length. Earlier, before the herds were hunted with such devastating effects, the mammals were said to have been even larger.

It is the shallowness of the icy waters in the Bering Sea which has always attracted great numbers of walrus. Their diving range is limited to 250–310 feet and they must surface for breathing within ten minutes. Unlike seals, which stay at sea for months, walruses spend much time resting out of the water, either on ice floes or on rocky beaches when ice is not available. The seasonal migration of the Bering Sea herds is dictated by ice conditions. In October they leave the Arctic Ocean for the Bering Sea before the Bering Strait is closed by ice. Arctic ice is too widespread and too thick to allow breathing holes in the winter, while the Bering Sea ice is less formidable. In the summer, a reverse migration takes place as the disappearing ice of the Bering Sea forces a northern exodus. For feeding convenience and for protection against predators, the walruses prefer freely drifting ice floes as their base. A reasonably close contact with ice is essential. For this reason the largest herds have always been found off the north and south coasts of the Chukchi Peninsula where the ice remains much longer than on the Alaskan side of the Bering Sea.

Mating occurs on the sea ice during February and March, and the calves are born on the ice, usually during the migration to the Arctic in April or June of the following year. Both events occur beyond the vision of human observers and have rarely been noted. This is quite a contrast to the mating of seals and sea lions which takes place on land rookeries and can easily be watched. Much uncertainty thus surrounds the walrus' habits. Whether the bulls contend against other bulls to maintain exclusive rights over their harem of cows, as do elephant seals and sea lions, is not known. In fact, it is not even known whether bulls have harems or are monogamous. Also unknown is the extent to which walruses congregate and migrate in family groups.

The most striking characteristic of the walrus is its ivory tusks, up to three feet in length, and weighing up to 10 pounds. With the help of tusks and flippers, the ponderous animal hauls its enormous bulk from the water to the ice floes where it spends most of its time. With its tusks the walrus plows the ocean bed for its shellfish food, kills and butchers seals, wars against its fellows, and breaks open breathing holes in the winter sea ice. The ivory of the tusks was the chief attraction of the white men in hunting these beasts, which was actually secondary to whaling.

WHALING SHIPS

New England whaling vessels were built for strength and durability rather than speed. They were squat but roomy, usually about 100 feet in length with a 25-foot beam and a 15-foot draft. Most were registered at 300 to 500 tons and were rigged as ships (square sails on all three masts) or barks (square sails on two of three masts). Late in the nineteenth century, vessels were generally equipped with steam engines capable of propelling them about eight knots an hour, a great advantage in ice navigation. Whalers, like the famed *Charles W. Morgan*, built at New Bedford in 1841 and now berthed at Mystic, Connecticut, as a museum attraction, were almost always sheathed in Australian green heart, a wood of great hardness, to provide protection against the wear of ice.

The particular needs of whaling dictated other special features of these ships. Tryworks for boiling the oil out of the blubber were fixed on the deck and consisted of two large cast iron kettles, with a 200-gallon capacity, enclosed in brick ovenlike structures so that fires could heat the kettles safely. Up to seven whaleboats were carried. These vital boats were the hunters' platforms and were of a uniform design for generations. Each was light enough to be propelled by four oarsmen in pursuit of their prey. They were twenty-eight or thirty feet long and six feet wide, graceful, and sturdy enough to carry a 2,000-pound load; easy to repair if damaged and not expensive to replace.

Below decks the captain occupied a large stateroom on the starboard side and just forward of this were small staterooms for the mates. Further forward the steerage compartment held eight bunks for ranking crew members, while the ordinary seamen were housed in the cramped, low-ceilinged forecastle. Forecastle conditions were unpleasant at best and could be squalid. Crude bunks lined the compartment in a double tier. Ventilation and light were minimal. A hole cut in the deck above provided the only entry and was the sole provision for light and fresh air. A bad enough situation in good weather, but in rough seas the deck hatch had to be closed. Smoky lamps used for lighting contributed to the stuffiness of these close quarters. Twelve bunks and as many foot lockers left little space for unencumbered movement. In such surroundings, seamen smoked, talked, quarreled, and otherwise diverted themselves over voyages which could extend up to four years.

Cramped quarters aside, the whaling vessels were splendidly suited to their purpose. Their design evolution occurred over many decades of practical experience. Although seldom praised for their beauty, these rugged floating factories withstood the rigors of equatorial gales and polar ice in dogged quest of their hapless victims. The *Charles W. Morgan* returned from her last voyage in 1921 and the *Wanderer*, the last of the square-rigged whalers, set out on its final hunt in 1924.

THE MEN OF THE WHALERS

> Oh, poor Reuben Ronzo,
> Ronzo, boys, oh Ronzo,
> Oh, Ronzo is no sailor
> So he's shipped aboard a whaler,
> Ronzo, boys, oh Ronzo.[5]

This derisive song expressed the contempt in which whalemen were held by merchant seamen. According to maritime historian Samuel Eliot Morison, the long whaling voyages "brought out the worst traits of human nature. Whalers' forecastles were more efficient schools of vice than reformatories." [6] Brutal treatment of seamen by officers was the rule. "Many whaling skippers, who on shore passed as pious friends or church members, were coldblooded, heartless fiends on the quarter-deck." [7] Ship owners and captains created conditions on shipboard which decent men would not willingly stand, then argued that the bad character of their crews required them to impose the harshest discipline. Morison's denunciation of whaling captains was savage; the "blackguards" in command "degraded the flag and the name of America." [8]

William Fish Williams, a New Bedford whaling veteran whose father was a captain, played down the brutality of officers. Stern discipline, he argued, was necessary because of the sharp decline in the quality of seamen after the Civil War. "The type of men found in the forecastle of sailing ships showed a very appreciable deterioration in character, both physical and mental." [9] With new industrial opportunities and easier access to the West, fewer young men of quality were willing to ship out in whalers. Captains had to convert "land-lubbers and semi-sailors" into sailors and did so, although "it took a lot of energy and profanity." [10] In Williams' view, a new set of standards was necessary; sailors had to be driven because they had no ambition and no courage. Williams claimed that seamen obeyed orders only because their fear of the officers was greater than their fear of the dangers attached to the execution of the order. "If the seamen were different, unfortunately the officers were as brutal as ever and maintained the conditions that had long given whalers the reputation of 'hell-ships.' " [11]

Conditions aboard whalers brutalized men, and the effects spread beyond shipboard. Such seamen, after long months of sea, had no qualms about debauching the natives of the Bering Sea. Sailors were not notably high-minded in such circumstances. They desired women and had the means to lure them to their bunks. Ship captains did not interfere with the lusty recreation of their crewmen. If the sailors were ridden with venereal disease, that was too bad for the natives—it was all part of the exchange. In Honolulu and other Pacific ports there were missionaries and other respectable folk to complain, however fruitlessly, of such debaucheries, but during the peak years of whaling in the Bering Sea, no similar resident group existed to admonish the lascivious seamen.

The seaman's life was hard, monotonous, and fraught with danger. Nor was the greatest danger associated with the hunt. Disease was a greater menace. Venereal disease was commonplace, and the crewmen's coarse diet of salt, meat, and biscuit and close confinement led to scurvy and organic disorders. Long exposure to extremes of climate encouraged tuberculosis, dropsy, and other chronic afflictions. Accidents, falls, fighting, and floggings weakened the bodies of the men; yet, unless crippled, they were forced to turn out in all weather to carry out their shipboard labors. Tyrannical officers sometimes drove seamen beyond the limits of physical endurance. In such circumstances they were even more subject to disease. Some were driven to mutiny, others to desertion.

Every year four to five thousand sailors deserted their ships on balmy South Pacific islands, and others were desperate enough to cast their lot among the Chukchi, Aleuts, and Eskimos of the Bering Sea and Arctic Ocean. Clearly, those who deserted in northern waters were not bemused by tropical skies and the promise of a languorous life among palm trees.

Whalemen did not receive wages for their services: they were apportioned a share of the net proceeds of the voyage known as a *lay*. A lay varied from $\frac{1}{8}$ or $\frac{1}{10}$, the captain's share, to the $\frac{1}{250}$ allotted to the cabin boy. The net proceeds upon which lays were based were determined after the cargo was sold and the expenses of the venture deducted. For example, in 1851 the *Benjamin Tucker* returned to New Bedford with 79,055 gallons of oil and 30,012 pounds of bone.[12] The cargo's gross value was $47,682.73 and expenses $2,362.73, thus the net was $45,320. An inexperienced seaman with a lay of $\frac{1}{200}$ received $226.60 for his many months of work. Sometimes 60 percent of the proceeds were reserved to the owner, while lays were based upon the remaining 40 percent.

On the return of the *Addison* from her 1856–60 voyage, the crew shared in $35\frac{3}{4}$ percent of net proceeds, totaling about $50,000.[13] Captain Lawrence got a $\frac{1}{4}$ lay, the chief mate $\frac{1}{18}$, the second mate $\frac{1}{35}$, the third mate $\frac{1}{55}$, boat-steerers—the key hunting personnel—received $\frac{1}{90}$, the cooper $\frac{1}{90}$. Seamens' lays varied from $\frac{1}{150}$ to $\frac{1}{250}$. Green hands, with a $\frac{1}{250}$ lay, earned $202.09 for the four years' voyage, while a lay of $\frac{1}{175}$ netted $288.71. This return, as miserly as it appears, does not actually represent the full picture. From these earnings, cash advances made for shore leave expenditures were taken out, as were the inflated costs of items of clothing and gear purchased from the ship's slopchest or store. Interest was added to all such charges. This pernicious system of remuneration was unique among whalemen. Whaling owners forced their men to share fully the risks involved in the venture, without providing them the chance of a substantial gain from the profits. If the profits were minimal, the crew gained nothing, but if the ship did well, the lesser members were poorly rewarded. It has been estimated that the average earnings of the lowest paid shore laborers during the same period were two to three times higher than those earned by whaling seamen. Little wonder that of the original crew of Captain Lawrence's *Addison*, only nine of the thirty-two completed the voyage. Fourteen men received their discharges at various times, seven deserted, and two were drowned.

These statistics speak volumes for the morale aboard whalers and should check any tendency to exclaim on the "romance of whaling."

PROFITS OF WHALING

Since time out of mind, the natives of the Bering Sea hunted whales and walrus for meat, skins, and oil. Today the walrus still provides the chief sustenance of the Eskimos of St. Lawrence Island and the Diomede Islands. The walrus is hunted by villagers dwelling both on Asian and American shores. The whale is also important to many northern peoples and is hunted each summer as it moves through the Bering Sea and into its Arctic feeding grounds. The walrus, whale, seal, sea otter, and sea lion have been depicted in native legends, contributing to a mythology in which the mysteries of nature were interwoven with the seasonal pattern of human life in the North.

But the white hunters eschewed mythology and mystery. Short on legend but advanced in technology, they invaded the Bering Sea whale grounds with relentless intent and in increasing numbers—cruising northern waters in response to the world markets for whalebone, ivory, and oil. By this time, the once prolific whale herds of the Atlantic and South Pacific Oceans had been ravished; now they had to move north. With deadly efficiency the hunters hounded the leviathans of the sea, filling their ships with the bountiful harvest of their exertions and enriching their backers.

For the captain and the ship owners, the rewards of whaling were substantial. Whaling was a profitable business, particularly during the "golden age." From 1835 to 1860 the annual imports of whale products to the United States averaged 117,950 barrels of sperm oil, 25,913 barrels of common whale oil, and 2,323,512 pounds of baleen, to total approximately $8 million each year. At that time, whale oil was used chiefly for candles and other illuminants. Later, the oil was used principally for soap making, leather dressing, and lubricants. Depending upon the skill or fortune of the captain, an individual whaling vessel could return a good profit to its backers.

New Bedford, in southeastern Massachusetts, eventually became the greatest whaling port in the world in the mid-nineteenth century, having grown steadily more prosperous since 1755, when its first whaler was outfitted. Other New England ports were active too, as the following list indicates:

New Bedford: 254 vessels	Mystic: 17 vessels
New London: 70 vessels	Nantucket: 75 vessels
Fairhaven: 48 vessels	Stonington: 27 vessels
Warren: 23 vessels	Provincetown: 18 vessels

Over 600 ships from these and other American ports were sailing to the North and South Pacific Oceans at mid-century. Hundreds of others sailed the Atlantic, Indian, and lesser seas. Captains and crews sighted whales and brought them back on a steady basis to serve a burgeoning market. For the thirty-seven years prior to 1872, the whalers averaged 524 ships a year on the oceans and brought back an average of 96,625 barrels of sperm oil and 172,448 barrels of whale oil. The average yield of a sperm whale was 25 barrels of oil, an indication of the great numbers of whales killed during this period. Catches of whales in Alaskan waters reveal the importance of its fisheries during this period.

By about 1880 whale and walrus oil lost value because of petroleum production. For some years the bone alone sustained the profits of the industry and shippers paid less attention to oil. Some whalers made it a practice to abandon the bowhead's carcass after severing its head. This saved a good deal of heavy work and increased the cruising range of ships. There was some complaint about such waste, although nothing could be done about it. In 1880 the *San Francisco Bulletin* complained about wasteful sea-mammal hunting, but there were no regulations or restrictions governing the Bering Sea-Arctic fisheries.

NATIVES AND THE WHALEMEN

"The natives were frequent visitors, but with very few and rare exceptions, they were to me extremely repulsive in looks and habits. They have a disgusting fad of making a hole through the cheek near the corner of the mouth, in which they place polished pieces of ivory or stone, and sometimes empty brass cartridge shells." [14] So spoke William Fish Williams in a lecture before a men's club in New Bedford, Massachusetts. Williams had firsthand experience with Bering Sea whaling. In 1873–74 he served on his father's ship, *Florence*, as a junior officer—the same vessel on which he had been born during his mother's 1858–61 voyage. Young Williams described the natives he encountered as shiftless and lazy; so much so that they sometimes failed to provide

WHALE CATCHES IN ALASKAN WATERS (1845–1890)

Year	Number of Ships	Total Catch Oil, Sperm, and Whale (barrels)	Total Value (including bone)
1845	163	250,600	$5,337,780
1846	192	253,800	5,542,990
1847	177	187,443	4,519,330
1848	159	185,256	4,198,637
1849	155	206,850	5,085,716
1850	144	243,648	7,186,549
1851	138	86,360	2,812,350
1852	278	373,450	14,118,900
1853	238	218,135	7,264,470
1854	232	184,063	6,506,976
1855	217	189,579	8,038,914
1856	178	146,410	6,651,156
1857	143	113,900	5,158,760
1858	196	121,650	4,625,620
1859	176	94,160	3,459,060
1860	121	62,678	2,297,511
1861	76	55,024	1,792,900
1862	32	19,525	785,217
1863	42	36,010	1,855,770
1864	68	35,490	2,725,612
1865	59	36,415	3,092,160
1866	95	56,925	4,301,250
1867	90	57,620	3,192,380
1885	———	20,817	———
1889	49	12,231	———
1890	48	7,452	———

sufficient food for their winter consumption and starved to death. "They early took the first two degrees in civilization by learning to use tobacco and drink rum." [15] After a trading transaction, Williams reported, the men went on a spree until the rum was all consumed. No one in Williams' audience inquired about the advisability of providing rum to natives in the first place. Whalemen were not charged with the responsibility for the wanton conduct of aboriginals, and Williams made only this passing reference to the liquor trade. In his address and in his published account of the *Florence*'s 1873–74 voyage, Williams had another purpose: As his modern editor put it, Williams' narrative "is a record for posterity about the glory of the American seamen." [16]

The glory of the American seamen and the profitability of whaling has been well established in the literature, dimmed only by a few crusty historians, like Samuel Eliot Morison and Elmo Paul Hohman, who pointed up the brutal treatment of seamen by officers. But the damning effects of the liquor trade were passed over lightly in whalemen's chronicles, and the sexual abuse of native women was never mentioned.

Virtually all the whalers doubled as traders. Natives had valuable stocks of whalebone and ivory which they would willingly exchange for firearms, ammunition, tobacco, liquor, and other items. The Russians had imposed a ban on the liquor traffic, but had no means of enforcing it. In fact, the Russians felt compelled to trade liquor themselves when commercial rivalry made it necessary. After Alaska was purchased by the United States in 1867, booze traders had to be more discreet; more than one stock of liquor was hurriedly thrown overboard on the approach of a Revenue Marine ship. But the Revenue Marine cruises in the Bering Sea were irregular until the 1880s, and by that time, the liquor trade had been flourishing for forty years. Even then, the few ships of the Revenue Marine were incapable of halting the flow of booze.

Belatedly, the whiskey and sexual abuses incident to trading were brought to the attention of the United States government in the early 1880s. Captain C. L. Hooper of the Revenue Marine called for the protection and education of the population of 3,000 Innuit Eskimos of Alaska's west coast. He observed that they were sinking lower each year, and were at the mercy of the whiskey seller.

Ivan Petroff, who made the first United States census of Alaska's population in 1880, reported on the decimation of St. Lawrence Island Eskimos that occurred in 1874, when 400 or more people succumbed to famine and disease. "Living directly in the track of vessels bound for the Arctic for the purpose of whaling and trading, this situation has been a curse to them; for as long as the rum lasts they do nothing but drink and fight among themselves." [17] St. Lawrence inhabitants, according to Petroff, refused to trade for anything but whiskey and firearms.

John Murdock, an American scientist who investigated the conditions of Point Barrow Eskimos for the Smithsonian Institution in 1887–88, asserted that "the unmitigated evil of the intercourse with whites has been the introduction of spirits." [18] Murdock also declaimed against "another serious evil, which it would be almost impossible to check, in the unlimited intercourse of the sailors with Eskimo women." [19] In fairness to the whalemen, Murdock admitted that the whites had not introduced fornication to the Eskimos, "but they have encouraged a natural savage tendency, and have taught them prostitution for gain, which has brought about great excesses." [20] Little study had been made of Eskimos at the time of Murdock's investigations, and he wondered whether the promiscuity stimulated by the whalemen had been responsible for the limited fertility of Eskimo women. Of the brighter side of white-Eskimo cultural contact Murdock had little to report except that natives had learned a few English expressions, notably "get out of here," a few Hawaiian words from Kanaka seamen, and some songs: "Little Brown Jug" and "Shoo Fly." What seamen in turn learned from Eskimos was not noted.

John Murdock and Captain John Healy of the Revenue Service were among the first American officials to call attention to yet another problem which evolved from the activities of whalers in the Bering Sea and Arctic Ocean. As a consequence of the trade with whalers, natives had acquired modern firearms, and their increased efficiency in hunting may have depleted the caribou herds which had provided a major portion of their sustenance. Caribou learned to avoid the coastal regions in their migrations, and their scarcity led to hardship and an increasing dependence on modern, efficient weapons. Bows and arrows would no longer do. This was perhaps one of the indirect results of white contact for which no one could be seriously blamed. Certainly it seemed beneficial to provide natives with weapons that would help them fill their larders; yet, as so often with technological advances, the end results wreaked havoc. Of course, the presence of whalers increased the demand for meat, and upon occasion, there were greater slaughters of game than might otherwise have taken place.

Governmental remedies were disastrous: A ban on the trading of breech-loading rifles to natives was enforced, but this did not bring back the caribou and severely hampered the efforts of hunters. For years, missionaries and other observers urged Washington to lift the firearm restriction, but to no avail.

An even more serious game shortage was directly attributable to the whalers. In 1890 the Presbyterian missionary Sheldon Jackson urged the government to alleviate starvation among Alaska's Eskimos. "From time immemorial they have lived upon the whale, the walrus, and the seal of their coasts, the fish and aquatic birds of their rivers, and the caribou or wild reindeer of their vast, wild plains," reported Jackson. "But fifty years ago American whalers, having largely exhausted the supply in other waters, found their way into the North Pacific Ocean." Thousands of whales were slaughtered in the Pacific, then the whalemen moved into the Bering Sea and Arctic Ocean. "In this relentless hunt the remnant have been driven still farther into the inaccessible regions around the north pole, and are no longer within reach of the natives." [21]

Captain Healy concurred with Jackson's alarm: "The results of the active and unscrupulous chase of their [native] pelagic food by the whalemen have already become evident; walrus are almost invisible on the ice floes within reach of the native hunters, while the flurried and galled whale makes its passage to the unknown regions of the Arctic Ocean at a speed which defies the natives to capture it." [22] The rhetoric of Jackson and Healy was directed to a particular remedy to the native food problem: the introduction of Siberian reindeer to Alaska. This imaginative scheme concocted by Healy and Jackson is among the brighter chapters in the history of government endeavors to help native peoples, even if it did not achieve all that had been hoped. Jackson launched his major effort to alleviate distress with the aid of private contributions; the effort was later supported by the government. An admiring biographer of the missionary claimed that the reindeer project "saved the Eskimo from extinction." Although this claim is something of an exaggeration, the attempt was certainly a praiseworthy one.

Some of the whalemen were conscientious. During the 1851 season, Eskimos from St. Lawrence Island and the Diomede Islands came aboard a New Bedford ship to beg for rum. "Notwithstanding all their gesticulations and grimaces," wrote one captain to a shipping newspaper, "they got nothing but cold water from the butt." [23] Strangely enough the Eskimos drank the water then pretended to be drunk, "their excellent mimicry showing that they had had some experience." [24] This captain found that the Siberian natives were less addicted to booze, and hoped that "our whalemen will do nothing to foster their appetite. These people are already wretched enough." [25]

The writer noted that rum had contributed to violent conflict between whalemen and natives in 1851. That year six ships were lost: the *New Bedford* off the Aleutians; the *Henry Thompson*, in the ice off the Diomedes; the *Superior* in the Anadyr Sea; the *Globe* at East Cape; the *Houqa* near Cape Oliver; and the *Armata* on a reef near Cape North. A trading vessel from Hong Kong was exchanging liquor for furs and ivory along the Bering Strait that season, and the natives were in a boisterous mood. In the course of abandoning the *Armata*, the seamen had trouble with drunken natives who were watching the stricken ship. The conflict resulted in the death of one sailor and eight natives. "I do not know upon whom the blame must rest," wrote the whaleman who reported the tragedy, "but I do earnestly entreat my fellow whalemen by every consideration of morality and of self-interest not to furnish these poor people with intoxicating drinks." [26] Whalemen were very much dependent upon natives if they were shipwrecked "and it is only prudent to keep them as simple in their habits as possible." [27]

Captain Frederick A. Barker of the *Japan* was one of the few whaling men to cry out against the wholesale destruction of the walrus herds of the Bering Sea. In a letter to the *Whalemen's Shipping List and Merchants Transcript* he warned New England whaling men that the practice "will surely end in the extermination of this race of natives who rely upon these animals alone for their winter's supply of food." [28] If the butchering of the walrus did not cease, the fate of the Eskimo was inevitable: "Already this cruel persecution has been felt along the entire coast, while a wail like that of the Egyptians goes through the length and breadth of the land. There is a famine and relief comes not." [29] Eskimos had often asked Barker why the white men took away their food and left them to starve, and he had no answer to give them. They told him of their joy when the whalemen first began to come among them, and of their growing despair as the hunters began to decimate the walrus.

"I have conversed with many intelligent shipmasters upon this subject," wrote Barker, "since I have seen it in its true light and *all* have expressed their honest conviction that it was wrong, cruel and heartless and the sure death of this inoffensive race." [30] Captains had told Barker that they would be glad to abandon walrus hunting if the ship owners would approve it, "but until the subject was introduced to public notice, they were powerless to act." [31] It would be hard to give up an enterprise that provided 10,000 barrels of oil each season. My advocacy "may seem preposterous and meet with derision and contempt, but let those who deride it see the misery entailed throughout the country by this unjust wrong." [32]

Captain Barker was not the only shipmaster to appeal for an end to the walrus slaughter, but he knew better than most what was happening to northern natives. Barker had taken his *Japan* into the Arctic Ocean in 1870 and had made a good catch. Whales were plentiful and the weather was good; so Barker was reluctant to return south through the Bering Strait. As the days grew colder and the shore ice thickened, Barker was forced to give up the chase and work the *Japan* toward the strait. Unfortunately, he encountered heavy fog which slowed his progress, then a storm which buffeted the *Japan* for four days. On October 9, 1870, the *Japan* was off East Cape, Siberia, and in serious trouble. "The gale blew harder . . . attended by such blinding snow that we could not see half a ship's length." [33] Although Barker had taken in most of his sails, the *Japan* was racing at breakneck speed before the gale. "Just then, to add to our horror, a huge wave swept over the ship, taking off all our boats and sweeping the decks clean." [34] The situation was critical. Barker steered for the beach and hoped for the best. An enormous wave hit the *Japan* and drove it upon the rocky shore. Miraculously, all the men got ashore safely, but their travails were just beginning. The weather was bitterly cold, and clothing and provisions had to be recovered from the disabled ship. Barker and his men struggled through the surf to the ship and back to the shore again and suffered fearful consequences. All were severely frostbitten, and eight of the thirty-man crew died in the effort. Natives came to the mariners' assistance. Barker was dragged out of the breakers, breathless and nearly frozen, loaded onto a sled, and taken to a village. "I thought my teeth would freeze off." [35] Barker scrambled out of the sled and tried to run, hoping the exertion would warm him. Instead he fell down as one paralyzed. The natives picked him up and put him on the sled once more.

In the village the survivors received tender care. "The chief's wife, in whose hut I was," wrote Barker, "pulled off my boots and stockings and placed my frozen feet against her naked bosom to restore warmth and animation." [36] With such care the seamen who had not died on the beach recovered. But for the natives "every soul . . . would have perished on the beach . . . as there was no means at hand of kindling a fire or of helping ourselves one way or the other." [37]

Barker and his men wintered with the Eskimos. They had no choice in the matter, as the entire whaling fleet had returned south before the *Japan* started for Bering Strait. It was during these months that Barker learned something of the Eskimos' way of life and became their advocate. Except for a few casks of bread and flour that had washed ashore, the seamen were entirely dependent upon their hosts. The men ate raw walrus meat and blubber that was generally on the ripe side. The whalemen did not relish their diet, but it sustained them. Prejudices against a novel food inhibited Barker for a time. He fasted for three days. "Hunger at last compelled me and, strange as it may appear, it tasted good to me and before I had been there many weeks, I could eat as much raw meat as anyone, the natives excepted." [38] Barker soon understood that the natives were short of food. "I felt like a guilty culprit while eating their food with them, that I have been taking the bread out of their mouths." [39] Barker knew and the Eskimos knew that the whalemen's hunting of walrus had reduced the natives to the point of famine, "still they were ready to share all they had with us." [40] Barker resolved to call for a prohibition of walrus hunting when he returned to New Bedford and further resolved that he would never kill another walrus "for those poor people along the coast have nothing else to live upon." [41]

In the summer of 1871 Barker and his men were rescued when the whaling fleet returned. Some recompense was made to the Eskimos for their charity; they were given provisions and equipment from the ships. The natives' plight was observed by other captains too. One wrote a letter to the *New Bedford Republican Standard* to describe the "cruel occupation" of walrus killing. Most of those killed were females which were lanced as they held their nursing offspring in their flippers "uttering the most heartrending and piteous cries." [42] Many whalemen felt guilty about this butchery, and they had to have very strong stomachs to carry out the bloody job under such circumstances. "But the worst feature of the business is that the natives of the entire Arctic shores, from Cape Thaddeus and the Anadyr Sea to the farthest point north, a shoreline of more than one thousand miles on the west coast, with the large island of St. Lawrence, the smaller ones of Diomede and King's Island, all thickly inhabited . . . are now almost entirely dependent on the walrus for their food, clothing, boots and dwellings." [43] Earlier there were plenty of whales for them, but the whales had been destroyed and driven north. "This is a sad state of things for them." [44]

Other captains reported that they had seen natives thirty to forty miles from land on the ice, trying desperately to catch a walrus or find a carcass that had been abandoned by the whalemen. "What must the poor creatures do this cold winter, with no whale or walrus?" [45]

Such appeals might have been effective eventually, though whether they would have led to a prohibition of walrus killing in time to spare the northern natives from famine is unlikely. But events took an unexpected turn in 1871: The ships which passed through the Bering Strait that season did so for the last time. The entire fleet was caught in the ice near Point Barrow, as the men—including the *Japan* survivors—hunted walrus and whale. Thanks to the Revenue Marine, the seamen were saved, but the ships were lost. This disaster, coming six years after the *Shenandoah*'s destructive cruise, dealt the whaling industry a blow from which it never recovered. But it may have saved the walrus and the northern natives from extinction. It was clear enough to the Bering Sea natives that they had benefited by the loss of the fleet. As an Eskimo or Chukchi of Plover Bay put it to a whaling captain when word of the loss reached Siberia: "Bad. Very bad for you. Good for us. More walrus now." [46]

THE JOURNAL OF MARY CHIPMAN LAWRENCE

August 28, 1857: "Arose this morning and found ourselves in a city of ships. Could count fifteen from off deck. Some were boiling, some cutting in, and other chasing whales. It seems very lively and pleasant. Our boats lowered for a whale in the forenoon; killed a very large one which sunk, but, three boats being fast to him, they succeeded after some time in pulling him up again, much to our satisfaction." [47]

This notation was not made in the conventional ship's log—that terse record of weather, ship position, and hunting activity which recorded the basic incidents of all voyages—but in the journal of Mary Chipman Lawrence kept aboard the *Addison* on its 1856–60 cruisings. Mary Lawrence was the captain's wife and one of the handful of women who preferred the maintenance of family life at sea to the widowlike existence allotted to the wives of most seafaring men. Mrs. Lawrence and her daughter, Minnie—five years old on her initial cruise—came to know the Bering Sea and Arctic Ocean and gain an intimate understanding of the whalemens' life and its dangers. It was because of the uncertainties and perils of whaling that Mary Lawrence decided to join her husband,

and she did not regret the experience. She shared the exuberance of a successful hunt and the bitter disappointment when, for days at a time, the *Addison* of New Bedford failed to find its prey. She watched her husband anxiously: "The trouble with the absence of whales wears upon Samuel. He grows thin and has lost his appetite, but it may be that all will turn out in the end." [48] She rejoiced when Captain Lawrence exhibited his seamanship and the courage of command: "I should never have known what a great man he was if I had not accompanied him." [49]

In Mary Lawrence's journal we can glimpse a less grim side to the whaling voyage. Not that the Bering Sea shed its fogs and rewarded the *Addison* with galeless seas just because the "Captain's best mate" shipped aboard, but her presence made life on the northern waters seem more pleasant. On Unimak Island of the Aleutians Mrs. Lawrence had time to land and gather "a large bunch of flowers for Minnie and myself, which delighted us very much, also about a dozen strawberries, blackberries, and huckleberries." [50] Flowers and berries on the "desolate" Aleutians? Other whaler crew members seemed not to have noticed that the rugged, volcanic islands bloomed profusely. Contacts with Bering Sea dwellers were pleasant too. Natives who boarded the *Addison* stared in fascination at a white woman and were amused by Minnie's attempts to converse with them. Probably the table of the *Addison*, at least the captain's table, was better for Mrs. Lawrence's efforts: "We have everything nice to eat, sweet and Irish potatoes, cabbages, onions, cucumbers, string beans, bananas, coconuts, melons, pumpkins, preserved meats, vegetables, oysters and lobster, sausage meat, etc., butter and soda crackers, tamarinds, preserves, arrowroot, pigs, turkeys, ducks and chickens." [51]

But Mary Lawrence's chief concern was not with flowers or gourmet foods. Always she noted the events of overwhelming significance to everyone aboard, the occurrences that had brought the ship to the distant reaches of the far northern Pacific:

> August 18. This morning we picked up a carcass. It had been dead too long to be of much use. We saved about 18 barrels from it and 100 pounds of bone—not much, but worth saving.
>
> August 19. Lowered for whales this morning, but immediately after a thick fog set in so that nothing could be seen. We fired guns and blew horns so that the boats might find their way to the ship, until Minnie thought it surely must be Fourth of July or some other great day.

August 22. A thick fog for several days. Today a gale of wind . . .
We are now living on fresh fish, which are very nice.

August 23. Calm again. Lowered for whales this morning, but they
very mysteriously disappeared; were not seen after the boats went down.

August 26. Nothing in sight that lives. Our company was beginning
to feel rather down again, when the cry of white whales resounded from
the head. The boats were lowered and about eight o'clock P.M. got a whale
alongside. Commenced cutting him in immediately, as the barometer gave
indications of another gale.

September 2. Whales in abundance. It is a grand sight to see them
ploughing through the sea, rising to breathe. If they were aware of their
strength, how few would be safe. Our boats went off in the morning for
whales. About 10 A.M. fastened to one which knew how to use his flukes
very scientifically. At dark they were compelled to cut from him, which
they did with a very bad grace.[52]

The 1858 cruise of the *Addison* was typical of those recorded by
Mary Lawrence. It began on March 23 from Honolulu where the ship
had been reprovisioned. Captain Lawrence sailed northwest, sweeping to
the west of the Aleutians and reached the Kamchatka Peninsula whaling
ground early in May. The *Addison* cruised the coast of Kamchatka until
July 17, keeping clear of the ice pack of the Bering Sea by skirting its
western edge. As the ice retreated in July, the *Addison* pushed north and
reached the Bering Strait. The *Addison* passed through the strait and
cruised the waters between East Cape, Siberia, and Icy Cape, Alaska, for
several weeks. On September 9 Captain Lawrence set sail for the south,
passed through the Aleutians on September 26, and reached Honolulu
again on October 15—completing an eight-month voyage.

The *Addison* experienced more than the usual travails of such a
cruise. Thick fogs and strong gales hampered hunting, and on June 17,
she struck a massive ice floe that stove in the starboard bow. The collision
did not imperil the ship, but it did open a leak that made repairs
necessary. Captain Lawrence brought the *Addison* into Masinka Bay, on
the Siberian side of the Bering Strait, to see to the damage. Fortunately
several other ships were anchored there and their carpenters assisted the
Addison men.

Mary Lawrence enjoyed the social opportunities presented by the
Addison's mishap. "Gamming"—conversations with people of other
ships—was the leading recreation of Bering Sea hunters. Mary Lawrence

visited other ships and exchanged gossip and news from home. Socializing, however, was not restricted to periods of harbor anchorage. On any fine day at sea, when activity was slack, it was the custom to exchange civilities. Officers and seamen would lower a boat and row to another ship, sometimes to sample a festive dinner, but more often to share notes on the hunt or to talk of home with neighbors from New Bedford, Salem, or Sag Harbor. Gamming offered a great relief from the tedium of long voyages. Merchant-ship sailors did not have leisure for such pleasures, but neither did they have to endure the monotony of such long cruises. With hundreds of ships in the Bering Sea, the *Addison* was seldom out of sight of other sails for more than a few days at a time.

CAPTAIN JOHN A. COOK

As whaling declined in the Bering Sea, the great fleets of New England no longer made their long voyage around the Horn to enter the Pacific Ocean. Such voyages were no longer profitable, and the center of whaling enterprise shifted to San Francisco in the 1880s. Whalers outfitted in the Bay City made the 2,200-mile voyage to the Aleutians, hunted along the edge of the Bering Sea ice pack in the spring, and followed the bowhead whales as they retreated into the Arctic Ocean during the summer months. In one season's hunt the whalers did not usually make a large enough catch to fill their holds with oil. The mammals had become increasingly scarce, and the ships commonly wintered over near Point Barrow or Herschel Island. After an inactive winter, the whalemen freed their ships from the ice and took up the hunt again. Once they had taken a full cargo, the whalers passed through the Bering Strait and Bering Sea and returned to San Francisco where their cargoes were shipped by rail to the east.

John A. Cook was one of the prominent whaling men of this second phase of Bering Sea-Arctic Ocean enterprise. Cook was a rugged character who knew his business thoroughly. He first went to sea in 1868 at the age of eleven and remained active for the next half century. In 1916 he became the owner of the famed *Charles W. Morgan*, the last of the square-rigged whalers, and managed it on its last cruises.

Unlike many of his contemporaries, Cook never lost a ship in the North. He experienced his only shipwreck as first officer of the bark *Ohio* when it grounded in dense fog on a reef off Nunivak Island, near the Alaskan coast of the Bering Sea.

Whalers in Arctic shore ice.
University of Alaska Archives

After a futile effort to save the ship, the forty crewmen of the *Ohio* scrambled aboard their five whale boats and managed to land on Nunivak Island without any loss of life.´ Once on land, they constructed tents out of boat sails and surveyed their situation. It was grim. Except for two sacks of hardtack they had no food, and there seemed little likelihood of finding any on the uninhabited island. Lacking fuel, they could not even build a fire for comfort or in order to signal other ships: Nunivak Island was treeless.

After an uncomfortable night, Cook was cheered to find that the fog had lifted. Far in the distance, beyond miles of ice-strewn waters, he could just make out the dim outline of a ship. Cook roused his boat's crew and ordered them to prepare for a dash to the distant vessel. Captain Gifford objected strenuously: "Mr. Cook it is sure disastrous for any boat to attempt to go through that ice while it is moving so rapidly with the current." [53] The captain's caution was understandable: the running ice could easily stove in the frail whaleboat, and even if this peril were avoided, the fog could descend at any time cutting off their vision of both ship and island. But Cook preferred the risk at sea to starving on the island and persisted, even after the captain forbade the attempt. "Well, Captain, I and my boat's crew are going," announced the adamant mate.[54]

"If it has got to the point where I must refuse to obey orders, I tell you now, sir, regardless of what may happen, John Cook and his crew are going to get out to that ship or die in the attempt." [55]

Technically, Cook's refusal to obey was not mutinous, since the captain's command had terminated with the wreck of the *Ohio*. By tradition, officers had charge of their individual whaleboats and could exercise command of their crews. The men of Cook's boat were more than willing to take the chance: "These men had been with me before and knew the ability of a Cape Cod man to handle a boat." [56] Accordingly, Cook launched his boat and set out, together with the like-minded men of the third mate's boat. "We started off amid the good-byes and groans of our companions who thought we were going to certain death." [57]

A blanket of fog soon enveloped the boats, but the men did not lose their bearings. The fast-moving ice floes were a menace. Three times Cook and his men had to haul their boat onto a floe to patch holes caused by the ice. But their luck held. After three hours the fog lifted and they could see the ship five miles distant. After more hard pulling the boats reached the whaler, *Ocean*, and were able to board. The *Ocean* then steamed to within three miles of the ice-choked shore of the island; Cook launched his boat once more, reached the shore, and led the remaining boats back to the *Ocean*. As was the custom among the Bering Sea whalers, the *Ohio* crew was distributed among several other vessels. Cook joined the *Josephine* and was granted a first officer's usual lay, though the cruise brought no profit. "That season was a very poor one in the Arctic. We in the *Josephine* got but one whale." [58]

Some time after the *Ohio* shipwreck Cook had another close call. He was in command of his first ship, the bark *John and Winthrop*, on a cruise of the Kodiak grounds in April 1890 when a fire broke out aboard. Summoned from his bunk at midnight, Captain Cook saw smoke billowing from the forward hold. He and other seamen clambered below and fought the flames amid suffocating smoke. With a well-directed hose and an efficient bucket brigade, the men were able to douse the fire before any serious damage had been done. Fire at sea was a dreaded threat to all seamen; yet Cook found an empty kerosene can and bits of charred paper in the hold—evident signs that the fire had been set deliberately.

A very grim, smoke-begrimed captain called the crew together. As the men gathered, Cook thought about the ten years' hard work he had put in before achieving a command, and about his family back in New England, with whom he had spent but five weeks in the preceding eight years. These reflections aroused in him a passion for revenge. Cook issued an ultimatum: "Men, some of you have set fire to this ship. You that did not do it know who did. If you shield them you are as guilty as they." [59] The captain did not waste words: "At six o'clock in the morning I shall come among you. I shall then know who set the fire or the whole twenty-two will hang from the yardarm, else I shall go over the side a dead man. Now, men, think what your answer will be in the morning, for you know that nothing but death will prevent me from carrying out my purpose." [60]

Cook did not have to carry out his threats. The crew must have been as frightened as the captain by the near disaster and, at the appointed time, they brought forward two men who admitted to the arson. The firebugs confessed that they set the fire in the hope of curtailing the voyage. They must have been either very stupid or driven to extreme desperation by their anguish. Cook had them write a confession, then clapped them in irons, where they remained for seven months until the *John and Winthrop* returned to San Francisco. In San Francisco Cook let the arsonists go without pressing charges. Involvement in a protracted trial did not appeal to him, and he was in a benevolent mood because the voyage had been very successful.

Whether Captain Cook treated his crewmen brutally is impossible to say. Certainly his book, *Pursuing the Whale*, allows no such inferences, but he could not be expected to admit misconduct. The charge of running a "hell-ship" was levied against him by a Nome newspaper, but the accusation could have been unfounded. Deserting whalemen were quick to defame their former officers, and there is no way of checking the truth of such reports. Desertion by sailors is not necessarily evidence of inhumane treatment.[61] Some historians of the whaling industry have argued that desertion was encouraged as a means of forfeiting the absconding seamen's lay; yet there are many recorded instances of the determined efforts of captains to seek out missing men. Probably the availability of suitable replacements was a significant factor. Cook tells of an incident that occurred in Japan when he encountered a deserter on the street who refused to return to the ship. After a lively discussion, Cook knocked the man cold, hired a rickshaw to convey his man to the dock, and carried him aboard ship. To insure that no others deserted, Cook banned shore leave—a common expedient practiced by whaling captains, and a measure that must have been frustrating to sea-weary hands.

John Cook lived to see the end of Bering Sea whaling. His had been a hard life but a profitable one. He had thrived on his adventures and had no regrets and many memories of the thrilling pursuit of the bowhead whale in the North.

9 — CIVIL WAR IN THE BERING SEA

To some Confederate strategists, sea power seemed to be the key to victory over the Yankees, and part of the Southern effort culminated in the most improbable campaign of the Civil War. The climax of this campaign occurred in the narrow waters of the Bering Strait off Cape Dezhenev, Siberia, when the *Shenandoah* destroyed the last victims of her long, victorious voyage. Southern forces suffered loss after loss through 1864–65 in battles waged thousands of miles to the east, but in the Bering Sea there was no check to Confederate supremacy.

The story of the *Shenandoah*'s marauding in the Pacific Ocean, Okhotsk Sea, and Bering Sea deserves remembrance as one of the great epics of maritime warfare. Certainly the raider's war cruise was one of the longest made in any war, longer by thousands of miles than the fatal voyage of the Russian fleet sent against Japan in the Russo-Japanese War (1905). As startling as the length of the cruise of the *Shenandoah* was the spectacular success of its predatory work. In all, thirty-eight ships were ransomed or destroyed, 1,053 prisoners were taken, and the monetary damage done totaled $1,361,983. Few more audacious schemes have been launched in any war; fewer still have achieved such results.

The bold voyage of the *Shenandoah* was a part of the sustained effort of Confederate agent James D. Bullock to counter the Union's maritime supremacy. Bullock was sent to England in 1861 to secure ships in aid of the Southern causes. Obstacles were formidable: The South could offer cotton in payment but not cash; vigilant Yankee diplomats were on hand to warn the British government that its laws forbade the delivery of armed ships to be used against a nation not at war with England. Yet there was no lack of sympathy in England for Confederate efforts and, for a price, warships could be built or purchased, despite the prohibitions of law. Bullock had two excellent ships built in 1861–62, the C.S.S. *Florida*, a 185-foot, heavily armed wooden gunboat, and the famed *Alabama*, which was to devastate Union shipping in the Atlantic. Bullock labored to produce a fleet of twenty-five iron rams to break up the Union blockade of Southern ports, but was thwarted by the opposition of the Union's ambassador to England, Charles Francis Adams. One of Bullock's rams was almost ready to go when Adams put pressure on the British government. Even one of these sleek, speedy, 220-foot vessels could have raised havoc with Union shipping, and Adams issued an ultimatum: If the rams left England in Confederate hands, the United States would declare war. This threat did the trick; Bullock had no choice but to sell the two completed rams to the Royal Navy.

By 1864 the Confederate cause was desperate, but Bullock was still active in England. He heard about the *Sea King*, built by the Glasgow firm of Stevens and Sons, one of the world's most distinguished shipbuilders. Bullock wanted a ship fast enough to outrun any ships of the Union navy, and the *Sea King* was reported to be the fastest afloat. On one run of twenty-five hours, the 790-ton ship under sail and steam power cruised 320 miles. Here was the last hope of the Confederate navy, a raider that could fulfill Bullock's dream of destroying the Union's Bering Sea and Arctic whaling commerce.

Secretly the *Sea King* was purchased for £45,000 and sent to Madeira. There in mid-October 1864 it rendezvoused with a supply ship, the *Laurel*, which had sailed from Liverpool with a cargo of guns, powder, and supplies and a number of Confederate officers and seamen. The *Sea King* was soon armed with eight guns, six of them heavy, sixty-eight pounders, and all the other necessities of a long war cruise. Then followed a short ceremony: Down came the Union Jack and up went the flag of the Confederacy. Captain Waddell took command and the *Sea King* became the C.S.S. *Shenandoah*.

Waddell spoke to the assembled crews of the *Laurel* and *Shenandoah* and revealed for the first time the destination of the sleek three-masted ship. His orders were clearly specified in a letter from Bullock.

> You are about to proceed upon a cruise in the far-distant Pacific, into the seas and among the islands frequented by the great American whaling fleet,

a source of abundant wealth to our enemies and a nursery for their seamen. It is hoped that you may be able to greatly damage and disperse that fleet, even if you do not succeed in utterly destroying it.[1]

Aside from the Confederate officers and seamen who had shipped aboard the *Sea King* as passengers, ostensibly bound for Bombay, Waddell depended upon the enlistment of sufficient seamen from the two ships to complete his crew. The *Shenandoah*, to be adequately manned as a warship, required a 150-man crew to handle her sails, guns, and steam engine. But few of the English seamen cared to volunteer, despite Waddell's assurances that the cruiser offered little danger. The ship was a raider—not one that would engage other men-of-war. Pay would be good and crew members could expect to share in prize money derived from captured merchant ships. Food would be of the best. Waddell spoke of another prospect—that of the adventure and excitement inherent in such an endeavor. No responsive fire was struck in the breasts of the English tars by this last appeal. Why should Waddell's words move them? The Confederate officer was neither eloquent nor charismatic. Truly, a passion burned in him, but not one that was infectious to the English. Probably Waddell's call to adventure had a hollow ring; after all, he was not himself an adventurer, but a cold, stern, duty-bound man dominated by patriotism and hatred of the Yankees. Even Waddell's dramatic gesture of displaying a bucket of sovereigns before the assembled sailors, as he raised the ante, had no effect. Initially he proffered £10 for signing on, with a £4 monthly wage for able seamen. Raising the bonus to £17 and wages to £7 did not help. Seamen were conservative of their necks and did not care to meddle in foreign wars. Nothing could be done; Waddell had to set off on his voyage with less than a third of the men required—only forty-three in all. He would do further recruiting among the crews of captured vessels.

The *Shenandoah* sailed for the South Atlantic Ocean and the Cape of Good Hope, but with no great haste to reach the distant Bering Sea. Chase was given to every vessel likely to be of Union registry. A couple of prizes were taken in November; early in December the first whaler, the *Edward* of New Bedford, was encountered off Tristan da Cunha. The *Edward*'s destination was the same as the *Shenandoah*'s, but she was not to course Arctic waters again. After some of the *Edward*'s stores and its crew were transferred to the *Shenandoah*, the hapless whaler was put to the torch.

In late December, Waddell rounded the Cape and moved into the Indian Ocean. The *Shenandoah* still had months of cruising ahead as 1864 ran out. On New Year's Day, Waddell reflected on his assignment and on war. He thought about his friends who had been killed in the war. Probably it was best for a warrior to hate his country's enemies and to be sustained by the unwavering certainty that his cause is just. "They have fallen in battle in defense of their homes invaded by a barbarous enemy." [2] War had been carried into the South by "unprincipled and brutal civilized men" who were more inhuman and savage than primitive peoples: "The Yankees in their invasions of the South came with all the vices and passions of civilized men added to the natural ferocity of the savage." Yankees were devoid of chivalry and magnanimity. "They fought on a calculation of profit." Such thoughts comforted Waddell, a cavalier of North Carolina bound on an avenging mission to the far Pacific and Bering Sea, and reconciled him to his destructive tasks.

The *Shenandoah* called at Melbourne for refueling, repairs, and mail. For the Australians the appearance of a ship of the Confederate navy was a sensation of great dimensions. Newspapers reported on the raider's deadly activities, while society received the ship's officers ashore. All this was a heady tonic to the men of the *Shenandoah*—an excellent morale boost for those who remained with the ships, and a fine invitation to desert for those who preferred to end their voyage. Waddell reduced shore liberty and increased recruiting efforts on the Melbourne waterfront. Meanwhile, William Blanchard, United States consul to Australia, fumed over the lionizing of the Confederates and urged government authorities to seize the raiding vessel as an illegal pirate.

After seeing to his needs in Melbourne, Waddell hoisted anchor and sailed into the South Pacific. Whalers were not easily discovered in the South Pacific near Australia—because the word of the *Shenandoah*'s presence and intentions had spread—but Waddell did find several American schooners at Ascension Island, one of the Caroline Islands. Among the booty taken were sailing charts which indicated the best whaling waters. The grim, avenging captain was very pleased: "With such charts in my possession, I not only held a key to the navigation of all the Pacific Islands, the Okhotsk and Bering Seas, and the Arctic Ocean, but the most probable localities for finding the great Arctic whaling fleet of New England, without a tiresome search." [3] This information was a windfall for the Confederates. Now they had the means to track down their victims in far northern waters. Meanwhile their April 1 catch at Ascension Island was a fine one indeed. Four whalers were taken:

Pearl of New London, valued at $10,000;
Edward Carey of San Francisco, valued at $15,000;
Hector of New Bedford, valued at $58,000;
Harvest of Honolulu, valued at $34,759.

In all, their crews totaled 130 men.

Now, as the season advanced, it was time for Waddell to turn north, where he could expect to run down the greater part of the whaling fleet. First the *Shenandoah* would hunt the Okhotsk Sea, north of Japan, then move into the Bering Sea. It was May 20 when Waddell first sighted the Kurile Islands, the long chain of mountainous islands stretching north of Japan into the Okhotsk Sea. Soon after, the Rebel pirate broke into the waters of the Okhotsk Sea and ran along the coast of Kamchatka. On May 20 Waddell captured and burned the whaling bark *Abigail* of New Bedford (value $16,705). At the time of this encounter, the *Shenandoah* was skirting an extensive ice field. It was the first time that a ship of the Confederate navy had experienced the novelty of ice navigation, and Waddell was very nervous about it. The *Abigail* made an easy catch. Her master assumed that the *Shenandoah*, which was flying the Russian flag, was a provision ship heading for the port of Okhotsk, and approached the raider directly to exchange information.

Amazingly enough, Captain Nye of the *Abigail* had earlier in the Civil War been a victim of that other famous Confederate raider, the *Alabama*. His ship had been taken in the Atlantic, and now he lost another, thousands of miles distant in the North Pacific. One of Captain Nye's mates took a cut at the skipper's luck: "You are more fortunate in picking up Confederate cruisers than whales. I will never again go with you, for if there is a cruiser out, you will find her." [4] Actually no one aboard the *Abigail* seemed to mind their capture, and several seamen agreed to join the *Shenandoah* crews.

Part of the *Abigail*'s cargo included liquor which was to be used in trading with the Siberian natives. The booze trade is rarely mentioned in the published memoirs of whaling men; they knew too well the devastating effect of alcohol on aboriginals. But the *Abigail*'s liquor posed no threat to Siberian natives once it was discovered by the *Shenandoah* crew, though it swiftly debauched the sailors of the raider. A *Shenandoah* boarding party found the liquor, broached a cask, and embarked on one of the most glorious drunks in Okhotsk Sea history. Waddell and his officers worked hard to snuff out this alcoholic blaze. The drunks were hauled back to their ship and locked in the forecastle. Those difficult to restrain were clapped in irons. While this was going on, other *Shenandoah* men got in on the party and Waddell had his hands full. "In brief," wrote ship's officer Cornelius E. Hunt, "I think it was the most general and stupendous 'spree' I ever witnessed. There was not a dozen sober men on board the ship except the prisoners, and had these not been ironed it might have proved a dearly bought frolic." [5]

Waddell brought his drunken crew under control but remained uneasy about navigation in the Okhotsk Sea. A sudden gale threatened to dash the *Shenandoah* against the ice and left the ship's rigging encrusted with ice. Seamen, wearing bulky woolens against the cold and fortified with extra rations of hot coffee and grog, had to be sent aloft to chip the ice off. It was time enough to leave the dangerous waters of the Okhotsk Sea and sail northeast into the Bering Sea. Waddell calculated that a good part of the whaling fleet would be cruising the Bering Sea by this time—mid-June. He was right. Fifty-eight ships were hunting their quarry between Siberia and Alaska or working their way even farther north into the Arctic Ocean.

Ships were encountered soon after the raider sailed into the Bering Sea. Two New Bedford whalers were seized and fired after their crews had been taken on the *Shenandoah*. These were the *William Thompson*, New Bedford's largest ship—valued, with its cargo of oil and bone, at $40,925—and the *Euphrates*, valued at $42,320.

Five whalers were encountered the following day. These were cruising along the edge of a huge ice floe and were caught easily. Their masters had seen the *Shenandoah* bearing down on them but assumed that the steamer flying American colors belonged to the fleet of the Western Union Telegraph Expedition. Whalemen who had been in San Francisco recently had heard a great deal about the plans to build a telegraph line through northern Canada and Alaska to the Bering Strait, and across the strait to Siberia. Men were being recruited in San Francisco for construction work and ships were being fitted out. All this was news to Waddell; yet he indicated no amazement that such a vast enterprise would be undertaken by a nation at war. Nor was he distracted by the fervent assertions of the captain of the *Milo* that the long struggle between the states was over. The whaler had no proof of this and was not believed.

The Bering Sea war went on. It is curious that all three naval wars of the Bering Sea's history have been marked by fiascoes: the Allied effort against Petropavlovsk in the Crimean War; the *Shenandoah* doing its deadly work weeks after the Confederate surrender; the American invasion of a depopulated island during World War II. Somehow the Bering Sea has not been a battleground on which warriors have been able to win distinction. It has been the graveyard of ships and of the reputations of commanders.

On the following day, Waddell took the brig *Susan Abigail.* Aboard he found San Francisco newspapers with news of the war. President Jefferson Davis had announced that the war would be carried on with renewed vigor, despite the Northern victories that had forced him to abandon the Confederate capital. This news was rather dated, but Waddell still maintained his vigor: He ordered his men to burn the *Susan Abigail.* Three of the captured crew agreed to serve under Waddell, which he took as "good evidence at least that they did not believe the war had ended." [6] Unlike all the other ships taken in the Bering Sea, the *Susan Abigail* was not engaged in whaling. The vessel's voyage from San Francisco to the Bering Sea was for the purpose of trading and must have been one of the pioneer efforts of California merchants to tap the Siberian trade. In exchange for furs and whale bone, the San Francisco trader exchanged clothing, tobacco, and whiskey.

The *Shenandoah* sailed north to the vicinity of St. Lawrence Island, its fires banked to conserve fuel. There was no hurry, no Yankee ship in the Bering Sea could escape the Confederate predators. Off St. Lawrence Island the Southerners met their far northern neighbors for the first time. Eskimos paddled out to the black-hulled raider in their graceful kayaks and engaged in peaceful trade.

The next day other neighbors were encountered. The *Shenandoah* steamed in chase of the *General Williams* of New London, which was captured and burned. The 26th of June was a big day. Six whalers were chased and captured. All were burned, except one which was ransomed. The ransom provided Waddell an opportunity to rid the *Shenandoah* of its captured seamen. All the captives were taken aboard the ransomed vessel for passage to San Francisco.

On to the north stalked the *Shenandoah*. Eleven sails were sighted off East Cape (Cape Dezhenev). "We lowered the smoke stack and continued in the rear of the eleven, keeping a close luff, and retarding our progress as much as possible, so as to arouse no suspicions amongst them." [7] The wind died down, the "game" could not evade the raider, which steamed into the bay with the American flag flying. All of the whalers were taken, including the *Favorite*, whose master was the defiant Captain Young. Young's attempt to stand off the raider provided the only comic relief of the campaign.

"Haul down your flag," shouted the Confederate naval officer. [8]

"Haul it down yourself, G——d d——n you, if you think it will be good for your constitution," replied the enraged master of the whaling bark *Favorite* as he aimed his bomb gun at the cutter.

"If you don't haul it down, we'll blow you out of the water in five minutes."

"Blow away, my buck, but I may be eternally blasted if I haul down that flag for any cussed Confederate pirate that ever floated," cried Captain Young.

The standoff did not long endure. A single man with a harpoon bomb gun could tear the entrails out of a whale but was no match for the guns of the raider C.S.S. *Shenandoah*. Captain Young's officers and men knew it. They discreetly lowered boats and abandoned the *Favorite*, leaving their master to man the bridge alone. The deserters were not craven, but only realistic. Their captain's courageous defiance could only be a gesture. Whaling men and their vessels were not equipped to combat a man-of-war. But the spirit of New England continued to oppose southern arms. Once more the order was given to haul down the *Favorite*'s flag.

"I'll see you dead first," shouted Young, now brandishing a whiskey bottle.

The *Shenandoah* officer sighted his rifle at the proud Yankee: "If you don't do it I'll have to shoot you."

"Shoot and be damned," roared Young.

Shooting was unnecessary. A boarding party from the *Shenandoah* scrambled aboard the *Favorite* without meeting any resistance. Repeated doses of whiskey had taken some of the fire out of Captain Young, who now rested heavily against the mount of the bomb gun. His defiance had never had much substance. Before departing the *Favorite*, her officers had removed the cap from the bomb gun to prevent Young from firing it and thereby exciting the Southerners to respond. The only resistance presented to the predations of the *Shenandoah* in the Bering Sea was ended when Captain Young was rudely carried from the *Favorite* and put in irons aboard the raider. Perhaps Young's whiskey-laced fortitude does not merit much acclaim; yet if one recalls the hundreds of monuments erected to commemorate Civil War heroes across the United States, it seems that there might be room for one honoring the old sailor. Imagine him in bronze—unmoved by either the tossing waters of the Bering Sea or the fiery spirits he has downed—standing by the bomb gun, scowling, cursing, shaking a cutlass in one hand and a whiskey bottle in the other. Does New England have any more impressive commemorative statues in its town squares than this one would be?

Waddell was not impressed by Young's grand and warlike display but he was amazed that the *Favorite* was not carrying a ship's register and was thus liable to seizure by any naval ship. This tells us something important about the conduct of Bering Sea fishery in the period. That an experienced shipper like Young, with a heavy stake in ship and cargo, would neglect the basic requirement of carrying his ship's registry aboard indicates that whalers did not expect to be challenged on their northern cruises by ships of any nation.

The men of the *Shenandoah* were impressed by Young's bravery and were not put off because the whaleman proved to be roaring drunk. "It was evident he had been seeking spirituous consolation, indeed to be plain about it, he was at least three sheets to the wind," commented officer Hunt, "but by general consent he was voted to be the bravest and most resolute man we captured during our cruise." [9]

The Confederate sailors had reason to be in good spirits. Their hunting that day had netted ten ships containing valuable cargoes of whale oil and bone that were thus denied to the enemy. The ships captured on June 28 are listed on the following page.

All these vessels hailed from New Bedford, except the *Nile* of New London and the *Favorite* of Fairhaven, and most shipped a crew of thirty-five men. The day's work also provided an opportunity to extend some Southern gallantry. On the *James Murray* the master had recently died and his widow and three young children were aboard. The bereaved

Ship	Value
James Murray	$40,550
Nile	25,550
Hillman	33,000
Nassau	40,000
Isaac Howland	75,112
Martha	30,307
Congress	55,300
Waverly	62,376
Brunswick	16,272
Favorite	57,896

woman, who had preserved her husband's body in a barrel of whiskey for burial ashore, was much frightened by the *Shenandoah* men but had the presence of mind to beg that her husband's ship not be destroyed. Waddell agreed to ransom the *James Murray* and directed it and the *Nile* to make for a United States port, carrying the crews from all the ships taken. The remaining eight ships were set afire, creating a dazzling spectacle as the oil-laden vessels were engulfed in flame. "It was a scene never to be forgotten by anyone who beheld it," wrote Hunt. "The red glare from the eight burning vessels shone far and wide over the drifting ice of those savage seas; the cracking of the fire as it made its devouring way through each doomed ship, fell on the still air like unbraiding voices." [10]

Aboard the *James Murray* and the *Nile* the whalemen watched with varying expressions. Some were angry and disappointed, some wondering and fearful as the blazing hulks, each in turn, went to the bottom of the sea, disappearing in a cloud of hissing steam and smoke as the waters engulfed them. This was the last act, Hunt noted, of the bloody drama of the American Civil War: "The overture was played by the thunder of artillery beneath the walls of Sumter . . . the curtain finally fell amid the drifting ice of the Arctic Seas." [11]

After disposing of his last catch, Waddell cruised through the Bering Strait to attain its farthest point north—sixty-six degrees, forty minutes. Ice floes were scattered over the sea all about the *Shenandoah*, and Waddell did not care to risk this kind of navigation. Nor did he want to chance being caught in the ice pack. The Yankee maritime was no threat to Waddell, but the icy sea was impartially hostile. The *Shenandoah* headed south and slipped by the Diomede Islands just as a vast field of floe ice was closing the strait. Off St. Lawrence Island the ship had a close brush with disaster. A dense fog obscured vision and, at the same time, the *Shenandoah* crunched into a field of ice. With great skill and caution Captain Waddell managed to extricate his ship and continue south. He had had enough of ice navigation.

The *Shenandoah* cruised out of the Bering Sea into the North Pacific by Amchitka Pass. Because of the almost constant fog navigation necessary in the pass, it was hazardous, and the sailors were relieved to encounter the clear skies of the North Pacific once the tricky passage was made. No mariner who ever made the Aleutian passage was unaware of the uniqueness and dangers of the Bering Sea.

Waddell planned to steam into San Francisco harbor and lay "that city under contribution." [12] But first prudence dictated that he see some recent newspapers from that city. Waddell halted and boarded a British ship and at last learned the ancient, irrefutable news of the war. "Having received . . . the sad intelligence of the overthrow of the Confederate Government, all attempts to destroy the shipping or property of the United States will cease from this date." [13] This log entry of August 2, .1865, marked the belated end of the Civil War for the last military unit that was still engaged.

Waddell steamed south, rounded Cape Horn, and eventually ended his long cruise at Liverpool, the city where his fabulous voyage had begun.

The war was over but not the rancor. United States officials were determined that someone would have to compensate shippers for the havoc wreaked by the *Shenandoah* and the *Alabama*. (The twenty-two-month cruise of the *Alabama* in the early years of the war had cost the Yankees sixty-six ships valued at $5,344,261.) [14] The dissolved Confederate government could not be made to pay, but the British—who knowingly allowed the raiders to be fitted out—could be forced to acknowledge responsibility. After months of diplomatic wrangling, the British gave in and agreed to pay $15,500,000 to the Americans. This compensation helped the Yankee shipping men, but the Bering Sea and Arctic Ocean whaling fleet never again recovered its former place. The Civil War had proved tremendously disruptive because of the *Shenan-*

doah's predations and the sinking of the "great stone fleet," another war measure that involved the sinking of stone-laden whalers off Confederate ports in an effort to blockade the ports.

Perhaps the only winners in the Civil War were the whales of the North. They would still be hunted for decades after 1865, but the size of the hunting fleet diminished continuously.

10 — TYING THE CONTINENTS BY TELEGRAPH

In 1856 an energetic American, Perry Collins, made a momentous journey across Siberia to the Pacific Ocean. He was a visionary, as the journal of his travels revealed: "I had already fixed in my own mind upon the River Amoor as the destined channel by which American commercial enterprise was to penetrate the obscure depths of Northern Asia, and open new world to trade and civilization." [1] After conferences with President Franklin Pierce, Secretary of State William L. Marcy, and the Russian ambassador, Collins secured an official appointment as commercial agent of the United States for the Amur River.

This designation, and letters of introduction to influential people in Russia, provided Collins with the opportunity to gather valuable information about commercial possibilities along the entire Amur River, the heartline of Pacific Asia.

In the meantime, telegraphic communication was developing into an ever-expanding network. Europe and the eastern United States were being crisscrossed with wires that speeded commercial and political information and decisions. Larger and larger networks were called for. The telegraph was fast becoming a vital part of nineteenth-century life. Cities such as Washington and Baltimore were connected as early as 1844. Rivers and channels were bridged. Dover and Calais were linked in 1851. England, Ireland, and Europe were joined three years later.

The next step was obvious: The continents of Europe and America had to be connected by submarine cable spanning the Atlantic Ocean. The paramount question at the time was whether technology was mature enough to fulfill the idea. A telegraphic hookup across the Atlantic would provide the New and Old Worlds with a vast improvement in communications.

In 1857 the first attempt to lay a submarine telegraph cable across the Atlantic failed. The following year, the Atlantic Telegraph Company tried again and failed a second time. Technology did not seem to be ready for such a scheme.

But Perry Collins was ready with another idea. He had traveled up and down the Amur River in Russia. He had made friends with many important foreign officials and had nurtured political contacts in Washington. He was convinced that an Atlantic cable could not be laid and offered an alternative plan: It would be easy to tie the continents over the fifty-odd miles of the Bering Strait.

Collins laid the groundwork of his enterprise. By 1860 he was ready to submit a report to Congress in which he offered a new plan for a telegraph connection. Collins stressed the fact that two attempts at the Atlantic cable had failed and that only fifty-six miles of waterway separated America and Europe through Asia on the Pacific side. He knew the Russian terrain by personal experience and knew the right people on both sides of the Pacific to develop a telegraph line to the West. What could prevent the construction of a Pacific line? A transcontinental line across the United States was scheduled to be completed to California in 1861 and would stretch northward to Oregon. It would just be a matter of extending it to the north. Samuel Morse, the inventor of the telegraph, could see no insurmountable difficulties. Hiram Sibley, founder and president of the Western Union Telegraph Company, thought the whole thing entirely practicable. Senator Milton Latham, a political backer of Collins, argued that the enterprise would strengthen America's power as a great commercial nation.

The United States was engaged in the Civil War at this time, but the "manifest destiny" of the United States to stretch from ocean to ocean was a vibrant motivating force even during the turbulent 1860s. The proposed telegraph line seemed logical and inevitable. Twice Congress recommended appropriations as results of Collins' reports, although no money was budgeted. The third request of Collins was recommended and approved: he received the grant of a right-of-way across public lands and the assurance of the U. S. Navy's assistance in constructing the project.

Collins sold the Western Union Telegraph Company the right-of-ways he had secured from the Russian government. The vast engineering and construction project got under way in 1865. The plan was to direct a line north from Vancouver, British Columbia, to the headwaters of the Yukon River, and from there along the Yukon to Nulato, north to the Seward Peninsula, across the Bering Strait, and south across Siberia to meet the Russian line from Europe at the mouth of the Amur River. The 5,000 miles of line was expected to cost one and a half million dollars or about $300 each mile. The Western Union Telegraph Extension Company (WUTE) was organized and stock distributed. The reunification of North America and Asia was underway.

Meanwhile, Cyrus Field, the promoter of the Atlantic submarine cable, had not given up his own dream. He had as much faith in the transatlantic telegraph line as Collins had in the trans-Pacific line. Field leased the ship the *Great Eastern* in 1865 for a second attempt at laying the Atlantic cable. In 1866 he tried again.

Western Union officials had more to fear from the work of the *Great Eastern* than from all the thousands of miles of wilderness to be surveyed, the immense distances of the north country, and the obstacles of rugged terrain and subarctic climate. It was to be a race against time. Nevertheless, the *Great Eastern*'s record of performance instilled a little confidence in Western Union men. The ship was five times larger than any other ship afloat at its launching in 1858, but the monster turned out to be a jinx. The ship disgraced herself by refusing to slide down the launching ways, and weeks later, when finally freed, the wayward leviathan crashed into another vessel. So it was on every cruise thereafter. Freak accidents maimed and killed crew members; lesser ships unfortunate enough to get in her way were mauled. Economically, the great iron ship ruined her several successive owners and finished her career ingloriously as an exhibition ship. She was the proverbial bull in a china shop. Yet, for all her bungling mishaps and catastrophes, she was to have her day of glory.

The Pacific enterprise was referred to as the Western Union Telegraph Extension, and sometimes the Collins Overland Telegraph. Charles S. Bulkley was the chief engineer of the project and began actual field work in 1865—a year before the *Great Eastern* began its second attempt at laying the Atlantic cable. Bulkley headed an army of over 1,000 men that included many of the most competent engineering and scientific talents the nation had to offer. The immediate goals were to survey a route for 5,000 miles of telegraph line and then build it through British Columbia, Russian America, and Siberia. An incidental goal was the gathering of scientific data. The little-known territory of Russian America was to be of particular importance to the scientists. For the purpose of gathering knowledge of Russian America, the Scientific Corps was formed and staffed by men suggested by the Smithsonian Institution in Washington, D.C. Among the corps' members were two young Americans who were later to publish accounts of their experiences, Richard Bush and George Kennan. Both men were keenly aware of the significance of the venture, though somewhat apprehensive as they—like virtually all the WUTE members—had had no previous experience in the North. As a youngster, Bush had been thrilled and chilled by the adventures of polar explorers like John Franklin, Elisha Kane, and Charles Hall. Were they, wondered Bush, going to encounter comparable perils and hardships in the little-known wastes of the Arctic? But, with a natural ebullience and optimism, Bush could banish such forebodings. "What man has endured . . . man could endure again; and as we were all young, stout, healthy, and ambitious, and the enterprise one we thought worth to chance one's life upon, we entered upon it resolved not to be alarmed at imaginary evils, but to push forward, accept whatever fate was in store for us, test the powers of these Polar denizens in actual encounters, and win, if possible; if not, succumb with the best possible grace." [2]

The *Olga* carried the Siberian division from San Francisco to Petropavlovsk in forty-seven days in the summer of 1865. The ship had been enveloped in fog throughout most of the voyage, and fog still persisted as the ship stood off Petropavlovsk, the Russian settlement on Kamchatka that was the expedition's destination. All that Bush had heard about Kamchatka suggested bleakness and desolation; yet, as the fog suddenly lifted, a much brighter picture presented itself—high cliffs sparkling in the sun, crowned with beautiful green slopes from which small rivulets dropped into the foaming surf. Flocks of sea birds circled above the cliffs. At the base of the cliffs, hundreds of seals could be seen basking in the warm sun and plunging through the surf. Quite near the *Olga*, gulls and ducks flapped about, breaking the stillness with their screams. All this lively activity and the grandeur of the view dispelled Bush's preconceptions of Kamchatka and the Bering Sea. "This unexpected display, enlivened by the flapping of ducks, the screaming of startled sea-birds, the hoarse, unmelodious bellowings of seal, and the deep thunderings of the surf resounding from the black caverns under the cliffs, aroused in us all feelings of most exquisite delight." [3] All aboard the *Olga* were eager to get ashore, shake off the effects of the voyage, and commence their great task. History was to be made along the Bering Sea shores, and they would have a share in it!

The town of Petropavlovsk was not as spectacular as its mountain-ringed setting. Low, log houses were scattered about, most thatched with bark or straw, and in their midst stood the small, octagonal, red-roofed church, topped by a green turret. Only 300 residents, including natives, inhabited the community, which had declined as a consequence of the Crimean War campaign a decade earlier. Although Petropavlovsk's port was still utilized by the Russian American Company, the fortunes of that once expansive Alaskan enterprise had dwindled to insignificance. Ships carrying cargo to and from the company headquarters at Sitka appeared only rarely and, in a very short time, this traffic was to pass into other hands.

The town had been founded in 1740, as a part of Vitus Bering's exertions in American discovery and Siberian development, and was named after Bering's two exploration ships, the *St. Peter* and *St. Paul*. George Kennan, not yet the Siberian expert he was to become in time, was not aware of the origin of the settlement's name. Somewhat mockingly he speculated that the two saints had not visited the Bering Sea; so the inhabitants must have hoped that, without inquiring too closely into their merits, Saint Peter and Saint Paul would nevertheless offer the town protection.

The northern base of the WUTE was made at Anadyrsk, a settlement of four villages on the Anadyr River about 250 miles inland from the Bering Sea. Anadyrsk had been a Russian military post in the eighteenth century after the Cossacks had defeated the Chukchi; but when the Russians withdrew most of their force to Kamchatka, the Chukchi were allowed to pursue their traditional ways. In 1866 when George Kennan and his associates set up winter quarters, the Chukchi— unlike the Kamchadals—were still a vigorous people, independent in spite of the presence of a handful of Russians—a priest, traders, and a few Cossack soldiers.

Three separate divisions were formed to carry out the work in the three major land areas of British Columbia, Russian America, and Siberia. Frank L. Pope led the British Columbia party and began line construction in the first season of actual operation. At first, Pope did not face the problems related to a remote, unknown country as did the other two divisions. Scouting and engineering parties led the way north. Over 500 ax-men who prepared poles followed immediately. Close behind them came the wire-laying crew. The telegraphers who put the system into operation came last.

The rugged and little-known region of northern British Columbia furnished increasing difficulties. Pope and Edmund Conway, chief of the British Columbia construction parties, had to explore a region that had not yet been mapped to locate the best route to the headwaters of the Yukon River. Other unexpected problems emerged. The U. S. Navy provided little cooperation for Pope's division, and the difficulty of hiring labor because of gold strikes in the North caused delays and hardships. But it is now generally agreed that Pope performed brilliantly. By spring, 1867, the line was operating as far as Fort Stager in Central British Columbia. The gain was a permanent one, since eventually the line between New Westminister and Quesnel was purchased by the provincial government and incorporated into the national Canadian telegraph system.

Equally spectacular was the accomplishment of the Siberian division. Serge Abasa, a robust, personable Russian, headed the Siberian survey party and galvanized his men with his own titanic energy. After the first season's work he was able to report jubilantly to Bulkley that a survey had been completed all the way from the mouth of the Anadyr to the mouth of the Amur River.

During the next season 1,500 poles were cut, a fifty-mile road was constructed near Okhotsk, and forty telegraph stations were built. All this was accomplished despite recurring food and supply shortages and the disheartening failure of the maritime division of Western Union Telegraph Extension Company to get the construction materials to the work parties in time for a full season of work.

But the Russian American division did not perform nearly as well as the others. The reasons are not entirely clear. Even the scientific achievements owe more to the work of William Healy Dall and others after 1867 than to the sponsorship of Western Union. Very little construction was carried out in the North. The illness and subsequent death of the party's leader, Robert Kennecott, on the Yukon River probably had much to do with the slight progress. Also, problems of food shortages and lack of dogs for transportation contributed to the very real hardship of exploring and working in the harsh winter climate of Alaska. From all evidence, the expedition members seemed to be too dependent upon the "excessively unreliable" Russians and the "lazy" Indians.[4] This, coupled with their lack of resourcefulness and inclination to bicker among themselves, was not a recipe for success.

William Healy Dall, a member of the Scientific Corps, had admired Kennecott and became embittered by his death and by the mismanagement of the expedition. When he heard of Kennecott's death he wrote the news to Spencer Fullerton Baird, head of the Smithsonian Institution. Dall blamed William H. Ennis for the tragedy. He told of the obsequious hounding that Ennis, second-in-command of the Russian American division, gave Major Kennecott. Ennis he described as "a man of frank address and excellent company, witty and well posted, notwithstanding which he is double faced, selfish and overreaching not only to but beyond the verge of honesty." [5]

Evidently, Ennis was a sycophant when face to face with Kennecott, but not so when out of sight. Dall wrote the following of Ennis:

> I have heard a statement from several parties to the effect that Ennis either wrote in the official journal, or in a letter to Kennecott words to the following effect. "If there had not been so much humbugging and foolishness on the part of our commander, we should have been at Fort Yukon long ago, and I shall report so to Col. Bulkley." I believe it to be true, that these words or words to the same effect were spoken or written by Ennis and in some way reached Major Kennecott.[6]

Dall had only hearsay evidence because he was not present at the time, but he was sure that Kennecott heard what Ennis had said and became unusually gloomy. The next day Kennecott was found dead on the ground about 300 yards from general quarters. "If any human being is responsible for his death and I believe one man is, partly responsible," asserted Dall, "God will be his Judge, and will punish him in his own good time; but if that man seeks to interfere or oppose the workings of the Scientific Corps in future, I will take a double revenge." [7]

Later he complained bitterly of the inadequate stock of provisions for the support of about fifty men. Eight thousand pounds of flour had barely lasted a year for fifteen men. For fifty men the company had 6,000 pounds of flour and other provisions. The preposterous folly of issuing food by ordinary rations to men in the Arctic was never more fully demonstrated.[8]

At least 600 pounds of flour, 8 pounds of sugar per month, and 3 pounds of tea, with bacon in proportion, was what men in the country considered to be the proper allowance for each man.

The general workers in the division were viewed by Dall as a lot of riffraff from San Francisco. Dall was eventually made the surgeon for the entire country but was not given proper medical supplies. He treated as best he could several men suffering from secondary symptoms of syphilitic disease. He protested to his superiors that these men be taken from the country or else they could very easily "introduce that scourge among the Indians." [9]

Dall's letter to Baird was a report on the progress of the work from September 20, 1865, to May 1, 1867. Clearly the bickering, inefficiency, and incompetence of the company officials and members of the Alaskan division slowed progress, and the *Great Eastern* was making a better pace in the Atlantic.

Nevertheless, some accomplishments were registered in Russian America. Several members of the party ascended and surveyed the Yukon River. William Ennis explored the region between Nulato and Bering Strait and was able to begin construction of the telegraph line during the second season. Fifty miles were actually laid north and west of St. Michael by one party, while another under Daniel B. Libby worked south from Port Clarence to string another thirty miles. A few poles were raised on January 21, 1867, at Unalakleet and celebrated with flag raisings and the downing of the last bottle of whiskey. But this was the extent of the Western Union telegraph in Russian America.

Frank Smith, a member of the work party, recorded his impressions in a diary during the 1866–67 winter. On February 6 he found the ground so hard that four steel-pointed crowbars were turned up and split as if they had been made of tin foil. The digging of postholes into permafrost was strenuous labor. On May 28 he reported bleakly: "Almost everything has been unfavorable for us this month. Weather bad, worse crowbars, dog feed scarce and poor of its kind, men living on two meals a day, one of which only can we afford to have salt meat. The ground as hard as a Pharaoh's heart." [10]

Smith greeted the news of the termination of the trans-Pacific telegraph project with pleasure, although most of the men of the three divisions were dismayed by its collapse. The news arrived on June 24, 1867, while Smith and others were working on the line between Unalakleet and Nulato. Smith wrote: "Company has suspended operations. Reason: the Atlantic cable is a success. We are all ordered home (much joy). United States bought Russian-America for $7,000,000.00 from Russian government. Torrents of news left us almost speechless." [11]

The ill-starred *Great Eastern* had won the day. In July 1866 she had carried the Atlantic cable from Ireland to Heart's Content, Newfoundland. Europe and America were connected. The transatlantic telegraph was a success.

The Western Union Telegraph Company waited exactly eight months to the day to see whether the cable would maintain operation. It did. On March 27, 1867, William Orton, vice-president of Western Union, wrote to Secretary of State Seward to announce that construction, after an expenditure of $3,000,000, had been discontinued.

The official news took another three months to reach the outposts in Russian America and Siberia.

Thus the great Collins Overland Telegraph undertaking came to an abrupt end. The race against time had been lost, and the attempt to reunify North America and Asia at the Bering Strait had failed.

Much of the equipment and materials on both sides of the Bering Sea and North Pacific were merely abandoned to the elements. Shiploads of insulators and brackets and other telegraphic equipment were never used in Siberia. Miles of wire left to rot were commandeered by the natives of Russian America and put to their own convenient use. Indians at Hagwilget, British Columbia, constructed a picturesque bridge suspended by telegraph wire across the Bulkley River. But for fate, that same wire might have tied the continents.

Although the WUTE had lost its race with the *Great Eastern* and the Alaska division, in particular, had suffered due to petty squabbling and the death of Kennecott, the two eventful years' efforts were to have some bearing on future events in the Bering Sea. In the course of his explorations of the Seward Peninsula, Daniel Libby discovered some very good signs of gold. At the time he was not interested in looking any further. He was sick of the North and anxious to return home after the venture folded up. But Libby was to return twenty years later with the glint of a gold seeker in his eye—after the 1897–98 Klondike stampede alerted the world to the mineral riches of the North. On his second journey to the North, Libby and a handful of other prospectors found rich ground and organized the recording district in which Alaska's greatest gold strikes were made, and which made Nome the leading metropolis of the Bering Sea.

George R. Adams and others of the expedition became smitten by the North and did not want to return to the States. Adams took a job with the Alaska Commercial Company, when the firm fell heir to the Russian American Company's interests on the Pribilof Islands, and became a storekeeper. When the Alaska Commercial Company moved into the Yukon valley, Adams worked in various river posts. In 1898, during the gold rush, Adams was still in the North. By this time he was an independent merchant and had established a mercantile business in the bustling town of Dyea. The *Dyea Trail* of January 19, 1898, reported on this venture by the "handsome and well preserved pioneer of pioneers." [12] Adams' hair and moustache were white but he remained "strong, active and full of hope" and the *Trail* went on to relate his adventures of "33 years ago" with the WUTE. [13]

William Healy Dall remained in the North because he recognized the scientific opportunities it offered to an ambitious, hard-working man. The most significant scientific investigations made in the Bering Sea since the days of Georg Steller were those carried out by Dall the year after the telegraph project failed, and in subsequent seasonal journeys.

The WUTE also left a literary heritage. A little newspaper was produced by hand at two expedition stations on the Bering Strait. The *Esquimaux*, which was later published in book form in San Francisco as a memorial of the WUTE, served as a cultural bridge to unite the members of the Siberian and Alaskan divisions, and was the first newspaper ever produced in northeastern Siberia and in Alaska.

The *Esquimaux*'s literary merits are slight, but it is an invaluable document for understanding something of the attitudes and aspirations of the members of the expedition. Volume 1, number 1 was produced at Libbysville, Port Clarence, Alaska. Libbysville station was named for its chief, Daniel Libby, and was to be the jumping-off point for the trans-Bering Strait line. Editor J. J. Harrington assured readers that the tone of the paper would be light and that he would keep "clear of the filthy pool of politics," provide some poems, humor, and information concerning the progress of the expedition.[14]

In the second issue, the editor noted proudly that the paper was up to six pages and called for contributions from other writers: "We can have here a literary world, which will astonish the older countries, and become a source of amusement to ourselves, of whose variety we will never tire." [15] Among the "latest intelligence" gathered from "Outside Barbarians" Harrington announced the marriage of the famed Emperor Norton, a colorful San Francisco character of the day, the surrender of General Lee's army, and the defeat of General Cornwallis' redcoats by the American rebels. On the more earnest side, an order from Libby was published: Looting of native graves for artifacts must be stopped.

Later in the year, Harrington made further reference to the natives. How should they be treated? "It behooves us to study some plan of action in our dealings with them." [16] We should take their different customs into account and understand that they believe whites have unlimited wealth. "What intercourse they have had with whalers and others, has not served to give them a very exalted idea of the white man's character." [17] Traders had always imposed upon the natives and in return they will try to profit from our stay. Let's agree among ourselves on the prices to be paid for articles purchased from the natives. "When they visit our houses, we should not roughly eject them, but in a kindly manner, explain to them the largeness of our numbers, and the cooped-up state of our dwellings, giving them to understand that we have built a house for their especial accommodation." [18] Strangers who come from a far distance for trading should be fed, but not "those daily pests, whose only object here, is the getting of American cow-cow." [19]

Until the navigation of the Bering Sea opened in late spring, food was a major topic of the newspaper. Poor planning had left the men short on food. Stocks of bread and flour had been used up, and everyone was wishing for the arrival of the supply ships. Eventually these did arrive and carried Harrington and other Alaskan division men across the Bering Strait to Plover Bay, Siberia. In July the *Esquimaux* became a Siberian newspaper without losing or gaining any quality.

A July issue reported on a visit Captain Libby had made to King Island and the pernicious effect of the liquor trade. Someone, presumably a whaleman, had given booze to the Eskimos, who, while drunk, attacked Libby's boat. Luckily, other Eskimos were sober and restrained their intoxicated countrymen. "The Esquimaux are like all other savages when they have whiskey in them," commented Harrington; "they are ready for all kinds of mischief." [20] The same issue announced the sad news of the abandonment of the telegraph work.

In August the last issue of the *Esquimaux* was published. Most of the men were anxious to return home now that their work was over. Harrington was eager to leave and marveled that anyone would want to stay in the North. One of the Siberian division members, named Brady, had in 1865 taken a liking to the country and to a native woman and had resigned from the WUTE to live with the natives. "He preferred rather to live on dried fish than return to his home," recounted Harrington.[21] "A strange freak for a young man brought up in a white man's country, and one that, we think, he will live to regret." [22] This terse notice is the only record of this company dropout, but it shows the fascination for the North and its peoples that captured some men. The WUTE left the North; but Brady, Adams, Dall, and others were to stay on and participate in the region's development. Most travelers to the Bering Sea were transients—mariners, fortune seekers, government officials, and the like; but a smaller number put down their roots at various places to become true pioneers. Not everyone needed a telegraph or the other amenities of the more cultivated world.

11 — THE UNITED STATES TAKES POSSESSION

$\mathbf{M}$ountains, harbors, islands, capes, coves, and a town in Alaska are named after Baron Ferdinand Petrovich von Wrangel, and if he had had his way in the 1830s, his namesites would today be in Russian America instead of the United States. Wrangel saw a brilliant future for his homeland in Russian America. He saw continuing Russian domination of the North Pacific, an extension of Russian territory into North America, and strong Russian economic and political power around the world.

Wrangel shared in the vision held earlier by Baranov and Rezanov, but realized that Russian expansion and the future of the Russian American Company depended upon the development of healthier financial prospects for the fur-trading enterprise. As governor of the Russian American Company from 1830 to 1835, he analyzed the reasons for the declining profits quite accurately. As always, the chief drain on the operation was in the high cost of provisioning the colony and transporting trade items. This familiar problem was complicated by the necessity of finding new sea otter hunting grounds as the resources of once rich areas became exhausted. The solution seemed clear to Wrangel: The agricultural colony at Fort Ross must be revitalized, and this could only be accomplished if more California territory could be acquired from Mexico.[1]

By the time Wrangel was appointed governor of the Russian American Company in 1829, official support for a strong Russian presence in the Pacific had waned. Sentiment was already moving toward the abandonment of the American colonies. The coastal waters no longer teemed with the valuable sea otter, and the company was not contributing to the St. Petersburg treasury as it once did.

Wrangel, though, was an excellent choice for the remote governorship. He was thirty-four years old at the time and had already distinguished himself as an Arctic explorer and naval circumnavigator. Baron von Wrangel found a wife willing to spend the next five years on the rainy, distant coast of Alaska. She was nineteen-year-old Baroness Elizabeth Rossillon who was married to Wrangel one month after they met. After a long journey across Siberia, Wrangel and his bride arrived in Alaska in the spring of 1830. His wife was the first woman of social standing and education to reside in Alaska.

The five years Wrangel was governor were filled with accomplishment, even though the decline of trade and the petty corruption of storekeepers was discouraging. As head of the new Russian territories, Wrangel encouraged exploration. In 1833 he sent one of his subordinates, Tebenkov, north to map the coast, investigate the Yukon River delta, and build a post in the area. Tebenkov could not find a suitable place at the mouth of the great Yukon River; so he built a fort just to the north, on an island in Norton Sound, and named it the Mikhailovski Redoubt (St. Michael). He also built other posts farther up both the Yukon and Kuskokwim Rivers. In addition, Wrangel found time to make a significant contribution to ethnological studies on Alaskan natives.[2]

During Wrangel's governorship there was a confrontation between the Hudson's Bay Company and the Russian American Company. This was precipitated when the British company's great trader and explorer, Peter Skene Ogden, traveled up the Stikine River in 1833 with the intention of establishing a trading station in the interior. Wrangel responded by sending a party to establish a Russian fort at the mouth of the Stikine River to prevent British navigation of the river.

Fear of both Russians and natives motivated Ogden's withdrawal and return to Fort Vancouver, although the Hudson's Bay Company did not give up the attempt to expand its fur-trading empire. Eventually, by more subtle diplomatic means, George Simpson of the Hudson's Bay Company negotiated with Wrangel—at this time a Russian American Company director—for a lease of part of Russian America.[3] Czar Nicolas I directed the company to accept Simpson's offer to lease the coastal strip of southeastern Alaska from Cape Spencer south to fifty degrees, forty minutes for ten years. Later, the wily British traders used the back door and founded Fort Yukon on the upper reaches of the Yukon River, well within Russian boundaries.

While Wrangel was still at Sitka he was able to secure tentative approval of his California expansion scheme from officials in St. Petersburg. He was authorized to travel to Mexico City after completing his term of governorship in 1835, and there try to negotiate with President Santa Anna for more land in California.[4]

Mexico had won her independence from Spain in 1821 but still suffered from internal conflict and from the threat of foreign invasion. The year of Wrangel's visit, 1836, was quite significant for the histories of both Mexico and the United States. This was the year that Texas proclaimed independence from Mexico and defeated Santa Anna in his effort to put down the rebellion. Perhaps it was not too auspicious a time for a foreigner such as Wrangel to ask for the acquisition of other parts of the northern provinces of Mexico. The Texas rebellion, though, probably had little influence on the response of the Mexican government to Wrangel's request.

The obdurate refusal of Czar Nicolas to offer the essential *quid pro quo* desired by Mexico was what destroyed Wrangel's hopes and set the stage for the eventual sale of Russian America. Santa Anna demanded that his new republic be recognized by Russia as a legitimate state. Wrangel was all for it. He argued that Mexico would appreciate the good will and would realize that the settlement of a few Russians in the northern Mexican territories presented no threat to the Mexican people. In fact, such a settlement might block the more dangerous encroachments of England and the United States.

Czar Nicolas I had other conflicting concerns. Not only did he fear that acquisition of more American territory might antagonize England, whose government was already alarmed by Russian expansion, but Nicolas favored unconditional support of legitimism. The rebellions of Spanish-American subjects could not be viewed by the czar with any satisfaction: The authority of the monarchs must be maintained. Nicolas' hope was that in the future Spain would be able to reassert control over its colonies.

The failure of the Russian American Company to enlarge its California holdings in 1835–36 foreshadowed the sale of the territory three decades later. North America was thrown away, and so were the opportunities for Russia to dominate the North Pacific. Wrangel fought hard against the proponents of the 1867 sale, just as he had labored to mend the company's financial woes in the 1830s. On both occasions his efforts were in vain. Others did not share his vision of Russian hegemony in the North Pacific.

Secretary of State William H. Seward was a redhead who wore his unleashed optimism as prominently as his aquiline nose.[5] Seward was an exuberant politician. He reveled in the political life, and his capacity for both hard work and social life knew few bounds. He, more than anyone else, typified the expansionist tendencies of the United States during the nineteenth century. He was one of the influential American leaders of the nineteenth century who was eager to gather new territories such as Hawaii, the Philippines, and California. A rather complex man, he is not easy to place in one of the standard slots of American political heroes. His ambition for public office reached for the presidency itself, but his ambition was never satisfied. He was a generous man, full of good humor and a great thirst for knowledge.

Russian America was only one area that Seward envisioned as a part of the United States. He also had aspirations to Canada, Greenland, and Iceland. Yet Seward was not the first to suggest the northward expansion of the United States into Canada and Russian America. The very real possibility that Russia would attempt to expand into Canada and the northwestern Pacific coast was one of the reasons behind the Monroe Doctrine of 1823, which was a warning from the United States that European intrusions into the Americas would not be tolerated. Twenty-three years later, Secretary of State William Marcy, under President Franklin Pierce, initiated an offer to purchase Russian America, but the time was still not ripe.

Meanwhile, conditions in mid-nineteenth-century Russia changed. Russian interest began to turn back to central Asia and the Amur Valley for a more logical land-connected expansion of territory. The czarist crackdown on the eastward movements of the lower class as a result of the laws of the 1760s that changed peasants into serfs had its effect in diminishing the population of Siberia and Russian America. The cost of maintaining the Russian American Company continued to rise, and the loss of the Crimean War in the early 1850s generally weakened the czarist regime.

The question was raised of whether or not Russia could defend its American colonies if her Pacific territories were attacked. In a memorandum to Finance Minister Knyazhevich, Grand Duke Constantin, chief of the Russian naval staff, reported that in a war with a naval power, Russia would not be able to protect her colonies.

At the same time Russia looked carefully at the unrelenting expansion of the American people. They heard rumors that Mormons were threatening to move from Utah to Russian America. California was already a part of the United States. Sooner or later the American people were going to push northward. If Russian America were in Russian hands, trouble would no doubt occur.

Word reached Seward that Russia was willing to sell Russian America. Seward saw the Russian territory as extremely valuable in terms of geography and political strategy. He was very willing to buy.

In late 1866 Baron Edward de Stoeckl, minister of Russia in Washington, was authorized by the emperor to sell the Russian colony to the United States for not less than $5,000,000. Three months later in March 1867, Seward and Stoeckl bargained until a purchase price of $7,000,000 was reached. A treaty was drafted and was made ready for presentation to the cabinet and Congress.

In the early morning hours of March 30, 1867, the treaty to transfer Russian America to United States possession was drafted for submission to the U.S. Senate.

Some American newspapers impugned Seward's motives in the transaction and argued that the administration was merely attempting to divert attention from its domestic woes. It was claimed that the purchase was an affront to Great Britain. To some, Alaska was a vast wasteland that held no potential value. But the majority of Americans shared Seward's expansionist sentiments. They may have had only a vague idea of the geography of Alaska, the North Pacific, and Bering Sea, but they felt it was a good thing to acquire the huge territory.

Seward prevailed, and because he did so, the character of the Bering Sea frontier was to be much altered. Beginning in the year 1867, maps were published showing the division of the Bering Sea—a firm line divides the Bering Strait, severs Big from Little Diomede Island, and cuts between the Aleutian and Commander Islands. No longer were the peoples of the opposite shores of Siberia and Alaska to share a common government. Yet geography could not be denied. The drawing of boundary lines cannot extinguish links of cultural and economic importance. The peoples of the two continents were to maintain some forms of contact and share, to some extent, a common destiny despite the political changes.

THE REINDEER PROJECT

Now that Russian America was in possession of the United States certain questions might logically have been raised: What did Alaska have in common with Siberia? Was there any Siberian resource development that could be a model for the Alaskan economy? Given the proximity of northeastern Siberia and northwestern Alaska, it is remarkable that these questions were seldom asked by United States officials charged with the administration of the newly acquired territory—particularly in view of the deprivations under which natives were suffering. Thorough investigations of native conditions and bold planning for the alleviation of distress were not characteristic of Washington bureaucrats. They moved slowly, if at all. Government inertia had contributed to the maladministration of natives in other western territories, and there was no greater concern for aborigines of the North. One thing seemed clear—the reservation system had not been beneficial in the west and could not be applied in Alaska. But no positive economic programs of any scope were implemented for Alaskans, despite the warnings and pleas of missionaries and resident government officials. The government would unbend enough to convey relief stores to starving people, but beyond this basic humanitarian response it had no initiative to offer.

Fortunately, there were a few men of vision who *did* look for parallels between Siberia and Alaska—men who knew both shores of the Bering Sea and saw something that suggested a solution to the impoverishment of American Eskimos. A captain of the U.S. Revenue Marine, Michael J. Healy, was one. His ship was almost as familiar in Siberian harbors as on the American side of the Bering Sea, and he was capable of making certain comparisons and reflections. Another was the missionary and U.S. commissioner of education, Sheldon Jackson, who was a frequent passenger on the Bering Sea revenue cutters and came to appreciate the geographic unity of the northern regions. Together, these men conceived and launched the reindeer importation project and eventually induced a reluctant government to come to its aid. Whenever heroes of the Bering Sea are noted, Healy and Jackson must be given a place.

Jackson's first suggestion for the importation of Siberian reindeer to

Alaska was made to the U. S. Department of the Interior, Bureau of Education, in November 1890. After detailing the impoverishment of Alaskan natives he suggested a solution of modest proportions that was to have far-reaching effects.

"In this crisis it is important that steps should be taken at once to afford relief. Relief can, of course, be afforded by Congress voting an appropriation to feed them, as it has so many of the North American Indians. But I think that everyone familiar with the feeding process among the Indians will devoutly wish that it may not be necessary to extend that system to the Eskimo of Alaska. It would cost hundreds of thousands of dollars annually." [6] Worse than that, Jackson alleged, it would degrade the natives. It would be cheaper and more humane to introduce the reindeer.

This scheme, Jackson argued, "would in a few years create as permanent and secure a food supply for the Eskimo, as cattle or sheep-raising in Texas or New Mexico does for the people of those sections." [7]

Jackson went on to explain the wonders of the reindeer:

In the Arctic and sub-Arctic regions of Lapland and Siberia, the domesticated reindeer is food, clothing, house, furniture, implements, and transportation to the people. Its milk and flesh furnish food; its marrow and tongue are considered choice delicacies; its blood mixed with the contents of its stomach is made into a favorite dish called in Siberia *manyalla;* its intestines are cleaned, filled with tallow, and eaten as a sausage; its skin is made into clothes, bedding, tent-covers, reindeer harness, ropes, cords, and fish lines; the hard skin of the forelegs makes an excellent covering for snow shoes.

Its sinews are dried and pounded into a strong and lasting thread; its bones are soaked in seal oil and burned for fuel; its horns are made into various kinds of household implements—into weapons for hunting and war, and in the manufacture of sleds.

Indeed I know of no other animal that in so many different ways can minister to the comfort and well-being of man in the far northern regions of the earth as the reindeer.[8]

He also explained the transportation potential of the reindeer, noting that the beasts could draw a load of 300 pounds.

Jackson's message was seconded by Captain Healy: "In Lapland there are 400,000 domesticated reindeer, sustaining a population of 27,000. In Siberia, but a few miles from Alaska, with climate and country of similar conditions, are tens of thousands of tame reindeer supporting thousands of people, and it will be a very easy and comparatively cheap matter to introduce the tame reindeer of Siberia into Alaska and teach the natives the care and management of them." [9]

A cruise on the U. S. Revenue Marine's *Bear* in the summer of 1890 had given Jackson his first opportunity of observing Siberian reindeer. The American government had wanted to show its appreciation to Koriaks who had aided whalemen, shipwrecked off the Siberian coast, by distributing gifts to villagers of Cape Navarin just south of Anadyr Bay. In contrast to the starving Eskimos of Alaska, Jackson found Siberians "a hardy, active, and well-fed people, owning tens of thousands of head of domestic reindeer." [10] Jackson returned to Washington to lobby for a reindeer appropriation, but the bill failed to pass in the 1891–92 congressional sessions. Undaunted, he made a public appeal through newspaper advertisements and received private donations of $2,146. This enabled him to make a start in 1892; subsequently, Congress passed a reindeer appropriation to sustain the fledgling program.

Siberian natives had never sold live reindeer prior to 1892, but they had confidence in Captain Healy of the *Bear*, and he helped Jackson gather animals on a summer cruise. It was not, as Jackson discovered, as easy as buying cattle in Texas. Time and patience were necessary. Natives flocked aboard the *Bear* at its anchorage off various villages, exchanged furs for flour, cloth, and ammunition and accepted the bread distribution that custom had sanctioned as their due. "They know perfectly well that we are after reindeer, but nothing is said about it. They have to feast first. They are never in a hurry and therefore do not see why we should be." [11] When presents had been given to the wives and children of leading men and all were in a good humor, the leaders were taken to the pilot house where negotiations commenced. After agreeing to sell, there was still a delay. Reindeer were not herded on the coast, and Jackson had to wait a week or more while the owners traveled to the interior to secure their deer. Siberians were somewhat reluctant to sell because they feared the economic consequences. "From time immemorial they have been accustomed to take their skins to Alaska and exchange them for oil. To establish herds in Alaska will, they fear, ruin

The *Bear* in icy seas.
University of Alaska Archives, Mulligan Collection

this business." [12] Healy was able to convince them that the sale of a small number of animals would not affect the traditional Bering Strait trade. His advocacy was enough to appease the Chukchi, but only temporarily; a few years later, the Russian government intervened to ban the export of live animals to Alaska. In 1892 only sixteen reindeer were purchased, though agreements were made to collect more the next year.

Five Siberian trips by the *Bear* in 1893 netted 175 reindeer. These were taken to Port Clarence, the nearest good harbor to Asia on the American side of the Bering Strait, and a station was established, named for a congressman, Henry M. Teller, who had supported the project. Teller Station was a good choice for the first herd. Ample pasturage could be found in the area, and there were no other commercial distractions. The Seward Peninsula was to remain the chief center of reindeer herding into contemporary times. Responsibility for the care of the nucleus herd and the training of Eskimo herdsmen was given to a white supervisor and four Siberians, who were hired for the purpose and taken to Teller.

According to Jackson's plan, the reindeer were to be controlled by the government for several years, until Eskimos acquired the necessary skills of herd management. The first years of the experiment were difficult. Although the Eskimos expressed keen interest in the reindeer, they disliked the Siberians and threatened their lives. Supervision of the Teller reindeer station was controlled by a white man who had to pacify the Eskimos and assure the Siberians of protection. The age-long enmity among the peoples of the Bering Strait—Eskimos and Chukchi—still existed, despite the fact that they had always traded with each other. The Siberians were not good teachers. Though obedient to the direction of the superintendent, they were easily moved to anger at Eskimo clumsiness in handling the reindeer. In 1894 Jackson began to recruit Norwegian Lapp herders to replace the Siberians. Lapps were more successful; many of them remained in Alaska for the rest of their lives. Some married Eskimo women, and today, a number of their descendants are still active herdsmen.

The early history of the reindeer industry can be traced in reports issued by Jackson from 1890 to 1910. Each year saw the increase of the herd. Without a doubt, the reindeer could flourish equally on both sides of the Bering Strait. But human beings are not always as adaptable as animals. To achieve the goals set out by Jackson, the Alaskan Eskimos had to be transformed. This required a major cultural assimilation by the Eskimo. Certain individuals and families did make the adaptation, but it became obvious that the majority were not making the desired cultural change. It was relatively easy to transport reindeer across the Bering Strait, but the bridging of the gap between traditional methods of subsistence—between sea and land mammal hunter and roving herds-man—was another problem.

The complexities of the adaptation could not have been anticipated by Jackson and other exponents of the reindeer scheme. When the Teller herd was established, the Eskimos were not a static community among which such experiments could be conducted under controlled circum-stances. Years of contact with American whalers had already disrupted the traditional economy of many Eskimos. And while the reindeer experiment was still in its infancy, an explosive influx of whites into the Seward Peninsula affected them tremendously. Whether the gold rush of 1899 significantly reduced the chances for making hunters into herdsmen cannot be determined with certainty, but assuredly it was distracting.

It would be presumptuous to call the reindeer project a failure. Even had it succeeded to the point of Jackson's highest expectations, the new concentration might have produced a situation more threatening to the Eskimo than that which he faced in 1890. Results of widespread change cannot always be fully anticipated. In truth, the success or failure of the undertaking has never been carefully assessed. Advocates of the endeavor despaired when Eskimos seemed more prone to kill off large numbers of the reindeer for food than husband the resource for a sustained yield. Yet, the Eskimo had always survived by taking the meat needed for subsistence when needed, without concern for the future. Even if his use of the animal did not conform to expectations, the Eskimo did use the reindeer in his own way. Huge herds declined as the animals were consumed. No vital native industry was developed; yet the food maintained life, at least for a number of years.

Sheldon Jackson, the splendid advocate of the domesticated rein-deer, had to report on the use of federal funds expended on the project each year. The obligation gave him the opportunity of defending the current program and pointing out other uses for the magnificent animal. In December 1894 he described the year's work as one of gratifying progress and success. After discussing the Teller herd, he suggested that the Aleutian Islands be stocked. In 1891 small herds had been loosed on

Unalaska and the Amaknak Islands and they were still thriving, though uncared for. Jackson urged that all the islands be stocked and pointed out that the decimation of the sea otter had left the Aleuts in need of a new food resource.

A disaster that had occurred on the Aleutians that year provided Jackson with evidence of other benefits. A whaling bark, the *James Allen*, had struck a sunken reef off the east end of Amlia Island and gone down. The crew took to their boats, but twenty-five seamen were drowned or died from exposure. Captain Michael J. Healy, of the *Bear*, eventually rescued nine survivors from Unimak Island. They had been eating the dead body of a companion who had died two weeks previously. To Jackson the lesson was obvious: If the islands had been supplied with reindeer much of this starvation and loss of life could have been prevented.

On the Aleutians, as the shrewd Jackson pointed out, reindeer would benefit whites as well as natives. But there was a potential use of the animals that would be of even more value to the territory's development—a service that would benefit whalers, the gold prospectors of the interior, and throw open the entire North. The reindeer could be utilized for a speedy, efficient mail service. This was something sadly lacking in the region.

This proposal was a farseeing one. As with most prophets, Jackson was in advance of his time. Reindeer would eventually be used for mail service but not on as wide a scope—and only after the Klondike and Nome gold rushes had increased the population of Alaska manyfold.

To Jackson, the reindeer experiment seemed to have been a great success. Once more a novel means had been found of bridging the Bering Strait gap.

12 — GOLD

Reindeer were carried from Siberia to Alaska in the hope of sustaining a people; yet, unknown to all, the shores of the Bering Strait were laden with wealth. That a small quantity of gold existed in many northern streams was known to the Russian fur traders, but their concern was with furs. In 1866, Daniel B. Libby and other members of the Western Union Telegraph Expedition "saw unmistakable evidence of the presence of gold" on Seward Peninsula, and "they made up their minds to prospect in that section in the summer of 1867," but instead, they left the North when the telegraph construction was abandoned.[1]

"Little or nothing more was thought about its gold at that time," wrote Libby in 1899, "and thus, the matter rested for more than a quarter of a century; until the great Klondike strike was heralded to the world." [2] When the gold diggings of Dawson City became the wonder of the world, Libby returned to the Seward Peninsula. In 1898, he and others made discoveries that sparked a great stampede.

News of the great finds on the Seward Peninsula traveled up the Yukon River. A great exodus of hopefuls commenced. Miners poured from Dawson and the other camps along the Yukon. Some drove dog teams during the winter to the diggings near Nome, but many more awaited the spring opening of the river to steamboat traffic. Several hearty adventurers bicycled down the frozen Yukon before the breakup.

By December 1899, approximately 4,500 claims had been recorded; a year later, thirty mining districts had been organized. Many men who came to Nome were destitute, suffering from scurvy and bitterly disappointed over the failure to find gold at the other locations they had worked. Some were riffraff, disgusted with the strictness of Canadian law. Their bitterness was magnified when they arrived at Nome and found that the entire region had been staked. Enterprising prospectors spent their first season staking claims in preference to working them. Optimists believed that gold was to be found in every stream, and they staked from beach to skyline in their own names, for others, with power of attorney, for their friends and relatives, as agents. The law required that a mineral discovery be made before a claim be staked and filed, but nobody had time to verify the presence of wealth. Claim-jumping and relocating resulted from this wild scrambling, and there would have been enough dispute to keep the court docket filled endlessly—if there had been a court.

As bleak as the town and its environs appeared, it was obvious that prospects of moneymaking were very high indeed, and public-spirited citizens with a respect for private property demanded that law and order be maintained. The Chamber of Commerce was the first organized body in the town, and its president issued a decree against violence: "We will hang the first man who unnecessarily spills human blood if we have to go to Council City to get the tree to hang him on." [3] Council City was a goodly distance to go for a hanging tree, which gave the determination credibility.

Actually, disease posed a greater threat than crime, since no sanitation system existed and the area was full of refuse and offal. Eventually, this was carried out onto the Bering Sea ice before the thaw, but not before typhoid and other diseases took lives and excited alarm.

The throngs of miners who reached Nome in the summer of 1899 came in time for the second stage of the drama—the discovery of gold on the sandy beaches of Nome. Never had mining been easier. No slow burning of a shaft through permafrost sixty feet to bedrock was necessary on the beach. A crude rocker set up on the beach was enough equipment for the job. The rich sand was shoved in and shaken down until the gold particles were trapped in the rocker. In the first season of the 1899 discovery of the beach gold, over $2,000,000 in gold was recovered by this simple process. During the same time, the creeks of the Nome district produced $1,000,000, though it was hard to keep miners working the creek placers so long as beach possibilities remained available. A year later, overall production rose to over $4 million and that figure was maintained for each of the next six years.

There were no claims on the beaches of Nome. Prospectors simply worked at a hole between high- and low-water marks as long as they could. The tide smoothed off all the diggings every time it came in. Then, once it had receded, the thick swarms of men would return to set up their rockers once more at one spot or another.

The noted geologist Alfred H. Brooks journeyed to the town in the fall of 1899. He reported that all the larger buildings in Nome were saloons or dance halls. Law and order was difficult to maintain because of the numbers of gamblers and con men who flocked to the camp. One means of keeping order was extremely effective if not legal. Spotting a dozen men in the camp who were well-known criminals, the city fathers asked the commander of the U.S. Revenue Cutter Service to take them outside on the last sailing, before winter closed the navigation season. Captain David H. Jarvis of the *Bear* accommodated, and the men were rounded up and taken aboard the *Bear* to Seattle where they were set free. None of the unwilling passengers sued the government for what could only be considered false arrest and false imprisonment.

Conditions were serene through the 1899–1900 winter. However, the balance changed for the worse after the rushers of 1900 hit the beach. Nome was easy to reach for all who had passage money from Seattle or other Pacific coast ports. As a result, all kinds of scoundrels and swindlers joined the throngs to the golden beaches of Nome. Brooks, back for another look at the camp, was appalled. He had been in every mining camp of Alaska and the Yukon; yet Nome was the only place where he felt the fear of robbery and violence. Like many others, he found it necessary to carry a weapon to insure his personal safety.

At one point during the summer, seventy ships were anchored in the open roadstead before the town. Thousands of men waded in the muck that passed for Front Street, where most of the business houses and saloons were located. Nome residences were mostly tents. All northern mining camps began as tent cities, but were soon transformed into log-cabin towns. This transformation was slow to come in Nome, where there were no trees in the immediate vicinity.

Blood-letting was frequent in Nome. The town was filled with rowdy and disreputable characters, and neither the military nor the town police made determined attempts to check lawlessness. A company of soldiers sent up from St. Michael did not actually have the authority to keep order in the community. Robberies occurred frequently and

The beach at Nome, 1900.
University of Alaska Archives

shootings were daily events. The situation dismayed even hardened miners who had been in the North for years.

In his book *Dog-Puncher on the Yukon*, Arthur Walden relates an incident indicative of the atmosphere in Nome that second summer. He found a diary lying on the beach in which the writer had recorded his travels to the Yukon over the White Pass, his experiences on the Klondike, and his voyage down the Yukon to Nome. When the owner arrived in Nome, he wrote on a full page in larger letters, "Drunk!" Here the diary stopped.

Walden noted robberies of every description going on in Nome. Legitimate claimants to expensive town lots were forced off at gunpoint, deputy sheriffs robbed drunks, bar patrons were rolled by proprietors, and frequent stick-ups occurred on the roads.

Still, plenty of fun awaited the tired miners at day's end. What made Nome singular in the annals of mining camps was the general level of prosperity of its thousands of miners. Even the miners who had staked creeks in the vicinity with the intention of working the placers by the conventional mining methods could take time off to grubstake themselves by doing a little shoveling and rocking on the beach. The beaches were open to all, and no one need be without the means to buy a drink. Wyatt Earp's saloon watered many each night. Earp, who, as a television hero, was portrayed as a frontier gunman who used his talent in early western camps, was known in Nome as a saloon keeper. The record reveals only one violent episode in Earp's Nome sojourn—an assault for which he was fined fifty dollars.

Wilson Mizner was a key figure both in the social world and the underworld of Nome. Handsome, debonair, unscrupulous, he dazzled the ladies and fleeced opponents at cards and gulls in badger games. He even had time to satisfy the camp's craving for sport by promoting several boxing matches.

All this unlovely camp needed to aid its swift transformation from chaos to civilization was a permanently established court maintained by honest officials. Instead, it attracted a couple of the most daring rogues in the country.

Alexander McKenzie hit the beach in July 1900, bringing in tow another no-good, Judge Arthur H. Noyes. Their aim was to corral all the gold of Nome for themselves, and they developed a fairly simple plan to that end. McKenzie had organized the Alaska Gold Mining Company and distributed shares to influential politicians in Washington. The politicians, in turn, arranged Noyes' appointment as federal judge for the Nome district. Immediately on his arrival in Nome, McKenzie hired a number of toughs to eject miners from five of the most valuable of the claims on Anvil Creek. Legal rationalization rested in the appointment of the Alaska Gold Mining Company as receiver for the Wild Goose and Pioneer Mining companies. McKenzie's papers were in order—Judge Noyes had signed them.

The miners protested to Noyes, but he refused to entertain their petitions. A representative of the evicted miners was dispatched to San Francisco where the circuit court of appeals ordered McKenzie to return the property to its legal owners. McKenzie, with Noyes' support, resisted until another appeal to San Francisco resulted in the dispatch of two court deputies to bring McKenzie in for trial. Noyes and McKenzie were convicted, but their political connections insured that their terms would be short ones.

The removal of Noyes did not end the legal chaos in Nome. Hundreds of cases remained to be settled, most suits arising from the claim jumping that was so persistent a feature of the Seward Peninsula rush. Judge Noyes' conspiracy had absorbed his efforts to the exclusion of all other judicial business. Not a single case unconnected with his audacious venture had been heard.

The task of restoring judicial authority in Nome fell to Judge James Wickersham, who replaced Noyes in September 1901. Wickersham and Noyes had both received their appointments from President McKinley the previous year. They met in Seattle, en route to their respective districts. Wickersham had envied Noyes' assignment to the Seward Peninsula where the gold excitement raged. Wickersham's Third Judicial District sprawled over much of the Alaskan interior and even took in the Aleutian Islands.

The new gold town of Nome developed rapidly into a cosmopolitan center. Originally, it was called Anvil City, after the creek on which the rich mineral discoveries had been made. Later, its residents decided to name it after the cape on which it was established. Cape Nome had been named under curious circumstances. A draftsman in the Hydrographic Office of Britain's Royal Navy was laboring over charts of the Bering Sea and could not find any identification of one prominent cape. Thus, he wrote *Name?* An engraver interpreted that as *Nome C.* or *Cape Nome,* a mistake that held.

Nome has many claims to fame. It could be seriously argued that professional prize fighting was born there, at least in the steel-trap mind of Tex Rickard. Rickard did not build a Madison Square Garden in Nome, but he might have conceived of the palace of boxing there as he watched pugs belabor each other in the rear of his Northern Saloon. Rickard promoted fights and drew good, thirsty crowds of spectators to the saloon. Boxing was still a smalltime, somewhat disreputable sport at the time. It lacked the glamour that Rickard and a few others were going to give it in the first decades of the twentieth century. It is curious how many men associated with the fight game turned up in Nome in 1899–1900. Just down the street from the Northern Saloon there was the Dexter Saloon. Bouts were put on at the Dexter under the direction of Wyatt Earp, who had a record of dabbling in prize fights and a reputation as a gun slinger.

Earp had played many roles before coming to Nome, including those of horse thief, buffalo hunter, miner, peace officer, and saloon operator. In 1896, he had acted as referee of the controversial Sharkey-Fitzsimmons fight. But in 1899, Earp added his talents to those of the other Nome characters who were intrigued by boxing, and what a galaxy they represented! Besides Rickard, who would later make the million-dollar gate commonplace, there were Jack "Doc" Kearnes, Tommy Burns, Wilson Mizner, and Mike Mahoney.

Kearnes was just a scrawny kid at the time, but he met the leading *bon vivant* of Nome, Wilson Mizner, and was introduced to the fight game. After taking a beating in a Nome match, he resolved to rely upon brains rather than brawn. This was a sound decision. In time, he was able to manage the elevation of the great Jack Dempsey to the world heavyweight championship.

Tommy Burns was to become the heavyweight champ a few years after leaving Alaska, but in Nome he suffered a setback in a fight with the great musher Mike Mahoney. Mahoney's preference was for a free style of fighting which did not bar kicking. Burns agreed to these rules and was knocked cold by a devastating kick to his solar plexus launched by Mahoney. Some years later, when Burns was champion, Rickard tried to lure Mahoney to New York for a return engagement with Burns—with no kicking allowed. Mahoney refused to accept such unmanly restrictions.

Wilson Mizner was a dedicated con man, but did find time for boxing when he was not fleecing newcomers to Nome or squandering his gains at Rickard's Northern Saloon and gambling emporium. After leaving Nome, he managed Stanley Ketchel for a time, before moving on to Hollywood for film writing and eventually to Florida for real estate speculation.

We cannot know how much the crisp air of the Bering Sea frontier contributed to the blossoming of professional boxing in the United States, but the key figures attributed their successes to their Alaskan days. When Kearnes and Rickard reached the top, they agreed that their talents had been honed on the golden beaches of Nome.

FAMED SHIPS

All the vessels that sailed and steamed through the waters of the Bering Sea were indispensable links between Nome, Siberia, and the outside world. The U.S. Revenue Cutter Service ship *Bear* was well known to Russians and Americans because it often carried passengers across the Bering Strait. One Russian counterpart of the *Bear* was the gunboat *Yakut*, which policed the coast of Kamchatka and northeastern Siberia and tried to curtail the booze trade of the Americans. Its service in the Bering Sea predated the Alaskan gold rushes. The crew of the *Yakut* had a hard time during the Bolshevist revolutionary strife. They supported the Whites against the Reds, and when the Reds gained control of Vladivostok, the *Yakut*'s home port, in 1919, the sailors did not dare to remain in Siberia. The *Yakut* steamed to Nome, where the crew was allowed ashore for a short visit. There was some sentiment in Nome for encouraging the Russians to stay on, but immigration regulations did not permit such informal entries. Carl Lomen felt sorry for the *Yakut* men, noting that the ship "was now without a country." [4] It would be interesting to know how many Russians had crossed the Bering Strait to take up permanent residence in America in the thousands of years the land bridge existed and subsequently.

The best-loved passenger ship to ever plow through the Bering Sea was the *Victoria*. In 1928, the *Seattle Star* noted that the *Victoria* was still going strong after completing her 171st round trip to Nome. At that time, the ship had been in service for fifty-eight years and was the only iron ship still afloat. The Scottish shipbuilders W. Denny and Brothers laid down the ship's hull in 1870. Named the *Parthia*, the flush-deck, open-bridged vessel served as the queen of the Cunard line on the Liverpool–New York passage for the next ten years. In 1881 the *Parthia* carried British troops under General Charles Gordon to Egypt to fight the Mahdi forces. Later, the iron ship sailed under the colors of the Guion line and ran to South America and Australia. The North Pacific career of the *Parthia* commenced in 1887 when the ship was purchased by the Canadian Pacific Railway for the passage between Vancouver, British Columbia, and the Orient. Later, the ship, now rechristened the *Victoria*, was sold to a Tacoma line, but remained in the Oriental traffic. With the gold rush to Nome in 1900, the *Victoria* began her long service to the Bering Sea. Some Alaskans referred to the ship as the "Holy Roller," but to most, she was "Old Vic." When passengers boarded her in Seattle, they already felt as if they were back home in Alaska, though the voyage to Nome was one of 2,300 miles.

The most famous skipper of the *Victoria* was "Dynamite" Johnny O'Brien, a fiery seaman whose maritime experience began on ships running between San Francisco and China. He interrupted his sea service to join the gold stampede to the Cassiar region of northern British Columbia in 1874. The *Victoria* usually called at Cordova on the return voyage from Nome and loaded a cargo of copper ore, which had been shipped to the coast from the fabulous Kennecott mines over the Copper River Railroad. He was the great friend of another Irishman of prominence in Alaskan history, Mike Heney, who built the Skagway-White Horse Railroad during the Klondike gold rush, and later directed the incredibly difficult task of punching the Copper River Railroad over glaciers, mighty rivers, mountainous terrain, and forests. The hard-charging Heney burned himself out and died before the job was completed, but he did not forget his old friend of the *Victoria*. O'Brien received $150 per month from Heney's estate for the rest of his life. Both men have been characterized in Rex Beach's novel *The Iron Trail*, which treats the story of the building of the Copper River Railroad.

The most disastrous voyage of the *Victoria* from Nome took place in 1918. A flu epidemic ravaged the passengers. O'Brien got permission to bypass Cordova in order to get his passengers to Seattle hospitals sooner;

but when the *Victoria* reached Puget Sound, it carried 31 dead. Carl
Lomen was one of the passengers who was not afflicted. In Nome, 187
Eskimos and 21 whites died.

The Alaska Steamship Company bought the *Victoria* in 1903 and
remodeled the vessel. Her decks were raised, a superstructure was added,
her bridge was closed in, and additional passenger accommodations were
added. From 1900 to 1930, either the *Victoria*, the *Corwin*, or the *Bear*
was usually the first ship to reach Nome after the ice went out of the
Bering Sea. This was always a joyous day for Nome. Relatives and friends
returned on the *Victoria* after wintering outside, and, for the first time in
months, fresh fruits and vegetables were available. On her return voyages
to Seattle, the *Victoria* hauled other passengers, gold, and, after the
Lomens founded their reindeer industry, the frozen carcasses of reindeer.

"For 58 years she has weathered gales on the seven seas," observed
the *Seattle Star*. "For 41 of those, she has been the proud old matron of
the North Pacific. Long may she sail." [5] This was the sentiment, too, of
all the residents of Nome.

Nome did not die as had other western-frontier gold towns,
although the demise of placer mining has reduced the number of
residents. These days, ships do not crowd the open roadstead before the
city, but it remains the service center for a vast region of northwestern
Alaska.

PROSPECTING IN SIBERIA

Like many 1898 voyagers to the Bering Sea, Washington B.
Vanderlip was a gold seeker. His wandering brought him to Kamchatka
in 1898. While thousands of adventurers landed at St. Michael en route
to the newly discovered gold fields of the Yukon valley, he was interested
in Siberia. It was a firm tenet among northern mining men—Americans
and Russians—that mineral conditions were similar on both sides of the
Bering Sea. If the Klondike and Alaska were rich in gold, so was Siberia.
It was just as simple as that.

Vanderlip had mining experience but no money; so he landed at
Vladivostok, the lively port and terminus of the Trans-Siberian Railroad,
looking for employment. Gold excitement was in the air. The merchants
of Vladivostok had had no chance to cash in on the Klondike but were not
adverse to grubstaking an American prospector who had the necessary
credentials. Vanderlip was commissioned to lead a party north. He hired

four helpers and outfitted his party at the store operated by Enoch Emory, a Yankee trader who had four business houses in the Amur River region. Emory, one of the most prosperous merchants in southern Siberia, dealt primarily in American goods which were shipped in from San Francisco.

Passage to Petropavlovsk was secured on a German tramp steamer, *Cosmopolite*, chartered to Kunst and Albers of Vladivostok for their annual provisioning voyage. Kunst and Albers maintained trading posts on the Bering Sea as far north as the Anadyr River and held a nominal monopoly on the fur yield of northeastern Siberia. In 1898 the company had a fairly secure position, although they had some rivalry from a few small, independent traders and American whaling vessels. At the turn of the century the tempo of trading was to accelerate, as Nome became the metropolis of the Bering Sea and Americans from Nome and the Pacific coast competed for the lucrative Siberian business. The American whalers in the Bering Sea were few in number by this time; yet they were still of concern to Russian officials, because they customarily ignored the ban on liquor traffic. Two Russian naval ships patrolled the long Siberian coast to enforce the prohibition, but it was difficult to catch traders in the act.

Petropavlovsk was still a sleepy outpost with a population of 300 Russians and half-caste Kamchadals, presided over by a magistrate and policed by 20 Cossacks. Vanderlip prospected unsuccessfully outside the town, then embarked for the west coast of the peninsula. Reports of gold prospects took Vanderlip from the west coast across the Okhotsk Sea to Gizhiga where he set up a base. From there he prospected the interior rivers, panning the sandbars for signs of gold. His methods were the same as those of Yukon River miners. When flakes of gold were discovered in suggestive quantity on sandbars, a discovery shaft had to be sunk to bedrock. As in Alaska and the Yukon Territory, digging was laborious. The ground was frozen just below the surface; the earth could only be removed after it was thawed by fires. It took several days of thawing and digging to reach bedrock, twenty-five feet down, and it was only then that it could be determined whether paying quantities of gold existed. None of Vanderlip's shafts revealed promise; so he set out on a long exploratory journey to the north. Despite the severity of the Kamchatka winter, travel was actually easier that season than in the summer—provided one used dog sleds for transport. In January

Vanderlip commenced a 2,500-mile trip starting and ending at Gizhiga, to prospect the rivers of northeastern Siberia that flowed to the Bering Sea.

Traveling through the Koriak country, Vanderlip noted the huge reindeer herds held by the natives of the interior and wondered why the U.S. government imported its Alaskan herds from Lapland, rather than Siberia. "If the government had sent a steamer a single day's run across Bering Sea, it could have purchased fifty-thousand reindeer right on the coast at a cost of one rouble, or fifty cents, apiece." [6] The American miner was not aware that the original Alaskan herd had been acquired from Siberia, though not as easily as he imagined, and that Lapland deer were only imported after further purchases from Siberia had been prohibited. Somewhat belatedly, the czarist government was trying to curtail foreign activity on the Bering Sea coast.

Vanderlip worked his way slowly through the Koriak country, camping along likely-looking stream beds, digging down to bedrock in a fruitless search for gold. When he approached the Bering Sea coast, he met Chukchi for the first time—"the Apaches of Siberia." [7] He had heard that they were "a rather ugly lot" whom the Russians had not been able to subdue and was warned to be wary in their country.[8] But the Chukchi were anything but menacing. They assisted the prospectors with transport and provided them with food, refusing recompense for all services. "I felt so safe among the Tchuktches that never once did I take my guns from the pack and bring them into the tent with me." [9] Vanderlip's travels among the Chukchi coincided in time with those of the English adventurer Harry DeWindt. The two men did not meet, but Vanderlip was later amazed to read DeWindt's highly charged account of the indignities he suffered at Chukchi hands during his abortive effort to travel from the Bering Strait across Siberia. Vanderlip stopped short of calling DeWindt a liar, but as he had traveled over the same ground, treated as an honored guest where the Englishman had raved of imprisonment and ill treatment, he clearly suspected that DeWindt's misfortunes were imaginary. Without reservation, Vanderlip described the Chukchi as "the finest race of savages that it has ever been my lot to meet." [10] The Chukchi did not love the Russians, but clearly differentiated between their old adversaries and other visitors. Americans were particularly popular because the whaling ships brought articles of trade that the Chukchi desired. The Russians wanted the foreign trade stopped but were not able to halt it by decree alone.

After a year of prospecting, Vanderlip returned to Vladivostok to report to his employers. In both of the regions searched he had drawn a blank; neither the streams flowing into the Okhotsk Sea nor the beach sands of the Bering Sea south of Anadyr Bay contained gold deposits. So much for the search for a Siberian Klondike. The most likely areas had proved barren, and Vanderlip—so he thought—was through with Bering Sea prospecting. But events determined otherwise. New gold discoveries on the Seward Peninsula of Alaska, just opposite Siberia on the Bering Strait, sparked a major Alaskan gold rush and created new interest in the potential of northeastern Siberia.

THE CHUKCHI GOLD RACE

Washington Vanderlip was relaxing in the United States, after his 1898–99 Siberian prospecting, when the news of the Nome gold bonanza reached him. The Anvil River discoveries had been followed in the late summer of 1899 by a discovery causing even greater excitement, when the beach sands fronting the new gold camp were found to be rich. Once more a tantalizing geographic parallel suggested itself—a much closer one than had existed between the Yukon valley and northeastern Siberia. What could be more striking than the similarities between the Asian and Alaskan shores of the Bering Strait? Only fifty-six miles separated the two shores. Why should not the beach sands of the Chukchi Peninsula have the same geological characteristics as those of Nome?

The Vladivostok company, which had employed Vanderlip the previous year, sent him a hurry-up call. Get back to the North, and this time investigate the region north of Anadyr Bay, they urged. And time was crucial to the second expedition. Newspapers had just announced that a mineral concession to the entire Chukchi Peninsula had been granted by the czar to two Russian nobles, Count Unarliarsky and Count Bogdanovitch. This concession would seem to exclude competition, but there was a catch. Any mining claims staked prior to the presentation of franchise authorizations to the governor of the Anadyr district would supercede the rights of the concessionaires. When this news broke, the winter ice still held the Bering Sea fast, closed to all navigation. If Vanderlip could reach the Bering Strait and stake a claim before the other

Russian company, all would be well. The concessionaires might not move as fast as their rivals, since they were unaware that there were any competitors.

Vanderlip moved with alacrity. He reached Vladivostok from San Francisco, hired fifty Russian miners, and chartered a Russian steamer, the *Progress*. By June 3 he was ready to set out and seemed to have a lead in the race. A cablegram from his employer's San Francisco agent revealed that the franchise holder's party, headed by Count Bogdanovitch and George D. Roberts, an American mining engineer, had chartered a Puget Sound lumber ship, the *Samoa*, and would depart on June 6. Vanderlip's ship was slightly faster and had a shorter distance to go. Even more vital, the *Samoa*'s party was still unaware that there was a race and planned to rendezvous at Anadyr Bay with a Russian gunboat. The Russian naval vessel, the *Yakut*, would drive away any American miners who were surreptitiously prospecting the Siberian shore. Some Americans were supposed to have made their way across the Bering Strait from Nome in hopes of striking a bonanza. Probably just a few individuals, if any, were involved, though alarmed reports to the Russian companies described an invasion of 3,000 miners.

A week after steaming from Vladivostok, Vanderlip's ship reached Petropavlovsk. Fresh water was taken on and the race north continued. Fog enveloped the Bering Sea as the *Progress* pushed northward into ice-strewn waters. Speed was reduced despite the urgency of the mission. A slight blow would finish the *Progress*; its steel hull was not reinforced for ice navigation, nor was it divided into watertight compartments.

Some of the Russian miners were put to work making a large United States flag, a decoy to lure natives aboard. Vanderlip had not forgotten the Chukchi's aversion to Russians. If he wanted to get any information from them concerning coastal prospecting activity, the *Progress* would have to appear as an American ship.

On June 16 the *Progress* reached Cape Chaplina (known as Indian Point to American seamen). No inshore passage was possible; a thirty-five-mile band of ice clung to the shore. Vanderlip steamed over to St. Lawrence Island to see if he could learn anything of the Siberian "invasion" from Nome. The Presbyterian missionary there had no information and had his hands full with epidemics of flu and measles. As isolated as the Eskimos of St. Lawrence Island seemed to be, they could never escape the ravages of imported diseases—or liquor.

Siberian Eskimos on board *Corwin*, East Cape, Siberia.
University of Alaska Archives, Charles Bunnell Collection

Vanderlip was on St. Lawrence Island when another ship loomed through the fog and cast anchor beside the *Progress*. This was a famous ship of the Bering Sea, the *Corwin*. The *Corwin* had been a tough, ice-ramming cutter of the U.S. Revenue Cutter Service before it was decommissioned and sold. It was now owned by Captain Ellsworth West, whose enterprises included coal mining at Cape Lisburne on the Arctic coast of Alaska. The *Corwin* had been the first ship to reach Nome in the 1900 navigation season, an honor it maintained for the following decade and more. To be first was a matter of profit as well as distinction: The *Corwin* brought miners their first fresh foods of the season and West made a handsome profit.

West agreed to batter a passage through the ice for the *Progress* to the Siberian shore. He was going there anyway to land a party of prospectors he had picked up in Nome. The *Corwin*'s capacity to force its way through ice depended on its special construction: a twelve-foot bow of solid greenheart timber and a four-foot sheathing of the same material along its sides. An ordinary ship could not be used as a battering ram, but the *Corwin* could be backed off heavy floes and then run forward under full power to smash its way through.

Following the *Corwin*, the *Progress* got through to Indian Point safely. West's service cost Vanderlip $500, but it was well worth it. Once ashore, Vanderlip inquired about American prospectors in the vicinity; none had been seen by the Chukchi. So far, so good. No rivals were in the field in advance of his expedition. Vanderlip hired a Chukchi to act as ice pilot and others to man a small boat for a coastal investigation. Thanks to the fact that American whalemen had often recruited Chukchi to serve as crewmen on Arctic Ocean cruises, the Indian Point natives were splendid oarsmen. With their help, Vanderlip made a circuit of St. Lawrence Bay, landing at various points on the Siberian shore to prospect the beach sands. The results were negative. Vanderlip had won his race against the concessionaires, but there was no golden prize. Contrary to the firm convictions of armchair geologists, the beach sands of northeastern Siberia did not resemble the golden sands of Nome.

Vanderlip then steamed to the two Diomede Islands which lay midway in Bering Strait. Prospecting there proved equally fruitless; so he steamed north to land at East Cape, the extreme eastern tip of the Chukchi Peninsula. The villagers there had lost half their inhabitants to an epidemic of flu and measles. Corpses were lying about, half-eaten by dogs. "A little child had a leather thong tied through the eye-holes of a skull, and was dragging it about for a cart." [11] It was a macabre and pitiful scene. Vanderlip blamed the American whalemen for the condition of the natives who had become slaves to liquor and censured the U.S. government for not interfering with the nefarious liquor trade. Legally, of course, the U.S. Revenue Marine Division had no jurisdiction in Siberian waters, and the Russian patrol consisted of a single small gunboat.

Vanderlip was now convinced that there was no Siberian Klondike to be discovered; yet, as subsequent events indicate, he must have retained his faith in the overall economic potential of eastern Siberia. Twenty years later he was to negotiate with Lenin for concessions on Kamchatka. But, for the time, he had had enough and brought the *Progress* into Plover Bay—on the south side of the Chukchi Peninsula— to await the arrival of his rivals in the *Samoa*. When the *Samoa* arrived, Vanderlip boarded her to convey his news to the Russian and American gold seekers. He thought he was doing them a favor by telling them of his unsuccessful search and probably could not resist the chance to show how he had beaten them. Count Bogdanovitch was not amused "and apparently wished me at the bottom of the sea." [12] The American miners were friendlier and listened to an account of his prospecting, but the quest for Siberian gold did not end with Vanderlip's failure. In time, gold was mined in Siberia.

13 — THE TRUMPETS OF COMMERCE

Although Washington B. Vanderlip was convinced after his 1898 and 1899 prospecting expedition in Siberia that the region did not share the mineral wealth of the Seward Peninsula, others thought differently. The Siberian share was so tantalizingly near to the gold-booming Seward Peninsula, it was bound to attract prospectors and promoters from Nome, Seattle, and San Francisco. The supposed mineral riches of Siberia were to remain a constant lure to Americans until well into the 1920s when the Soviets finally shut the gate to Yankee enterprise.

Nome newspapers often reported the potential of Siberia, though with some caution. "Siberia may be a promising gold field; but there's plenty of land on this side of the straits." [1] All-out boosting was reserved for the yet underdeveloped resources of Alaska—especially the Seward Peninsula. In 1901 editor J. F. A. Strong noted the arrival in Nome of D. V. Evanoff of St. Petersburg, a representative of V. N. Wonlarlarsky, holder of a mining concession for all northeastern Siberia. Evanoff assured Strong that a Russian consul would be established in Nome in the next year for the benefit of American miners wishing to voyage to Siberia. The import of all this was clear to *Nome Nugget* readers: if Siberian miners outfitted in Nome, it would greatly benefit the gold town's economy and establish its importance as an international commercial center. And it seemed likely that some of the gold mined in Siberia would find its way to Nome.

Clearly, during the summer of 1901, the developments that would bring the Asian and American continents together were moving swiftly. Gold was important, but there were other links as well. A herd of reindeer was being shipped to Teller from Siberia to augment the government-administered herds intended to benefit Eskimo villagers. But most significant of all prospects, backing had apparently been secured by American financial interests for the construction of the grandest railroad of them all—the one that would join America to Asia by bridging or tunneling the Bering Strait.

HARRY DeWINDT

General public interest in connecting the Asian and North American continents by rail was sparked by the completion of the Trans-Siberian Railroad in 1901. The discovery of gold in Alaska that suggested a rich economic potential for the North Pacific region provided an additional incentive to extend the North American railroad network northward. That same year the English traveler Harry DeWindt journeyed from Paris to New York via the Bering Strait. In 1896 he had tried to make it from the west and failed. A Franco-American syndicate hoped to tunnel or bridge the Bering Strait and run a branch line from the Trans-Siberian Railroad across to meet a proposed Alaskan railroad. On the 1901 journey, DeWindt investigated the feasibility of the route for the syndicate. He traveled 4,000 miles in nine days by rail from Paris to Irkutsk and then continued by sleigh for the remainder of the trip. East Cape on the coast of Siberia was 11,263 miles from Paris along the route DeWindt traveled.

DeWindt relied upon the U.S. Revenue Cutter Service to cross the Bering Strait to Cape Prince of Wales, Alaska, where he turned south to Nome and the gold rush boom there. He continued the rest of the 18,494 miles to New York and there made his report. DeWindt's conclusions on the feasibility of a rail route were pessimistic: It would cost too much to bridge or tunnel the strait. He did not recommend the proposal, but he was certain that one day a railroad would eventually be constructed across the continental gap.

The first person to conceive of the possibility of traveling from Europe to the Atlantic coast of America via the North Pacific was the American adventurer John Ledyard, who accompanied James Cook on his third circumnavigation. Ledyard planned to cross over to Alaska from Siberia and then proceed overland to the Atlantic. His hope of making the first crossing of America north of Mexico, however, was frustrated in 1788 by Russian authorities who stopped his progress at Yakutsk.

Evidently Ledyard had been too impatient in St. Petersburg to wait for authorization of his journey. He traveled over 4,000 miles from St. Petersburg to the Lena River but was stopped and escorted back to the capital.

The earliest visionary to suggest a railroad to link Asia and North America was William Gilpin, the first territorial governor of Colorado. Gilpin first predicted that such a link would be built in 1849. In 1861, when he became governor, he argued that Denver deserved to be the center of the world by virtue of its location. A railroad should cross the continent from New York to Denver, turn north to the Northwestern Territory (present Alberta), Alaska, and the Bering Strait where a ferry could take the trains across to Siberia. There the railroad would meet the connecting links to Europe.

Gilpin's railroad views appeared in *The Cosmopolitan Railway Compacting and Fusing Together All the World's Continents*, which was published in 1890. "The more I investigated," wrote Gilpin, "the more practical the plan appeared." [2] He noted that the Russians were constructing a Siberian railroad while "several systems in America are drawing nearer and nearer toward the narrow strait which separates the oldest continent." [3] The prospects excited Gilpin. A railroad would be another "link in the great chain of progress." [4] All the worlds' people would be connected in the near future.

Another proponent of the Bering Strait railroad was a man who knew the region from personal experience. Frederick Whymper, an English artist, had been a member of the Western Union Telegraph Expedition (1865–67), and the potential of a rail link seemed a logical extension of the telegraph project. In his narrative of his Alaskan travels, Whymper argued that a rail connection would be practical and could be accomplished without much difficulty.

Harry DeWindt, a thin-faced little man with an imperial moustache and slick black hair, attempted to travel by land from North America to Europe in 1896. He journeyed through Alaska to the Bering Strait and was taken across the Pacific by the U.S. revenue cutter *Bear* to Kamchatka. His trip was thwarted by uncooperative Chukchi natives who would not provide him with the means of transportation.

DeWindt reacted hysterically to the delays and uncertainties posed by the Chukchi upon whom he and his "body servant," George Harding, depended. The Chukchi leader was drinking and treated the Englishmen insolently. A winter in a Chukchi village seemed to be unendurable: "We turned our eyes seawards, where the foot ice, already over a mile in breadth, had come to stay, and our hearts sank within us at the thought that another ten days at the most would entomb us securely and hopelessly as a vault at Kensal Green Cemetery." [5] What could be done? George Harding had an inspiration: "I watched him," wrote DeWindt, "as he walked through the gathering gloom to the beach, and fixed it to an old whale rib that had once formed part of a hut. And, as the Union Jack fluttered gaily out on the evening breeze, I wondered whether the lady who had given it me in far-away England had ever realized that the lives of two men would one day depend upon that tiny bit of bunting." [6]

In these melodramatic terms, "traveler and explorer" Harry DeWindt described his terrible experiences among the Chukchi. Earlier their expedition had seemed such a grand idea; they would be the first men to travel from New York to Paris by land. Now "we looked hopelessly through the grimy window at the mournful poverty-stricken huts looming through the dusk, and cursed the scheme that had landed us among them and their foul inmates." [7] Everything had gone awry.

The first terrible disappointment of the journey had been encountered at St. Michael, Alaska, when DeWindt was told that a winter crossing on the Bering Strait sea ice would be dangerous. He had so wanted to cross the narrow fifty-six-mile gap on foot. Why he yearned to cross in this manner when ferry service was available is not too clear. At other stages of his journey he had walked only when no other alternative existed. Trains, steamers, and riverboats had carried him from New York to St. Michael, save for a short stretch from the Alaskan coast over the Chilkoot Pass to the upper Yukon River. And that one pedestrian excursion had not been a happy one—at least judging from the harrowing account he gave of its hazards and rigors. Perhaps the greatest feature of his disappointment was in having to wait five weeks at St. Michael until the U.S. Revenue Cutter Service's Bear arrived to provide transport across to Indian Point, Siberia, once a popular resort for American whalers.

But to return to his immediate perils and the hopes he had vested in the bravely fluttering Union Jack; why was it that DeWindt's life depended upon the chance sighting of the flag by a whaling vessel?

Starvation was no immediate threat; shelter was available; the Chukchi were difficult and disinclined to carry them to Anadyr by dog sled, yet posed no physical threat. Why then the hysterical reaction?

One must look deeper into the situation to find out the unpleasant truth—which was that DeWindt, despite his fiercely aggressive moustache, was unworthy of the tradition of British empire builders. Alas for the shades of the like of Alexander McKenzie, David Livingstone, and Richard Burton. DeWindt, despite his exertions as a traveler to out-of-the-way places, did not have the necessary mettle. Too much time in the cafés and racetracks of Paris had sapped his initiative. He was but a pale shadow compared with the great travelers of the day, and he was a liar. Happily, an American whaler spotted the flag and took the two travelers to Nome.

DeWindt's achievements as a traveler brought him an invitation to lunch with President Theodore Roosevelt. Roosevelt knew a great deal about the North and was not impressed by the railroad idea. "The president seemed to derive infinite amusement from the idea of connecting the two continents by rail and especially when picturing the condition in which unfortunate passengers might be expected to emerge from the train, after a breakdown in the glacial neighborhood of Bering Straits!" [8] Still Roosevelt "grandly commissioned" DeWindt to place a car at his disposal on the first New York–Paris express. [9]

Things often went wrong for DeWindt. He did not seem to care much for people or for the places he journeyed to so strenuously. Alaskan Indians were "the laziest and most impudent scoundrels" he had ever seen until he encountered the Chukchi. [10] Nome, St. Michael, and other Alaskan towns were repellent to him, and he could not understand why travelers praised the beauty of Japan. Too many Americans he met were without good breeding and hence, distasteful to the fastidious traveler. Even the presidential luncheon went awry: The company was good, but wine was not served!

THE VIEW FROM NOME

Nome gold discoveries and the possibility of similar mineral wealth in Siberia sparked interest in an Alaskan-Siberian railroad connection in 1901. But visions of rails bridging continents were not enough for tight-fisted financiers: They needed substance, some solid assurance of gain; and the sudden emergence of a populous, thriving Bering Sea settlement suggested a genuine economic potential for the scheme.

A front-page story in the *Nome Nugget* of August 30, 1901, heralded the newest railroad project. "James Hill is interested." [11] Hill was the famed builder of the Northern Pacific Railroad, and if he took an interest, the project could be no chimera. "A dispatch from St. Paul says it is no myth." [12] Miners in Nome were having their woes in 1901. The corrupt federal judge Alfred Noyes and the powerful Republican politician Alexander McKenzie were making a brazen attempt to steal the richest mines from their discoverers, but they could not help but be excited by the news from St. Paul. If a railroad were to be built, the Bering Sea frontier could become one of the bustling trade centers of the world!

On October 18, 1901, the *Nugget* had more particulars on the proposed railroad. A ferry would carry the cars across the Bering Strait. This seemed a fine and economical solution to bridging the gap. It would do well for the summer season, but no one had suggested how traffic would pass through the ice-strewn waters the other eight months of the year. But the Trans-Alaska Company of Denver had been formed. J. J. Frey was president. The company had been incorporated in Washington state and would issue $50,000,000 in stock.

Hopes remained buoyant throughout 1902. The iron trail must surely come. Readers of the *Nugget* were treated to the comprehensive reflections of the editor on the railroad and on Siberia development generally. Editor Strong reflected on the entire Siberian scene in a statesmanlike way. He had some doubts concerning "the status of those persistent promoters who claim to be in the possession of large Russian concessions, and on their strength try to induce American capital to invest in some Siberian scheme." [13] Such promoters had been quite visible on the Pacific coast for years "and have naturally penetrated to the new field of Nome of late. If they are not outright imposters or frauds, they have simply exploration permissions and letters of introduction to Russian officials in whichever territory they intend to operate," documents which were a far cry from legally established concession rights.[14]

Strong reviewed the history of the American-Russian trade relationship as it was understood in Nome. Russia was set in her ways and too "far-sighted today to let trading concessions for the sake of a little extra revenue" if it would interfere with "established customs and police regulations on its Pacific frontier." [15] Strong pointed out that when the United States government asked permission to establish a reindeer-purchasing station on the Siberian coast, approval was not given directly; yet Russian officials were willing to shut their eyes if such a station was set up. "Likewise, Russia has been willing to shut its eyes to the trading by the American trading vessels with the native population along the Bering sea coast of Siberia." [16] Russia could stop this trade any time, Strong believed, but rather than establish a customs service on the Bering Sea, it had preferred to let this smuggling and trading go on unmolested. "During the last twenty years only three small trading vessels have been seized there by the Russian cutters, and these were all caught in the open and direct act of selling whiskey to the natives." [17] American vessels were often boarded by Russian officials who examined their papers and made superficial searches for contraband cargo, but if the American "happened not to be an outright blockhead," he was treated politely enough.[18] "On general principles they would, of course, be warned and requested to leave the waters in a specified time." [19]

Things would change now. "With the discovery of gold at Nome a new epoch has begun." [20] Russian officials would understand that trading and other activity is bound to increase and would establish custom houses and ports of entry north of Petropavlovsk. Russian statesmen would be as farsighted now as they had been earlier in selling Alaska to the United States, predicted Strong. Transportation systems would be developed. "For the last twenty years all Russian military maps of railroads and projected railroads have shown a projected road extending to the Bering straits." [21] Russia needed such a road in its operations in eastern Asia and against China. In time, the Russians hoped the Celestial Empire would become a dependency of Russia. All this would be greatly facilitated by a Bering Strait railroad which would carry the manufactured products of America to Russia. "Alaska should be made the needed storehouse, from which Russia could draw as required all the supplies needed to carry on its aggressive policy." [22]

A few days later the *Nugget* assured readers that the railroad would be built. "Let him scoff who will." [23] Strong was neither the first nor the last to prophesy on the glowing future of Alaskan-Siberian commercial ties and to argue for the necessity of the railroad. He was an intelligent and cultured man and in time became governor of Alaska. But alas, when he left office in 1922, the two great continents were still unbridged by a railroad. Yet something of what he predicted did occur, if only fleetingly. During World War II, Alaska was to some extent "the needed storehouse," helping Russia carry on "its aggressive policy." The air transportation link developed at that time did not owe its origin to any change in Bering Sea geography—but to Russia's military needs.

In the spring of 1902 a Seattle entrepreneur, John Rosene, organized the Northeastern Siberian Company for the exploitation of Siberian minerals. Technically the firm was based in St. Petersburg to suggest Russian ownership, but in fact its operation was to be directed from Seattle. Rosene had secured V. M. Wonlarlarsky's Chukchi Peninsula mineral concession and retained the Russian as the figurehead director of the corporation, assuming the modest title of American and Siberian manager for himself. Besides taking on the development of a mineral industry in Siberia, Rosene intended to establish trading outlets in Siberia and Alaska, build railroads in Alaska, and provide steamship service to Siberia and Alaska from Seattle.

Rosene was a capable organizer. In May he chartered the S.S. *Manauense*, took on a cargo of supplies, and steamed from Seattle to Vladivostok. There he hired 125 Russian miners and carried them north to St. Lawrence Bay, Siberia. At St. Lawrence Bay he established the company's first trading station. Others were set up at Emma Harbor (Plover Bay) and East Cape, Siberia. Prospectors soon reported promising indications of gold and silver. All prospects seemed bright. There was plenty of ivory, furs, and whalebone to be gathered in exchange for trading goods. Prices were favorable. For one brick of tea and a two-pound bundle of tobacco Siberian trappers were pleased to offer the prime pelt of a white fox. Rosene figured that the company could eventually extend its operations into other enterprises. The Bering Sea salmon fisheries were among the most prolific in the world and should be developed by the company.

In July 50 prospectors hired by the company were shipped from Nome to Emma Harbor. Nome, at least in the summer, would be the hub of much of the Siberian activity. All the mail for company personnel and a good portion of company supplies would be directed to Siberia by way of Nome.

One of the men taken on at Nome was a down-and-out prospector named W. B. Jones. He was glad to get the work after a jobless winter hanging around the Northern Saloon. Tex Rickard of the Northern Saloon was a generous man, but there was a limit to the hospitality he would extend. Jones and other Nome men wrote to friends of their Siberian experiences; so the Nome newspapers did not have to depend upon company publicity handouts to learn what was going on.

Some of the American miners did not feel comfortable on the Russian side of the Bering Strait, but to most it was all in a day's work. They were used to the climate, the tension, and the isolation. As experienced northern mining men they went to work with a certain *élan*.

> Forty strapping miners,
> With shovel, pick and drill,
> Were ripping up Siberia
> From mountain peak to rill.
>
> They broke into the treasures,
> Down in the soaking mould,
> Where the hoary ice-bing
> Had stored his virgin gold.
>
> They sheared the Laurentian mountains
> With graphite laden deep;
> They drained the mossy marshes
> Where silver lay asleep.[24]

So sung John Kelly, one of the company men.

In April of 1902 rich gold strikes were reported in Siberia. Captain Seim gave a lecture to the literary society concerning his own travels in northeastern Siberia. The gold was there and the rails would follow. Throughout the spring and summer, Nome newspapers reported on the Rosene company's activities in Siberia. Rosene was interviewed by the *Nugget*. He was optimistic and hoped to be able to say someday, "Have a nugget with us." [25] Great days were coming.

In July the *Nugget* reported a great gold strike made in eastern Siberia. This was significant, but not too important for Nome, since it was supposed to have been made near the Manchurian border.

An interview with E. B. McCowan, a prospector, appeared in an August edition of the *Nugget*. He had just returned from across the Bering Strait and expected "word of a big strike each day." [26] There were also signs that Plover Bay held immense quantities of petroleum.

Morale was high among American miners in Siberia. They were treated like princes by Rosene.

The Russian revenue cutter *Yakutsk* reached Nome in September, with the acting governor of Siberia aboard. He had come to confer with Rosene about mining and trade matters.

One of the American miners wrote a friend in Nome. He was leaving the Rosene company. Nothing of importance had been found. He was going to get a dog team "and strike out for the tall timber" in November on his own.[27]

Nome newspapers had little to report of Siberian or railroad affairs during the 1902–3 winter, but the tempo picked up in the spring. Rosene was in Paris during March and would soon leave for St. Petersburg to make arrangements for a "large development" of mining and fishing.[28] The company had a large tract of gold land. A supply ship would leave Seattle for Siberia on April 15. It was also announced that Rosene's Northwestern Commercial Company had contracted with the American government to buy and deliver Siberian reindeer to Alaska. Later this transaction was nullified by the czar's government: Americans were denied permission to buy reindeer for exportation. Aside from this, the August news from Siberia seemed good. Vague reports of important mineral discoveries continued to circulate. Rosene's partner, Colonel William Perkins, called at Nome en route to Siberia to inspect the company holdings. Huge coal fields, "just a short distance from Nome," were allegedly found in Siberia.[29]

Editor J. F. A. Strong reviewed the Siberian prospects for *Nugget* readers in September. Recently a Russian warship, the *Manchur*, had called at Nome, and the crew had been amazed to find the amenities of civilization on the Bering Sea: electric lights, railroad, and waterworks. All this came about because of gold, and fortunately the gold was also to be found on the Asian side of the strait. "Nome certainly has nothing but the good hand for Siberian adventurers." [30] The gold city was the "natural base" for the supply of its vast neighbor and recently most of Siberia's supplies had come from Nome.[31] The future promised equal prosperity to the people on both sides of the Bering Strait.

The steamer *Tacoma* of the Northeastern Siberian Company brought a fine cargo from the Anadyr region into Nome in July—whalebone, ivory, and furs. The company prospectors were still in the field and "hopes were still high." [32] Rosene had other good ideas about opening up

Siberia. Tourism had some possibilities, and there was no point in keeping company vessels idle. Round trip excursions from Nome to Siberia were organized. For only $25, Nomeites could satisfy their curiosity regarding their Asian neighbors. It was a popular outing, but the Alaskans were not particularly charmed by what they saw in Siberia. "Siberia may be rich in everything," wrote one excursionist, "but give me Nome, sweet Nome, every time." [33]

Each October saw the return to Nome of the prospectors of Rosene's company. It was becoming a fixed routine. Rosene's Nome agent, Count Podharski, would issue the usual messages of optimism in regard to the next season, the last steamer would depart for the outside, and Nome would settle down for the winter. Podharski was a Polish nobleman who had something in common with a countryman, Count Benyowsky, who had earlier created a stir in Siberia. Both the eighteenth-century adventurer and Podharski were ladies' men, but this amicable weakness was to bring Podharski to a tragic end. He made the mistake of seducing or raping the wife of Jack Hines, a *bon vivant* of Nome, who did not regard the affair lightly. In fact, Hines tracked Podharski all over the states; he finally caught up with him in Goldfield,

Approaching Nome across the frozen Bering Strait. University of Alaska Archives

Nevada, where he shot and killed Podharski.

The year 1905 resembled those that had preceded it. Gold had not yet been discovered in Siberia but the search went on. Anyway the railroad was coming. "Construction may begin soon," headlined the *Nugget* in June.[34] John J. Healy headed what appeared to be the most serious railroad concern.

John J. Healy made his intentions to build a Bering Strait railroad known in the spring of 1904. Healy had headed the North American Transportation and Trading Company in the 1890s—a firm which provided the Yukon River gold towns with stores and steamboat service. He was a respected pioneer and businessman who had secured powerful backing from the Cudahy family of Chicago for the North American Transportation and Trading Company and could perhaps attract the vast amounts of capital needed for railroad building. Healy predicted that five major railroads would be built in Alaska and one of them would cross the Bering Strait. Editor Strong found Healy and his forecasts worthy of praise. Captain Healy had always been an optimist and was "probably born one so is not to blame. His optimism is of such a cheerful encouraging kind that some people might call it by another name." [35] But

The *Diamond L* on a seal hunt.
University of Alaska Archives,
Lomen Family Collection

not newsman Strong. Healy was a "pathfinder of the Alaska wilds," who has never failed to back his projects "with his own money as well as other peoples'." [36] Furthermore, Healy's knowledge of the North "was not gained from the deck of an excursion steamer," but came from "brushing up with the country itself," so when he spoke of Alaskan railroads, he knew what he was talking about.[37] "He is a wise seer who dips into the near as well as the remote future and sees visions of what is to be." [38]

Of course, Healy was not one of the best-loved Alaskans. As an early trader on the Yukon he had been tightfisted and ruthless. His company had not even given credit to miners. And the real pioneers recalled how Healy had destroyed the healthy, manly independence of the miners of Forty Mile in 1895 by calling on the Canadian government to provide police protection. Before the Mounties reached the upper Yukon River, the men governed themselves through periodic miners' meetings —a system that was revered by some as the parent form of democracy and damned by others as lynch law. But despite his shortcomings, Healy knew Alaska and could probably get the job done. The *Nugget* described the journey that would soon be possible. One would board a Pullman at Nome and, after a few days of easy traveling, would arrive in Paris.

Nome to Paris—a convenient link between two of the most romantic cities in the world.

It is interesting to note that some Siberian natives had become well known to the considerable number of Nomeites who spent part of the year on the opposite coast of the Bering Strait. "I Hope-So" was one character familiar to visitors, and he was not well liked. The *Nugget* was pleased to report that the "old Chukchi, full of years and cannibal honors, was hanged at St. Lawrence Bay." [39] Another notorious character of Plover Bay, Koharra, "chief highbinder of Indian Point" who had maltreated traveler Harry DeWindt in 1896, made the news too.[40] He had been presented with a watchman's scarlet coat and cap by the Russians because he looked after an American natural museum collector in 1900.

In December 1905 word reached Nome that the railroad company headed by John Healy, Baron Loicq de Lobel, and a former newsman and Klondike stampeder, Tappan Adney, had failed to secure the necessary concession from the czar. The *Nugget* did not comment editorially but reprinted a story from the *Dawson News* which expressed no sorrow over the collapse of the New York–Paris railroad. "A much less colossal undertaking would serve to open up the North," argued the *News*; and anyway there would be no traffic for the grandiose Bering Strait railroad to handle.[41] Boosters of Nome were used to such sour and jealous reflections emanating from Dawson City. They could understand the sour grapes tone of the fading gold town on the upper Yukon River that had been surpassed by Nome and would probably be overshadowed by the new Alaskan gold town of Fairbanks.

But John Healy had not given up. He was in Seattle in the spring of 1906 boasting of the railroad prospects. "By 1907 we'll be at work on both sides of the Bering strait." [42] Healy cited the successful trip of Harry DeWindt as clear proof of the feasibility of the whole venture, saying that the czar *would* grant them a concession. The project had "passed by the dream stage," and his company was about to purchase three steamers to carry materials north from Seattle.[43] Tunneling the strait would not be difficult. At a depth of forty feet the sea floor was of granite which would provide a solid foundation. The job would be easier than building the New York subway. Though the costs would be about $1,000,000 a mile, the money "will be forthcoming." [44] So much for the critics of progress: The rails would yet link the continents.

In reality Healy was a discouraged man. Not only was the necessary concession from the czar hanging fire, but money was proving very hard to come by. The chief asset of his Alaska-Siberia Development Company was the control of property at Port Clarence where wharfs and warehouses would be built. But until the rails got to Port Clarence, the value of such property would remain highly speculative. Healy lobbied desperately in Washington for government aid. At the very least, the government should undertake to survey the route. In New York, Chicago, and Seattle he besieged every financier he could get to, painting rosy visions of tremendous future profits. Adverse comments in the press injured his cause. A New York newspaper considered the Bering Strait tunnel a "folly," a project of no value except as an "engineering stunt." [45] There would be no traffic between Alaska and Siberia so what was the point of the enterprise? Seattle newspapers were kinder and more optimistic. After all, Seattle businessmen had a very large stake in Alaskan development. The *Seattle Post Intelligencer* had some doubts about the potential of Siberian commerce, but none at all about Alaska's. A railroad was needed and would come in the future.

In 1907 it appeared that the czar would grant Healy a concession.

The promoter was ebullient. Then suddenly the axe fell. In St. Petersburg, the czar's minister announced firmly and clearly that no such rights would be granted to foreigners. The more the Russians heard from rail promoters of the brilliant future of Siberia once the rails spanned the Bering Strait, the more they worried. Dreams of financial gain were offset by the specter of trainloads of Yankee hustlers invading the Russian provinces, gobbling up all the lands, and dominating the entire national commercial system. No, it would just not do to give the expanionist-minded Americans that kind of a foothold in Russia. Once they got in they would take over everything.

This news finished John Healy. He died soon after, a bitterly frustrated man. John Rosene's company had also fallen on hard times. His trading activities in Siberia made some money, but not enough to finance the disappointing search for mineral wealth. In 1909 he suspended all prospecting work on the Chukchi Peninsula and closed his stores. Efforts that year to raise fresh capital had not been successful. In 1910 Rosene turned to railroad promotion. Rosene was finished with mining but he had other visions. His Trans-Alaska-Siberian Railway system would link Controller Bay of south-central Alaska to rich coal fields of the interior then go on to tie the continents. "The resources of Alaska for the people" was the slogan of his Northern Exploration and Development Company. His advertising brochures urged Americans to be patriotic and invest in an enterprise that would provide American coal to the ships of the U.S. Navy. "Foreign ships now carry our fuel to United States ships." [46] Investors could expect to gain a 25 percent return on their holdings each year.

Rosene launched another rail scheme in 1911. The Alaska Midland Railroad would link the coast at Haines with the interior. Travelers would be able to travel from Seattle to Dawson, Eagle, Circle, or Fairbanks in one-half the time the journey now required.

Neither of these railroads were ever built, but Rosene did join forces with the Morgan-Guggenheim syndicate in 1911. The syndicate built the Copper River Railroad from Cordova to its fabulously wealthy copper mines at Kennecott, and operated it until the mines were worked out some twenty years later.

But the greatest ghost railroads of them all have not yet been built. One can ponder over a map showing the Bering Strait, think about the dreams of Rosene, Healy, DeWindt, Strong, and others, and reflect on what might have occurred had the gleaming rails been laid. In a sensitive mood you just might hear the faint, muffled steam whistle and the labored chugging of a hard-driving locomotive emerging from the Bering Strait tunnel. "Ifs" can be compelling. What might have been our political relationships with Russia in this century if the road had been laid? Would the Russian Revolution have been prevented if America had rushed aid to the czar across the Bering Strait? We might speculate on and on concerning how different things might have been, but we can never be sure what might have happened. Clearly there would have been momentous divergences from the present state of the international situation.

REINDEER

The members of the remarkable Lomen family remained in Nome when gold no longer was easily available and after most of the 30,000 stampeders went elsewhere. G. J. Lomen, an attorney and later a federal judge in Nome, was head of the family. His children included sons Harry, Alfred, Ralph, and Carl, and a daughter, Helen. Carl became the best known of the Lomens. He became head of the celebrated reindeer business, in partnership with Jafet Lindeberg after his father's retirement, and published an account of his unique experiences.[47] The reindeer industry of the Seward Peninsula was, except for mineral production, the only large-scale commercial enterprise the region has ever known.

The Lomens became interested in the marketing possibilities of reindeer meat in 1913 and purchased their first stock from some of the original Lapp and Eskimo owners in that year. Other Lomen businesses at that time included a photo studio and drug store in Nome, and they eventually acquired interests in stores at Egavik, Golovin, Nome, Candle, Teller, and Baldwin, as well as warehouses, docks, and lighterage equipment at all of those places except Baldwin.

Their business venture was unique, and the Lomens saw themselves as something beyond the ordinary entrepreneur. As Judge G. L. Lomen expressed it in his unpublished *In Reindeer Realms*, "The reindeer industry, young as it is, already looms large on our Northern horizon, and is destined to reclaim barren wastes and frozen tundras surpassing in extent the empires founded by Alexander the Great or Genghis Kahn." [48] To create a rich industry for the North, where the natives had always maintained a perilous subsistence standard of living, was certainly a significant undertaking and, for a time, it appeared that this revolutionary effort would be achieved.

First the Lomens had to learn everything they could about the reindeer; later they would educate the rest of the nation. The beast weighed about 300 pounds at three years of age and stood about four and one-half feet high, measuring six to seven feet from nose to tail. Its useful coat varied in color from chocolate brown to white, depending upon the season and the animal. Since its sharp hoofs enabled it to dig through the snow to reach the lichens on which it fed, its maintenance was no burden to the owners. It provided milk, meat, clothing, and even transportation once it had been broken to a sled harness. Thus the reindeer grew fat and multiplied prolifically on the frozen Arctic tundra, a region not generally thought of as rich in natural bounty. Wolves were the only natural enemy of the reindeer, but in the first years of the Lomens' work, they were not too much of a problem. In the 1930s there was a substantial migration of the large Alaskan gray wolf to the north. These powerful animals often weighed as much as 150 pounds and were capable of ravaging a herd.

The family worked together on every phase of the reindeer operation. As the herds grew, the supervision of their ranging, tagging, slaughtering, storage, and shipping necessitated a great deal of travel. There were five big ranges for the Lomen animals, centering on Kotzebue, Buckland, Teller, Golovin, and Egavik. In addition, they experimented with stock on Nunivak, an island south of the peninsula in the Bering Sea, which was rich in reindeer feed. Today a larger U.S. government reindeer herd and meat-processing facility can be found on Nunivak, as well as an experimental musk-ox herd.

With the herds increasing rapidly, the Lomens had to prepare cold storage facilities and provide for means of shipping to the States. Initially, they depended upon the ships of established lines, but in time, they purchased and operated their own vessels. The venture began to pay off as the annual shipments increased from 10,650 pounds in 1916 to 257,000 pounds in 1920. Even so, there was an urgent need to build a larger market for reindeer meat, and Carl spent several winters outside for promotional purposes.

One gimmick that gained much publicity for their product was the exhibition of live reindeer in several cities of the west and east. Many children enjoyed seeing Santa Claus pulled through town on a reindeer-powered sled, while their elders were introduced to the novelty of reindeer chops. Tracing the organization of the Santa Claus campaign increases one's respect for the business acumen of the Lomens. The promotion opened on the first of October, not too early for the cooperating department stores around the country to begin reminding customers that Christmas was coming. Telegrams began to appear in the newspapers of Seattle, Portland, San Francisco, Philadelphia, and elsewhere, describing the activities of Santa Claus in preparing to bring toys to America's children from his northern workshop. From Icy Cape he announced he was "leaving today for Kringle Valley to get my six reindeer left to graze there on Arctic moss and hay since Christmas. Will arrive . . . via Nome, Juneau, Seattle, Chicago about December first. Please notify little boys and girls." [49]

From Icy Cape Santa drove his reindeer sleigh to Nome for sea passage to Seattle, thence taking to reindeer power once more to cross the Rockies to reach the expectant children of the east. Millions of people had their first look at the fabled northern animal during the Christmas season of 1927. The children were ecstatic, and their parents, now being familiar with the handsome reindeer, would hopefully flock to the market to buy the tinned "fancy roast meat balls" or the various fresh cuts.

When the Great Northern, Northern Pacific, and Milwaukee Railroads agreed to serve reindeer meat on their diners, it seemed a significant breakthrough. Special reindeer menus called attention to the novelty, and passengers were given recipe books so that they could repeat the culinary experience at home. But, unfortunately, pressure from the cattle country put an end to this. The railroads were given an ultimatum by the cattle interests: If they wanted to handle cattle shipments, they would have to serve beef. Thus as Vilhjalmur Stefansson put it, "the souvenir menus were destroyed; the cookbooks were thrown away; the reindeer meat was withdrawn from the dining cars." [50]

The peak years of the business were 1928 through 1930 when 30,000 carcasses were sent to the States. These deer were much larger than those of the original herd because of the successful experimentation on Nunivak Island in using the reindeer's cousin, the heavier caribou bull, for breeding. There was also a good market for hides, particularly for the manufacture of gloves. Still another product was the manufacture of feather-weight flying suits from reindeer fawn furs—but the days of open cockpit planes were numbered.

In seeking capital investment for the reindeer corporation and a wider market for the meat, the Lomens had to be imaginative. It was not enough to advertise that reindeer had "the juiciness of beef and the texture of lamb—and a delicate flavor." They had to issue special recipe leaflets that showed the best ways of preparing the meat as "Reindeer Hunter Soup" or "Reindeer Goulash Hungarian Style." Their advertisements had to emphasize that "Reindeer is not venison" and that the meat was more economical and nutritious than beef, pork, and lamb.

In the latter argument, they made use of the testimonial of a "world famous dietitian" who assured Americans that when they learned to "eat reindeer meat at least once a week they will be a healthier race." Much was made of the healthiness of the reindeer themselves. They were free from contagious diseases, as beef cattle were not, and the Lomens' advertising copy—without too blatantly raising the specter of tuberculosis—suggested that its human victims would benefit from a reindeer-meat diet.[51]

Another advantage to the business came from the prophecy in the 1920s that the nation faced a beef shortage. The *Brooklyn Daily Eagle* of April 10, 1927, devoted a page to a story headed "When Beef Gets Scant on Bill of Fare." Experts, including Chicago meat packers, saw a scarcity developing within eight years. Happily for the meat eaters, a spokesman for the U.S. Department of Agriculture argued that the gap could be filled by the reindeer industry of Alaska, where herds up to 444,000,000 could be supported. Without reservation, the Lomens were delighted to confirm their ability to prevent any such catastrophe to the national well-being.[52]

The threat of the coming population explosion even assured the Lomens the support of William Randolph Hearst. Hearst's New York editor, Arthur Brisbane, wrote Carl that he anticipated a New York population of 50,000,000 people by 1978 and considered the reindeer an important source for the necessary increase in food supply.

The Great Depression hit the Lomens as hard as it did any other business. Not only did the reindeer industry encounter the opposition of American livestock interests, which urged retailers to boycott the northern meat, but they were undercut by federal competition at the same time. Reindeer meat purchased from Eskimo herds was marketed by the U.S. Department of the Interior in Seattle, at from nine to ten cents per pound, when the Lomens were asking twelve and one-half.

This was only one instance of the adverse effect on the Lomens by government agencies. Carl Lomen showed much less bitterness in his published autobiography than he did in his private letters on the government's role. Although all businessmen feel themselves at times to be the victims of high taxation and excessive government regulation, it seems clear that the Lomens had genuine cause for complaint. It was not just the intermittent confusion over whether U.S. game regulations applied to reindeer, nor the frequent investigations by Congress and the administrative agencies into the relations of the Lomens with the natives—but that the government plainly wanted to force them out of the reindeer business.

To many people it seemed wrong that a firm operated by non-natives should be profiting from an enterprise that had been originally intended to aid the natives. Time and again the Lomens tried to point out that in maintaining a payroll of 579 full and part-time Eskimo workers (1929), they were the largest employer of native labor in the North. Earnestly they asked critics to observe that their herd ownership did not prevent natives from maintaining their own stock, and that their leadership stimulated the industry and created a market for the product. Yet it seemed there could be no end to the complaints originating from missionaries, government officials, and the natives themselves.

Finally it dawned upon the Lomens that the Department of the Interior had simply reversed its earlier policy of favoring non-native stock ownership—and that nothing would do but that they sell out. Of course it is hard to judge a specific situation of this nature. One can appreciate the indignation and discouragement of the Lomens, who rightly felt themselves to be benefactors of the North and its people, and still understand why the Interior Department might have considered it better to leave the industry to the natives. Yet, in a region where industry unsubsidized by government has rarely existed, one can sympathize with the free-enterprising Lomens (though it should be noted that the Lomens had attempted to get government subsidies because of their employment of natives)—without accepting their views.

But the U.S. government did not actually buy out the Lomens until 1939. In the interim the most dramatic of all their adventures occurred. This was the great reindeer drive—an attempt to deliver 3,000 animals to Canadian officials east of the Mackenzie River delta. Lomen described this as an unusual trip, and that was an understatement for a route that passed through the Kobuk Mountains, the Brooks Range, crossed hundreds of rivers and lakes over an 800-mile stretch of the most desolate and least inhabited portion of North America. At temperatures as cold as sixty degrees below zero, in driving blizzards, a handful of Lapp and Eskimo herdsmen and their dogs were expected to keep control of their herds and keep them moving toward their destination. It was not so easy, especially when wolves scattered the reindeer and the weather or terrain made it impossible to keep the beasts together. A further detriment was the powerful homing instinct of the animal itself: Whenever possible they would try to return to their home range.

None of the Lomens personally accompanied the drive, but its organization and maintenance demanded much of them. Communication between the herders and headquarters was infrequent, and this added to the anxiety over the safety of men and animals. The drive started from Nabachtoolik on December 26, 1929, and since the summer thaw of the tundra would prevent travel during the warm season, it was expected that a second winter would be needed for the journey. Instead, despite the competence of the organization and the skill of the leadership, it took five years to complete the drive.

Drive leader was Andrew Bahr, one of the original Lapps brought to Alaska to train Eskimo herders. The Lomens were delighted to be able to lure him out of his comfortable retirement in Seattle because no one was so able a reindeer handler. Bahr did all that was humanly possible to keep his herd together, but it was a futile struggle. There was a continual loss along the way, and the original stock dwindled greatly. Happily, nature sustained the size of the herd as each spring's fawns joined the herd. The herders had their increase too. After two years on the trail the Eskimos requested their wives, and the Lomens had them taken by ship to a Beaufort Sea rendezvous. At least one baby was born before the Mackenzie River was finally gained.

In the summer of 1933 the Lomens got word that Andrew Bahr was failing; so they dispatched another deputy to take over the drive. As it turned out, this probably was the cause of a year's delay. Contrary to report, Bahr's competence was unimpaired, but that winter the new man ordered a start which turned out to be too early in the season. They were forced to turn back and lost the whole season's opportunity. Lomen indicates in his book that Bahr had full control of the operation, but the latter's plaintive letters make it clear that the new man was making the decisions—and made a bad one.

Finally, the long travail was ended. Emitting their own formidable cloud of ice fog, the weary animals were at last driven into the Canadian corrals. Only 10 percent of the original stock remained, but there were, nonetheless, almost the 3,000 head that had been contracted for.

Though the sales price amounted to $154,830, it is unlikely that the American company made any profit on the transaction. Each year of the prolonged drive cost more than $30,000 in expenses, and the herd had been on the move for five years. Nevertheless, Carl Lomen expressed great satisfaction at the success of the drive because the reindeer were to serve as the mother stock for the development of a Canadian herd. The Canadian government hoped to provide the same resource for its natives that the Americans had. This was not, incidentally, the only Canadian effort to develop reindeer herds. Vilhjalmur Stefansson, the great Arctic explorer and publicist, maintained a long correspondence with Carl Lomen and was encouraged by the Lomen success. In 1921 Stefansson interested the Hudson's Bay Company in the enterprise and was accordingly made a director of the Hudson's Bay Reindeer Company which established a herd on Baffin Island. An unfavorable report on the quantity of foliage available on Baffin Island led to the abandonment of this project in 1927—much to Stefansson's annoyance.

When the Lomens went out of the reindeer business, they estimated that there were about 1,000,000 animals in Alaska; one quarter of this number were owned by the firm, while the others were native-owned. An immediate decline in the number of stock followed the sale of their business. There was no outside market for the meat; so the herders slaughtered for their own use. Besides that, the ranges were severely overgrazed from the vast herds and required a long recuperation period. Wolves were a constant menace to the defenseless beasts, and little vigilance was exercised against their depredations.

According to a recent study of the industry, there are only 30,000 head in Alaska today—17,000 of which are privately owned by natives—who alone are permitted to own reindeer. Eleven herds are located on the Seward Peninsula; there is one large herd on Nunivak Island, and the U.S. Bureau of Indian Affairs maintains a model herd at Nome. Economist Dean Olson—whose "Reindeer Ownership in

Alaska" is the source of these contemporary figures—is pessimistic about the future of the industry, since federal law now prohibits field slaughter of meat to be sold. Owners are now required to drive their herds to a packing plant in Nome, an economic inconvenience as well as a disruption of traditional practice.

Carl Lomen observed this decline, in the years following the firm's withdrawal from the industry, with sincere regret, never losing his confidence in the value of the animal. "We are convinced," he wrote in his autobiography, "that the reindeer industry can once again prove of great value to the people of Alaska and the far North. A domesticated animal that can live without shelter in the Arctic the year round and feed itself, that lives free of disease and furnishes fine meat and beautiful skins to make the warmest garments ever developed for Arctic wear, is certainly worthy of further serious study and development by both government and private industry." [53]

Lomen wrote in 1954, Olson in 1968. Now as oil derricks are raised on the once empty plain across which the great reindeer drive to the Mackenzie delta was made, and construction of an oil pipeline is underway, there seems even less cause for optimism. For better or worse, the day is gone when the Eskimo culture might have maintained itself by adapting itself to reindeer herding. The failure, at any rate, was not the fault of the ambitious and persevering Lomens of Nome.

14 FUR SEALS AND INTERNATIONAL CONTROVERSY

Russian fur traders destroyed the Aleuts who resisted their intrusions and enslaved the survivors without stirring world opinion to any extent. They hunted the sea cow to absolute extinction and almost hounded the Bering Sea otter out of existence—and no one complained. American whalemen reduced the whale and walrus population of the Bering Sea drastically, affecting the capacity of Eskimos to maintain the modest catch that was necessary to their survival—and no effective protest was made. Then it was the turn of the fur seal to face the threat of extermination and, at last, there was an explosive response to the decimation of a Bering Sea resource. Times and conditions had changed. The first great international controversy over the exploitation of the Bering Sea erupted with a shock that led to the dispatch of ships of war into the troubled waters, caused the arrests of ships and crews, and brought harried diplomats to the conference tables. Now the issue was not one of the oppression of an aboriginal people, nor the conservation of valuable mammals—though conservation sentiment was drawn upon— but an issue of national interest. And national interest, fomented by powerful economic concerns, made all the difference. Quite suddenly, the Bering Sea was in the international limelight. Events there had significance. Clamors and alarms sparked by the outraged sensibilities of nationalists raised clouds of war, and it was high time for statesmen to ponder over maps of hitherto neglected regions and wonder how to avert an armed conflict.

224

THE FUR SEAL ROOKERIES

The cause of all the furor was an inoffensive marine mammal that inhabited two specks of islands in the Bering Sea. St. Paul and St. George, two tiny islands forming the major land areas of the Pribilofs— named for the Russian fur trader, Gavrila Pribylov, who discovered them in 1786—are unique in being the breeding grounds for the northern fur seal. These islands and the Commander Islands—of which Bering Island is the largest—and Robben Island near Sakhalin Island, are the destination of the Pacific Ocean fur seal, which migrates to the northern islands each summer for a few months to breed.

About the first of May, the date varying with the seasonal breakup of the ice pack, the first bulls haul ashore on the Pribilofs. The earliest arrivals seem to be scouts whose purpose is to investigate the security of the designated rookeries, and they are soon followed by other veteran bulls. Once ashore, the bulls take their positions as beachmasters, establishing a small territory of their own. In June the cows gradually appear and land on the rocky shores, where they are rounded up into the harem of the nearest bull. Up to a hundred cows—though the average is usually thirty—form a harem watched over zealously by a single bull, who drives back any cow venturing to escape back into the sea. Within a month, the pregnant cows give birth, completing a ten-month gestation cycle. Very soon afterward the females are in heat and the rookery scene becomes enlivened.

The harem bulls then begin servicing the cows, each in turn, but not without considerable turbulence. There is no pell-mell mating practice among fur seals. Only the dominant, fully mature males hold the privilege, one that they must defend vigorously against the encroach- ments of the bachelor bulls who reach the rookery soon after the arrival of their seniors. Bachelors establish themselves in less accessible parts of the shore, where they are cut off from the sea by the bulls and their harems. Their opportunity for mating depends upon their resourcefulness and strength. Once the cows have pupped, usually within a week of their arrival, the bachelors attempt to break up a harem and drive some of the cows to their own ground. The harem bulls defend their cows with a fierce fighting instinct, roaring defiance and lunging at the intruder. In the struggle that continues throughout the mating period, the old bulls either prove their fitness to survive as beachmasters or go under. During this entire three-month sojourn, the beachmasters never leave their position for food, but must subsist on the fat stored during their winter feeding. Cows, however, slip away from the rookery from time to time, swimming as far as 300 miles in search of feeding grounds, and return within a day or two to nurse their pups.

In actual fighting, as distinguished from the sham combats that occur in defense of their chosen ground before the cows arrive, beachmasters strike with their sharp teeth at the invader's foreflipper. If the serpentlike stroke is well aimed, a bloody gash results; if the flipper is protected, each mammal seizes the other's shoulder or breasts with powerful jaws, clinching and tugging to overturn or push off the other. A marked disparity in strength soon results in the retreat of the weaker. In a more equal conflict, the bulls throw their 500-pound bulks forward again and again, until one yields or succumbs to exhaustion and loss of blood. Cows stand by, seemingly indifferent to the struggle waged over them, though they are sometimes fatal victims of rough handling themselves, if they persist in trying to escape the rookery. Cows are much smaller than bulls, weighing about 100 pounds, and when a bull wants to move his mate, he grips her neck with his jaws and carries her where he pleases.

All this activity produces a deafening din. "To appreciate fully this picture of the animated life of the fur seal rookery, one must take into account the medley of sound that accompanies it," wrote one nineteenth-century observer.[1]

> The bulls are giving vent at intervals to their savage roars of defiance. In their more subdued efforts to maintain discipline in the harem they are constantly whistling, chuckling and scolding in various notes. Mingled with all this is the shrill bleat of the female and the answering call of the pup, which correspond to the voice of the sheep and the lamb, though greater in volume. When it is understood that thousands of these animals are calling and answering all the time, some idea of the uproar and confusion incident to rookery life is possible. Nor is the din and noise peculiar to the day. It can be heard at all hours of the night; in fact, the activity is, if anything, greater at that time.[2]

Equally characteristic of the seal rookeries is the all-pervading stench emanating from the animals' waste—an odor that the wind can carry far out to sea to announce the existence of a rookery.

By the end of July the bulls, having completed their task of impregnating their cows, start to leave the rookery. Weakened by their long fast and their sexual and martial adventures, they gradually move off to catch the fish on which they feed and recruit their strength for the long southerly migration. For many months they will remain at sea until nature again compels them to swim north to their breeding grounds. Bachelor seals, cows, and pups are then left with the freedom of the rookery. Pups first take to the water at an age of one month and by mid-September, still sustained by their mother's milk, become expert swimmers. At the first approach of winter, usually in November, the cows and pups leave the rookery together. By this time, the pups have been weaned and have learned to subsist on fish. Ashore, the pups' numbers have been reduced by fatalities. Some are crushed by the thrashing bodies of their elders, others die of starvation if their mothers meet with some mishap on sea-feeding excursions. Still others have been taken on their tentative swimming expeditions by their greatest enemy— the rapacious killer whale *(Orca orca)*. But most survive to begin the long voyage to southern waters.

BERING SEA CONTROVERSY

"All waters within that boundary to the western end of the Aleutian Archipelago and chain of islands are considered as comprised within the waters of Alaskan Territory." [3] So read one provision of the Treaty of Transfer signed by the United States and Russia, the terms of which seemed to make the eastern three-quarters of the Bering Sea American waters. This division appeared reasonable enough to the negotiators: it protected the Russian coastline and assured that the Aleutian Islands fell within the U.S. sector. It did not, however, anticipate questions that might arise if other nations contested maritime rights in the Bering Sea. In 1867 it was a well-settled proposition of international law that a sovereign power had exclusive control to offshore waters of any part of its land territory extending three miles seaward. An exception at law was recognized in the uncommon instance of a *mare clausum,* a closed sea—one considered to be so intimately a part of the surrounding land as to be acknowledged as belonging to it. The United States made no such claim for the Bering Sea at the time of the acquisition of Alaska and had no reason to do so. Practically, the interests of the United States were confined to the land and nearby waters. Furthermore, the dividing line left waters adjacent to the Siberian coast to the Russians, which would seem to have constituted a disavowal of a *mare clausum.*

In 1870 the United States Congress prohibited the killing of seals and other fur-bearing animals within the dominion of the United States in the Bering Sea and approved a twenty-year lease of the Pribilof Islands to the Alaska Commercial Company—originally Hutchison, Kohl Company. A year later, the company secured a twenty-year lease on the Commander Islands from the czar's government, thus apparently gaining a monopoly of the Bering Sea fur-seal industry. All the breeding rookeries of the northern fur seal were located on the small islands of the Pribilof and Commander groups. In a sense, the shrewd San Francisco merchants of the Alaska Commercial Company had tied together what the Treaty of Transfer had separated. Once again—at least as far as the fur seal was concerned—the Bering Sea was united under commercial aegis. The Alaska Commercial Company maintained a store in Petropavlovsk for the transshipment of seal pelts to China and the purchase of Siberian-land furs for the same trade; though the great bulk of the Bering Sea seal catch was conveyed to San Francisco, and from there to the fur-processing and trade market in London. The arrangement was a happy one for the ACC. The company controlled the only significant industry in Alaska and became, in effect, the heir of the Russian American Company.

One of the founders of the ACC reached Sitka in 1867 to purchase the assets of the Russian American Company. For $155,000 the ACC acquired the Russian ships, merchandise, and buildings—including those on St. George and St. Paul. ACC officials considered their rights to the seals paramount and opened negotiations with the United States government for a leasing arrangement. Before the lease was granted in 1870, the ACC had some lively competition. In the summer of 1868 two other San Francisco merchants sent ships to gather seal skins. Some 365,000 seals were killed that season for the benefit of the California fur dealers. The Russians had been taking only 76,000 skins each year in an effort to conserve their resource, but the Americans were out to reap a quick yield. Aleut sealers were paid in liquor for their butchering, while the American traders caroused with their women. This wanton decimation of the herds and debauchery of the Aleuts was halted in 1869 when the U.S. revenue cutter *Lincoln* landed a party of soldiers and a special

Treasury agent to keep order; the 1870 lease agreement prevented the recurrence of uncontrolled slaughter.

International complications concerning the Bering Sea arose with the development of the pelagic sealing industry. In 1879, commercial interests—mainly of San Francisco and Victoria, British Columbia—began outfitting schooners for the hunting of migrating seals at sea. Schooners watched for seals off the Washington coast in February, then pursued them north as they headed for their Bering Sea rookeries. From a total of 16 schooners in 1879 the pelagic fleet increased to 34 in 1883, when the hunters began to operate in the Bering Sea, and 115 in 1889. Their take rose to 15,000 seals a year in 1882 and 60,000 by 1895. Even if these figures represented only the actual kill, their numbers would have been significant; but, in fact, the recovery of animals shot at sea was a precarious endeavor. A yield of 15,000 pelts entailed the killing of 120,000–150,000 seals, many of which were pregnant cows. It was an ugly, wasteful hunt that threatened the extermination of the Pribilof herds and might have achieved it had not the United States government intervened. Fortunately for the continued existence of the fur seal, there were effective lobbyists in Washington, D.C., who were quick to defend the interests of the ACC.

In 1886 three Canadian schooners were seized and taken to Sitka by the U.S. revenue cutter *Corwin.* England immediately protested this violation of the freedom of the seas. Suddenly the Bering Sea became the focus of international attention. For the next twenty years, the rights of maritime nations and the welfare of the northern fur seal was to occupy diplomats of several nations. Initially, the United States defended its seizure of foreign vessels on historic rights it had inherited from Russia. America's diplomats argued that the Bering Sea was indeed a *mare clausum,* a sea closed to all but Americans by virtue of historic usage. In support of its shaky position, the United States cited a Russian ordinance directed against foreign traders—most of them Americans—in 1821. In that year, Czar Alexander II answered the complaints from the Russian American Company concerning the intrusion of American whalers and merchant ships into the North Pacific by proclaiming that Russia's domain extended to the fifty-first parallel, i.e. to the Alaskan-Canadian boundary. A clear ban was issued against "the transactions of commerce, and the pursuit of whaling and fishing, or any other industry on the islands, and in the harbors and inlets, and, in general all along the North West Coast of America from the Bering Sea to the 51st parallel." [4] Only Russian subjects could engage in fishing or commerce in Alaska, Siberia, and the Kurile Islands and their adjacent waters. The restrictions were all exclusive; rights of foreign vessels beyond the three-mile limit were not recognized. Section two of the ordinance or *ukase* asserted that "no foreign vessel shall be allowed either to put to shore at any of the coasts and islands under Russian dominion . . . or even to approach the same to within a distance of 100 Italian miles . . . subject to confiscation." [5] An exception was permitted in the case of ships in distress.

Both England and the United States immediately protested Alexander's *ukase*. John Quincy Adams, then secretary of state, fiercely resisted what he termed a new pretension, pointing out that Americans had long been trading at Sitka and Kodiak with the full approval of the Russian American Company. The czar backed down and made new treaties with the United States and England in 1824 and 1825, giving foreign traders a right to call at Russian ports with the permission of local authorities. Although they were not rescinded, the Russian claims were ignored by tacit agreement.

With the uproar over the arrest of British ships, the Foreign Office swiftly reminded the Americans of the earlier protest against the 1821 *ukase*. The United States State Department defended its stance on the ground that the Bering Sea had not been in question in 1821; deliberations had concerned only the North Pacific between the 51st and 55th parallels. The 1824–25 treaties, insisted the United States, "left undisturbed the right of strict control by Russia 'over all interior waters and over all waters inclosed by Russian territory, such as the Sea of Okhotsk, Bering Sea or the Sea of Kamchatka.' " [6] This was true. Adams had not been interested in the Bering Sea in the 1820s as the area did not attract American commerce. Whether he would have protested the czar's claims if American shipping had been active in the Bering Sea cannot be known, but his protest did vitiate the American hopes of relying on the Russian pretensions in their entirety. It was also difficult for the Americans to maintain their *mare clausum* case in the face of the Treaty of Transfer. Obviously, all the waters of the Bering Sea were no longer enclosed by the lands of one nation. Geographically the Bering Sea had not changed in 1867; politically, it had been severed—its legal unity, if it had ever existed, had been disrupted. Thus the decision of the Paris

Arbitration Tribunal issued in 1893 rejected the position of the United States. The United States had no "right of protection or property in the fur seals frequenting the islands of the United States in Bering Sea, when such seals are found outside the ordinary three-mile limit." [7] The tribunal established a protected zone of sixty miles around the Pribilof Islands; prohibited pelagic sealing during May, June, and July; banned hunting by motor vessels and the use of firearms. These restrictions applied only to citizens and subjects of the United States and Great Britain.

The Paris Arbitration Tribunal's judgment did not end the fur-seal controversy, though it did overthrow American claims. The United States continued to negotiate with other interested powers for the protection of the fur-seal industry. The lengthy correspondence and reports germane to these negotiations fill many volumes. Russia, Japan, the United States, and Britain were the principal parties in a number of discussions carried on over the years. Each party had its interests and arguments, but the chief obstacle to an English-American accord was America's insistence on honoring its commitment to the lease holders, who depended upon their land kill, while calling for a ban on sea hunting. Britain argued long and hard that if, as the United States stridently maintained, the fur seal faced extinction, hunting on the Pribilofs should be curtailed severely.

THE PELAGIC HUNTERS

Pelagic seal hunters were despicable predators to American government officials and to most of the public; yet their side of the story never did receive a fair hearing. They had developed an industry of major proportions that Northwest coast Indians had originated and practiced on a small scale.

The United States government would have been spared much pain and conflict, and the considerable costs of law enforcement by the U.S. Revenue Cutter Service and naval ships, if it had compensated the sealers for their losses of profit opportunities. But this measure seemed never to have been considered seriously. As is usual when the government has turned its attention to the matter of preservation of a natural resource, the struggle to bring it about becomes so demanding that the legitimate interests of involved parties were trampled.

Sympathy for the plight of the American sealers was largely confined to the west coast. The *Portland Oregonian* reviewed the controversy in 1909 in an editorial that was reprinted in the *Pacific Fisherman.* From the start, the United States government's management of Alaskan seal herds was "a grand fiasco." [8] The seals might just as well have been left with the Russians. Government seizures of schooners in 1886 caused particular hardship. Five American and six British ships were taken and their crews were thrown into "squalid Alaskan prisons." [9] Worse yet, the captain of the *Alpha*—which was seized while hunting well outside the three-mile limit—suffered a tragic end. Weakened and demented by the hardships he experienced, the mariner wandered into the forests near Sitka, raging like a maniac, and died there. Claims for compensation for seizures which American sealers put forward were ignored, though the United States government eventually had to pay Canadians $425,000. "The government did not protect its own," and Americans were driven to change their home port to Victoria, British Columbia.[10]

An Alaskan journalist, John Underwood, complained at the discriminatory effects of extending the three-mile offshore limit of jurisdiction. The British did not protest too much, according to Underwood, because London fur dealers handled the pelts taken on the Pribilofs. Their profits were assured and no one cared very much about the rights of individual sealers. "Then arose the term *seal poachers.* Any pelagic sealer—whether he remained outside of Bering Sea or went into the 'grave-yard of the Pacific'—was blazoned to the world as a poacher." [11] Real poaching was in landing on the islands and killing seals, but "not more than four such attempts were made." [12] Sealing captains became outlaws, argued Underwood, because American and Russian governments decided that "the only proper, sportsmanlike, and humane way to kill seals is to wait until the animals have hauled themselves out on the beach, a sanctuary to which they resort for breeding purposes, where they have no chance to get away, and then, when the poor, harmless animals are absolutely defenseless, bravely and intrepidly beat them to death with a club." [13]

Underwood also had harsh words for "certain willing and mercenary scientists" who went to the islands and gathered a "vast number of affidavits to prove 90 percent of the seals killed in the open sea were females, frequently with young." [14] Yet British officials had no trouble getting counter affidavits to present to the Paris Arbitration Tribunal and the "American representatives were confounded." [15]

In Lewis and Dryden's *Marine History of the Pacific Northwest,* a classic of maritime history published in 1895, the sealing matter was presented succinctly—from the seaman's point of view. The ACC resented the pelagic hunting because it lowered the price of furs; so the *Corwin* was sent north to seize sealing schooners. "This act was the beginning of one of the most disgraceful and unjust policies to which the United States government has ever been a party." [16] Peaceful sealers were taken on the high seas. "The *Corwin* swooped down on them, took possession of their schooners, turned part of their men adrift several hundred miles from their homes, without food or shelter; while others, masters and mates of the captured vessels, were thrown into prison and fined." [17] The powerful ACC got its way.

Whatever one concludes about the justice of the restrictions put upon the Bering Sea fur-seal hunting, it does offer an interesting example of international cooperation in the preservation of a natural resource. To accomplish such a thing is no easier today than it was in the nineteenth and early twentieth centuries; yet who can doubt the urgent necessity of fishery and mammal regulation today? The means by which the goals of preservation can be reached will always be a matter of dispute—and, indeed, should be. But a consideration of the Bering Sea controversy indicates that those who take extreme positions can never be reconciled to a position of compromise.

THE NAVY TAKES A HAND

As the international dispute over the question of sealing rights raged on, the U.S. Navy was assigned the task of assisting the U.S. Revenue Cutter Service in policing the Bering Sea. In 1890 the *Alert* patrolled the disturbed waters and boarded suspicious-looking schooners. This was a cat and mouse game that taxed the skill of navigators, and the fog was an ally of the poachers. One naval man observed that the schooner captains had the advantage, with their smaller vessels and their experience in sighting seals and whales at sea. If schooners were apprehended with a cargo of furs, they were arrested and taken to Sitka. When there was no evidence found aboard that would support a conviction, the schooners were ordered out of the Bering Sea.

The 1892 naval fleet sent to the North was commanded by a famed captain, Robley D. Evans, more familiarly known as "Fighting Bob." Evans was a testy character who was willing to take chances on an international confrontation. By this time, England's Royal Navy was also patrolling the Bering Sea and its purpose was also to police, as well as to protect the Canadian schooners against unwarranted interference from U.S. officials.

Evans decided to strike at the support vessels that serviced the Canadian fleet and carried their seal catches back to Victoria. It was a risky venture and Evans knew the odds. "It is sometimes an officer's duty to do a thing that his Government must afterward disavow and punish him for having done." [18] His orders from Washington were stated ambiguously; yet it was clear the authorities wanted the supply ship to be apprehended. There would be no problem if Evans found the ship in an Alaskan port with skins aboard, but a capture on the high seas was quite another matter. "I made up my mind to get her legally if I could, illegally if I must." [19] Even if he were punished, he would have done his duty, and that was his paramount consideration.

While looking for the supply ship, Evans also apprehended several American schooners. Off Kodiak Island "we caught a fool of a schooner captain who had been violating the law; he thought I did not know it, and gave us some trouble." [20] The schooner skipper tried to get away and Evans cut him off, ordered him aboard the U.S. *Yorktown,* and read him the riot act. "I never saw a man so scared in my life." [21]

"Fighting Bob" learned something of Alaskan conditions in the course of his cruise. "The people up here seem to think I am some kind of military governor, or something, and come to me with the most absurd complaints." [22] Evans despised the missionary school teachers who complained to him interminably and advised him on what the government should do. Other Alaskans seemed all right to him, at least in comparison with the missionaries. "They nauseate me. The conditions up here . . . are about as bad as they could be, and the whole business is a disgrace to our government; but I am a policeman this trip for sealers only." [23] Evans was only one of many government officials who joined the chorus of complaints from Alaskans who felt their needs were being neglected. This neglect became even more obvious in the 1898–1900 gold rush era when the lawlessness of Skagway and Nome revealed the inadequacy of the government's administration.

When Evans heard that the supply ship had been seen in Prince William Sound, he dispatched the *Corwin* to make an arrest. The *Corwin* caught the steamer taking on skins in Port Etches, a clear violation of American law, and Evans was most pleased. At Sitka the supply ship was released on a $600,000 bond which, Evans reflected, "paid most of the expenses of our summer's work." [24]

The *Yorktown* found most of the sealing fleet between Prince William Sound and Unalaska. His officers boarded all of the schooners, ordering them to stay out of the Bering Sea. Cruising on through the Unimak Pass of the Aleutians, Evans chased a schooner that attempted to run from the *Yorktown*. Three shots from the naval ship's guns, the last of which splashed within a few feet of the schooner, ended the pursuit. As it turned out, the fleeing vessel was a whaler bound for the Arctic Ocean. Evans commented disgruntledly: "If the people we sometimes hear of who think the navy has nothing to do could come up here among these islands and see the work the navy is doing here and hear the things that are said of it, they would change their minds—if they possess such a thing." [25]

The *Yorktown* continued its patrol of the Bering Sea through fog so thick that "it seemed as if one could make a hole in it with the finger, the finger would pop, like a cork out of a bottle, when it came out." [26] Ship captains rarely dared to leave the bridge for their bunks while navigating the Bering Sea.

Evans took his ship back to Unalaska Island for refueling, and there found something to enjoy: "the mountains covered with snow, and long arms of it running down into the valleys and right into the grass and flowers. No one would credit a picture of it." [27] He was astonished to observe that in five days after the snow melted the grass was knee high and there were lilies, violets, lupines, anemones, and beautiful orchidlike blooms to be seen everywhere.

Leaving Unalaska, the *Yorktown* passed close by Bogosloff Island, a land mass that had arisen from the sea in 1874 as a result of a volcanic eruption. At the time the navy men saw it, it was still active; clouds of smoke rose from its burning surface and rose hundreds of feet into the air.

The *Yorktown* cruised off St. Paul Island of the Pribilofs. No sealers were seen and the crotchety captain had time to worry about more mundane affairs. He heard that Congress was going to give admiral's pay to two captains commanding squadrons and thought he should be one of them. "I command more vessels than both . . . and do more work in a month than they do in a year." [28]

Evans and his sailors got ashore at St. Paul to stretch their legs and look at the seal rookeries. The diversion was welcome, though the Pribilofs—despite a profusion of flowers and the novelty of the virile, teeming rookeries—did not attract Evans. "I begin now to understand why the seals selected these islands for their home: they felt that nothing but a seal could stand the climate." [29] Patrolling the fog-bound waters was a strain on the commander of the *Yorktown*; it was dangerous and monotonous. He would have been glad to give all the seals back to Russia "and these blessed islands with this beastly fog, too." [30]

The Revenue Marine ship *Rush* caught the Canadian schooner *Winifred* and consulted Captain Evans. This was a supreme test of his diplomatic powers which, judging from his memoirs, could not have been his strongest asset. He knew the skipper of the sealer as "the most noted pirate in Bering Sea." [31] The year before, the pirate had raided St. Paul and carried off 400 seals on his *Borealis*; a year before that he had killed 350 seals in a raid with the schooner *Adele*. Evans knew that if the sealer were turned over to the British, no punishment would be inflicted on the poacher, and he was determined to see the man tried in an American court. After much discussion and correspondence with his Royal Navy opposite, Evans got his way. "No one who has not seized an English sealer under the guns of the English navy can know just how much writing that calls for—not to speak of the bluff." [32] The event produced a few more gray hairs for Evans. "I have fits of the shakes when I think of the volcano that was under us, and how close it was to the surface." [33] The American succeeded but it was true that a diplomatic Bogosloff Island had been a distinct possibility.

Evans had landed a naval party on the Aleutians near False Pass to watch for sea otter poachers. Some Aleuts hunting in kayaks were apprehended and forced to give up skins and guns. The navy men also had a brush with a small steamer on a poaching mission. Fog permitted the steamer to escape after the navy personnel had fired 500 rifle rounds at it. "The whole place is a perfect nest of pirates," thought Evans, "but I have not the time to treat them as they deserve, as we must keep constantly moving in order to prevent our Canadian friends from poaching." [34] Russian ships were also on patrol off the Siberian coast and took five Canadian and one American schooner in 1892. All the schooners were condemned and burned. Evans heartily approved of such retribution. "They have a good way of treating such chaps over there." [35]

The Russians kept the skins and left the sealers to find their own way home.

Curiously enough, the United States government did not share Evans' views on the Russian seizures and made a claim on behalf of the sealers that was eventually settled through international arbitration. The *C. H. White* of San Francisco, a sealing schooner, was seized near Copper Island. The schooner and its crew were taken to Petropavlovsk. There the vessel and its cargo were confiscated after the master "was compelled, under duress and by threats of deportation to Siberia, to sign a paper which, being in the Russian language, an unknown tongue to the said master, he could not understand." [36] Russian officials in Kamchatka did not treat prisoners with tender care. The American seamen were closely confined and were not given any medical attention. The skipper of the *C. H. White* fell ill because of this harsh treatment.

One of the most notorious of sealing captains, Alexander McLean, was also arrested by Russians in the Bering Sea near Copper Island. McLean defied the Russians and tried to run from the Russian gunboat *Aleut*, but could not evade pursuit. A Russian boarding party had to fight their way aboard the *James Hamilton Lewis* and subdue the American by force of arms. McLean and the crewmen were taken to Petropavlovsk and later to Vladivostok. The Americans were put to hard labor for a time and miserably lodged "in an unwholesome and vermin-infested building, and inadequately fed." [37] Two of the seamen contracted smallpox; one of them died of the disease.

Several other American skippers were taken by the Russians during the same period. Some were clearly intent upon poaching on the rookeries; others were carrying on what they considered a legitimate pelagic hunt. Either way, they were following a perilous trade.

At last, on September 30, Evans was able to end his patrol. There were now no poachers in the Bering Sea, and the closing of navigation was near at hand. In the last weeks of the patrol gales had been terrific. Evans considered the Bering Sea "the worst patch of water it has ever been my lot to handle: and I sincerely hope I do not have to do it again." [38] To keep order in the Bering Sea the ships under his command had logged 38,398 miles.

CONSERVATIONISTS AND THE ACC

"Here is exhibited the perfect working of an anomalous industry, conducted without a parallel in the history of human enterprise, and of immense pecuniary and biological value," wrote Henry Wood Elliott of the Alaska Commercial Company's Pribilof Islands sealing enterprise in 1886.[39] By 1886 Elliott had long been a recognized expert on the fur seal, whose breeding grounds he first observed in 1872–74. His report for the U.S. Department of the Interior in 1874 had also been full of praise for the ACC, and his enthusiasm for the "wonderful seal islands" was unbounded. Company stockholders reveled in Elliott's writings and congressional testimony; they could not praise his sagacity and sound judgment enough. Other Alaskans cursed him because his optimistic reports on the northern territory were confined to the Pribilofs. Though Elliott knew virtually nothing at first hand of the rest of Alaska, his ignorance did not inhibit him. Though he admitted that mineral discoveries could conceivably lead to some further Alaskan development, Elliott was not sanguine. The lack of agricultural potential would, he argued, prevent substantial settlement. In all probability the vast region would remain a wild, unexploited frontier. This dismal forecast caused others to gnash their teeth in frustration. Most of Alaska's white residents shared one unimpeachable article of faith, namely, that the "Great Land" needed federally funded improvements in transportation, communication, and economic development which, if forthcoming, would reveal the region's riches.

Henry Elliott's emphasis on the Pribilofs was quite in keeping with that of the United States government, from the time of Alaska's acquisition to the end-of-the-century gold rushes. It was as if all Alaska consisted only of the tiny islands of St. Paul and St. George in the Bering Sea. Compendious reports based on investigations ordered by Congress were published in the 1880s and 1890s, while the rest of Alaska was comparatively ignored. The controversy over pelagic sealing was the chief reason for concern with the Pribilofs and inquiries focused upon the fur-seal population and its conservation. Another reason for congressional interest arose out of charges levied against the ACC. Vociferous opponents of the company who did not share Elliott's belief in "the perfect working of an anomalous industry," claimed that provisions of the twenty-year lease had been violated, that the killing quotas had not been observed, and that the Aleuts were being mistreated.

According to the terms of the 1870 lease, the ACC was permitted to kill 100,000 seals each year. In return for this exclusive privilege the company was to pay a yearly rental of $55,000 and a revenue tax of

$2.63 per skin shipped from the island. The killing of female seals or seals under one year of age was prohibited; killing could only be carried out in June, July, September, and October, and no firearms could be used. Aleuts were to be paid forty cents for each seal they skinned and one dollar a day for any other labor they performed. In addition, the company was to provide housing, schooling, firewood, and some provisions for the natives. This paternal status of the ACC was unique to the Pribilofs. No other Alaskan natives were protected in the same way; nor was any other commercial enterprise granted similar rights and obligations. In effect, it was a means of continuing the Russian system of wardship, while securing some economic benefits to the Aleuts. Although the provisions made for the Aleuts were generous, the situation was an unusual one, and it provided the ACC's opposition with an inflammatory point of attack.

Attacks on the ACC originated in a San Francisco newspaper, the *Alaska Herald*, edited by a Russian, Agapius Honcharenko. The *Herald* commenced its semimonthly publication in 1868 with articles in Russian and English. Honcharenko, who styled himself "Bishop of Alaska," proclaimed that his chief purpose was the defense of Alaska natives against commercial exploitation. But he and the other backers of the newspaper had other interests as well, particularly in the development of Siberian and Alaskan trade.

"The trade with Alaska and Siberia is becoming larger every day," announced the *Alaska Herald* to its advertisers in 1870. "These countries have immense and rich resources, and all supplies for them must be drawn from this city." [40] Merchants wishing to do business with the Russian-speaking population in Alaska or Siberia should advertise in this paper, "so that their houses may be known throughout Siberia, the Aleutian Islands and Alaska." [41] San Francisco was indeed the center of northern trade from the time of the Alaska purchase until the 1898 gold rush, when Seattle took the lead; and the pages of the *Alaska Herald* provided all the shipping news and propaganda a reader could wish for.

Agapius Honcharenko was actually the spokesman for the merchants of San Francisco, who had been outraged when the Alaska Commercial Company was given an exclusive lease to the Pribilofs. At that time it looked as if the withdrawal of the Russian American Company from Alaska would precipitate a tremendous boom in the North. Enterprising Americans flocked to the old Russian-American capital of Sitka and started to boost the region's prospects.[42] A continuing wave of emigration from the south was stridently predicted by the merchants of Sitka. There seemed to be no limit to what could be accomplished now that Alaska was in American hands. But interested San Francisco merchants knew that it would not do to allow the ACC to reap all the gains that were to be made.

In June 1868, the *Herald* reported that the last governor of the Russian American Company, Prince Maksoutoff, had been hired by a San Francisco firm to dissuade the Russians in Alaska from returning to their homeland. Since the *Herald* spoke for all peoples of Alaska—Russians and natives—Honcharenko did not hesitate to encourage Alaskans to resist the prince. "Break away from your old imperialistic notions of abasement to family, rank or show nobility, conferred on men whose honesty even you cannot confide in." [43] If even a prince tries to enslave you by force or threats, or appeals to your ignorance or timidity, "fear not, let him find out that you are free men indeed." [44] What Honcharenko was really saying to the Russians of Alaska could always be determined by a close reading—don't hire out to that perfidious San Francisco firm that is seeking to dominate northern trade.

According to the *Herald*, a certain firm was out to destroy it in order to block circulation of Alaskan news, "but we are glad to say they did not succeed." [45] The *Herald* was a fearless advocate of truth and would fight the monopolists on behalf of all who were against the granting of exclusive privileges.

In a later issue, the *Herald* identified the firm which it feared.[46] It was, of course, the Hutchison, Kohl Company, later to be the Alaska Commercial Company. This firm dared to offer Honcharenko money if he would stop writing about monopolistic practices and about Prince Maksoutoff, but the *Herald* still speculated on what was happening in Alaska. Could it be that the U.S. Customs agent and first American mayor of Sitka, William Summer Dodge, was in the pay of the Hutchison, Kohl Company? Dodge, who was Sitka's number-one booster and the owner of many town lots, struck back with an article in the *Alta California*, another San Francisco paper, charging the *Herald* with making false charges and praising the Hutchison, Kohl Company.[47]

Despite the *Herald*'s attacks, the ACC did get its monopoly in 1870, but Honcharenko did not lose interest in Alaskan affairs. He was, after all, the Bishop of Alaska and had the spiritual and physical welfare of the natives at heart. An editorial entitled "A Voice from the Indians of Alaska" cried out against despotism, the debauchery of the liquor trade, and the brute force by which traders "seduced, polluted and ravished our daughters, our wives, and even our mothers." [48] When natives protested this treatment, they were denounced as "brutes and savages."

The *Herald* continued to denounce the ACC and defend the cause of Alaska natives for years. Its reporting on the natives did not reveal much editorial knowledge of native culture, nor did its stories reflect a genuine understanding of what was actually taking place in the North. Humor seldom intruded the self-righteous pages of the *Herald*, though one story about Aleut customs came close to it. Aleut women place fur seals before the shrine of the Virgin when they hope to have an easy birth. "The priests 'lay hands' on the valuable offerings, and thus the double swindle of the immaculate deception and the immaculate conception go hand in hand." [49]

Another publication, a pamphlet which appeared in 1875, "A History of the Wrongs of Alaska, an Appeal to the People and President of America," was a widely distributed assault on the ACC and the lease arrangement. Publication of the pamphlet (which was credited to the Anti-Monopoly League of the Pacific Coast) and the fulminations of the *Herald* resulted in an investigation by Congress in 1876. Testimony before a House committee revealed a connection between the *Herald*, the Anti-Monopoly League, and a combination of San Francisco fur merchants who resented the profitable ACC lease. A man named Robert Desty testified that he had written for the *Herald* for six years but had since decided that its slanders of the ACC were false.

Desty claimed to have written nearly all the attacks against the ACC that appeared in San Francisco papers from 1869 to 1876 and, in a letter to the House committee, repudiated his slanders. "Being a poor man, and a writer, I wrote upon this subject such things as I was required to write by those who employed me; and being a radical in politics, of the French school, I was the more easily deceived." [50] Desty confessed that the purpose of the fur merchants "was to raise a clamor against the Alaska Commercial Company and by charging fraud and oppression continually, make the company so odious to the public that congress would take action toward the abrogation of its contract of lease." [51]

Desty's testimony concurred with that of several fur traders who admitted that their attacks on the ACC were based on false information and motivated by self-interest. Accordingly, the House committee exonerated the ACC.

Other investigations confirmed the compliance of the ACC with their lease and defended its treatment of the Aleuts. Henry Elliott drew a sharp contrast between conditions under Russian rule and those he observed in the 1870s. Under the czar's rule, the Aleuts' life was miserable. "They were mere slaves, without the slightest redress from any insolence or injury which their masters might see fit, in petulance or brutal orgies, to inflict upon them." [52] They lived and died, "unnoticed and uncared for, in large barracoons half under ground and dirt roofed, cold and filthy." [53] But with America's acquisition of the islands, the changes had been marvelous: "In the place of the squalid, filthy habitations of the immediate past, two villages, neat, warm and contented," housed the Aleuts. "Each family lives in a snug frame-dwelling; every house is lined with tarred paper, painted, furnished with a stove, with outhouses, etc., complete. . . . There is no misery, no downcast, dejected, suffering humanity here today." [54] Less fortunate Alaskan natives, Elliott asserted, referred to the Pribilof inhabitants as the "rich Aleuts."

Elliott considered the Aleuts one of the "lower races," likely to relapse into drunken orgies when the opportunity was provided and too much addicted to gambling. Yet he found them gentle, well mannered, and pious supporters of their Russian Orthodox Church. A modern historian of the Pribilofs, stung by his reference to "lower races," has wondered that Elliott considered "liquor suppliers and gambling instructors" racially superior to the Aleuts.[55] "The sealers interested him" wrote Fredricka Martin, "only because geographic and historic accidents had made them the natural custodians of his fur seals." [56] Martin's strictures on Elliott's racial attitudes were perhaps harsh in view of her own evaluations of comparative animal values. She thought that the sea otter and fur seal were superior to Russian hunters: "When the hunters staggered, besotted, from their dirty lairs to kill, they were murdering their betters." [57] In truth, both Martin and Elliott were unreserved admirers of the fur seal, whatever their reservation about certain people—Russian or Aleut. Elliott lobbied for years against their threatened extermination while Martin charted their sufferings in two passionate books. In the 1870s and 1880s Elliott had been sure that the fur-seal herds were inexhaustible and that the commercial killing was no threat to their existence. In 1890 new census figures showed an alarming decrease in the herds which shattered Elliott's belief in both contentions. It had become apparent that commercial killing and pelagic sealing were capable of destroying the fur seal just as Steller's sea cow had been destroyed. For the next forty years Henry W. Elliott was the outspoken champion of fur-seal conservation. Again and again he appeared before congressional committees to cry out against a commercial exploitation he had once lauded; time after time he issued warnings in testimony and in vehement letters to newspapers. Fur interests and government officials vilified Elliott and tried to destroy his reputation with every devious trick at hand, but he kept at it.

Henry Elliott was an amazing man—passionate, disputatious, tenacious, and devoted to a single cause—the fur seals of the Pribilofs. As he sat for hours, during his initial sojourn on the islands, making wonderful paintings of the rookeries, he was in ecstasy. He and he alone could interpret Alaska and the fur seal to the world. No one knew what he did. Even Georg Steller had not understood the fur seal. It was clear to Elliott that he was the premier scientist of the Bering Sea of his century—and probably of all time.

Elliott was certain of his destiny, but he had vociferous critics. When William Gouverneur Morris, a U.S. Customs official stationed in Alaska, read Elliott's *Our Arctic Province* in 1878, he delivered his judgment to a *San Francisco Chronicle* reporter: "He is the enemy and natural foe of Alaska. He can discuss nothing that is valid in the Territory beyond a fur seal, and although he married into the Aleutian tribe, he persistently decries the country and belittles it on every occasion." [58]

Scientists were not concerned with Elliott's assessments of Alaska's wealth, but were critical of the methods he used to estimate the fur-seal population on the Pribilofs in 1874. Elliott had grossly overestimated the number of animals, and his error contributed to the severe depletion of the rookeries in later years. If the herds were as huge as Elliott had claimed, why should not the Alaska Commercial Company be permitted its annual harvest of 100,000 pelts? This was the government's reasoning and Elliott heartily concurred.

David Starr Jordan, president of Stanford University, reproached Elliott, both for his inaccurate counting in 1874 and his overreaction to the ACC after his second observation of the rookeries in 1891. After seeing the depletion of the herd in 1891, Elliott became a violent critic of the killing practices of the islands' lessee. Elliott was obsessed with the idea that the herd had dwindled sharply because the ACC and the government believed that the prohibition of the killing of female seals was a sufficient protection to the herd. Not so, thundered Elliott before congressional committees, in magazine articles, in newspaper interviews, in public lectures, and in every other forum he could find. Killing of the male animals must also be greatly reduced. The continuance of the lease stipulations would bring about the extinction of the precious fur seal.

Elliott's insistence and flair for publicity pained Jordan and other scientists, who had studied the rookeries between 1890 and 1895 to prepare reports for the Paris Arbitration Tribunal. Jordan believed that the fur seal was threatened by the continuance of pelagic hunting rather than by the ACC's harvest. Elliott's sharp attacks on the ACC, the company he had once praised, detracted attention from the real problem, the urgent necessity of restricting the hunt of migrating seals.

One must pity the government officials and diplomats who were involved in a consideration of the long dispute. A rational regulation of the killing on land and on the sea had to be based on scientific opinion, and what were harassed officials to do when the scientists themselves disagreed on remedies for the herd's protection?

Jordan believed that the 1911 treaty resolved the preservation issue in a sound way. Japan joined in the agreement, and all parties had reason to be content. Killing at sea was prohibited, but the islands' lessee could take an annual harvest that was to be shared with the Japanese, Canadians, and Russians. But there was one man who thought the treaty perfidious. This was Henry Elliott "whose abusive letters to the press over false signatures" flowed in an unremitting stream of denunciation of the government's approval of the rookery harvest. "All scientists," argued Jordan, "knew it was nonsense to stop killing males." [59] Except, of course, Henry Elliott. "The scorn of government employed scientists," as Fredricka Martin pointed out, "had no effect upon the fur seals' representative." [60] Elliott had been wrong once in his appraisal of the benevolence of the ACC, but he had repented and could never be convinced that he was mistaken on the best conservation practices. Elliott was certain and he was wrathful. It is unlikely that any Alaskan interest has ever had as fiery and persistent a lobbyist as the fur seal had in Elliott.

LIFE ON THE PRIBILOFS

Life was curious on the Pribilofs. A U.S. Treasury agent was stationed there throughout the commercial leasing period to supervise the seal harvesting and look after the interests of the Aleuts. During the turbulence of the 1880s, when the poaching threat was at its height, the islanders lived in a state of wariness. The report of a strange vessel lying off one of the rookeries would result in spirited defensive activities. Natives would lay down their skinning knives, grab up rifles or clubs, and dash to the point of the threatened raid. Often it was a false alarm, but each report had to be followed up. Each season a U.S. Revenue Marine cutter patrolled the waters, but the Treasury agents always insisted that more protection was necessary. The poachers were cunning and ingenious, their movements were obscured by the fogs. It was essential that armed men be stationed on both islands.

Aleut diet was a matter of concern. The lease allowed for some seal pups to be killed for food, and some agents felt that this practice should be prohibited. The ACC was willing to provide more canned beef and condensed milk. One agent was against this plan and argued that it would be undesirable to feed Aleuts salt meat all winter when they had no vegetables or other antiscorbutic foods. "If any people may claim to have an inheritance from nature these islanders could hardly be condemned for dismal forebodings at the thought of being deprived of the luscious pup." [61]

In time the Aleuts came to disdain seal meat, and as a result of an increasing dependence on white men's food, they declined physically. The Aleuts seemed to have fared better during the period of commercial leasing than they did later when they became wards of the federal government. Their evacuation during World War II caused serious health problems. A physician who examined the Aleuts in 1946 after they had been returned to the islands wrote an outraged report. "The Islanders are almost without exception undersized and unable to do hard manual labor. This is attributable to the fact that they do not get enough to eat, nor of the right kind of food." The doctor called the food schedule "one of the archaic documents in existence" and questioned the mistreatment of the expert sealers who provided the government millions of dollars by their services. "No fresh meat is available on the schedule except seal meat. AND THE ISLANDER IS NOT ALLOWED TO BUY ANY. Half of the Islanders eschew seal meat and the loss in weight during the last sealing season varied from 2 to 18#." The schedule gave 1,700 calories to each person, while "Uncle Sucker is giving the Germans (prisoners of war) 1,900 calories." What the government had overlooked is that the Islanders were no longer Aleuts: "They are white people and can no longer receive the physical treatment that was accorded to the aborigines who were first brought from the Aleutian islands." [62]

Earlier medical reports had sounded a warning but apparently no notice had been taken because of the war emergency. In 1942, before the Aleuts were moved from the islands, the resident physician called the diet "absolutely inadequate" and pointed out the prevalence of boils and other infections. "This inadequacy starts at the age of 3 months. Under existing conditions a child up to the age of 2 years is issued milk only." [63]

But in the 1870s and 1880s the physical debilitation of the Aleuts was still in the future. They were able to club and skin the seals and scramble over the rocks to defend the rookeries against poachers. The poachers were bold men. In 1876 a Captain Butler and Dr. Thatcher brought a crew of pirates into the Bering Sea on a ten-ton schooner, the *Ocean Spray*. Besides the normal complement of sailors they had picked up twenty-six Indians from British Columbia. Their plan was a simple one. They would seize Otter Island, a small unpopulated rock near St. George and St. Paul Islands, and hold it by force. Otter Island had a rookery that could be easily exploited. Fog defeated the aims of the plunderers. Thatcher and a canoe of Indians went aground on St. Paul and were captured by island officials. The pirates were given a "severe warning" and allowed to go back to their schooner.[64] The *Ocean Spray* proceeded to the Aleutian Islands where the Indians, who were denied their promised plunder, mutinied.

Aleuts were expected to take turns standing watch over the rookeries, but no funds were provided for their pay. In 1882, the natives refused to stand guard without pay and went on strike. This antagonized treasury officials who wrangled among themselves about what action to take. One called for severe punishment and advised that the store be closed and all pay for sealing be stopped. These measures were not carried out, and the matter was settled peaceably when the chief agent insisted that the watch be maintained.

A year earlier the Aleuts had also gone on strike. The issue was a familiar one. Aleuts were accustomed to brewing an alcoholic beverage, *quas,* from sugar, molasses, or whatever sweet substances were available.

Treasury agents always hoped to wean their charges from this practice, which was considered even more pernicious than speaking the Aleut tongue. As agent Harrison G. Otis, who was later to head the *Los Angeles Times*, informed officials in Washington: "Raw quas takes rank as the most villainous compound that ever traversed the human gullet, making the drinker not only drunk but sick also and unfit for work, even after the stupor has passed off." Otis refused to issue any sweets to St. Paul villagers, and they promptly laid down their clubs and refused to do any work. "No sugar, no seals will be." [65] Otis negotiated most forcefully. Unless the workers promised to stop drinking quas and return to their jobs, he would promote the Aleuts from Unalaska to the sealing work. The Unalaskans did the less glamourous and poorly rewarded menial work on the Pribilofs, and the sealers, horrified by the prospect of being supplanted, went back to work.

15 — FORBIDDEN SEAS

"We went north, even to the Pribilofs, and killed the seals in herds on the beach, and brought their warm bodies aboard until our scuppers ran grease and blood and no man could stand upon the deck. Then we were chased by a ship of slow steam, which fired upon us with great guns. But we put on sail till the sea was over our decks and washed them clean, and lost ourselves in a fog." [1] Thus did the Aleut Ulysses Naass, describe his pursuit of the "yellow haired wanderer." Naass was the hero of a Jack London story, "An Odyssey of the North," and a traveler whose peregrinations were even more extensive than those of Count Benyowsky, that superlative travel liar of the eighteenth century. Naass' lovely wife, Unga, was seduced from him by the blond wanderer who was a notorious pirate of the Bering Sea and for years the Aleut from Akutan Island ranged the world to hunt the elusive couple down. While this tale is not among the most convincing of London's works, it does indicate the writer's fascination with the Bering Sea and its real poachers.

"It is said . . . that the yellow-haired sea wanderer put into the Pribilofs, right to the factory, and while the part of his men held the servants of the company, the rest loaded ten thousand green skins from the salt houses . . . the northern seas rang with his wildness and daring, till the three nations which have lands there sought him with their ships." [2] In the end it was not the American, Russian, or Japanese navies who ran down the wanderer, but the vengeful Aleut, who looked on as his rival died of starvation, then killed Unga when she resisted him. Even such proteans as the wanderer could not withstand the purpose of the single-minded Aleut prince of Akutan. It was quite a chase, and the story

248

is neatly tied into the northern gold rush adventures upon which London's fame was established.

But Jack London was not the only writer who was lured by the legends of Bering Sea poachers. Earlier, the great English author Rudyard Kipling had succumbed to the theme with "The Rhyme of the Three Sealers" written in 1893.

Unlike London, Kipling had had no firsthand experience in what he aptly called the "smokey sea," but it is known that he wrote the poem in Japan. In Yokohama he visited the Yokohama Club, a resort of English and other foreign residents and probably heard there of the daring poachers of the Bering Sea. It is quite likely that his informant was H. J. Snow, the English sea otter hunter and sometime seal poacher. Snow was articulate and a member of the Royal Geographical Society, and the two men could have been acquaintances, although none of Kipling's biographers mention Snow. At any rate Kipling's imagination was sparked, and the saga of the schooner *Northern Light* was conceived. The competitive aspects of sealing seemed to have fascinated all those who became interested in it. This poem focused on the rivalry between two sealers and a dramatic incident on another level of excitement and danger beyond that incident involved with evading the protectors of the rookeries. His characters face the constant hazards of foul weather, Russian gunboats, and the vindictiveness of their own kind. Jack London also introduced a deadly rivalry in his sealing novel, *The Sea Wolf.* His rivals were the two brothers Larsen, each of whom was a seal poacher who would run from a patrol boat. But, if their ships met in the Bering Sea, they would joyously engage in combat. London's interest in the two-brother theme probably came from his friendship with Daniel and Alexander McLean, the San Francisco-based sealing captains.

The McLeans prospected for gold in Juneau, Alaska, before they were attracted by seal hunting in 1883. Initially they sailed together in the *San Diego* with the first white crew to hunt seals, then each got his own schooner. Daniel McLean made the record catch in 1886—4,268 skins—on a voyage with his *Mary Ellen.* The U.S. Navy ordered him out of the Bering Sea in 1888, but he went back to the hunt every season throughout the 1880s and 1890s. In 1891 he evaded the Russian patrol vessels and got 2,100 skins from Copper Island. Conditions in the Bering Sea grew hotter, and from 1892 to 1894 he confined his hunting to the Japanese and Kurile Islands.

Alexander McLean skippered the *Favorite*, the *San Diego*, and the *Mary Ellen* in various seasons. His *James Hamilton Lewis* was seized by the Russians off Copper Island in 1892, and he was jailed for four months. After his release he went right back to the Bering Sea, a warier but undaunted hunter. In successive seasons he commanded the *Rose Sparks*, the *Alexander*, and the *Bonanza*.

Where fact and fiction concerning poachers merge and when one derives from the other is often difficult to determine. One of the rousing anecdotes told by Charles Madsen in *Arctic Trader* involves Alexander McLean and concerns an incident similar to that told by Kipling. McLean and another Nome-based freebooter, Captain Herman, got word that the Russian gunboat had departed from its Commander Islands patrol and raced there to grab seal skins from the lightly protected warehouse. Herman and his crew abandoned the skins and sailed away to escape capture. McLean, whose schooner had been disguised as the patrol boat and equipped with a smoke-making apparatus, landed and gathered up the skins. Most of the events Madsen described can be verified, but the Kiplingesque rivalry between the two sealing captains he described cannot be. The events may have occurred, but it is not clear who the protagonists were, nor at what time the incident actually took place. Madsen, like Kipling, gained his information from hearsay; but Kipling wrote in 1893, during the period when poaching was at high tide. Whatever the truth, the legend remains vital. Many a reader who would not otherwise have been conscious of the "smokey sea" or predatory sealers has been captivated by the "Rhyme of the Three Sealers" and, in imagination, has sailed the dangerous waters of the Bering Sea.

H. J. SNOW AND PELAGIC POACHING

"To the strict moralist some of the episodes herein related may appear to savour somewhat of the freebooter," admitted H. J. Snow in his narrative describing twenty years of sea otter and seal hunting in the Okhotsk Sea and the Bering Sea.[3] "The sea-otter hunter and sealer has been called . . . [by rivals] poacher, freebooter, pirate and even worse. He, however, is not nearly so black as he is painted by these unscrupulous slanderers." Snow's defense of the island poaching of pelagic hunters was straightforward. "Certainly sealers sometimes visited rookeries on islands leased to commercial interests, but "almost always with the connivance, invitation, or consent, of the natives themselves." In Snow's long experience, no poacher had ever stolen skins or attacked natives, yet "scores of men engaged in pelagic hunting have been shot down and murdered while hunting near the land, without ever a shot being fired in retaliation by those attacked." [4]

In all the uproar over pelagic sealing and island poaching that ensued during the international controversy that erupted in the 1880s, it was generally conceded that the free-lance hunters of the Bering Sea were a nefarious lot. If Snow's account does not wholly counter this consensus, it does provide us with the point of view of the much traduced men. The strongest point of his defense, the connivance of island natives in poaching, has some merit. If an island's inhabitants benefited by receiving goods from schooners in exchange for allowing sailors to make a kill at the rookery, why should the world's opinion be outraged by a slight loss to absentee concessionaires? And why should such mercantile concern be applauded for arming natives with automatic weapons and compelling them to murder adventurous seamen? Poachers, in Snow's opinion, were explorers who risked capital and lives to reveal undiscovered resources, while the concessionaires were "like that pirate of the gulls, the skua, amongst the kittiwakes, who, instead of seeking his own food, watches until another bird captures a fish, and then swoops down upon him, compels him to give it up, and swallows it himself." [5]

Snow was an Englishman who resided in Japan and owned his own schooner. His chief hunting ground was off the Kurile Islands, that chain of islands stretching north of Hokkaido over 600 miles to approach the southern tip of Kamchatka. For years Russia and Japan competed for dominance of the small, barren, volcanic islands and their Ainu inhabitants, until the czar relinquished claims to the southern part of the chain to Japan in exchange for Sakhalin Island. In the foggy waters of the islands, Snow and his small Japanese crew searched for the valuable sea otter which fed in the many kelp beds adjacent to the shore. Small boats were launched from the schooner for the actual hunting. It was cold, wet work and extremely hazardous. On his first cruise in the early 1870s Snow used an old-fashioned firearm—a Kentucky muzzle loader. Later, a heavy American rifle with a very small bore was preferred. Standing in the bow of the boat, regardless of the rocking sea, the hunter aimed his Winchester at a sleeping otter and fired at the instant the mammal awakened, raised his head, and prepared to dive. The shot was usually taken at a distance of 200 yards. It was hoped that the wounded otter would emerge from his dive within the triangle formed by three hunting boats. Otters had learned a good deal of hunters since Steller's day. They hid behind rocks, taking short dives as the hunter approached, then staked their survival on a long dive that might carry them out of range. Some ran for four hours, diving repeatedly to dodge the bullets. In such a chase hunters expended up to 400 shots, though, on the average, the hunter got his prey within an hour, firing 40 to 50 shots before successfully hitting the otter just as his head emerged after a dive.

The sea otter hunt was exciting, but not too profitable, though each skin was worth $80–$90. Snow killed 1,000 otters on his various cruises from 1872 to 1895, far fewer than Russian hunters used to bring back after one season's efforts in the Aleutian Islands in the mid-eighteenth century. Some years were a total loss because otters were so scarce. On one occasion Snow's schooner was wrecked on rocky, fog-bound reefs. It was this uncertainty of profit from sea otter hunting that lured the hunters to the Bering Sea seal rookeries. Yet to take seals on Bering Island, Copper Island, or the Pribilofs entailed the risk of being shot by the armed guards and ship and catch being confiscated.

Snow listed fifty-two vessels which engaged in pelagic otter hunting in the Kuriles over the last quarter of the nineteenth century. Most of these schooners were from San Francisco, and there were never more than twelve in northern waters during any single season. This fleet was distinct from that which fitted out in San Francisco, Victoria, British Columbia, and other Pacific coast ports for pelagic hunting in the Bering Sea. Kurile Island schooners did not compile an enviable record of achievement. Of the fifty-two vessels, thirteen were lost with all hands; seventeen wrecked with the loss of twelve lives; five were seized by the Russians. By 1895 there was not a single ship fitted out solely for sea otter hunting in the Kurile Islands, though Bering Sea sealers sometimes tried their luck there.

In 1883 Snow and his *Otome* ran afoul of the law when he attempted to poach seals on Bering Island. On his first approach to an island rookery he was seen by the Aleut inhabitants. The Aleuts were armed with clubs and rifles, "and, their actions not appearing to be of a friendly nature, we pulled back on board our vessel." [6] But this inhospitable greeting did not dissuade the skipper. The season's hunting of sea otters had been very poor, and Snow hoped to cut his losses with a load of seal skins. A party from the *Otome* landed some distance away from the point of the initial encounter, under the cover of fog, and the men quickly clubbed 600 seals to death. Skinning took several hours and was interrupted by the appearance of 30 armed Aleuts. Snow's men dropped their knives, dashed for their boats, and rowed out to the *Otome*, while Snow, cut off from his boat, hid ashore. Eventually he made it back to his schooner. Instead of fleeing, Snow took a nap until the *Otome* was boarded by a party from the *Alexander*, an Alaska Commercial Company ship. The ACC held the fur-seal concession for the Commander and Pribilof Islands under contracts granted by the Russian and United States governments. Snow had not anticipated trouble with the *Alexander* but was disabused when Russian naval officers aboard arrested him and proposed to take him to Petropavlovsk. Because the *Otome* had no seal skins aboard, it was not held; its captain was cheered to see it sail away as the *Alexander* made for Kamchatka. Once in Petropavlovsk, Snow had no trouble convincing the Russian naval authorities that he was the innocent victim of excessive zeal, and he was allowed to leave Petropavlovsk on a Russian ship. Just as he was congratulating himself on the successful conclusion of the affair, the *Otome* sailed into the harbor. This time his schooner was seized; crew and ship were taken to Vladivostok where Snow spent weeks protesting the confiscation to Russian authorities and the British Embassy. In the end he recovered the *Otome*'s stores but lost the vessel. It was a bad year for poachers.

In 1885 Snow returned to Bering Island with the *Nemo*, his new schooner. This time he made an agreement with the Aleuts and managed to secure 674 seal skins and avoid any run-ins with Russian or ACC ships. A few years later, in 1888, Snow ran into more trouble. While innocently hunting sea otters off Copper Island, Snow's boat was fired on from the shore. Three of his men were killed, and he suffered several wounds before managing to get his boat back to the schooner.

After this disaster Snow gave up hunting for the vanishing sea otter. The *Nemo* was converted into an auxiliary steamer and Snow joined the pelagic seal hunters in the Bering Sea. Snow tells little about this phase of his career in his book, *In Forbidden Seas*, which is largely devoted to sea otter hunting. Apparently, he had his share of adventures which he planned to record in another book but never got around to doing it. If the evidence provided by his book can be accepted at face value, Snow seemed to be a wide cut above the more ruthless exploiters of the Bering Sea, the savage "sea wolves" of legendary ill fame. He frankly admitted his poaching which, according to his principles, was justified. Whether he debauched natives with liquor cannot be known—he does not mention it. He was tough enough for a rugged maritime activity, capable of thrashing his crew to keep them in line, yet enjoyed a good reputation. Scholarship attracted his interest. The results of his observations on the fauna, flora, and meteorology of the Kurile Islands were published by the Royal Geographical Society and his navigational charts were utilized by the British admiralty. Writing in 1910, he summed up: "I found life worth living during the twenty-odd years I spent in hunting, and whatever other people may have to say about the morality of the calling, it is greatly to be preferred to a life spent in cheating your neighbor in trade, or in other sharp practices which are so prevalent in these days." [7]

THE SEA WOLF

Wolf Larsen, scowling fiercely, paced the bridge of the *Ghost* restlessly. Where were the migrating seals? When will the infernal fog of the Bering Sea lift to permit a safe passage through these dangerous waters? Is that damned Russian patrol boat on the trail of the *Ghost*?

Larsen was a strange, complicated man—half savage, half philosopher, a man of immense strength, powerful drive, and boundless tenacity of purpose. As articulate a man as ever sailed the seas, a true intellectual; yet he was as cruel and merciless as a Tartar warrior. A captain who drove his crew by means of fear, he treated any defiance as a personal challenge and beat offenders with gusto. Murder was not beyond his ken. He was a sailor who worked at a demanding game, who risked his life and his schooner in the hazardous hunting of the northern fur seal, an activity proscribed by the laws of the two maritime nations exercising dominion over the Bering Sea. Larsen was an outlaw, a pirate, a buccaneer, an unashamed plunderer who knew no fear of God or man, nor feared death.

The *Ghost*, after crossing the North Pacific from San Francisco, picked up the cruising seal herd off the coast of Japan and followed it north, "ravaging and destroying, flinging the naked carcasses to the shark and salting down the skins so that they might later adorn the fair shoulders of the women of the cities." [8] It was a wanton, continuous slaughter. The day's end usually left the deck of the *Ghost* running with gore, slippery with fat, and the men exhausted from their bloody work of removing the precious skins. Until a man got used to it and found his stomach, it was a revolting trade. But men will labor at all sorts of disgusting jobs to earn a living.

Only the savagery of the elements could halt the gory execution. With only the fleetest of warnings the *Ghost* was ripped by a storm characteristic of the roaring, higher latitudes of the North Pacific. The wind flung the *Ghost* about like a toy—indeed the tiny schooner was a trifling, insignificant object among the mountainous waves of the angry, tumultuous seas. "It seemed that the end of everything had come. On all sides there was a rending and crashing of wood and steel and canvas. The *Ghost* was being wrenched and torn to fragments. The foresail and the fore topsail . . . were thundering to ribbons, the heavy boom threshing and splintering from rail to rail. The air was thick with flying wreckage, detached ropes and stays were hissing and coiling like snakes, and down through it all crashed the gaff of the foresail." [9] But worse than the plight of the *Ghost* was that of the hunters who were out in their tiny dories when the storm struck. While the *Ghost*, a mere cockle shell, was battered and swept before the raging wind, the ship boats were scattered and swamped. The hunters who could not hang onto the overturned boats were lost. Larsen was able to rescue some of them before the numbing cold of the water curtailed their struggle for life. Others died. A man could only last about an hour in such frigid seas.

Eventually the storm blew itself out. Then the routine was recommenced. On and on to the north drove the *Ghost*. Emergency repairs were quickly made. No time for more than that. The seal herd would not wait; its leaders were moving into the Bering Sea, answering their instinctive siren call, swimming faster now toward their island breeding grounds.

Wolf Larsen, too, was responding to some terrible signal. A malignancy within his powerful body tore at him relentlessly, ravaging the great butcher of the sea as surely he had ravaged the migrating seal herds. Larsen met his end on Endeavor Island, one of the rocky, desolate fur-breeding islands of the Bering Sea. Until his death he remained a potent threat to the other protagonists of Jack London's fast-paced novel: the lovers who were carried unwillingly on the *Ghost*'s last voyage and survived a Robinson Crusoe experience on the lonely, and fictional, Endeavor Island.

Wolf Larsen was a creature of the surging imagination of a young writer who had already won fame by turning his personal experiences into vivid stories. In 1898 the footloose London had stampeded to the gold mecca, Dawson City, with thousands of others. Like most of the other gold seekers, London failed to strike a mineral bonanza, but, a writer born, he fashioned the Klondike excitement into numerous short stories and novels, launching a brilliant career and earning a lasting reputation as an interpreter of the North. In 1903–4 London conceived the story of *The Sea Wolf*, Wolf Larsen. Again the writer drew upon incidents familiar to him. London had been only sixteen years old when he was attracted to the seamen of the sealing fleet who wintered in the Oakland Estuary near his home. As young as he was, he had already had stirring adventures at sea, as an oyster pirate and member of the fish patrol, and on land as an exuberant hobo—adventures which he later mined as effectively as he did his Klondike travels.

In January 1893 London signed the articles of the *Sophia Sutherland* as an able-bodied seaman. The *Sophia Sutherland*, a three-masted schooner of 150 tons, was much larger than most of the sealing vessels, and the young man was delighted to have secured a berth. London made just one voyage as a sealer, following the route traced by Wolf Larsen's *Ghost*, across the Pacific Ocean to Japan, then north into the Bering Sea, before sailing south again to Yokohama—for a riotous shore leave—and returning to San Francisco. But one voyage was enough to provide the foundation for one of his best novels. Who was Wolf Larsen? Certainly not the skipper of the *Sophia Sutherland*, but an unlikely compound of the themes of a strong man and primitivism that the writer was entranced with.

MAX GOTTSCHALK

If Wolf Larsen had never peered through the Bering Sea fog in the flesh, there were other reckless mariners who did exist and were endowed with at least some of the brutal and conniving qualities immortalized by London. There was Max Gottschalk of Nome for one. Gottschalk was something of a legend among the predators who debased Siberian natives with rot-gut whiskey to glean their furs cheaply; engaged in pelagic sealing; and, if the occasion presented itself, raided the seal island rookeries for valuable pelts. According to Judge G. J. Lomen of Nome, Gottschalk would have been a truer model for Wolf Larsen than the veteran sealer Alexander McLean, who was an acquaintance of London's and probably the prototype for the terrible master of the *Ghost*. McLean's exploits were but "milk and water" to the "strong rum of Max Gottschalk's true experiences in his trading along the Siberian coast." [10]

Gottschalk was born in Lithuania; "he was as strong as a bull and knew no fear of man, weather or beast." Lomen saw Gottschalk often on the streets of Nome and knew his reputation for lawlessness, yet admired the pirate's devotion to his family. Gottschalk had paid $2,000 to an Aleut family to secure their beautiful daughter for his wife. "They had several children and oftentimes I have seen him walking the streets of Nome with a child perched on each shoulder and others swinging along by his hands." [11]

For years Russian governments, czarist and Soviet alike, had a price on Gottschalk's head; yet he never hesitated to sail to Siberia for trading. Siberian natives cared nothing for government restrictions on foreign traders. Gottschalk was as welcome to them as more respectable merchants, if he brought what they desired. And the Nome trader knew what that was. Lips smacked as he rolled a fifty-two-gallon barrel of rot-gut whiskey onto the beach and traditional bargaining commenced. One season Gottschalk had trouble with the Chukchi of Cape Serdez. For a time the village had been a dumping place for troublemakers of other regions, and these outlaws resolved to practice a little extortion on their visitor. According to the story Gottschalk told Judge Lomen, the natives demanded $500 to give him his freedom, then added insult to injury by boarding his schooner and stealing another $250. But Gottschalk came out on top in the end. He concealed his wrath, invited the Chukchi to drink heartily of his trading alcohol, relaxed until all the villagers were blinded and befuddled by the tainted spirits, and sailed off with their entire store of white fox pelts.

Gottschalk was no more tender in his dealings with whites. One season his schooner was caught in the ice pack off the Siberian coast and had to be abandoned. He and his partner managed to cross the frozen Bering Strait to Big Diomede Island, where Eskimos fed and housed them until they recuperated. The traders bought a dog team from their hosts and set off for Cape Seward, on the Alaskan side of the Bering Strait, carrying two bundles of valuable furs which they had salvaged from their schooner. Gottschalk, "a man of iron on the trail," plowed ahead of the team on snowshoes, tramping a path for the dogs.[12] Midway across the ice, Gottschalk heard a shout from behind. His partner had fallen into an open lead in the ice. Too bad for him. Gottschalk wasted no time on rescue efforts but took over the team and mushed on to safety. Now he would not have to divide the furs.

Miraculously, his partner was able to save himself. He clawed his way onto the surface of the ice and crawled back to the Big Diomede Eskimo village. Once again the Eskimos tended the white man whose feet were badly frozen. In time he was able to make it back to Nome and promptly sued Gottschalk for recovery of his share of the furs. The pleadings in the legal case make fascinating reading. Sworn statements of the parties tell of Gottschalk's brutality to the people who succored him, of sneaky attempts to hide the furs while the partners were still resting on Big Diomede. Still more strange, they tell of the remoteness of life in a winter-bound Bering Strait village, where the rule of law could not apply, but the strong terrorized the weak. How does a court in Nome deal with the chicanery on Big Diomede Island—a Russian outpost? Did an American court even have jurisdiction? The issue was eventually settled when the disgruntled partners divided the furs equally without testing the competence of the court.

Another season, Gottschalk and two partners ventured off to trap on St. Matthew Island, a small Bering Sea island lying midway between the Pribilofs and St. Lawrence Island. That St. Matthew Island was a designated game refuge, hence closed to trapping, was an opportunity rather than an impediment. A winter's trapping yielded rich results. White foxes and other fur animals abounded. All went well except that thieves are inclined to fall out. The key man of the party was the engineer who alone could keep the one-lung auxiliary gas engine of the schooner going. Gottschalk and one of the other partners were skilled trappers but, they brooded, what if the engineer chose to make off with the schooner and the furs and maroon them on the desolate island? A position of dependence did not suit ruthless men. Then they got an idea. When the warm weather of spring began to break up the ice-clogged sea, Gottschalk chained the engineer to the schooner's gas engine, securing the chain with a padlock from his sea chest. A man who loves his work should not mind a little imposition, Max figured.

When ice conditions permitted, the trappers left St. Matthew Island and landed at a trading post on Bristol Bay. There they planned to dispose of their furs. Dealers and government officials in Nome might be suspicious; it would not do to take the furs there. But the engineer, still

Max Gottschalk.
University of Alaska Archives

chained to the engine, thwarted Gottschalk's plans. While the two trappers were ashore negotiating with the local trader, the engineer filed off his chains, hurriedly raised anchor, and sailed off with the fur cargo intact. The stranded men found an old dory, rigged up a sail, and started in pursuit. Gottschalk reached Nome several days after the engineer and, oddly enough, did not resort to self-help to recover the furs. Instead, righteously indignant and perhaps confused by his arduous exertions, he swore out a complaint for the arrest of the treacherous engineer.

On trial day the courtroom was packed. Everyone was entranced by the new role pirate Max was assuming: that of an injured, law-abiding citizen. The trial was swiftly consummated. The judge asked, reasonably enough, where the furs in question had been gathered. Amazingly, Gottschalk blurted out the truth. "Case dismissed and furs confiscated. St. Matthew Island is a game preserve!" declared the court.[13]

Max Gottschalk's closest brush with death and most daring adventure was also vouched for by Judge G. J. Lomen—who was an assiduous collector of anecdotal material on the colorful characters of Nome. Once the hull of Max's schooner was gouged by an ice floe off the Siberian coast. Max and his partner hauled the vessel ashore and set about repairing the damage. This was soon accomplished, and the men waited for the next tide to refloat the schooner. It was not well for a mariner of Gottschalk's renown to be immobilized within Russian territory. As luck would have it, the Russian patrol boat discovered the Americans before they could clear the beach. Both men were arrested, secured, and thrown into the hold of the Russian ship, which then towed the schooner to Emma Harbor. With unceremonious haste, the Americans were bundled into the log cabin that served as the local lockup. Their fate was uncertain. Would they be taken to Petropavlovsk for trial or just be dispatched on the spot? Max would not risk either eventuality. His warders had made only a superficial search of his person for weapons. They had not discovered the two sticks of dynamite strapped to Max's leg—a little protection he carried against just such a situation.

Gottschalk waited through the night following his imprisonment until all was quiet. At 2 A.M. a thundering explosion shook the village. Gottschalk had placed the dynamite charge between two of the logs of the cabin wall then fired it while sheltering behind a hastily constructed barrier. Before the smoke settled, the two prisoners dove through the ruins of the jail wall and dashed for the dock. Their schooner was tied to the dock but hemmed in by a larger Russian trading schooner. While confusion still reigned in the village, the Americans had time enough to board the Russian vessel, slash the dock lines, and put to sea before a hue and cry was raised. Fortunately for the Americans, the Russian patrol boat was anchored in the harbor at some distance from the dock. Gottschalk glided by the patrol vessel without disturbing the sailors' heavy slumber—induced by the libations taken that evening in celebration of the capture of the notorious freebooter.

The exchange of schooners was advantageous to Max. The Russian boat was larger and better appointed. Better yet, it was loaded to the gunwales with furs, ivory, and seal hides. Once safely in Nome, Gottschalk sold the cargo and reaped a handsome return. No one in Nome questioned his right to sell the Russian goods. It was not that the Bering Sea neighbors did not have a history of good relations. Russian patrol boats often called there and officers threw parties for Americans aboard their ships and went ashore to be entertained in return. It was the same when U.S. Revenue Cutter Service vessels called at Siberian towns. Hospitality and aid was generously proffered. There was sometimes a little difficulty with language, but good fellowship and bountiful toasts eased the strain. "All men are brothers," cried the toastmaster. "We will look forward to full cooperation and good will," cried another. But that era of brotherhood was complicated and altered by the Russian Revolution. International policies governing Americans were not worked out among the pioneers at the Bering Sea—but in Washington, D.C. And Washington decreed that all diplomatic and trade relations between the United States and its citizens, and the Soviet Union and its citizens, be severed. Such weighty decisions did not end the Bering Sea trade carried on by Nome's mosquito fleet, but they did make it possible for marauders like Gottschalk to evade Russian law enforcement. Nome traders were grateful. There was money to be made on the Siberian shore—and adventure enough to stir a warm-blooded man. It was not the easiest or safest of commercial pursuits, but if one had a taste for it, there were ample compensations.

16 — AMERICANS IN SIBERIA

In 1900 Olaf Swenson, a lanky Swedish-American lad of seventeen, left his home town of Manistee, Michigan, for his first voyage to the Bering Sea. Gold discoveries in the North induced Swenson, like thousands of others, to seek his fortune on the distant Seward Peninsula of Alaska. The great bonanzas that lured men north eluded Swenson but working for a mine owner brought him $30 a day for the few weeks the job lasted. It was rugged work; for the first few weeks his fingers were so stiff he had trouble buttoning his trousers. When Swenson was laid off he did not join the majority of disappointed stampeders who abandoned their hopes and took passage south before the close of the navigation season. He reckoned there was money to be made in the North for those who could stick it out—and the setting agreed with him. Having decided to hang on, he cast about for opportunities; if gold was hard to come by, he would try something else. With something of the Viking spirit of adventure in his makeup, Swenson was ideally suited to the raw North.

By chance, Swenson eventually became a Siberian trader—one of a band of Yankee entrepreneurs who dominated the commerce of the Bering Sea frontier. He was not among the first in the field by any means. American traders had been active among the Siberian and Alaskan natives for a good half-century, dating back to the first penetration of the region by the stout whaling vessels of New Bedford and Nantucket. Free-lancers of Swenson's stripe found the coastal villages of Siberia and Kamchatka a particularly lucrative market. On the Asian side they did not have to compete with large, well-established organizations. Russian merchants, after the demise of the Russian American Company, scorned the remote Pacific frontier, and enterprising Yankees filled the gap. A traveler to the Chukchi Peninsula in the late 1890s, Harry DeWindt, reported that Americans were more familiar to Siberian natives than were the Russians.

Swenson was recruited in Nome by an American mining company which held a concession for the exploitation of precious minerals in Siberia. After working for the company for a season, he left to take a job in Seattle for a time before returning again to the North. His subsequent career there was to span forty years. Swenson first got involved in trade when a company ship went aground at the mouth of the Anadyr. His offer to salvage the ship in return for the cargo of nonperishable goods aboard was accepted, and he soon had an inventory of slightly salty flour, tea, and tobacco. Customers were not wanting in the Anadyr country because the Russo-Japanese War activity had affected the supply of provisions. Disdaining war profiteering, he sold the flour at $1.75 a sack, though the going price had skyrocketed to $11. Buyers flocked from hundreds of miles around and "left with a comfortable feeling that they had been treated fairly." [1]

It was not hard to give up mining. The Northeastern Siberian Company, the American firm under whose concession Swenson worked, was forced out by a revocation of its mining privilege; so Swenson was free to consider other possibilities. The young man soon proved himself a natural trader. One of his first innovations established his reputation: He broke down all of his trade goods into packages of uniform size that would fit easily on the Chukchi backpacks and sleds. Early on, he fixed on strict honesty as the best policy: "I knew that if I dealt unfairly in one season I would not get their furs the next." [2]

Furs constituted the most valuable trading item proffered by the natives. Certainly 150 years of intensive harvesting had reduced the huge resource discovered by the *promyshlenniks* of the eighteenth century, but the region's wealth was far from exhausted. "The northland was like a huge plantation to us," Swenson wrote, "divided into many fields, each of which produced a different crop." [3] Along the coast of the Okhotsk Sea ermine and squirrels were gathered. Kamchatka produced "the finest red foxes (cherry red) in the World" and the sable "for which our company became famous." [4] Nor were the needs and returns of the Arctic coastal natives overlooked: white foxes, cross foxes, wolves, wolverines, deer skins, polar and brown bears' skins, ivory, whalebone, and seal skins were gathered from them.

In time Swenson and his partners owned several ships which plied the Bering and Arctic Sea coasts during the short summer navigation season. Ships like the *Polar Bear* and the old whaler *Belvedere* were well-known veterans of the North long before Swenson acquired them. Their appearance off a native village signaled a period of brisk trading. Between trading calls, the ship's crew hunted walrus along the edge of the pack ice for its hide, ivory, and oil. Occasionally the *Belvedere* took a bowhead whale, and the crew would recall the palmy days of whaling when hundreds of vessels hunted the northern sea leviathan.

FROM NOME TO SIBERIA

Among the commercial firms of Nome involved in the Siberian trade was the U.S. Mercantile Company of Ira M. Rank. Rank had been interested in the potential of the trade from the early years of Nome's establishment, and in 1910 established a store at Teller that would be a more convenient jumping-off place to Asia than Nome. Rank was the kind of trader who was willing to grubstake a man who appeared capable of success. In 1903 he was impressed by a nineteen-year-old Danish immigrant, Charles Madsen, who wanted to set up as a trader. Madsen was to have a long career in the North as trader, guide, and hunter; but at the time, he had come to Nome only because his uncle lived there. Soon he fell in love with a fifteen-year-old Eskimo girl who attended the mission school and married her. Charlie borrowed a thirty-four-foot schooner from the mission for which his wife sewed sails; then took on a stock of Winchesters, flour, sugar, tobacco, and calico contributed by Rank and sailed off into the Bering Strait. Madsen's first season's trading at East Cape was a success, and for the next year he secured a larger schooner, the *Mary Sachs*, a vessel which in 1913 would be utilized by Vilhjalmur Stefansson's Canadian Arctic Expedition.

Neither of these schooners suited Madsen because they lacked auxiliary engines. Ice and gales were constant perils to unpowered vessels, and Madsen resolved to get a more suitable vessel. Rank came through once more and let him take the *New York* for the following season.

Needless to say, the Siberian traders of Nome engaged in cutthroat competition. Time was of the essence. The first trading vessel of the summer to East Cape or Anadyr could cream the stockpile of furs and ivory. Any delays during the short navigation season could be disastrous. All ships were supposed to call at Anadyr for trading permits, but few of the mosquito fleet skippers bothered. They would lose time—and money. The Russians levied heavy fees for the permits, and the traders preferred to take their chances with the patrol boats. Even if they were caught, as long as they had no significant store of liquor they were treated leniently. The Bering Sea frontier had never lent itself to rigorous law enforcement. How could it be otherwise in such a rugged and remote setting, so lacking in civilized amenities and formalities?

Perhaps unjustifiedly, Madsen distinguished himself from such freebooters as Max Gottschalk and Alexander McLean. He made no mention of trafficking in booze in his published memoir, *Arctic Trader*; yet Harold McCracken, who hunted brown bears with him in later years on the Alaska Peninsula, heard some spicy anecdotes. Madsen told McCracken that he had been the unofficial leader of "the whiskey smugglers of the Polar seas" and during one period had to stay away from Nome for two years to avoid arrest.[5]

One of the incidents described by Madsen concerns the efforts of a Russian official to restrict the sale of liquor by the Anadyr agent of John Rosene's Northeast Siberian Co. The post was manned by an American named Beck and by a footloose old Australian, Charlie Carpenter. Carpenter had been a gold rusher to Nome in 1899–1900; then he moved to Siberia, where he set up a household with a Chukchi woman and took up trading. In 1908 the Cossack official in charge of Anadyr confiscated Beck's liquor stores, but the American managed to turn the tables on him. Beck's cook presented himself as a U.S. marshal from Nome who had been secretly investigating the trading company's operation and called upon the captain of a Russian patrol boat to arrest the Cossack for unlawful confiscation and convey him to Nome. If Madsen can be believed, this ruse was so successful that the Cossack was taken to Nome and fined $500. A good story that may have at least partial substance.

The extent of the activities of the mosquito fleet of Nome in Siberian trading can be traced through reports of shipping appearing in Nome newspapers. Voyages noted in 1910 include those of John Kelly, skipper of the U.S. Mercantile Company's *Bender Brothers*; Charles

Madsen in the *Edna*; Captain E. T. McIntyre and his *Louise*; Max Gottschalk and his *Luella*; Louis Lane with the *Helen Johnston*; the gas schooners *Hattie B. Hazel* and *New York* (no captain identified); the schooner *Martha Wilkes*, chartered to the Arctic Trading Company and skippered by C. B. Owen; Gus Johnson and his *Arctic*; Captain M. Talentine, manager of the Arctic Trading Company and his *Sea Wolf.* Probably there were other schooners that were unreported, but with just these ten vessels undertaking several voyages each, it is clear that the Siberian trade was becoming a lively enterprise. Gold could not sustain Nome indefinitely, but its depletion would not destroy the town if it became a thriving commercial center.

Russian officials were aware of the increasing trade and hoped to discipline the Americans. In September of 1910 the patrol boat *Shilka* called at Nome to return the crew of the *Martha Wilkes*, which had been wrecked in Anadyr Bay. Lieutenant Takeshvitz of the *Shilka* explained Russian trading regulations to Nome newsmen. They were clear enough: "No liquor, no mining rights," and traders must have an American passport countersigned by a Russian consul.[6] A trader living with a Siberian native woman, but not married, could keep a store and trade in her name; but if legally married, the woman lost her rights to hold a license. If, like Charlie Carpenter, a trader became a Russian citizen, he had the full rights granted any Russian to carry on trade. No posts could be established at any village where there was not a Cossack official in residence. The Russians were equally clear on the position of Russians who voyaged to Nome without authorization. The previous year three Russians had disembarked at Nome from a Norwegian steamer, the *Vargon.* Nome's Bureau of Immigration officer allowed the men to land, and they camped on the sandpit near the center of town. They had no money, could speak no English, and could not get work. After they had starved for four months they were arrested on vagrancy charges so that they could be housed and fed in the Nome jail. When the *Shilka* arrived, the unhappy immigrants asked to be taken back to Siberia. The *Shilka*'s captain replied that they "could stay in America for all eternity" unless they had passports.[7] Sometimes officials had to be lenient to Americans who broke Russian laws, but that gentleness would not be extended to subjects of the czar. It would not do to allow Russians to be lured by the glittering reputation of Nome. Good frontiers make good neighbors.

The editor of the *Nome Nugget* called on the Siberian traders to respect Russian regulations, "to stick to useful trade goods and legitimate means in order to protect what is becoming an important economic asset to Nome." [8]

The *Nugget* also reported that Russian officials were planning to educate Siberian natives. Unlike the "free" Eskimos of Alaska, the Siberian natives had neither education nor industry. Obviously the United States was doing a superior job.

Just when prospects for the Siberian trade seemed brightest, alarming news reached Nome. A Siberian Eskimo had purchased the *Hattie B. Hazel* of the Nome mosquito fleet for $2,200 and would operate it with a native crew "in competition with white traders." [9] This was a dire portent indeed. The *Nugget* commented editorially: "Soon they will corner the market and skim off the cream." [10]

But there was no point in worrying too much. The navigation season was soon to close for the winter. Time enough next year to worry about Russian regulations and native competition. Meanwhile, there were diversions. The *Hattie B. Hazel* arrived from Siberia, carrying another one of those crazy pedestrians who was walking around the world via the Bering Strait. This one was a Frenchman, Henri Mosse, who hoped to win a $10,000 bet and, of course, glory.

The peak year for the Siberian-Alaskan trade appears to have been 1911, when approximately $200,000 in furs and ivory were landed in Nome. Trade fell off in 1912 and 1913 but was still respectable, with $115,000 of business each of those years. Various explanations were given for the decline. The *Nome Nugget* asserted, "The falling off is due to the efforts now being made by Russian traders to obtain some of the benefits from the growing importance of the Siberian coast opposite Nome." [11] American traders muttered about this rivalry for commercial gain in a region they had been exploiting for many years. They had developed a market where none had existed before the first New England whalers sailed into the Bering Sea in mid-nineteenth century. Now the damned Russians were trying to horn in. Where's the justice?

Had the grumbling traders been able to foresee the future they would have been even more depressed. In 1913 the world stood on the brink of a war that was to alter many things. Even remote Siberia was to be affected by the cataclysmic events and, especially, by the revolution that shook Russia to its foundations.

But in July 1913 the people of Nome were unaware of all this and

The *Nokatak* of Nome's mosquito fleet after polar bear hunt.
University of Alaska Archives, Lomen Family Collection

very pleased at the bustle in the roadstead as several ships were fitted out for an Arctic expedition. The Canadian Arctic Expedition was the greatest effort that had been made by Ottawa to increase the geographic and scientific knowledge of a part of its northern regions, and Nome residents were proud to participate. Polar explorers had always been well received in the Bering Sea metropolis. In 1907 several thousand dollars had been raised for the benefit of Ejnar Mikkelsen, whose Beaufort Sea venture had been curtailed by shipwreck. But 1909 was a banner year. It was then that the great and determined Norwegian Roald Amundsen dropped anchor off the town, after having completed the first navigation of the long-sought Northwest Passage.

In 1913 Nome was honoring Vilhjalmur Stefansson, the Canadian Arctic Expedition's commander, and the scientists who were to act under his direction. Stefansson—a brilliant, articulate, and personable man—formed lasting friendships with several Nome people, including Judge G. J. Lomen, Carl Lomen, and other members of that remarkable family. From 1913 to 1918, news of the travails and successes of the Canadian Arctic Expedition often reached the outside world by way of Nome. Some of the news was disastrous indeed. The expedition had hardly gotten underway before the *Karluk*, the Canadian expedition's flagship, which had originally been a tender for Alaskan fisheries, was caught in the ice east of Point Barrow and drifted to its destruction. Many of the *Karluk* crew died after the doomed ship went down to the strains of Chopin's "Funeral March" issuing from Captain Bob Bartlett's Victrola. Bartlett, a famed Arctic navigator, survived after crossing to the Siberian coast from Wrangel Island and, with the help of Siberian natives and traders, reached St. Michael. Another reported disaster turned out to be the crowning achievement of the expedition. Stefansson and two companions set out on a long trek over the Arctic sea ice with a bravado that some of his men felt would lead to their certain end. After some months, their loss was generally reported; yet Stefansson did accomplish his mission and demonstrated that skilled hunters could "live off the land"—and frozen sea.

Russia had launched a major Arctic exploration effort of its own a few years before the Stefansson expedition set out. In 1910 two icebreakers—or at least what passed for icebreakers in the primitive era of ice navigation technology—steamed to the Bering Sea after a long voyage around the Horn and across the Pacific. The men of the *Taymyr* and the *Vaygach* were determined to restore the reputation of the Russian navy which had been much tarnished by its farcical performance in the 1905 Russian-Japanese War. In that conflict the ancient, ill-prepared Russian fleet steamed from St. Petersburg around the Horn and crossed the Pacific. By the time the battered ships finally engaged the well-manned ships of the Pacific's emerging naval power, they were fit only for surrender. Instead they fought an unequal battle and were devastated by the overwhelmingly superior Japanese.

But the Russian maritime had once attained some distinction. In the early nineteenth century, several notable circumnavigations had been made by talented commanders like A. J. Krusenstern and Baron von Wrangel. The navy had demonstrated its capacity to support the Russian American colony in the North Pacific and the Bering Sea, and with Otto von Kotzebue's 1815–18 voyage, had demonstrated its ability to explore the Arctic Ocean by way of the Bering Strait. So there was a glorious tradition to which the naval men of the *Taymyr* and *Vaygach* could hope to live up to, and there were very practical goals too. If the two ships could penetrate the ice-choked seas of the Siberian Arctic, it could be that a northern sea route between Europe and the Bering Sea could be developed. Of course the passage could be made. Adolf Nordenskiöld had shown that in 1879 by completing the passage across the top of Europe and Asia. Yet this achievement did not immediately open a passage of commerce over the length of the Northeast Passage. It did, however, help foster the development of the Kara Sea route that linked European Russia and western Siberia; but much more needed to be learned of navigation conditions of the Arctic Ocean off eastern Siberia, and the seamen and scientists of the Russian icebreakers were to devote five years to such investigations.

The first port of call for the Russian ships was Petropavlovsk. It seemed "sleepy, deserted, almost extinct." Yet there were 600 inhabitants, and a resident told the naval officers that the "town was in full swing with Russian, Japanese and American ships arriving," and trappers from all over Kamchatka were coming for the annual fur auction.[12] This supposed excitement was lost on the navy officers, but they observed that the square in front of the trader's store was paved with vodka bottles, bottoms up.

On its first of five cruises to the North, the icebreakers called at Emma Harbor and met the American Billy Thompson, "one of the predators who brazenly fleeced the naïve and honest Chukchi and Eskimo." [13] L. M. Starokadomskiy, a member of the expedition, whose account of the naval expedition was not published until 1959, made other adverse comments on the foreign merchants. It is possible that these comments were made for him by the editor of his work, in the spirit of Cold War fury that has diminished the stature of Russian scholarship in modern times. "Foreign traders and predatory liquor runners to whom the Eskimo was obliged to sell their goods had created among them a totally false idea of the true value of goods." [14] Starokadomskiy tendered hard cash to an Eskimo in exchange for a polar bear skin, but would not meet the "absurd price of $200." [15] The Eskimo was willing to deal swiftly if the Russian would give him a bottle of vodka. Perhaps the problem was partly linguistic. Starokadomskiy admitted that communication was difficult because Bering Sea natives did not know Russian.

What the Russian officers learned of the foreign traders' nasty practices confirms what had been reported by Charles Madsen and Olaf Swenson and censured by Nome newspapers. American schooners evaded the Russian liquor prohibition and evaded patrol boats. They traded a concoction of "molasses, kerosene and sweet water" in casks that were falsely labeled; they bribed Siberians to carry liquor inland for trading; they made tremendous profits by exchanging cheap rot gut and baubles for valuable furs.[16]

Emma Harbor was a wretched place, and Starokadomskiy was forced to revise his impressions of Petropavlovsk: "Now Petropavlovsk seems the acme of culture and prosperity by comparison." [17]

After departing from Emma Harbor, the Russians steamed as far north as Cape Dezhnev, a point marked by a massif rising out of the sea to a height of 2,500 feet. From this point they could make out Cape Prince of Wales on the opposite American coast. There was no opportunity to push into the Arctic. It was October and ice had already thickened the sea. According to plan, the two ships turned south for Vladivostok for wintering.

The next season, 1911, the Russians returned to Bering Strait. At Emma Harbor they encountered a Russian steamer from Vladivostok which was bound for the Kolyma River. Its trading mission marked an upswing in Russian commercial interest in northern Siberia: It was the first attempt to convey freight to the Kolyma by sea—at least the first Russian effort. Traders from Nome may have made the voyage earlier.

Later in the season the Russians met the motor schooner *Katie Ewer* from Nome heading for Nizhne Kolymsk on the Kolyma. The Americans planned a return to Nome the same season but had provisioned for a year, just in case they could not make it back through the ice. The two Russian ships separated at Emma Harbor. The *Vaygach* headed for Wrangel Island to establish Russian sovereignty there, while *Taymyr* surveyed parts of the Bering Sea coast.

Wrangel Island, which a few years later was to excite the adventurous spirit of Vilhjalmur Stefansson, was a "blank on the map almost unknown." [18] The Russians intended to put the island squarely on the map—the map of Russia—and were to show in time that foreign encroachment there would not be tolerated. Using language that tolls suspiciously of vintage 1959 rather than vintage 1911, Starokadomskiy (or his editor) noted that the island had been discovered by "Captain Kellett, one of the American agents, who penetrated into Russian waters under the pretext of searching for the last Franklin expedition in 1849." [19] In reality, of course, Captain Henry Kellett was an officer of Britain's Royal Navy, whose voyage had been one of the many sent out to search for Sir John Franklin and his men. Historical inaccuracies have not uncommonly enlivened Cold War rhetoric, but the Russian attitude toward the American whalemen's penetration of the Bering Sea and Siberian Arctic had not altered over the period of a century. In the mid-nineteenth century, Russian American Company officials had protested the American intrusion, and in 1959 Starokadomskiy's editor recalled "another predatory American, the whaler Thomas Long," who named Wrangel Island in 1867, while he was engaged with the "profitable extermination of whales in alien Russian waters." [20] But these and later American intrusions on Wrangel Island which threatened Russian territorial sovereignty could not prevail. The *Vaygach* men would survey the island thoroughly for the first time, make astronomical observations, and even set up a navigation beacon.

Starokadomskiy's book is extremely valuable, because it reviews many of the important events of Bering Sea history and fixes firmly the canons of Soviet historical revisionism. Of the 1865–67 Western Union Telegraph endeavor to tie Asia and North America by cable, an enterprise that was heartily supported by the czar's government, we are informed that the Americans' intent extended beyond telegraph construction. "This was a reconnaissance—in-depth of Russia's North Eastern territory, to which the greedy hands of foreign traders had long been grasping." [21] Predators, predators everywhere; that much is crystal clear. Starokadomskiy does mix up events. He correctly observed that the 1899 gold rush to Nome also stirred American interest in Siberian gold, but oddly finds that "the construction of the telegraph line was associated with this 'gold fever.' " His association of events was confused.

On another visit to Emma Harbor the Russians met the American trader Billy Thompson once more. Thompson complained about the drop in whalebone price on the Nome market. No sympathy was forthcoming from the navy men who had heard that the foreign traders took 400,000 rubles from the Chukchi villages in exchange for 50,000 rubles in trade goods. In contrast, Russian traders exchanged 20,000 rubles in goods for a modest 36,000 rubles in furs and other products.

Everywhere on the northeastern Siberian coast the American presence dominated and grated on the sensitivities of the Russian officers. The village of East Cape "could be on the American shore." [22] There was nothing Russian there. The store was run by Americans who had recently forced the closure of a rival store established by a Vladivostok merchant, "who could not stand American competition." [23] Indeed it was a strange state of affairs. It was as if the Bering Strait gap did not exist—as if the Americans had, throughout modern history, attached northeastern Siberia to North America by a force of commercial domination that eradicated geographic reality. No patriotic Russian could view this situation with equanimity.

Americans could not be trusted. They even dared to evoke the cause of science to mask their exploitative purposes. At Emma Bay the schooner *Abler* arrived from Nome. Its skipper requested permission of the Russian government official there for a landing on Wrangel Island to study the flora and fauna there and to make a film. Starokadomskiy was certain that the *Abler*'s so-called "scientists" were simply poachers, "illegally making a living from marine animals." [24] The captain's "appearance and reputation as a well-known walrus hunter makes us doubt the trip's purpose." [25] The films, if they were made, would make money in America, but what would Russia benefit?

Louis Lane was the captain who roused the suspicions of the Russians. He was a colorful veteran of the Siberian trade and the son of Charles D. Lane, one of the principal gold-mine operators in Nome. Among Lane's passengers was "the millionaire milk man," John Borden of Chicago, who had become fascinated by Alaska and the North.[26] The voyage terminated abruptly when the schooner was wrecked off St. Matthew Island. No lives were lost, and when Borden got back to Chicago, he commissioned a massive trophy as a prize for a marathon dog-sled race he helped organize in Nome.

Other traders were having trouble in 1916 too. The schooner *Hattie B. Hazel* was seized by Siberian officials, and the Nome Chamber of Commerce protested the action to Alaska's sole congressional delegate, James Wickersham. Wickersham was asked to obtain permission for Nome traders to carry on "without molestation" until a customs house was established at East Cape.[27]

In the same month, a trader returned to Nome from Siberia to report that the notorious sea wolf Max Gottschalk was in deep trouble. Russians had tried him for "selling liquor and resisting an officer" and laid a sentence of five years' hard labor on him.[28] It was getting harder for Americans to carry on their traditional Siberian enterprises. How Gottschalk got away from the Russians is not clear. Stories have been told of a daring escape, but according to one report, he volunteered to serve in the Russian army on the Western front.

By 1916 the war seemed finally to have reached Siberia. Russians were being drafted for the armed forces and sent west. Trader Olaf Swenson noticed a change of attitude among Siberians. Earlier they had been optimistic and were untouched by the conflict; now "there is an air of indifference with a certain amount of disquietude, due to the possibility that many may soon become involved." [29]

Captain Joe Bernard of Nome decided to give up Siberian trading and venture into the Canadian Arctic with his *Teddy Bear*. He planned a two-year expedition to traverse the Northwest Passage but did not actually go east of Coronation Gulf. Bernard was different from other traders in having pronounced scientific interests. He became a skilled collector of natural history specimens and Eskimo artifacts.

Captain James Crawford decided to go east, too, and prepared his schooner *Challenge* for a trading expedition to Herschel Island and Banks Island.

In August the *Nome Nugget* reported a rumor that several people in Nome were planning to make for the Siberian coast "with a heavy supply of liquor" for trading, as soon as the Russian patrol boat headed south near the end of the navigation season.[30] The editor lectured those planning such unethical conduct, pointing out that such tricks would severely hurt those involved in legitimate Siberian trade.

At the same time the schooner *Alaska* arrived at Nome with most of the members of the Canadian Arctic Expedition that had fitted out there in 1913. Stefansson was not among them; he needed more time to complete his work.

But to return to the observations of the Russian naval officers: They were told that Americans swept up virtually the entire fur yield of the Anadyr region. Earlier things had been even worse. Americans had been given a mining concession to the whole Chukchi Peninsula and "could plunder here with the blessing of higher authority." [31] The old rulers must share the blame for American intrusions. "Thus were the resources of the Far North 'utilized' by the Tsarist government." [32] Foreigners were permitted to decimate marine mammal resources. They wanted walrus tusks only, and wasted the meat and hides. This had always been the case. After having "bought Alaska for a song," Americans "plundered" its resources and "ignored natural conditions." [33]

Still there were some advantages in having progressive neighbors on the Bering Sea. On their 1913 cruise, the icebreakers called at St. Michael. There the Russians took on coal, overhauled their ships' engines, and used the telegraph to report to St. Petersburg on their activity. Reports were sent regularly, but little use seemed to be made of them. "Most Russian newspapers were not interested in our expedition story." [34]

Good neighbors did not mind reciprocating favors. When Captain Bob Bartlett reached St. Michael in 1914 and heard about the Russian icebreakers which had recently left, he telegraphed Ottawa and Washington, D.C., requesting that the Russian ships and the U.S. revenue cutter *Bear* be asked to assist the *Karluk* survivors he had left on Wrangel Island. At Emma Harbor the Russian naval officers got word of the *Karluk* disaster and crossed over to St. Michael once again to consult with Bartlett. Bartlett, meanwhile, had gone to Nome and the icebreakers followed. At Nome the Russians received wired approval from St. Petersburg: The *Vaygach* could try to penetrate the ice pack to reach Wrangel Island. Neither the *Vaygach* nor the *Bear* was able to get to Wrangel Island in the 1914 season. The ice defeated both sturdy ships.

Just when the rescue attempt was underway, news of the outbreak of World War I reached Nome. The *Taymyr* was still there and received

$25,000 worth of furs from Siberia landed at Nome, July 1909.
University of Alaska Archives, Thomas Cader Powell Collection

orders from St. Petersburg by wire. Despite the emergency, the rescue voyage was to proceed. Both Bob Bartlett and Vilhjalmur Stefansson wrote later that the *Vaygach* abandoned its effort to reach Wrangel Island, when the icebreaker was quite near its goal, in response to the war outbreak. In fact, this could not have been true, because the *Vaygach* was not within reach of radio reception from Nome, Siberia, or anywhere else and could not have known of recent events.[35]

Starokadomskiy did not comment on this question but had something to say about Stefansson's ingratitude in sending a colonization expedition to Wrangel Island in 1921. "While we were trying to get to Wrangel Island, we did not realize our efforts to help would injure us later." [36] Stefansson required Russian help "yet tried to annex" Wrangel Island to Britain.[37] And Stefansson had a " 'worthy' partner" in Carl Lomen of Nome, who took over Stefansson's interest on the island and tried unsuccessfully to get the United States government to claim the territory.[38] Lomen "amassed a fortune in unrestrained exploitation of Eskimos." [39] While one can understand Starokadomskiy's ire at Stefansson's colonization scheme, it is difficult to see where ingratitude was a factor. Certainly the Russians tried to rescue the *Karluk*, though they failed. It was an errand of mercy, and yet one of considerable political importance for naval ships that were charged with putting Wrangel Island on the Russian map. His gratuitous assault on Carl Lomen is hard to connect as well. Russians could be annoyed at Lomen's Wrangel Island involvement, but had no reason to know about his "unrestrained exploitation of Eskimos"—even if this did have some relationship with the Wrangel Island squabble.

The war curtailed Russian scientific activity in the Bering Sea and Arctic. Both icebreakers steamed back to Europe the long way. They were needed elsewhere. The opening of the Northeast Passage—if, indeed, that had been as significant a part of their program as it was made retrospectively—would have to wait.

WRANGEL ISLAND ADVENTURE

Knud Rasmussen, whose plans to visit East Cape Eskimos were thwarted by Siberian officials in 1924, attributed some measure of his inhospitable reception to the Wrangel Island affair. Though Wrangel Island is not in the Bering Sea—it lies in the Chukchi Sea 100 miles off the Arctic coast of Siberia and about 300 miles from the Bering

Strait—its colonization was launched from Nome, and the consequences of the scheme certainly had reverberations on Siberia's Bering seaboard. Wrangel Island, a sizable land of 2,000 square miles lying on the 180th meridian, was first discovered by Captain Henry Kellett of England in 1849. The first recorded landing by a Westerner was made by an American whaleman, Captain Thomas Long, in 1867, who named the island for Baron von Wrangel, an explorer of Arctic Siberia and once a governor of Russian America. In 1881 the United States flag was raised over the island by an officer of the U.S. Revenue Marine, but no official territorial claim was made by the United States or any other government until the colonization venture focused attention on the island.

In September 1921 a party of three Americans—Fred Maurer, Milton Galle, and Errol Lorne Knight—headed by a young Canadian, Allan Crawford, arrived in Nome and began quietly to outfit an expedition. They had been instructed by their backer, polar explorer Vilhjalmur Stefansson, to be secretive concerning their plans, which were to establish a colony on Wrangel Island and claim the territory as a British possession. Stefansson considered the venture a legitimate one. Russia had claimed sovereignty over the island shortly before, but Stefansson ignored the claim; he did not believe that an island's contiguity to mainland created a territorial right superior to discovery and possession.

No history of the Bering Sea could be complete without a review of one of the most remarkable men of the twentieth century, Vilhjalmur Stefansson. Stefansson's great travels and explorations were in the Beaufort Sea and Canadian Arctic islands; yet his province as advocate-prophet encompassed the entire Arctic and Subarctic. By 1920, when the Wrangel Island project was planned, Stefansson had completed over nine years of polar exploration work and had commenced the second phase of his energetic career. For over forty years, until his death in 1962, Stefansson wrote books and articles, lectured, advised, and pleaded—for one single cause. In essence, he advocated that the Arctic Ocean should be recognized as a polar Mediterranean that should be rationally utilized as the world's crossroads. Concomitant with this thesis was an insistence that northern development offered no formidable obstacles. Ignorance and prejudice rather than remoteness and severe climate retarded the exploitation of the ample resources of the North.

Wrangel Island would be of great benefit to the British Commonwealth, argued Stefansson to government officials in Ottawa in 1921 and London in 1923. Its situation would make it an ideal fueling stop for airplanes which would one day undertake transpolar flights, and its resources in fur-bearing and marine animals were bountiful enough to sustain a colony. Ottawa officials were interested in Stefansson's proposals but had not reached the point of commitment by the time the Stefansson Arctic Exploration Expedition sailed from Nome in the chartered *Silver Wave.* By this time, Stefansson felt sure that governmental concurrence would be forthcoming—particularly when the colonization proved successful—and in 1923, he traveled to London to put his case.

Meanwhile, on September 15, Captain Hammer of the chartered *Silver Wave* left the four men and an Eskimo woman from Nome, Ada Blackjack, the party's seamstress, on Wrangel Island. Returning to Nome, Hammer reported that the Union Jack was now flying over Wrangel Island. A Nome newspaper published the story, causing a number of Alaskans to protest to Washington that a British colonization had been launched from Nome. The Canadian press complained that the scheme was crazy because Wrangel Island was valueless, while the English press feared a jeopardy of British-American relations. American newspapers raged against the fostering of British imperialism by a British subject who resided in the United States. Stefansson had been born in Canada but had lived most of his life in the States. This unfavorable publicity disturbed Stefansson because he hoped to get the help of Canada in reprovisioning Wrangel Island in 1922, but at least the Russians had not yet protested.

The Canadian government contributed toward a relief charter in 1922, although not before the close of the navigation season. Stefansson had not waited for government action before pledging his slender resources for the charter of Captain Joe Bernard's *Teddy Bear.* Bernard was a well-experienced navigator of polar seas; yet ice conditions in August prevented his passage to the island. Stefansson was not too alarmed by this failure because the party's provisions had been calculated to sustain them through two winters and the men were experienced hunters.

The little colony on Wrangel Island came to a disastrous end. Several men of the party tried to duplicate Captain Bob Bartlett's feat of a few years earlier and cross the ice to the Siberian mainland. They were never seen again. When rescuers finally reached the island, only the

Nome Eskimo woman Ada Blackjack remained alive. The rescue party included the nucleus of a new colony made up of Charles Wells and several Nome Eskimos. Stefansson had commissioned Wells to trap furs on the island and hoped to recover the expenses of the colonization venture through the sale of the furs.

But the Soviets were having none of this. The government was eager to carry through the explorations commenced by the icebreakers *Taymyr* and *Vaygach* in the years before the war and was eager to assert its sovereignty over Wrangel Island. In August 1924 a naval ship, the *Red October*, steamed north from Petropavlovsk and arrived at Wrangel Island. Wells and the Eskimos were carried from the island and their furs were confiscated. The red flag was raised over Wrangel Island at last. No foreign adventurers would be permitted to claim Russian lands. And it was also high time to curtail the activities of the American traders of Kamchatka and northeastern Siberia, who had been for so long defying the national interest of Russia.

17 — RED FLAG OVER SIBERIA

In the early 1920s the remotest regions of Russia were affected by the revolutionary conflict, including the Bering Sea frontier, where outposts like Petropavlovsk were alternately held by White and Red combatants. Obviously, such civil conflicts affected the foreign traders of northeastern Siberia adversely despite their best efforts to stay out of politics and carry on business as usual. Just as obviously, it was not a good time to launch a new commercial enterprise and engage in trade competition with established American merchants like Olaf Swenson; yet the oldest trading company in North American did just that. In 1921 Canada's Hudson's Bay Company—founded in 1670 and granted a monopoly of the fur trade of northern North America which it exercised for over 200 years—extended its operations to eastern Siberia. The governors of the ancient Hudson's Bay Company were seeking new fur regions and assumed that with the company's wide experience and efficient organization it could thrive in a territory where wide-scale operations were unknown. Some logic supported the Bay Company's expansionist hopes. No Russian or United States concern could command the shipping resources or the worldwide commercial status of the Hudson's Bay Company. Far less could any rival call upon the know-how of the Bay Company's organization in dealing with native peoples of the North. But all these pluses could not sustain the company in the tumultuous era of revolution, civil strife, and rampant patriotism that, as far as the triumphant Reds were concerned, were sometimes expressed in xenophobic reaction to Western nations and their agents. Unfortunately for its success, the Bay Company's officers gravely miscalculated the Bering Sea situation.

Captain L. R. W. Beavis, Vernon W. Elphick, and Anton Hoogendijk headed the Bay Company's first assault on Siberian commerce in 1921. Three ships carried trade goods to Petropavlovsk from Vancouver, British Columbia—the company's *Casco* and *Baychimo* and a Japanese charter, the *Koyo Maru*. On their arrival at the Kamchatka port the managers carried a long purse to smooth over any anxieties on the part of Russian officials. For the right to trade, he paid "taxes, tolls, and bribes," presumably to Red authorities.[1] The payment of just tributes and palm greasing in cementing good relations with the Siberians did not exhaust the trader's goodwill policies. Petropavlovsk was not an imposing place and did not contain many reminders of its past grandeur, but it did have one—this was the memorial that had been raised to honor those killed in the repulse of the combined English-French attack on the port in 1854. Perhaps Beavis was stimulated by national feeling as well as sentiments of friendship, since most of the memorialized dead were English, but, at any rate, he offered to have the monument repaired. Just previously the Reds had occupied Petropavlovsk and had damaged the monument.

All pressing matters of license, extortion, and patriotism satisfied, Beavis rented the second largest building in town, caused it to be inscribed "Hudson's Bay Dominion," and rested from his exertions. But he had not reckoned on shifting events. In the middle of a night's sleep he was rudely awakened by four soldiers of the White Guard who demanded that the two small power launches carried on the *Baychimo* be turned over to them. These launches, designed for river navigation, would have been very useful to the counterrevolutionary forces; but Beavis, in anticipation of a forcible requisition, had dismantled them and buried the engines on the beach. Thwarted in their demands, the soldiers announced that the trader's salary would be confiscated, a measure that was effective in coercing reluctant Russian officials, but, as Beavis pointed out, could not be applied to a foreigner whose salary was paid in Vancouver, British Columbia. "At that they released me with many curses," Beavis reported, and he was somewhat disillusioned to discover that the White soldiers "were no better than the Bolsheviks." [2] Obviously neither Reds nor Whites had a firm grip on Kamchatka.

The Hudson's Bay Company managers left Petropavlovsk to establish trading stations at various places on the west coast of Kamchatka: Bolcheretsk and Tigil were chosen despite the lack of good ports. These posts were to be managed by local personnel, but the company had a difficult time recruiting competent managers. Beavis then took the *Casco* across the Bering Sea to Nome, where freight shipped there from Vancouver and Seattle was picked up and taken across to Siberia. A station was established at the mouth of the Anadyr, the most northerly point of the Russian telegraph network, and at East Cape on the Bering Strait opposite Nome. At East Cape, Beavis met an independent trader who had been resident there for many years, Charlie Carpenter, an Australian.

In returning to Petropavlovsk, Beavis called at the government offices to test the political atmosphere, just before returning to Canada. People he met were polite and "aloof from politics." [3] It is unlikely, however, that officials could afford to be indifferent to political events, though such an attitude would benefit the Bay Company's interests. In fact, officials were aware enough to have two sets of pictures available for office display—one of the czar and czarina; one of Lenin and Trotsky. On his first visit to the government offices, Beavis observed the Lenin-Trotsky portraits; on his second, the images of the czar and czarina held place of honor; and on his third observation, the revolutionary leaders were back.

Vernon W. Elphick and Anton Hoogendijk, the Bay Company's Siberian managers, looked hard at Swenson's company, the Hibbard Swenson Company of Seattle, and its other rivals. They were surprised to find that Swenson had stores only at Anadyr and East Cape and conducted most of his trade through local merchants and from his ships. They did not figure that it would be difficult for a major company to run Swenson out of business, but they were more concerned about the Denbigh Company established at the mouth of the Kamchatka River. Denbigh had two large fish canneries, a store, and a fleet of motor launches for the transporting of goods upriver. But he was distrusted by the trappers, and the Hudson's Bay Company could force him out too, were it not for the fact that Denbigh made use of an immense quantity of cheap Japanese alcohol for fur-barter purposes. The managers reported that Swenson and Denbigh cooperated on some ventures, notably on the trading cruise of a small steamer to the Okhotsk Sea. The *Tungus* "is also a great alcohol-bacilli spreader, visiting as she does all the places on the coast." [4] The Seidenberg and Wittenberg Company was already on the ropes. Except in Petropavlovsk, where a store was maintained, the firm was hardly known. Most of their business was carried out through agents. "Their influence in Kamchatka," reported the managers, "is hardly to be reckoned with." [5]

Once the managers had sized up the Bay Company's rivals, they were prepared to set up a trading network that would lead "to the eventual liquidation" of the competition.[6] Arrangements were made to cooperate with a veteran trading firm, the Karieff Brothers, and a large stock of goods was purchased from the American firm of Seidenberg and Wittenberg. The Americans had warehouses at Anadyr, Nome, and Teller, and the Hudson's Bay Company bought all they had.

Although the Bay Company had been granted trading privileges by Soviet officials in Moscow, local government officials had the authority to tax and could determine whether the license should be renewed or extended. In 1921 the company's manager asked officials at Petropavlovsk to grant permission for trading in 1922 so that preparations could be made. He also made a request for a monopoly of the fur trade on the Commander Islands. The officials at Petropavlovsk referred the Bay Company's manager to the head commissar of the Kamchatka district, who was then in Shanghai. The manager called on the commissar in Shanghai and impressed him with the "earnest intention of the Company to do their utmost in the interests of the population." [7] The commissar agreed to ask Moscow for approval. He was anxious "to encourage concerns like ours and thereby reduce the influence being rapidly gained by the Japanese in Siberia." [8]

For all the optimism of this 1921 report to the head office of the company, the managers had a shock on their return to Kamchatka in 1922. Their agent in Ust Kamchatka had been "overwhelmed by the competition and trickery of the Denbigh Swenson organization." [9] Denbigh had frequently entertained the Bay Company's agent to help him pass the long winter days, and in this friendly setting "no business secrets were kept." [10] The agent also sold most of his goods to other merchants and had little left with which to buy furs. To bring about the Bay Company's ruin, "our competitors have resorted to every trick imaginable." [11]

In June of 1922 Beavis arrived at Petropavlovsk again with two shiploads of trade goods. Now the Whites were in control, while the officials with whom Beavis had negotiated the previous year were besieged in a blockhouse some sixty miles up country. Naturally there were new taxes and bribes to be paid, and the trader complied cheerfully. He had also brought a new Crimean War monument provided by the British admiralty—a cross fashioned from British Columbia fir and suitably inscribed. With proper pomp, after a Russian Orthodox Church service, the memorial was unveiled.

Beavis made the round of the Hudson's Bay Company posts and noted the political uncertainty. At Bolcheretsk the White flag was flying as the Hudson's Bay Company ship approached the town, but the flag was pulled down because officials feared the ship might be manned by Reds. Once Beavis landed and declared his neutral intentions, the White flag was hoisted again, but not for long—as all White resistance was to be crushed in 1922.

Beavis established other stations on the Okhotsk Sea, did some trading, and saw indications of civil turmoil. In one settlement he encountered a party of twenty-five American gold miners who had been prospecting in the interior until the appearance of Red forces.

Off the Bering Sea coast of Kamchatka, the Hudson's Bay Company suffered a misfortune at the hands of nature. A gale drove the *Baychimo* ashore, and a $50,000 cargo had to be jettisoned before the ship could be refloated.

The 1922 trading season was a disappointment to the Bay Company, and conditions did not improve in 1923. Yet the company's managers thought prospects were brighter for 1923. In March they had been able to get a firm contract drawn up and signed in Vladivostok by a Soviet foreign-trade official. The Hudson's Bay Company would deliver goods valued up to $350,000 to Kamchatka and the Chukchi Peninsula. The profit margin was fixed at 20 percent. The Hudson's Bay Company would collect furs at certain points and conduct a coasting trade. A 10 percent slice of the furs' value would be taken by the local government. The managers were happy with these terms and did not mind agreeing to provide free medical treatment to inhabitants of the main centers of its activity—Anadyr, Kluchi, and Tigil—and to carry government officials on its cruises.

When Beavis reached Kamchatka in 1923, he found that the Reds controlled the peninsula. New taxes had to be paid, and other obstacles to calm, profitable trading were encountered. Revolutionary officials ordered Beavis to convey captured White soldiers to the Okhotsk Sea on the Bay Company's *Ruby* and bring back personnel of the victorious Red army and the head of the former White governor of Gizhiga. Nor were the elements favorable. The earthquake that had devastated Tokyo and Yokohama that year affected shipping in the Okhotsk Sea and the Bering Sea and damaged the *Ruby*. Beavis recruited some of the stranded American miners he had met the year before, and with their help managed to get the *Ruby* back to Vancouver.

In 1924 the Hudson's Bay Company made its last effort to get its Kamchatka venture moving. The *Baychimo* steamed north, but when reports indicated that conditions in Kamchatka would not be favorable to the company, the ship was recalled before it reached a Siberian port. Thus, after four frustrated years, the Hudson's Bay Company's adventure in Siberia ended. What had made the situation for foreign traders perilous was the opposition in Moscow to Lenin's "New Economic Policy" of granting concessions. As the secretary of the Bay Company noted: "With the death of Lenin the opponents of the new policy assumed control and power. The decree went forth that private business must be curtailed: Communism was to be reestablished and the war on Capital was resumed." [12]

THE KHAN OF KAMCHATKA

Among the foreign businessmen who wanted to take advantage of Lenin's liberalization of trade restrictions in 1920 was an American who was very much interested in northeastern Siberia: Washington B. Vanderlip, the mining man, who had prospected in Siberia in 1898 and 1899 without making any gold discoveries. Vanderlip was aware of the economic potential of the region. In August 1920 he negotiated with Maxim Litvinov, the Soviet ambassador to Denmark, and impressed him with his business acumen and political connections. Litvinov suggested that the American travel to Moscow and lay his proposal before Lenin. The opportunity of talking directly to the great Lenin was not available to many foreigners, and Vanderlip headed for Moscow with high expectations. Vanderlip probably gained entry to see Lenin because of the Russians' misconceptions of his identity. Soviets had confused him with the New York financier Frank A. Vanderlip, and the mining engineer did nothing to clarify the error.

Vanderlip claimed to have much political power. He told Lenin that he had been assured by Warren Harding that the United States would recognize the Soviet regime if the Republicans were able to win the next presidential election. Lenin was willing to go along with Vanderlip's request. In October the Soviet press announced a lease arrangement. The American syndicate represented by Vanderlip was given a sixty-year lease of territory east of the 160th meridian, an area of 400,000 square miles of northeastern Siberia and Kamchatka. Exclusive mineral and fishery rights were included in the concession.

Lenin acted from several motivations in granting the concession. One important reason for his action was his belief that the concession-aires would thwart Japanese expansion into Kamchatka. If the Japanese and the Americans wanted to fight each other over the exploitation of Kamchatka, the Soviets would gain by their conflict. "When two thieves battle each other, honest folk win out." [13] Lenin also believed that the resources of northeastern Siberia were boundless, and American aid in development would strengthen the Soviet economy without depleting the resources to any great extent.

Vanderlip had handled Lenin rather crudely. He had gone so far as to claim that only the grant of a lease to Kamchatka could cause Americans to favor the Soviet government. He also played on Lenin's distaste for the Japanese and predicted an American war against Japan, which the United States would win with the aid of Kamchatka's oil. Whether Vanderlip actually discovered signs of oil during his Siberian gold prospecting travels is not clear.

Vanderlip's backers were largely businessmen of Los Angeles. They were possessed by grandiose dreams and looked forward to American expansion in the Far East. Japan had to be foiled, they believed, and eventually the United States should purchase Kamchatka.

After securing the lease, Vanderlip traveled to Sweden and England, reveling in the international publicity which attended his progress. In the press he was hailed as the "Khan of Kamchatka," and he liked that title. But before Vanderlip left London, news of a speech by Lenin was reported in the press. Lenin had made it clear that the concession was intended to be of only brief duration, and was designed only to create conflict between Americans and Japanese. Vanderlip returned to Los Angeles and a corporation was formed. He remained optimistic, but his backers were less so: The company's capitalization was a meager $100,000.

Vanderlip returned to Moscow to lobby for his project and other new schemes he had in mind. Soon he informed the press that he had

Washington B. Vanderlip at Indian Point, Siberia, 1899.
University of Alaska Archives

obtained two naval bases from the Soviets. One was on Avacha Bay near Petropavlovsk; the other was near Vladivostok. The latter, he stated grandly, he would willingly turn over to the United States. No one paid much attention to his claims of success.

Nothing came of Vanderlip's schemes. The United States did not recognize the Soviets and added insult to Vanderlip's injury by revoking his passport because he had not received authorization for the second journey to Moscow.

No more was heard from Vanderlip, but Lenin did grant some Siberian concessions in addition to that given to the Hudson's Bay Company. One was to a firm directed by Olaf Swenson of Seattle.

OLAF SWENSON

In 1921, the year of the Hudson's Bay Company's first attempt to establish itself in Kamchatka, the veteran Siberian trader Olaf Swenson ran into serious troubles. In April Swenson sailed from Seattle, his outfitting headquarters, with his company's M.S. *Kamchatka* to make his customary calls on the Bering Sea coast of Siberia. The *Kamchatka* was a sturdy ship that had once been a whaler. Years of whaling service in the Bering Sea and Arctic Ocean had soaked the ship's timbers in whale oil, but this did not worry Swenson. He considered the *Kamchatka*'s strength for ice navigation superior to any other vessel. Besides the usual trading items—clothing, food, firearms, and hardware—the *Kamchatka* carried 1,000 cases of ammunition and a deckload of gasoline in drums. About two weeks out of Seattle, during a heavy storm, the *Kamchatka* caught fire. It was Friday the 13th and events confirmed Swenson's abiding superstition concerning this date. Panic reigned among the twenty-three-man crew when the ship lost its electrical power. No calls for assistance could be sent: Seas were raging. They were 500 miles from land on a burning vessel loaded with a flammable, explosive cargo. There was nothing to be done but abandon ship. Eventually, after five anxious days, the castaways reached the Shumagin Islands just south of the Aleutians.

Within a few weeks Swenson made it back to Seattle, then sailed to Japan where he chartered a ship and loaded a cargo of trading goods. He was determined to salvage the 1921 trading season despite the loss of the *Kamchatka*, but more misadventures were ahead. At Okhotsk, a White force had just driven the Reds out of the town, and its officers were pleased to accept money from Swenson in return for permission to do business. Even established traders had to adapt to the revolutionary scene, and Swenson was ready to deal with whoever held power. Trade was brisk; there were 1,000 Korean gold miners in town eager to exchange dust for goods, and Swenson cleaned up $14,000 in gold—then almost lost it. A White officer stole the gold, but Swenson retrieved it, then made a hasty departure.

But Swenson's travails with the revolution were just beginning. Later he admitted somewhat ruefully that he should have stayed away from Siberia during these troubled times. But business must go on. Thus in 1922 Swenson returned to Petropavlovsk on his usual voyage. White forces were in control everywhere and the town was full of eager customers. Clothing was in particular demand. The Russians were deliriously happy to replace tattered sheepskin coats and astrakhans with American mackinaws and caps. Some even bought clothes to ship to relatives in distant Moscow. Although trade was good, revolutionary involvement could not be avoided. Under threat of losing his ship and furs, Swenson was ordered to carry ninety men—presumably Red sympathizers—away from Okhotsk. As he foresaw, this could cause him trouble.

In 1923 Swenson did not return directly to Siberia. By that time the Reds' forces were reigning and had confiscated his property and issued a warrant for his arrest. Precise charges were never actually pressed, but Swenson understood that his competitors had accused him of selling guns to the Whites—accusations prompted by envy "because I had dealt fairly with the natives and gotten along with them better than they had done." [14] Proceeding with caution, Swenson traveled from Seattle to Peking, China, secured a Russian visa from the Soviet ambassador there, then went to Habarovsk to inquire into his affairs. Nothing could be done in Siberia so Swenson went on to Moscow and, after months of complaining, arranged negotiations. The Russians decided that the American company owed taxes covering the six-year revolutionary period, assessing these at $340,000. Swenson managed to get this figure reduced to $62,000. Confiscated property still had to be settled. Swenson had to sell his accumulated furs to the government for less than their market value. Losses suffered by this transaction and through the spoilage and pilferage of trade merchandise mounted alarmingly. In addition, he was subjected to numerous civil suits brought by other businessmen, though he won them all in the "admirably fair" worker courts.[15]

Despite all this, Swenson wished to continue trading in Siberia, and the government granted a one-year contract in 1925, then renewed it for five more years in 1926. Each summer Swenson was permitted to take goods to the Bering Sea to sell them at cost price, plus a fixed commission, in exchange for furs—the prices of which were also fixed. This was a profitable arrangement despite the restrictions, and Swenson came to appreciate the revolutionary regime, especially in its effects on the Russian people. On his last Siberian voyage his ship was caught in the ice off North Cape and held for the winter. A mixed crew of Americans, Scandinavians, Irish, and Germans bickered and grumbled at their imprisonment. In contrast, the crew of a Soviet ship, also ice-bound nearby, "were having a beautiful time, with no trouble at all." [16] Illiterates among them were learning to read and write, others were busily studying foreign languages and other subjects.

Swenson did not believe, however, that the Soviet rule benefited the material welfare of Siberian natives. In his time (Swenson wound up his Siberian ventures in 1933) the government's price-fixing policies reduced the natives' income from fur sales; nor did the Soviet trade monopoly provide the varied goods that foreign traders had stocked:

> We brought foodstuffs, canned milk, canned fruits, clothing of every kind (including frilly things for women), hardware of all kinds, toys for children, a great many luxuries which many of them had never known before. Now, with the Soviet monopoly in force, they got only such things as the Soviets saw fit to send them, and the government showed less imagination in its selections than we had done. Luxuries were completely taboo and the natives had to content themselves with a pretty grim, dull selection of absolute necessities.[17]

One might have difficulty sharing Swenson's gloom at the denial of frilly clothes and other "luxuries" in a region where famine was not an infrequent visitor, even if his dismay at the downfall of free enterprise can be understood. Incidentally, a recent Soviet history of the Russian North brands Swenson, in passing, as a "predator." This derogation prompted an English reviewer of the book to question the ranking. "Possibly he was," observed Terence Armstrong, "but the only evidence quoted in support of this view is his [Swenson's] own autobiography, which does not give this impression." [18]

Swenson's last Siberian adventure involved the tragic loss of one of Alaska's famed pioneer bush pilots, Carl Ben Eielson. The episode was noteworthy as an example of American-Soviet cooperation between Bering Sea neighbors that foreshadowed the ferrying of bombers from Alaska to Russia during World War II. Swenson outfitted the motor schooner *Nanuk* in 1929 for a voyage to the Chukchi Sea via the Bering Strait. His mission was to carry provisions to another of his ships, the *Elisif*, which had been caught in the Arctic Ocean ice the previous winter, and collect the furs aboard the *Elisif* and those stored at various company stations. By the time the *Nanuk* reached North Cape, the *Elisif* had managed to break free from the ice, and both ships steamed west for the mouth of the Kolyma River. En route, the *Elisif* smashed into a huge ice floe which gashed a five-foot hole in her hull below the water line. Her captain beached the *Elisif* and carried her crew safely to Nome in the ship's launch, a distance of 600 miles. Meanwhile, Swenson continued on to Kolyma, picked up the largest quantity of furs ever taken in one season, and started back for the Bering Strait. Off North Cape, near where the *Elisif* had spent the previous winter, the *Nanuk* was jammed in by ice floes and could go no farther. The year before, Swenson had been on the *Elisif* in the same situation, but rather than remain with the ship for the winter, he had made a long, hazardous journey by dog team to Yakutsk in southern Siberia—a distance of 4,500 miles. Before leaving the ship he had contemplated an alternative that had only recently been available to Bering Sea voyagers—the charter of a commercial aircraft from Alaska. He rejected it as too expensive, and also because he wanted to take the adventurous sled trip. When the *Nanuk* was caught he decided against repeating the 1929 journey and contracted Alaska Airlines in Fairbanks by radio. Several things influenced his decision to fly out. He did not want to expose his seventeen-year-old daughter, who had accompanied him, to a winter sled trip, and he was anxious to get his furs to market while prices were high. The *Nanuk*'s furs were worth over $1,000,000 at the current prices.

Carl Ben Eielson of Alaska Airlines agreed to transport furs and crew to Fairbanks. Rates for the fur were to be $4 per pound; each passenger would be charged $750. Eielson was one of the several Alaskan bush pilots who pioneered commercial aviation in America. It was in

Alaska, with its vast distances between population centers, where the technological and commercial feasibility of air transport had its chief testing ground in the 1920s and 1930s. Eielson was a highly regarded pilot who had earlier achieved fame in flying Sir George Hubert Wilkins, the polar explorer, from Point Barrow to Spitsbergen.

On his first flight to the *Nanuk*, Eielson landed on the ice and picked up six crewmen and a load of furs. Flying weather was perfect, and the first of the six round trips necessary to convey furs and crew went without a hitch. On the 9th of November Eielson and his mechanic, Earl Borland, set out from Fairbanks once more, this time in very thick weather. After two days, the plane had not reached the *Nanuk*, and a search expedition was organized. Other Alaskan bush pilots flew to North Cape and made the area a base for the search. Swenson flew on some of these flights, and landings were made at Siberian villages to interview natives. Several Siberians reported having heard an unfamiliar and terrible noise which had frightened them, but none had seen the airplane. From these reports it was clear that Eielson had made it across the Bering Strait to Siberia.

Relations between the United States and Soviet Russia were strained. The American government still withheld recognition of the new regime, but United States officials requested help from Russia and received a wholehearted response. Dog-team expeditions were organized in several Siberian villages, and Moscow offered a reward to searchers who could track the missing airmen. It was January before the wreckage of the lost plane was discovered by Alaskan pilots, and February before the bodies of the men were found. Apparently they had been killed instantly on crashing. The recovery of a defective altimeter indicated that Eielson probably misjudged his altitude as he tried to find his way through a roaring blizzard.

In early February, Swenson, his daughter, and the furs were taken to Teller, near Nome, and eventually back to Seattle. His daughter had become something of a celebrity through dispatches she had sent from the *Nanuk* to *The New York Times*. For a time, the Eielson search stirred the world and made newspaper readers aware of events occurring on the distant Bering Sea and Arctic Ocean. Despite the tragic overtones, aviation history was being made, and the publicity highlighted the potential of aircraft operations in the world's worst flying climate.

Newspaper coverage did not put Bering Sea commerce in the limelight. For many decades Americans and other non-Russians had been trading in Siberia without attracting much attention. There was nothing sensational in this, nothing to interest those who were not directly involved. But it was an exploitation of geographic proximity of historic significance, and one that was not to survive Swenson's retirement from the field. When Swenson terminated his Siberian venture, the commercial back door to Russia was effectively closed. Except for a brief time—because of the exigencies of World War II—the Bering Sea and Strait were not to be so closely linked as in earlier times. This is still true today; yet one would not have to be much of a prophet to foresee that this situation seems likely to change. Political events closed the Bering Sea to commerce, but political-economic realities could soon alter this.

Olaf Swenson was the last of the American traders in Siberia. For thirty years he had withstood "the hazards of the cold, white trail, the squeeze of ice floes, the filth of a Chuckchi hut, and the gnawing hunger which dogs and men feel during bad winters along the Siberian coast." [19] Writing in 1944 he recalled the pleasurable aspects: "the friendly simplicity of the Chuckchis, the hospitality which was perfect and unmixed, without any hope for personal gain . . . the pleasures of gossip around an Arctic campfire, the thrill of danger." [20] He was content with his memories, satisfied that his robust body had served him well, and pleased that his honest dealing had brought him prosperity. "I had my fill of life during those years and can live now in the memory of them." [21]

SCIENTISTS IN KAMCHATKA

Despite the unsettled conditions in Kamchatka, the Soviet government allowed an expedition of the Swedish Geographical Society to travel there in 1920–22. The party of six Swedish scientists, headed by Sten Bergman, steamed from Japan in June 1920 to the Okhotsk Sea on the armored steamer *Commander Bering*, bound for Petropavlovsk. There was little room aboard; the Swedes had to make their berths in open lifeboats on deck, but they were assured that the cruise would only take six days. En route, the Russian navy men maintained a sharp lookout for unauthorized ships in Russian waters. Too many foreigners, mostly Americans, were defying the restrictions on trade that had been imposed by the Soviets. Guns aboard the *Bering* were ready for action. During the nights, despite the fog, the ship ran without lights; a wartime atmosphere reigned. "The Russians rubbed their hands with joy at the prospect of capturing some schooner perhaps next day." [22]

But in the dense fog of the North Pacific the prey were often safer than their hunter. Early one morning a sickening crash shook the *Bering* from bow to stern: The steamer had crashed into a hidden rock which tore a huge hole in its bottom. Swiftly the *Bering* had to be abandoned and left to its fate. Fortunately, the ship was just a few miles off the southern tip of the Kamchatka Peninsula and everyone aboard got to shore safely, though the scientists had to abandon some of their equipment. Once ashore a camp was set up, salvaged provisions were distributed, and hunting parties were organized. Ten tents housed the fifty-three castaways and above that of the leader, a Red commissary agent, waved the Soviet Red flag, inscribed "Long Live the Democratic Republic!" The castaways were rescued after a few days, but in the interim, Bergman came to appreciate the Bolshevists. In Sweden he had heard of innumerable bloody atrocities perpetuated by the Reds; now he was amazed to find them such pleasant people. Their rescue was brought about by Japanese ships, and the Swedish scientists eventually made an unconventional entry into Petropavlovsk aboard torpedo boats of the Japanese navy.

Petropavlosvk did not have a very prosperous appearance. Empty-looking shops, most of them run by Chinese, lined the main street, and there seemed to be no great bustle among the town's inhabitants—Russians, Chinese, Koreans, and a few Kamchadals. Pigs roamed the town's three streets, and householders emptied slop pails into the streets directly from kitchen doors. Bergman rented a house from a Chinese businessman and received the local gossip daily from the Russian priest who spoke perfect Swedish. In substance, the priest reported that most of the town's citizens were rogues and rascals. Another acquaintance was the school principal, a Kamchadal who had studied in Tomsk, spoke excellent English, and was a keen botanist. Still another informant was the veterinary surgeon of the district. Although the surgeon had been in Petropavlovsk ten years, he had never undertaken any professional work. The shock of discovering that his district included the entire Kamchatka Peninsula, the Anadyr region, the Chukchi Peninsula, the Arctic Coast, and even Wrangel Island had staggered the doctor; he had resolved to vegetate in town. No one minded. His salary was paid despite his inactivity.

The American shop, Seidenberg and Wittenberg, was the best-stocked one in town. Wittenberg was the Seattle-based businessman whose schooner *Bender Brothers*, on which August Masik was mate, was due to arrive soon. At Wittenberg's store one could buy "Swedish Primus stoves, preserved fruits from California, matches from Japan, and everything else you can reasonably desire in such a place as Petropavlovsk." [23]

Much of our knowledge of Siberia's Bering Sea settlements during the 1920s comes from traders like Olaf Swenson and August Masik, men who were affected adversely by the change of government and the revolutionary turmoil. Bergman's observations are valuable because, as a scientist, he remained undisturbed by economic vicissitudes; yet his impressions did not counter those of more committed visitors. Prior to the revolution, supreme authority in Kamchatka had rested with the governor; now the Revolutionary Committee of Kamchatka reigned. A proliferation of bureaucracy was evident as a couple of hundred officials were installed "with commissioners and departments for everything, and any number of typewriters." [24] Settlements like Petropavlovsk gained substantial police forces, imposing men armed with big sabers and revolvers, wearing bright-red bands. "Their principal duty would seem to have been the confiscation for their own benefit of spirits on the Russian steamers which arrived." [25] Police posts were much sought after.

The new regime did not quicken the pace of things in Kamchatka. "In contrast with the gold-mining cities of Alaska, where energy and feverish industry give a stamp to the life, the atmosphere of Petropavlovsk is marked by lethargy and sloth. Time has no value. What is not done to-day can be equally well done to-morrow." [26] Russians of Kamchatka have two mottoes, asserted Bergman, "There's no hurry" and "It doesn't matter." [27]

Bergman took passage on a Russian steamer bound for the North on a trading voyage. Because the coastal service between Vladivostok and various Bering Sea ports was so infrequent, the ship was jammed with passengers and cargo. Passengers fought to get aboard and find space in the hold or on deck. To a passenger aboard ship, it appeared that traffic along the coast was heavy indeed; but actually the crowding occurred because of the short navigation season and the paucity of shipping. Kamchatka and northeastern Siberia did not attract shipping interests any more than it did large Russian trading concerns.

Before shipping on the Russian trading vessel, Bergman had arranged to go on a Russian war cruiser, the *Magnet*. This voyage was canceled at the demand of the crew. If Kamchatkans were largely unstirred by revolutionary fervor, the same could not be said for Red sailors. Many sailors from the *Magnet* deserted at Petropavlovsk, and the remainder threatened to quit too unless the captain abandoned the planned cruise to the North and headed south for Vladivostok. The sailors found Bering Sea duty dull and tiresome, but they did want to make their fortunes before returning to more civilized regions. To this purpose they demanded that the *Magnet* sail for the Commander Islands. Once there they hoped to exchange liquor for blue fox skins, having heard that the Aleuts, who had been settled in the islands in the previous century, were favorably disposed to such a trade. "A fine specimen of a war cruiser!" commented Bergman.[28]

In his months of travel in Kamchatka, Bergman visited scores of wretched villages in which the decline of the natives was depressingly obvious. "Here live the last remnants of a race which will soon be wiped off the face of the earth." [29] On the western coast of Kamchatka some natives still retained their language, but on the Bering Sea, it had been forgotten. But everywhere "civilization has set its mark on what is left of the inhabitants, for every one of them—men, women and children— suffer from hereditary syphilis introduced long ago by Russians." [30] This malady had raged, in the absence of medical assistance, to weaken and destroy a once hardy people. "In addition, the Japanese and Chinese and Russians vie with each other in drenching the degenerate villagers in spirits, which, in their miserable condition, they value above all else." [31]

Interestingly enough, Bergman does not indict American traders in his censure of the liquor trade, though he visited all the major trading stations in Kamchatka. During the 1921–22 winter, Bergman made a dog-sled journey to the central part of the peninsula, halting at Klutchi (or Kluchi) and other villages. Klutchi, a large village on the Kamchatka River fifty miles from the Bering Sea coast, had 500 inhabitants including Russians, Chinese, Koreans, and even Aleuts. In its beautiful situation at the base of a volcanic mountain, residents were able to fish all year. As in every other settlement in Kamchatka, trade centered on the fur industry. A Hudson's Bay Company post and other stores were to be found in Klutchi, but the biggest store was that of the Olaf Swenson Company. Swenson's "name is known and esteemed in every dwelling throughout the entire peninsula. Every spring Swenson comes over from Seattle with his steamer, which is laden with everything imaginable that Kamchatka can stand in need of." [32] While some of Swenson's stores were transferred to his coastal stations or shipped from the coast to stores at interior places like Klutchi, customers at smaller villages on the coast could go aboard his ship to exchange their sable, fox, otter, and bear pelts for guns, cartridges, traps, motorboats, sewing needles, and a most popular item, chewing gum. Swenson's reputation for honesty and a liberal credit policy made him popular. "Any customer with any credit at all is trusted to an astonishing extent." [33] Siberians "are very apt to sell their bear's skin before they have shot their bears!" [34]

Bergman observed that word of Swenson's arrival always reached villagers in advance of his schooner, and his customers had their furs ready when the trader appeared. "When in this very honourable way he has skinned Kamchatka, he proceeds on to Anadyr and the Chukchee peninsula. Should time permit, he swings over to the Arctic coast and returns in the late autumn to Seattle, with his American goods replaced by furs to the value of millions of dollars. Throughout his whole journey he keeps himself posted up as to the fluctuating prices on the world's fur markets by means of his own wireless." [35]

Bergman, who arrived at Petropavlovsk on a Japanese naval vessel, found that the Japanese dominated the commercial fishery industry of Kamchatka. After the Russo-Japanese War, Japanese were granted rights to fish for salmon off the coast and operate canneries. Each summer several thousand Japanese came to Kamchatka to pack salmon caught by their fleet. The canned salmon was then shipped to Japan, while Siberian natives continued to rely upon their own river fisheries which were closed to foreign fishermen. Throughout the 1918–22 period of military intervention, when Japanese forces were opposing the Red army on the Amur River, and elsewhere in Siberia, the Japanese fisheries in Kamchatka carried on. In reaction to some looting of their cannery facilities, Japanese warships were stationed in Petropavlovsk to proctect the industry, a deterrent that seemed sufficient to keep the peace. Bering

Sea Siberians often enough suffered because of their geographic isolation, but they certainly benefited during the trouble years of 1914–22 by their distance from most of the militant disturbances.

Bergman avoided politics as he traveled throughout Kamchatka, making two long winter journeys to gather ethnographical material for the State Museum in Stockholm. When he returned to Petropavlovsk after his second trip, the White and Red forces were struggling for control of the region, but the scientists were not bothered by either combatant as they passed through the lines. Save for a touch of rheumatism, the Swedes had completed their scientific investigations without any physical distress. If they had been less discreet or if Kamchatka's revolution had been livelier, the results might have been different.

AUGUST MASIK

By his own admission August Masik, a huge, blond, blue-eyed Estonian, was a pirate, but only because he found the restrictions on Siberian trading irksome. He had been a merchant sailor for several years before ending up in the United States, where he worked at construction and other odd jobs. Eventually he wound up in Seattle and shipped aboard a fishing boat for Alaska. Next he took up mining—laboring in Juneau, Alaska, and Dawson, Yukon Territory, before moving north to Nome in 1914 for employment at the United States lifesaving station there. For two years, 1917–18, he was a member of Vilhjalmur Stefansson's Canadian Arctic Expedition and participated in long treks over sea ice and tundra. Stefansson praised Masik, considering him among the most able of the nonscientific members of the expedition.

After all this diverse experience, including eight years in Alaska, the young Estonian felt equipped to cut himself loose from conventional employment and take up the independent life of a Siberian-Alaskan trader. In 1920 he took a chief mate's berth on the *Bender Brothers* of Seattle, commanded by Captain Walls, bound for Kamchatka, with the understanding that he could be discharged in Siberia or Alaska. The schooner was owned by "Papa" Wittenberg of Seattle.

On arrival at Petropavlovsk the traders found that the revolutionary party was in charge. The Reds would not allow any trading until Olaf Swenson arrived on his annual voyage from Seattle. While the delay was irksome to Wittenberg, nothing could be done about it. Swenson was the

American trader who commanded the greatest respect in Siberia, and his position had to be accepted. Once Swenson arrived with his ship, the *Kamchatka*, the traders agreed on prices and business went on, though not too profitably, as Wittenberg had to accept 10,000,000 rubles in valueless currency issued by the Whites before any Japanese money—the only other available currency of value—was tendered. When the *Bender Brothers* left Petropavlovsk to begin its circuit of Bering Sea villages, a representative of the revolutionary committee went along to supervise the trade. Obviously things had changed; the old, easy days of the czar's reign had come to an end. Red officials would see to it that villagers were not exploited and, at the same time, their presence would indicate a new order of government to remote areas. While the United States government refused to recognize the Red regime, American entrepreneurs engaged in Siberian trade could not ignore realities.

When Wittenberg and Masik got to Anadyr their Red official remained ashore. A government steamer from Vladivostok had arrived at the same time as the *Bender Brothers*, and government officials busied themselves explaining the revolution to Anadyr residents and inquiring into murders of officials and traders the previous winter. Wittenberg had to go to Nome to pick up another trading cargo, and it was on this voyage that the *Bender Brothers* carried fifteen White sympathizers to Nome. Masik heard later that two of the exiles had taken the *Victoria* from Nome to Seattle and were arrested there on charges of embezzling government money in Siberia and were returned to Nome for transport back to Siberia.

Masik also encountered the Japanese torpedo boats that were patrolling the Kamchatka coast to protect the Japanese canneries. Masik, who liked to identify himself as a "good Bolshevik," did not approve of the Japanese. "It looked as if they were trying to claim Kamchatka, for they took a census of all the towns, which seemed to me to be none of their business." [36]

Further employment with Wittenberg did not interest Masik, who was keeping his eye out for opportunities of his own. When the *Bender Brothers* called at Karaginski Island, Masik sensed the chance he was watching for. Because it was forbidden by the Red official who accompanied them, the American traders were not permitted to land on the island, which is situated twenty-five miles off the Bering Sea coast of central Kamchatka, but they learned about affairs there. The island had been utilized as a fur-raising farm, but when the czar was overthrown, the two supervisors on the island were recalled. Now the island was untenanted—save for the lovely foxes. Just the thing for an enterprising man who did not disdain taking a few risks!

In Nome, Masik terminated his employment with Wittenberg and took a partner, Pete Jaeger. They bought a small schooner, fitted it with a motor, and rigged a mast that could be lowered on the deck when hiding the vessel was necessary. Masik met "the famous Siberian pirate, 'Mike Kochak,'" probably Max Gottschalk, who made Nome his home base. Max was interested in all Bering Sea activity and offered to carry Masik to Siberia in his fine schooner but Masik hesitated to do business with the notorious freebooter. Masik and Jaeger left Nome without informing anyone of their destination and voyaged to Karaginski Island. The island proved to be occupied by twenty Siberian natives, but Masik landed at some distance from their settlement. Through the winter the two men hunted and trapped. Foxes were scarce, but they gathered a fair number of sables, and in the summer of 1921 left the island to return to Nome. Calling at Anadyr, en route, Masik was forbidden to land. All American boats were barred. Masik claimed to be from the south rather than from Nome and was allowed ashore. Soon he made friends with an official, a fellow Estonian, and this cleared the air. Several American mining parties were prospecting in the region, and Masik considered joining them but was unable to make contact. Officials of the revolutionary committee were confused by the legal situation in regard to mining. The czar's laws were ineffective and they had no new instructions. Masik would have been permitted to mine until things were clarified but decided instead to return to Nome. Apparently he had gotten away from Karaginski Island none too soon. A Russian patrol vessel arrived at Anadyr seeking the American schooner that had been reported at the island. "Oh, I'm sure I don't know who it could be," bluffed Masik.[37] "Those damned Americans are getting all over the country. Chances are they came from the opposite direction and not from Nome at all!"[38] After a friendly political argument over revolutionary events in Siberia, Masik was permitted to leave.

Masik only stayed a short time in Nome before setting out for East Cape and the Kolyma River. He joined a party of traders who wanted help in salvaging the *Polar Bear*, a schooner that Masik knew from his service with the Stefansson expedition. Masik wintered on the Arctic coast at the mouth of the Kolyma, did repair work on the *Polar Bear*, and ran a trap line under a permit issued by local Red officials. Before the end of the 1921–22 winter, the resurgent Whites took over on the Kolyma and elsewhere, including Anadyr on the Bering Sea. Some thirty Kolyma River Reds were summarily executed during the winter. Though he sympathized with the Reds, Masik tried to stay out of politics; yet his trapping license was revoked after taxes were collected from him. When no one was watching, he ignored the ban against private traders and did some business. But it was an uneasy winter. At times Masik feared for his life and, with the coming of summer, was glad to set off for the Bering Strait. Because of ice conditions, Masik's schooner could not make it through to East Cape. Masik decided to winter over in 1922–23 at Cape Billings, 300 miles east of the Kolyma River, just opposite Wrangel Island. Had he realized that the Stefansson expedition was on Wrangel Island and in difficulty, he might have been able to go to their relief. While he was comfortably settled in a cabin he built on the coast, three of the Stefansson party perished on the sea ice as they tried to reach the mainland. Masik had been in Nome while the Wrangel Island party was quietly outfitting, but had not heard of their plans.

In April of 1923 Masik set out for East Cape by dog sled, taking the furs collected over two seasons. At Whalen the furs were confiscated by the Reds. In June the U.S. revenue cutter *Bear* called at East Cape and Masik managed to get aboard and return to Nome. Another *Bear* passenger, for whom Masik helped arrange transport, was a man posing as a Yakut trader, who later admitted to being a White leader responsible for some of the Kolyma executions of Reds.

All kinds of travelers arrived at Nome during the revolutionary period. Just after Masik arrived on the *Bear*, a trading schooner, the *Iskum*, also reached the gold town. The *Iskum*, operated by an American, Johnny Fickel, had been arrested at Anadyr. Two Red customs officers were put aboard while preparations were made to unload the confiscated cargo. Fickel, a resourceful man, jumped the officers, tied them up, and steamed out of the harbor under cover of a thick fog. Once in Nome, Fickel looked after the Russians until transportation to Siberia was arranged.

THE *RIM OF MYSTERY*

In June of 1921 John B. Burnham steamed from Seattle on the *Victoria* for the 2,300-mile voyage to Nome. From Nome Burnham planned to cross over to Siberia and hunt for mountain sheep. Because of a Pacific coast shipping strike, the *Victoria* was sailing several weeks later than customarily, but, as usual, it was the first ship of the season to head north. The tough, old *Victoria* was a familiar and much loved ship to Nome passengers. Launched in 1869, it had once been the queen of the Cunard Atlantic fleet and holder of the transatlantic speed record. New luxury ships had replaced the *Victoria* on the Atlantic run, and during the Nome gold rush the steamer had been put on the Bering Sea route. Although the Seattle-Nome voyage lacked the glamour of the *Victoria*'s previous career, the ship gave good service for many years. To make an early passage into the Bering Sea a ship had to brute its way among receding, but still dangerous, ice floes, and the *Victoria*'s heavy iron hull was up to this job.

Burnham shared a cabin with Carl Lomen, the reindeer king of Nome and a veteran of twenty years of mining and commerce in the North. Everyone aboard knew Lomen. His cabin was a nightly rendezvous for old northern hands eager to exchange gossip. "One after another the men of action came and went leaving stories of the sea and ice, fighting, romance and tragedy until it seemed that nowhere else in the world to-day can so many daring Argonauts be met at one time and place as on the *Victoria*'s first trip." [39] These social sessions were an eye-opener to Burnham, who was making his initial voyage to the North, which he later described in a book entitled *Rim of Mystery*. Clearly the age of adventure still prevailed on the Bering Sea, and the gatherings of rugged characters who smoked and talked into the night gave ample evidence of it. Burnham was bound for northeastern Siberia and so were some of the other passengers aboard the *Victoria*; but there was no passenger service from the Pacific coast directly to Siberia in 1921. In fact, there had never been a commercial passenger service to Siberia, though for many decades ships of all kinds—small trading schooners, fishing boats, sealers, and whalers—put out each summer from Seattle, San Francisco, Vancouver, and other Pacific coast ports for Siberia. But the chief port of embarkation for Siberia—and the only one for those without their own vessels—was Nome. This had been true from the time of the founding of the Bering Strait gold town in 1899. Burnham had never thought of Nome as a cosmopolitan trade center; yet, he was to discover that "into Nome the traders bring not only polar bear, and white fox skins and walrus ivory but such things as bricks of Russian tea looking like black decorated tiles and hard as stone, Japanese goods and even the magnificently regal skins of Manchurian tigers." [40]

People from Asia came to Nome as well, and sometimes under strange circumstances. Just the year before Burnham's voyage, the *Bender Brothers*, on which August Masik was chief mate, carried fifteen Russians from Anadyr to Nome. The Russians were fleeing from the vengeance of the Bolshevists who had just taken over northeastern Siberia. In the see-saw conflict of the revolutionary turmoil, these Russians had represented the precarious hold of White forces on eastern Siberia and had executed Red officials and sympathizers. But for their escape on the trading schooner and an approval for landing telegraphed from Washington, D.C., to customs officials in Nome, it would have been their turn for the firing squad.

Discussion of the Bolshevist revolution was a major topic on the *Victoria*. Some of the traders aboard left partners in Siberia to carry on while they had wintered outside. Now the reports of a Red reign of terror during the winter made them fearful for the safety of the Americans. But there was much else to talk about as well. Two American missionaries aboard were hoping to establish a mission in Siberia. Charles Brower and Tom Gordon, the Point Barrow traders and whalers, were returning to their station and were rich in Arctic lore. Oil prospectors commanded attention too. Once the *Victoria* reached Nome there would be a race to stake oil claims on the Arctic shore. Bob Adams had chartered the *Silver Wave* and a party of Standard Oil men chartered Captain Joe Bernard's *Teddy Bear*. Gold rushes were an old thing in the North, but the search for petroleum was a novelty.

A joyous tone of unrestraint ran through the conversations of Johnny Fickel, E. T. McIntyre, Alex Smith, Bob Adams, Tom Peterson, and Jack Matthews which Burnham listened to. It was as if some of the speakers were old-time buccaneers. One Siberian trader had tried to buy a secondhand four pounder and a machine gun to arm his schooner. His object was to raid Siberian villages for furs. "Their government is not recognized by ours, what could they do after I got away?" [41] Then ensued a discussion of the best way to raid the Russian fur-seal islands of the Bering Sea, "with profits of the trip increased by contraband pelts of sea otter picked up on the way." [42] According to reports, the much hunted sea otters were still reaching the market despite the prohibition on hunting by the United States and Russia.

Another trader admitted he sold whiskey to Siberian natives. "A trader has to get skins," he affirmed. "Competition was severe, and the best was always saved for the man with the booze." [43] Unlike more unscrupulous traders he "never peddled whiskey in coal oil cans," but expected to get $20 in fur for $3 in trade goods.[44] For one fox skin he gave a bottle of cheap whiskey that cost 80 cents before he watered it.

Such discussions of piracy were surprising to Burnham, who was accustomed to more law-abiding communities, but the Bering Sea was still an untamed frontier. Lawlessness had characterized the eighteenth-century expansion of the Russian fur traders into the region until it was checked by the Russian American Company's monopoly. In the nineteenth century, the Russians had not been able to restrict American whalers nor police their trading with natives. After the purchase of Alaska, American authorities waged a constant battle against illicit traders in Alaska and against the seal rookery raiders and pelagic hunters. Russia's involvement in World War I and the subsequent revolution crippled its policing of Siberia and encouraged a flaunting of Russian authority. This turmoil attracted American freebooters to Siberia. The United States had a firm control of its Bering Sea frontier by this time, but the Soviets were still struggling against foreign interlopers. The daring, adventurous characters Burnham met were having their last fling before the Soviets were finally to close the Bering Sea to plunderers.

In Nome Burnham met Max Gottschalk, one of the legendary predators of the region. Gottschalk was willing to take Burnham and his horses across the strait to the Chukchi Peninsula, but Burnham knew better than to get involved with Gottschalk. Apparently the Bolshevists had offered a reward for Gottschalk's capture—dead or alive. The previous season, Gottschalk had taken a load of coal from Emma Harbor under the pretense of carrying it to another Siberian port under orders of the Anadyr revolutionary committee. Instead, he sold the coal in Nome for $25 a ton. "I did not steal their coal," said Gottschalk, "I was just collecting a debt." [45] According to the trader, the Bolshevist officials had "grafted" $500 from him when he landed a passenger, then stole $250 from him. "I bought my head fair and square for $500, those bastards want graft first and blood afterwards, but while we were drinking to the bargain they snitched the $250. They had my cash so I took their coal." [46] To Burnham, Gottschalk personified the Bering Sea buccaneer. "The story of Max's exploits would fill a dozen volumes. He is a man in the raw, unmoral rather than immoral, a careless gambler with death." [47] Just before the revolution, Gottschalk had been captured on the Bering Strait, taken by Russian officials to Vladivostok, and sentenced to death. Before he could be executed, the czar was overthrown and all the prisoners in Vladivostok were released. "A few weeks later he sailed back North with a vessel and a cargo he had requisitioned. When Nome becomes untenable he has a rendezvous arranged at the tail end of the Aleutians from which to carry on." [48]

There was no regular passenger service from Nome to Siberia in 1921, although earlier—during the peak of the Nome gold development —scheduled excursions across the Bering Strait were common. However, each summer one of the ships of the U.S. Revenue Marine was in and out of Nome and, if one had proper connections, ferry service to Siberia could be arranged. Burnham secured passage on the most famous of the Revenue Marine vessels, the *Bear*, which was carrying scientists and a U.S. Bureau of Education party to various places. The *Bear*'s first stop was at King Island just south of the Bering Strait. This precipitous rock 700 feet high and about a mile long was the winter home of 200 Eskimos, who lived in walrus-skin dwellings lashed to the face of a cliff. It was an unlikely place for a village; yet it provided a favorable base for walrus and seal hunting, and the Eskimos had long since established their homes on the steep cliff. Each summer the entire population voyaged by kayak and umiak to the Alaskan mainland for a few months. There the Eskimos had room to stretch their legs and, after Nome was founded, they customarily camped near the town, where they sold the intricate ivory carvings for which they were well known. Today the King Islanders are permanent residents of Nome and their singular handicraft is still much esteemed.

After leaving King Island, where the ship's surgeon set the broken leg of an Eskimo boy, the *Bear* called at St. Lawrence Island, though the rugged vessel had to buck ice floes to make its anchorage place. Material for the construction of a new school and a crew of carpenters were landed. Some years before, a number of reindeer had been taken to the island by the U.S. Revenue Marine for the benefit of the 300 Eskimo residents. Six of the animals were rounded up by Eskimos, shot by Burnham, and butchered for the *Bear*'s larder.

The St. Lawrence Island Eskimos had had their ups and downs in the fifty-odd years since the United States had acquired Alaska. They had suffered severely during the peak whaling period of the mid-nineteenth century, particularly through the introduction of liquor, but now seemed to have recovered from this devastation. The gold rushes of 1898–1900 had not affected them much, though, like other Alaskan natives, they had been hard hit by the flu epidemic of 1916–17. Mortality rates on the island had been one in ten, though some villages on the lower Yukon River had been virtually exterminated. Burnham praised the American school teacher who nursed the Eskimos through the epidemic and otherwise provided sound guidance. Dupertius "has not ridiculed their traditions but has encouraged them to live up to their inherited beliefs. As a result he has succeeded to a great extent in bringing back to these islanders their former honesty and self respect, qualities which were commonly lost after the advent of the whalers." [49] At Gambell, one of the villages, Burnham noted that the Eskimos owned twenty good whaleboats, two motor boats, and numerous skin boats and maintained a high living standard. Traditionally, St. Lawrence Eskimos depended upon the walrus for their sustenance—just as they do today. Reindeer meat was also available at the time of Burnham's visit, but reindeer breeding did not prove to be a long-term success.

St. Lawrence Island missionaries had not always been highly regarded by visitors. The Danish explorer Ejnar Mikkelsen, who called there briefly in 1906 en route to the Beaufort Sea, was sharply critical of Dupertius' predecessor, Dr. Campbell. According to Mikkelsen, Campbell operated the trading post as well as a mission, making a lucrative business of the post. Alaskan missionaries, Mikkelsen claimed, became men of substance in a short time because of profitable sidelines like store-keeping and profit-sharing in whaling boats. Mikkelsen was convinced that the missionaries were interested primarily in personal gain, but the evidence does not confirm his opinion. In Burnham's time, however, the village store was a cooperative operated by an Eskimo.

On June 30 the *Bear* crossed the Bering Sea from St. Lawrence Island to Emma Harbor, one of several good Siberian ports on the Anadyr Gulf. Emma Harbor had been named by one of the American whalers which customarily halted there; not far away was Plover Bay, another popular whaling base and, in 1865–67, a station of the Western Union Telegraph Expedition. Burnham's hopes of securing a permit for mountain-sheep hunting were dashed by the local revolutionary committee leader, a man called Vassily who was the bane of all foreigners who

King Island.
University of Alaska Archives, Lomen Family Collection

put into Emma Harbor. Vassily ordered Burnham and the *Bear* to leave, despite Burnham's insistence that he was a scientist who had nothing to do with American traders.

Burnham tried to secure a permit from other Siberian officials by telegraph without success; so he eventually moved up the coast beyond Vassily's jurisdiction and set off on his inland excursion without troubling any further about approval. This willingness to disregard the new Russian government did not ease the temper of Siberian officials, nor their disinclination to distinguish between foreign traders and scientists—as Knud Rasmussen, the great Eskimo authority, discovered on landing at East Cape three years later.

Rasmussen, whose scholarly field work among Eskimos is unparalled, traveled by dog sled across Arctic North America from 1921 to 1924. Once he reached Nome he was anxious to cross the Bering Strait to observe the small Eskimo population of northwestern Asia. From Nome he could have chartered a trading schooner to cross the strait but did not want to prejudice his relations with natives by association with traders; so he wired Washington, D.C., requesting passage on a U.S. government boat. This was denied because of the possibility of "grave political complications." [50] Accordingly, Rasmussen arranged passage with Captain Joe Bernard in the *Teddy Bear*. Bernard was a veteran Siberian trader, and the *Teddy Bear*'s landing at East Cape was not well received. Soviet officials ordered Rasmussen to leave because he did not have authorization for Siberian travel. The Danish scholar pleaded his scientific interests to no avail. His nationality was no help—Denmark's king was a cousin of the fallen czar, and his scientific endeavors were not of interest to the officials. "Scientists do not seem to be popular," noted Rasmussen, "after Vilhjalmur Stefansson planted the British flag on Wrangel Island." [51] Just a short time before, a Soviet ship, the *Red October*, had removed the party of Nome settlers from Wrangel Island, thus ending efforts to colonize the island. Consequently, Rasmussen's hopes of visiting Nuvoquaq, a village of 400 East Cape Eskimos, were dashed.

Rasmussen did have a chance to talk to some Chukchi who were disenchanted with the Soviet trading restrictions. At the time, Russian trading goods were not available; yet the natives were forbidden to do business with foreign vessels. Rasmussen had the impression that the restrictions were reasonable. Licensing was required, and the American traders did not want to pay for them.

Perhaps the Communist government would have curtailed foreign commerce and prohibited scientists in Siberia regardless of the provocation of unscrupulous free-lance traders. Yet their intrusions clearly aggravated the situation. That a franchise had been granted to Olaf Swenson indicates that an honest business traffic was respected by the Reds.

SOVIET HISTORIANS AND THE PREDATORS

There is some Cold War rage in Soviet historical writing that treats America's involvement in Siberia, but the interpretation of events subscribed to in the U.S.S.R. is not generally a fantastic one. In a long, scholarly article published in 1949, S. V. Slavin reviewed the entire history of Americans in Siberia. He argued that the trade carried on along the coast from the mid-nineteenth century slowed the development of the region and disrupted the efforts of Yakutsk merchants to supply goods. A Russian government bulletin issued in 1890 complained that in "treating the trade like their own property, they have for many years enriched themselves to the direct detriment of the local population, together as well as to the government." [52] It warned that whales were likely to be wiped out just as seals and walruses had been. The writer of the report did not know how many American ships traded along the coast each season but calculated that at least ten large ships hunted whales. Other ships took salmon in Russian waters, and one San Francisco merchant was eager to exploit the timber of Kamchatka. The report also noted the adverse effects of the liquor trading which the Americans indulged in.

In the early twentieth century, according to Slavin, the Americans became interested in territorial annexation. The franchise given to John Rosene's company was gained by fraudulent means. Rosene's partner, Wonlarlarsky, a Russian citizen, was the nominal head of the company, but Rosene was actually running things. Slavin was right about this transaction, but exaggerated somewhat in arguing that Rosene's mineral and fishery concessions were just the thin end of a wedge he was using to take over Chukchi entirely. There is no clear evidence that this had ever been Rosene's intent.

Slavin saw the same kind of manipulation in the various trans-Bering Strait railway schemes. A battle raged within Russian government circles for years over the concession requested by Captain John Healy's agent, Loicq de Lobel. The American's scheme "sufficiently concealed the intentions of the American expansionists, who tried to penetrate economically speaking into the depths of the country by means of the concessions, and thereby preparing the tearing away of large territory of the northeast of Asian Russia." [53] American propaganda efforts led to the publication of 2,500 newspaper articles on the Paris–New York railroad, according to Slavin's count. The American's "imperialistic lust" led them to demand a right-of-way eight miles wide for a ninety-year term.[54] The effect, if the concession had been granted, would have been similar to the American take-over of Panama after building the canal. "The Americans thus would acquire the spring board for the development of their aggression." [55] American colonization of northeastern Siberia would have followed in due course. The syndicate would probably not have constructed a railroad at all but used the concession as a means of exploitation.

Fortunately, the czar's officials saw through this nefarious plot and refused the concession. Certain measures were also taken to bolster Russian presence in northeastern Siberia. In 1911, an annual trade run of a steamer from Vladivostok to the Kolyma River was commenced, and more officials called at Bering Sea villages. "The supply of Russian goods lightened the situation a little, but it could not, however, dislodge the Americans, who strengthened their position during the many years of controlled management." It took the revolution and Soviet power before "American expansion on northeast Russia land was forever halted." [56]

18 — WORLD WAR II IN THE ALEUTIANS

> For ne'er can sailor salty be
> Until he sails the Bering Sea,
> And views Alaska's dreary shore
> And fills himself with Arctic lore.
>
> Columbus and Balboa too,
> With Nelson form a salty crew,
> But they are fresh to you and me—
> They never sailed the Bering Sea.
>
> So when you boast of fiercest gale,
> That ever ocean you did sail,
> You cannot salty sailor be
> Until you cruise the Bering Sea.[1]

Indeed, as the sailors' song proclaimed, the Bering Sea theater of World War II was singular. When the Japanese invaded the Aleutian Islands in June 1942 to open a fifteen-month campaign, American military planners were compelled to counter an unexpected attack that threatened a poorly defended sector of continental defenses. The conflict raged in a region offering the worst weather in the world for sea or air navigation. "Both sides," opined the disapproving naval historian Samuel Eliot Morison, "would have done well to have left the Aleutians to the Aleuts for the course of the war." [2] But it was the misfortune of the Aleuts, and the 10,000 Japanese, Americans, and Canadians who lost their lives there, that Admiral Isoroku Yamamoto was in an expansive mood in early 1942. For the Aleuts, who had long suffered invasions of Western peoples, the war was a fatal blow. For the half-million soldiers and sailors of several nations, the Aleutian campaign was punishing, frustrating, and tedious.

Admiral Moshiro Hosogaya commanded the Aleutian invasion. His supply base was Paramushiro, one of the Kurile Islands just off the southern tip of Kamchatka, 1,200 miles from Tokyo and 650 miles west of Attu Island in the Aleutians. The Japanese had no plan to invade the Alaskan mainland, though the Americans could not have known this; nor had it been a firm part of American strategy to direct its offensive operations against Japan by way of the Aleutians. Yamamoto's plan was to draw the American fleet out to defend Midway Island. His attack on the Aleutians was to be only a diversion. Once the U.S. Navy left the safety of Pearl Harbor, Yamamoto's stronger fleet would pounce on the Americans. This strategy proved disastrous to Japanese hopes of a swift victory in the South Pacific. The battle of Midway was fought, but not according to the Japanese plan. The U.S. fleet savaged the Japanese, to win its first major Pacific encounter and stem the tide of Japanese aggression. Yamamoto's fleet, weakened by the absence of aircraft carriers and other capital vessels that were sent north, lost the most decisive battle of the entire Pacific war.

But this result was not anticipated as Hosogaya's task force penetrated the fog-bound Bering Sea to land troops on Attu and Kiska and launch carrier planes to bomb Dutch Harbor off Unalaska Island. Dutch Harbor was the only American naval and seaplane base in the Aleutians, and nearer by 1,000 miles to the Alaskan mainland. But the Japanese command decided to land troops on Attu and Kiska at the western end of the chain, rather than at Dutch Harbor, out of fear for a too lengthy supply line.

Seemingly, the Japanese invasion vindicated the views of a handful of visionaries who had long urged that the North was the key to American continental defenses. But only partially, since the Japanese did not have the planes necessary to hold the Aleutians. General Billy Mitchell had urged as early as 1923 that Alaskan defenses be built up in anticipation of possible air attacks over the high latitudes. Other military strategists rejected Mitchell's warnings, and his public rows with the establishment over the role of airpower led to his court-martial. He was a prophet far in advance of his time. Another prophet, Vilhjalmur

Stefansson, writer and lecturer, had been arguing since the 1920s for a recognition of geographic reality—that the transportation routes of the future would utilize the short polar distances to the major world population centers. After the experiences of World War II—with the stimulation of the Cold War tension between the U.S.S.R. and the United States—the messages of both men gained acceptance. America and Canada built the Distant Early Warning radar stations across the Arctic, while commercial airlines developed their polar routes between Europe and the United States.

Another alarm and call for defensive measures had been sounded in the late 1930s by Alaska's delegate to Congress, Anthony Dimond. Dimond was not alone in suspecting that the future would bring Japan and the United States into conflict, but his emphasis on the vulnerability and strategic importance of Alaska did not influence opinion in Washington to any great extent. Unlike the United States military, Japanese strategists had long appreciated the peril poised by a Bering Sea approach to their islands. In negotiations between the two Pacific powers that led to the Treaty of Naval Limitation in 1922, the Japanese insisted that the United States desist from fortifying the Aleutian Islands. In the treaty the United States acceded to Japanese sensitivity on this point, and after its expiration in 1934, no bases were constructed west of Dutch Harbor until after the Japanese invasion. After the war it became clear that the Japanese possessed better charts of Aleutian waters than the U.S. Navy; some Alaskans were certain that the Japanese made a number of coastal surveys of the islands during the 1930s. According to this somewhat hysterical view, this was done stealthily from Japanese fishing boats. Alaskan fishermen claimed to have observed this activity and alerted Delegate Dimond. Cassandra-like, Dimond cried out his warnings against Japanese intentions before Congress, in press interviews, and in published articles—but to no avail. The Bering Sea simply did not loom large in strategic thinking in United States military and naval circles. And Dimond's colleagues in Congress could not help suspecting that the delegate's alarms owed something to a concern that the territory share in the bonanza of public expenditures. But in June 1942 Admiral Yamamoto's designs put the Aleutians and Bering Sea quite squarely on United States strategic maps. He demonstrated that the fears of Mitchell and Dimond had some substance, that their early warnings had been more reasonable than the military's indifference.

In 1939, when the war broke out in Europe, all Alaska was defended by 300 soldiers, most of them at Chilkoot Barracks in southeastern Alaska. A small base at Sitka and a radio station at Dutch Harbor constituted the naval facilities. The American military reassessed the Alaskan situation immediately, and by the time of the Aleutian invasion, territorial defenses had increased dramatically. The navy was developing seaplane bases at Dutch Harbor, Kodiak, and Sitka, while army airfields were under construction at Anchorage, Fairbanks, and Seward. Ground forces stationed at various places in Alaska—primarily at Anchorage and Fairbanks—were up to 35,000 men, and 100 aircraft of various kinds were available.

In the spring of 1942 there was some pressure on the U.S. War Department to open a Bering Sea front for the invasion of Japan. Winston Churchill wrote President Franklin Roosevelt on March 5: "Particularly I shall be glad to know to what point your plans for operating from China or the Aleutian Islands have advanced." [3] At that time, American planners were considering the possibility of exploiting the Bering Strait route to Asia. Forces would be sent from Nome to northeast Siberia, Kamchatka, then by way of the Kurile Islands to Japan. An aerial survey of a railroad route from Prince George, British Columbia, to Nome was ordered, but preparations never got beyond the tentative stage. Consideration was also given to the extension of the projected Alaska Highway from Fairbanks to Nome. Overland routes to the Bering Strait had been proposed before, and indeed would be again in more peaceful times, but international conflicts doomed the scheme in 1942. Soviet cooperation was required for the use of this invasion route and was not forthcoming. The hard-pressed Russians were pressuring the Allies to open a second front in Europe that would divert the Germans. A movement of Allied troops from Siberia to the south would not answer their military needs; its effect would involve the Russians with the Japanese without improving the European situation. It was not until Germany had been beaten, and the Soviets had little to fear from an attack on Kamchatka and southern Siberia, that they declared war on the Japanese Empire.

MAJOR EVENTS OF THE ALEUTIAN CAMPAIGN

The Bering Sea war opened with bombing attacks on Dutch Harbor's military base on June 3–4. Some damage was done to shipping in the harbor and planes on the ground, but the attack did not echo Pearl Harbor in devastating effects. The few destroyers in the harbor discouraged the attackers with antiaircraft fire and defensive planes downed eight Japanese. Even more discouraging to the Japanese was the discovery of its carrier task force by a roving Catalina patrol bomber. After this raid, other ships landed troops on Attu and Kiska. These islands were undefended, and the Japanese began building airfields and barracks. A retaliatory air attack by American army bombers and navy planes on Kiska on June 11–13 sunk a Japanese transport with the loss of three PBY's. A large Japanese convoy, including four aircraft carriers, reached Kiska at the end of June and landed reinforcements—1,200 men, doubling the occupying forces. American submarines harassed Japanese shipping, sinking several destroyers and subchasers. Judging from their success in July, the subs would have been a more effective force in the foggy and storm-lashed region than aircraft, but they were needed elsewhere. In August the Guadalcanal campaign began, and most of the subs were despatched to the South Pacific. By contrast, Japanese submarines, most of them midgets, accomplished little during the campaign.

Before the summer was over the Japanese lost the initiative. Admiral Yamamoto ordered the four carriers and other capital ships south on July 7–8, leaving Hosogaya with only a small naval force. Work on airfields for Attu and Kiska was hampered by lack of construction equipment, and his flying boats did not attempt any offensive attacks after July. Operational losses in thick weather and the American defenses reduced Japanese airpower to insignificance. At this point, wrote naval historian Samuel Eliot Morison, in looking back at events: "It would have been wiser in the long run to have left the Japanese in Kiska and Attu alone to get frostbite on the muskeg—the Arctic counterpart of that 'withering on the vine.' " [4] (Admiral Morison's several references to "Arctic" and "long Arctic night" are odd considering the southerly latitudes of the Aleutians and his well-demonstrated knowledge of geography.) But, of course, Washington lacked the advantage of hindsight and could not ignore the potential threat to the Pacific Northwest. The American command determined to dislodge the Japanese from the Aleutians, and the Japanese were equally resolute about remaining in occupation.

The war went on. In August a United States naval bombardment of

Kiska did some damage to ships in Kiska Harbor. But the operation, as usual, was hampered by fog. Admiral R. A. Theobald next moved to establish an airfield at Adak, 200 miles east of Kiska, so that fighter escort could be offered bombers from Cold Bay—on the tip of the Alaska Peninsula—for their runs over Kiska. With lightning speed, army engineers made an airfield by draining a flooded tidal basin. Adak was occupied on August 30; within ten days the airstrip was ready for both fighters and bombers. In late August and September the Japanese withdrew from Attu to concentrate their forces on Kiska, then reoccupied Attu in October, after they discovered the Adak base. Adak's occupation revived Japanese apprehensions of an attack on Japan via the Kuriles, and another 1,115 troops were sent from Paramushiro to Kiska in December. These troops would otherwise have been sent to Guadalcanal.

A winter campaign in the Aleutians was no picnic. Admiral Morison graphically described the labors and hazards of maintaining the American planes. "Blow high blow low, thick weather or clear, they had to fly. This meant warming up the engines with blowtorches; scraping snow and melting ice off the wings; loading heavy bombs or torpedoes with numbed hands; taking off in the dark, sometimes down-wind with an overloaded plane; and, if the plane were water-based, with frozen spray obscuring the windshield. Aloft in dirty weather, radar navigation prevailed, radio aids to airmen in the Aleutians being few and far between. The altimeter, calibrated on barometric pressure, could be very misleading if the plane flew through a weather front where the pressure changed. Any craft forced down into the open sea was doomed, and unless rescued promptly, the survivors died of exposure. On the flight home there was always the danger of being dashed to bits against a mountain, while the plane 'hung on the props' over the field, waiting for a hole in the overcast." [5]

Naval ship operation was hazardous in the stormy Bering Sea, but the most uncomfortable service was that of the motor torpedo boats. PT boats were sent to the Aleutians in the belief that the almost perpetual fog would make it easy for them to torpedo enemy ships. A small boat division made the 2,500-mile voyage from Seattle to Dutch Harbor under its own power, then it was assigned to protect Adak against invasion, scout for the enemy, and lay mines. PT boat duty was much glamorized during the war, but Bering Sea duty afforded little romance. The rough

U.S. Navy sub arriving at Dutch Harbor, Unalaska.
University of Alaska Archives, San Francisco Call-Bulletin Collection

sea bounced the little boats about and icing on deck and rigging made them dangerously top-heavy.

In January 1943 the American forces moved still closer to Kiska. Amchitka, a large island with a good harbor, 140 miles west of Adak and 60 east of Kiska, was occupied. Because of this, the Japanese command was forced to make a decision. Unless their airfield on Kiska could be completed before the Americans invaded, there was little hope for containing the enemy. A withdrawal would have made sense; yet this would leave the Kuriles open to attack. A direct order, issued by Imperial Headquarters on February 5, settled the dilemma: "to hold the Western Aleutians at all costs and to carry out preparations for war." [6] The Japanese forces were unable to do either—they could only sacrifice themselves to a lost cause.

BATTLE OF THE KOMANDORSKI ISLANDS

The greatest naval battle ever fought in the Bering Sea took place in March 1943, one that, according to Samuel Eliot Morison, "has no parallel in the Pacific war." [7] Admiral Charles H. McMorris' flagship, the light cruiser *Richmond*, with a destroyer squadron and the heavy cruiser *Salt Lake City*, was cruising west of Attu when it encountered the enemy's entire northern fleet. The Japanese ships were protecting two transports and a freighter carrying reinforcements to Attu when contact was made. Admiral McMorris was outnumbered two to one but, spoiling for a fight, he tried to intercept the transports. The Japanese were able to screen the transports and bring the *Salt Lake City* under heavy fire. A long, classic battle ensued as the two fleets engaged continuously for three and a half hours at ranges of eight to twelve miles. Neither combatant had the help of effective air spotters; thus the conflict resembled those of the pre-airpower age. Essentially the United States fleet fought a retiring action after failing to close on the supply ships. The Japanese were superior in speed and firepower but were held off by the screen of American destroyers and a daring torpedo attack. The Americans were aided by the weather as well. For once there was no wind and a smoke screen laid down by the American ships hid their movements. None of the torpedoes launched by Japanese destroyers found their mark, but the *Salt Lake City* received four shells, the last of which left her flooding, listing, and reduced in speed—yet still capable of returning fire. Suddenly the *Salt Lake City* went dead in the water, just as

Japanese cruisers and destroyers were closing in for the kill. But for the smoke screen which hid its plight and an audacious foray by the American destroyers, the cruiser would have been easy prey. Then, miraculously, the Japanese broke off action. Their supplies of fuel and ammunition were low, and they feared the arrival of American bombers from Adak. Bombers had been ordered to the rescue, but necessary preparations and a snow storm had slowed their response. Yamamoto would have plenty of time to get the *Salt Lake City* and probably the *Richmond* too. As it was, he returned to Paramushiro. His flagship had been heavily mauled and, more important, the transports and freighters returned with him, without landing troops and supplies at Attu. The *Salt Lake City* recovered her power and the proud but battered American fleet steamed east to Dutch Harbor. A retiring action is never as glorious as a victorious attack, but McMorris' men had reason for self-congratulation. Morison's multivolumed history of the naval war holds accounts of many more decisive battles than that waged in the Bering Sea; yet the historian rated the Komandorski affray highly. "That moment in the gray subarctic noon just as the enemy turned away, when *Salt Lake City* lay dead on a glassy sea but still firing, with *Richmond* firing as she closed, and three destroyers going in for a torpedo attack, deserves to be depicted by a great marine painter." [8]

RETAKING ATTU AND KISKA

The amphibious attack on Attu, the more westerly of the two Japanese islands, was carefully planned. In April the Seventh Infantry Division of the U.S. Army, after extensive drill in landing tactics near Monterey, California, steamed north for the jump-off point at Cold Bay. Naval forces to support the invasion were supplemented by the addition of three battleships, several cruisers, and an aircraft carrier. In all, the task force was to include over thirty major ships and as many smaller vessels. Efforts had been made to keep the destination of the forces secret. Troops had been lectured on tropical diseases; winter clothing had been kept hidden. Kiska was bombed continuously in April while Attu was left virtually untouched. Patrol planes maintained constant surveillance of Japanese movements without any opposition from enemy planes. Even so, news of the plan somehow leaked. Tokyo warned the Attu defenders to expect an invasion but could promise no reinforcements before late May.

Landings were made on Attu, an island only thirty-five miles long and fifteen miles wide, on May 11 without resistance. One landing site was Holtz Bay on the northern side of the island, the other at Massacre Bay on the southern side. Foggy weather had delayed the assault but the sea was calm when the troops were put ashore. Colonel Yamazaki, in command of the Japanese garrison, made no attempt to defend the beaches, though he had ample warning of the invasion. His defensive forces numbered only 2,630 soldiers, and his heavy armament was limited to a few antiaircraft and coastal defense guns. All he could do was plan a delaying operation, a blockade in the valley connecting Massacre and Holtz Bays, that would prevent a joining of the invasion armies.

The American invasion force of 11,000 troops had all the advantages: Field guns, trucks, and other mobile equipment were plentiful, though hampered by the spongy muskeg. Their advance was assisted by heavy naval bombardments, though not by aircraft. A thick fog kept American planes grounded and slowed the ground attack against the well-dug-in defenders. In the first forty-eight hours after landing the southern force moved only 4,000 yards. Its commander complained of the rugged terrain and enemy resistance, called for more troops and

American troops landing at Attu.
University of Alaska Archives,
San Francisco Call-Bulletin
Collection

road-building equipment, and predicted a six-month campaign. This hysteria was too much for operation commander Admiral Kinkaid, who swiftly replaced the dilatory general. By May 17 the two invading divisions made contact, and the Japanese retreated from the valley eastward to Chichagof Harbor, fighting all the way. All they could do was make a last stand against the overwhelmingly superior strength of the Americans.

Yamazaki refused to surrender. Instead, on May 29 he led one of the biggest banzai charges of the entire Pacific war, an attack on the main American camp. Before the assault, a Japanese officer made a last entry in his diary: "The last assault is to be carried out. All patients in the hospital are to commit suicide. . . . Gave 400 shots of morphine to severely wounded, and killed them. . . . Finished all the patients with grenades. . . . Only 33 years of living and I am to die here. I have no regrets. Banzai to the Emperor. . . . Goodbye Taeke, my beloved wife." [9] Then a screaming horde of 1,000 soldiers, some armed with only bayonets tied to sticks, overran two American command posts. The attackers were soon contained but would not be taken alive. The survivors, 500 in all, destroyed themselves with their own hand grenades.

This ended the Japanese resistance. It had not been a pretty battle. Only 28 Japanese prisoners were taken; the other 2,351 soldiers were killed. American casualties were 549 dead, 1,148 wounded, and 932 disabled by exposure, disease, accidents, and mental breakdowns. The Japanese government lauded the suicidal heroes of Attu as representative of the people's fighting spirit—as indeed they were. American commanders studied the mistakes made during the amphibious operation and resolved to do better in the future. The navy had been fortunate: Fog prevented Japanese planes from Paramushiro from delivering a heavy blow; yet cautious ship commanders had stood too far from the coast of Attu to bombard effectively. Army casualties were high, considering their dominant manpower. Army generals showed poor leadership, while the inexperienced troops—although they had been trained for desert warfare —did not show much verve in the ghostly fog of the Bering Sea. The chief distinction of the battle of Attu was the high attrition suffered by the Americans. In proportion to the opposing numbers it was, save for Iwo Jima, the most costly battle of the Pacific war.

Kiska was the next target and Kinkaid ordered daily bombings— weather permitting. The invasion force would be even larger; 34,426 combat troops practiced amphibious landings during the summer months. Meanwhile, naval patrols went on, and several enemy ships were destroyed by surface vessels and submarines. From June 1 to August 15, 1,454 sorties were made over Kiska; 1,255 tons of bombs were dropped. Some planes were lost to enemy antiaircraft fire, but more were lost to the weather.

On July 22, naval ships pounded the rocky island relentlessly. After the ships ceased firing, American and Canadian planes bombed and strafed probable enemy positions. Despite this pounding, the well-entrenched defenders suffered few casualties; but they had to keep their heads down.

A strange naval battle was fought after a Catalina reported radar contact with seven ships 200 miles southwest of Attu. The contact, which led to the farcical and entirely one-sided "Battle of the Pips" had been made on July 23. Three days later, Admiral R. C. Giffen disposed the task force used in the bombardment of Kiska 80 miles south of the island. Several ships reported radar contacts, and gun crews zeroed in on the supposed targets. For thirty minutes, gunners of fleet battleships and cruisers fired continually, adjusting their aim as radar operators advised corrections and lookouts reported on flares and lights. Over 1,000 shells rained down on the phantom fleet of the enemy. Finally, in the light of dawn, an observer plane looked over the area bombarded. Instead of savagely mauled Japanese ships and floating debris, the pilot saw only the empty sea. Phantoms seen on the radar screen, perhaps return echoes from the mountains of Amchitka, had misguided the American navy.

Had the navy been a trifle more alert it would have had a genuine battle. On July 21 a Japanese task force departed from Paramushiro to evacuate Kiska. Fog could be friend or foe in the Bering Sea. On this occasion it perfectly screened the Japanese fleet of sixteen ships from patrolling planes and ships. The fleet reached Kiska on July 28, and in one hour loaded the 5,183 men of the garrison, slipped away into the fog, and reached Paramushiro on July 31—entirely undetected all the way.

The attack on Kiska by the unaware Americans began on July 30 with a crashing naval bombardment. For two weeks various divisions of the fleet, at sporadic intervals, rained shells on the hapless rock and muskeg of the island. The army air forces were more regular; twice each day enemy positions were bombed and strafed. Intelligence officers submitted gleeful reports of damage done to Japanese installations. Photographs actually revealed a general destruction. The enemy had blown up buildings and stores before departing.

After these softening operations the invasion was carried out on August 15. Almost 35,000 American and Canadian soldiers and 100 vessels took part in the fiasco. For a week, troops searched the island to find only a few stray dogs. Still there were casualties, 313 in all, as the invaders shot at each other or tripped mines. The military commanders were extremely embarrassed, though some of the GIs thought the operation was very funny. The dogs inspired a ballad, "Tales of Kiska":

> You've heard the bloody tales of old
> Of fearless knights and warriors bold,
> But now the Muse pens Tales of Kiska,
> Or, how we missed them by a whisker.
>
> One hundred thousand men at muster,
> Admirals, generals adding luster;
> Two hundred planes, as many ships—
> All were bound for Kiska's Nips.

And now we come to how and when
"Dog-day" got its cognomen—
"Dog-day's" evening found our log
Quoting capture of one dog.

"Dog-day" plus 1 and 2 and 3
Found three more in captivity;
But as for Japs we couldn't say
We'd seen one either night or day.

We searched volcanic craters vast
To catch a glimpse of one at last;
It took three days before we learnt
That more than dogs there simply weren't.

Refrain

O here's to mighty ComNorPack
Whose kingdom lay at cold Adak,
Whose reign was known in fame for fog
And capture of two couple dog! [10]

The circumstances were less humorous to embattled American commanders elsewhere in the Pacific who could have used the troops and ships delayed in the Bering Sea. But at least the job was done. There would be no more battles in the Bering Sea and no more Japanese troops on American soil. Some of the American forces were shipped off to other fronts, but a good number remained to garrison the Aleutians for the remainder of the war.

The Bering Sea war brought Russians back to the region they had once colonized. The operation was highly secret because the Soviet Union had not yet declared war on Japan, but a Russian base was established at Cold Bay on the Alaska Peninsula some months before V-E Day. There, in conditions very similar to those of the Kurile Islands, Russian troops trained in amphibious landings. Like many other wartime projects, this one came to nothing. Atomic bombings brought about Japan's surrender before it was necessary to launch an invasion from the north. But military strategists had been preparing for a joint Russian-American attack from Siberia and the Aleutians.

In all the wartime excitement, the plight of the Aleut residents of the Aleutian and Pribilof Islands was overlooked. The war was an unmitigated disaster to the descendants of natives who had suffered through the invasions of Russian fur traders and Yankee whalemen. Evacuated from their island homes, the Aleuts of the Aleutians were never to return.

After the war, the Aleutians remained a key defensive area for a number of years. Defense thinking changed in the 1950s, however, and the Aleutian bases, except for Attu, were reduced in importance. Anchorage and Fairbanks became the principal northern defense centers. The Cold War had something to do with the shift, but other factors—advanced aircraft, the attraction of better flying weather, and the DEW Line—were more influential. It is unlikely, however, that the strategic possibilities of the Bering Sea will be overlooked in the future as they were prior to the war. Samuel Eliot Morison's history of the Aleutian Campaign was first published in 1951—at the height of Cold War tension. Future international conflict was not alluded to directly by the navy's historian, but he did refer to the importance of the North. "For it may well be that, in the future, the Bering Sea, and not the Caribbean or the South Pacific, will be America's 'Sea of Destiny.' " [11]

19 TODAY AND TOMORROW ON THE BERING SEA FRONTIER

The international boundary line that has appeared on all maps of the Bering Sea since the United States acquired Alaska runs between two little islands in the narrow Bering Strait. Big Diomede is a part of the Soviet Union, Little Diomede is on the American side of the line. Imaginary lines cannot separate people related by ties of blood and culture, although Cold War politics can create barriers. In the spring of 1973, for the second consecutive year, the people of the Diomedes met on the ice near the islands to talk and exchange gifts. A few years earlier the Big Diomede Eskimos had been moved from their island to a village on the Siberian shore. Now they are just visitors to their former dwelling place. The easing of relations between the United States and Russia made the informal meeting possible. Earlier, while Big Diomede was still populated, the Soviet government frowned on any contact between the peoples of the two islands.

But one suspects that politics has never been a matter of urgent concern among the Diomede Eskimos. At their 1973 meeting the talk was lively but centered on the kinds of goods which were exchanged. The Americans enjoyed their gifts of reindeer meat and vodka, while the Siberians relished the cigarettes and candy they received. The exchange that raised the most comment was that of a twenty-one-jewel Russian-made watch for an American Timex. All agreed that the American got the best of the deal. It was a happy meeting and plans were laid for 1974. This time the Siberians hoped to have visas which would permit them to visit their ancestral homes on Big Diomede. Then there would be leisure for much more talk, trading, and, perhaps, even the traditional sports the Eskimos love so well.[1]

The Americans have aspirations too. They want to remain on their island but would like to be less isolated. During the winter, airplanes land regularly on the sea ice to bring mail, newspapers, and goods; but in the summer, planes are not able to land. Little Diomede is only a mile and one-half long and three-quarters of a mile wide and no one has ever tried to carve a landing strip out of the sloping, granite-faced terrain. So when the ice breaks up, the islanders, for the most part, depend upon their skin boats for transportation to the mainland. Fortunately, most of their year's supplies are shipped to them each year on the *North Star III*, the supply ship maintained by the U.S. Bureau of Indian Affairs, which services all the villages of the Bering Sea and Arctic Alaska.

In 1973 the *North Star III* made a special trip to Little Diomede with 400 tons of building material. Now the villagers will have new housing to replace the dilapidated, cratelike houses they have long occupied. But the fixtures will not be modern: Seal-oil lamps will still provide heat and light. The eighteen new, one-room homes will house the entire population of the island with some comfort and safety. Lengths of cable were provided to secure the houses to their rocky perches and prevent them from being swept by severe winds into the sea.[2]

On St. Lawrence Island the Eskimos of Savoonga have been benefiting for several years from the use of a refrigerated storehouse for their seasonal walrus catch. Before this cleverly designed unit was conceived and built by Phil Johnson, a University of Alaska engineer, the walruses were piled in a wooden shed, where the meat tended to ripen as time passed.

Like the Diomede people, St. Lawrence Islanders have social expectations. Their ancestors had migrated to the island from Siberia, and there had long been an easy traffic between the island and Siberian mainland. This communication was severed after World War II; but now there seems to be a chance for a restoration, at least partially. The islanders want to visit Indian Point, Siberia, and have asked the U.S. Bureau of Indian Affairs to try to arrange it. The U.S. State Department has asked approval from Moscow and it seems likely to be granted. Once permission is given, Foster Aviation of Nome will fly the Americans over without charge.

What of the traditional umiaks? Yes, skin boats are still in use, but the islanders are perhaps a less daring maritime people today than their ancestors were. "We might get over there and not be able to get back," commented one.[3] The distance is forty miles and even in July, the best month of the year for such a voyage, the weather is unpredictable. "It would be better to fly—then we could go any time." [4]

One of the larger towns in Alaska is on Adak Island in the Aleutians, but there are few Aleuts to be seen there or anywhere among the islands. After World War II, most of the Aleuts found homes on the Alaska Peninsula or other places in Alaska. Their evacuation had been a necessary war measure, but in the chaos of the emergency, it was badly bungled. The poor Aleuts have always stood in the path of invaders and have suffered for it. Aleuts were taken to southeastern Alaska during the war and dumped there with inadequate housing and food—and worse, with absolutely nothing to do. Most of these Bering Sea people had never seen anything resembling the towering forests of southeastern Alaska and were completely disrupted by the move. In a sense, their nineteenth-century ancestors, who were carried to the same region for sea otter hunting by the Russians, had it better: They, at least, were able to carry on their traditional hunter's life.

The big base of Adak is populated by 5,000 people, mostly military personnel who man U.S. Naval and Coast Guard facilities there. Elsewhere in the Aleutians the dwellers are very thinly stretched out. The raging williwaw winds still bluster crazily, and the driving, almost horizontal rain still falls; but outside of Adak and other radio and military stations, there are few people to be discomforted among the island bird sanctuaries.

Traditions have been maintained to some extent on the Pribilofs. The Aleuts there were evacuated during the war but most returned to their villages. The islands are still rich in resources. Bellowing seal beachmasters still dominate their harems in the rookeries of the rocky shores, and a number of the bachelors are clubbed each summer to provide something of an industry. Aleuts do the clubbing but need the help of imported college boys for the skinning. Many of the natives had become too weakened by conditions of their relocation to wield skinning knives with their former skill.

One recent visitor to the Pribilofs described the villages as the most depressing places he had ever seen. Money is abundant. Young boys ride their motorcycles round and round the limited road and trail network and race their motor boats in the lagoons before the villages, but do not dare to take the boats beyond the safety of the lagoon. Once the short seal-killing season is over, there is not much to do on the Pribilofs. Traditions do not hold the young who are in a confused suspension between the Hollywood glitter of a modern world they have never actually experienced and a now meaningless ancient pattern of life. This problem is a serious one for all the bush people of Alaska. It is the old dilemma of clashing cultural change. Money could help, and the settlement of the native land claims is producing some of that. Perhaps more important is the emerging assertiveness of peoples who have been long submerged and depressed. Native leaders fought hard and lobbied long to gain the land settlement, and out of the fire of their struggle developed political knowledge and administrative skills that can now be applied to the problems of economic development.

Education will be important too. Better schools and better opportunities for vocational training, professional study, and an education more relevant to native life must be provided by the State of Alaska and the U.S. Bureau of Indian Affairs, which share the educational burden. One bright light on the horizon is in the growing concern for providing natives instruction in their ancestral languages. "Natives can learn in schools where all instruction is in English, just as a violinist can learn to play his instrument while riding a bicycle, but there are some handicaps involved," as Dr. Michael Krauss puts it.[5] Krauss is a University of Alaska linguist who has spearheaded a program to develop instructional materials in all the native languages still in use. It is an uphill struggle and a race against time. Languages must be saved if a cultural heritage is to be held together. In most villages only the elders speak their old languages; in some, the traditional language has been eradicated. This is the result of an educational effort of a century, a program of relentless, well-meaning destruction of traditional languages and cultures.

The correspondence files of the Alaska Commercial Company and the U.S. Treasury yield numerous examples of the battle waged against the use of the Aleut tongue. "School is on but not much is gained," wrote one Treasury agent from the Pribilofs in 1888. "Too much of their own jargon is being used by pupils outside of school hours." [6] There was never any problem regarding language during school hours on the Pribilofs or any other place in Alaska. English was the only language which could be spoken, and any student who lapsed was swiftly disciplined. After all, unintelligible mutterings were a threat to a teacher's superior position.

Nor was the U.S. Bureau of Education—the federal agency charged with Alaska native education from the 1890s to more recent times— solicitous about the cultural ties between Alaskans and Siberians. In his 1915–16 report, the teacher at Cape Prince of Wales complained of the visits of Siberian Eskimos. "They don't compare with ours in intelligence or physique." [7]

An exchange of visits was disruptive to the sincere, often frustrating, work of the teacher. "At such time ancient customs, songs, and dances are revived, all tending to a retrograde movement." [8] And as for family ties: "The older Wales native is a hopeless case, and unobstructed advancement will only begin when he is gone for good." [9] Today we can be sure that the elders in question are "gone for good," but we are not so sure that the teacher or his successors were wise. Clearly, they prevailed. A culture was dismantled and no one was able to replace it with another meaningful one. The teachers and bureaucrats in their arrogance and stupidity acted according to fervent general beliefs that had long guided white Americans in their administration of aboriginal peoples.

In many ways the bush teacher had to be admired. The teacher at Ugashik on the Alaska Peninsula in 1916–17 worked zealously—and not just at instruction: Each week he supervised the bathing of his pupils in the school washtub. He also managed the village reindeer herd and was consulted on virtually every aspect of village life. On occasion heroic performances were demanded of him. When a flu epidemic swept through the community he had to dash to a neighboring village for medicines. This involved a 570-mile round trip to Nushaguk by dog sled and it almost cost him his life. A snow blizzard swept across his route, and he was forced to hole up in the open for two days and three nights before the weather lifted. But there were compensations for all this: "We have the good will of every native within a radius of 300 miles and a feeling that we have done our duty to those in need." [10]

Bush teachers usually had the support of their wives and that lightened their burdens. But these dedicated couples were agents of changes too complex for them to understand clearly. During the same year the Ugashik teacher was struggling to provide medical care for the villagers, the teacher's wife on Atka Island expressed concern for the health of Aleut women. During the winter months while their husbands

Interior of Eskimo school at Golovin, Seward Peninsula.
University of Alaska Archives, Lynn Denny Collection

were away the women traditionally whiled away their time weaving baskets, superbly crafted objects of practical and aesthetic value. "This is very tiresome, close work, and we are discouraging it to some extent. We tell them to get out and walk or fish on nice days." [11] She also taught them less demanding skills of fabric sewing and "fancy work."

On the Siberian side of the Bering Sea a more enlightened educational philosophy has prevailed since the Soviets have turned their attention to their remote frontier. It was not until the late 1920s that remote Bering Sea villages were provided with schools; but once the effort was launched, it was carried along with sustained enthusiasm. In 1928 Tikhon Semushkin arrived at Penkegnei Bay, a village 120 miles south of St. Lawrence Bay, Siberia, to establish a cultural center. The year before, a congress of Soviets had been held with the participation of all of Siberia's natives. The Russian officials had been shocked to discover that none of them spoke Russian. Something had to be done about that right away.

The Siberian bush teacher faced many of the problems his counterpart in Alaska encountered. He, too, had to supervise baths and counter the resistance of parents to sending their children away from their villages for education. But he had an advantage unknown to Alaskan teachers and their charges. Although Soviet educational policies have had their turns and shifts, it was decided early on that the use of instructional materials in native languages encouraged the learning process. It was also Soviet policy to protect that traditional culture of each of its many native peoples—so long as this did not interfere with other economic and social goals. Thus when L. M. Starokadomskiy flew to Emma Bay in 1934—to visit a region known to him from his 1910–15 service on the icebreaker *Taymyr*—he was proud to observe the new school and a "local newspaper in Chukchi, Eskimo and Russian," and hear pupils sing Red army songs in Chukchi.[12] A process of cultural change was taking place in Siberia—as in Alaska—but in a gentler, more intelligent way.

Of course, one cannot accept all the fulsome praise the Soviets heap upon themselves for educational enlightenment. Researchers who have been interested in gathering hard facts and figures on Siberian village life and education have met with staunch resistance, but with serene assurances that everything, in every way, is going beautifully. Official propaganda beclouds the scene, discourages truth, inhibits scholarly exchange, and wearies the reader or auditor with its monotonous tone.

Russian professionals have attended international conferences on cross-cultural education in recent years but have never overstepped the barrier that divides propaganda from truth.[13] Maybe the propaganda is the truth. Who knows? Visits of foreigners to northern Siberia are sharply restricted. A few foreigners have been allowed to see something of the Siberian North, but not Kamchatka or northern Siberia, and Westerners known for their expert knowledge of Siberia have not seen much of any part of the North.

Whether in recent years any foreigners have been allowed to travel to Petropavlovsk or more remote places like East Cape is difficult to discover. Travelers have written back describing their Siberian journeys; yet there is a time-honored convention of travel narration that allows the author to avoid implicit clarification of the places he saw or just heard about. A recent English traveler, George St. George, devotes a long section to Kamchatka. The section is interesting because St. George had grown up in Irkutsk years before, then spent his adult years outside Russia. In his youth, Russians believed that "Kamchatka was the end of the world." [14] No one would go there of their own free will. The region was not even used as a place of exile or imprisonment because it would have been impossible to get anyone to guard them.

Population growth was slow because of the province's remoteness. Petropavlovsk, the chief town, had only 1,000 people in 1917, according to St. George's statistics. Other travelers of that earlier period found fewer than that. By 1939 the population was 35,000 because of the "search for gold in Siberia." [15] Growth was even more spectacularly accelerated by the return of the Kurile Islands to Russia after World War II. Figures for 1968 indicated a population of 126,000.

Petropavlovsk is centrally heated by the thermal sea that underlies it in the same manner as with Reykjavik, Iceland—an instance of clever utilization of a natural resource, noted by St. George, though he does not indicate he visited the town. Since the whole peninsula rests on a bed of thermal waters which emerge as geysers and hot springs, Russian engineers were able to tap this bountiful source of energy for heating buildings and the development of large-scale hothouse agriculture. This natural advantage has made Kamchatka the center of hydrothermics for the entire Siberian North.

Glowing reports have always been issued from time to time of the mineral wealth of Kamchatka and northeastern Siberia. A 1971 report described the discovery of a great potential for gas production in the Anadyr basin, the remote region which had historically depended upon its fur and maritime resources. One can assume that such petroleum resources as may exist in the northeast will only be developed when fields much closer to large population centers and transportation systems have been exhausted.

Kamchatka's chief riches today, as earlier, are in its fisheries. Various fishes and crustaceans abound in the waters of the peninsula where biological conditions have created a prolific feeding ground. Early in the century, Japanese fishermen were greatly attracted to the Kamchatka fisheries; but today, the industry is entirely in Russian hands.

Future economic development depends to a large extent upon the scale of utilization of Russia's northern sea route or what used to be referred to as the Northeast Passage. For years, seasonal use has been made of the Arctic passage, and the government has recently announced its intention of keeping the passage open the year round. Icebreaker technology in Russia is far in advance of that of other nations, and there is every likelihood that the Soviets can accomplish their purposes. The atomic-powered *Lenin* has been operating since 1960, and another atomic icebreaker, the *Arktika*, was launched in 1973.[16] This latest addition to Russia's Arctic fleet is supposed to be larger and twice as powerful as the 16,000-ton, 44,000-horsepower *Lenin*.

The launching of a new icebreaker, the first built in many years, in the United States in the fall of 1973 suggests similar technological developments that could affect the American side of the Bering Sea. The United States has lagged well behind the U.S.S.R. and Canada in icebreaker construction, but it is conceivable that the development of Alaska's Arctic petroleum resources will soon bring about a concentration of effort on the creation of a significant icebreaking fleet for the U.S. Coast Guard.

MARINE MAMMAL AND FISHERY PROTECTION

As a result of the waves of conservationist sentiment of recent years, the Bering Sea-Arctic Ocean marine mammals have come under new consideration. Congress held hearings on the best measures of protecting the mammals and, as usual, all views were represented. Members of Friends of the Earth called for an end to all killing. Fortunately for Alaska's coastal natives, a compromise was reached in the Marine

Mammal Protection Act of 1972. Natives are permitted to carry on their traditional subsistence hunting in order to gather meat for their larder and hides and ivory for their handicraft. Scientists, like Robert Elsner of the University of Alaska's Institute of Marine Science, think the regulation is necessary, but are concerned about the way the act will be interpreted. He is concerned that scientific research will be inhibited under federal regulation. Scientists cannot gather specimens for study unless they are granted a permit, and the permit system is a cumbersome one. Other Alaskans are pained because the act took away the state's power of fishery protection and believe that the state would have been able to do a better job of administering the act than a federal agency.

An explosive situation exists in regard to the fisheries of the Bering Sea. Only rarely does a ship penetrate the Bering Sea during the winter, but in the summer, hundreds of fishing vessels—Russian, Japanese, Korean, and American—scour the rich fishing grounds. International conflict is a common enough occurrence. U.S. Coast Guard vessels patrol the waters throughout the season and arrest foreign vessels which violate the three-mile limit. All maritime nations are examining their positions in regard to the distance of offshore territorial limits, and an international "law of the seas" conference is underway. Conflict can only grow more frequent as fishing activity is intensified, and its resolution in the Bering Sea and elsewhere depends upon negotiations that will have to be carried on for years.

Bristol Bay fishermen are alarmed at the depletion of the salmon run in recent years and have been vociferous in demanding that the United States extend its offshore sovereignty or otherwise find some means of restricting overfishing by foreign vessels. Salmon have always been the most highly sought catch in the Bering Sea; but shrimp, Tanner crab, King crab, herring, pollock, cod, perch, and halibut are taken.

The Japanese fishermen first came into Bristol Bay in 1930 because the Russians restricted their fishing off Kamchatka. They came each season, to the growing concern of Alaskans. Protests finally led the Japanese government to declare in 1938 that its fleets would no longer fish Bristol Bay. After World War II the Japanese, Korean, and—in ever increasing numbers—Russian vessels began to take annual catches. Even in winter Russian fish for herring in the Bering Sea in the area between the Aleutian Islands and the pack ice.

Alaskans do not always share the view of conservationists, but many of them applauded when the Friends of the Earth called for a 200-mile jurisdiction. Congress is considering bills introduced in both houses to this effect. "Biologists believe," argued a leading conservationist, "that another season of Japanese netting will cut so critically into the salmon runs that the Bristol Bay fishery will be destroyed, and the survival of the species jeopardized." [17] One Alaskan fisherman was sure that in ten years he would only be able to show his grandchildren red salmon by visiting a museum in Juneau. Clearly, there has been tremendous pressure put on all Bering Sea stocks. The total catch has risen from 28 million pounds in 1954, to 5 billion in 1973. How long can this measure of depletion go on before a disastrous collapse of the whole fishery occurs?

MARINE SCIENTISTS IN THE BERING SEA

Scientists customarily publish the results of their investigations in scholarly journals or in reports that do not have a wide circulation. Often their work is only known to other professionals with the same kinds of interests. This is unfortunate because there is much going on that is exciting and portentious. It is one of the ironies of our civilization that we often neglect the study of very important matters in favor of lesser, more exotic subjects. Scientific research of the Bering Sea does not have a high priority in any of the countries that border it; yet an intensive international research effort is critically needed. The bountiful sea is uniquely productive, and its stocks of whales, pinnipeds, and fishes are harvested by fishermen from the United States, Japan, U.S.S.R., Canada, and Korea. Despite the dependence of several nations on the richness of the sea, attempts to understand Bering Sea oceanography and to develop its resources nationally have been sparse.

We can grasp something of the wonders and mysteries of the northern waters from the reports of the marine scientists who are most concerned about the area. Among the unique qualities of the Bering Sea is the extensiveness of its continental shelf, which accounts for the high productivity of its waters. The shelf extends into almost one-half of the entire area encompassed by the Bering Sea.

Another unique feature—one that has been touched on many times in this book, but in quite a different context—is the nature and quality of the region's atmosphere. While mariners have complained endlessly of the winds, the marine scientist is enchanted with the "maximum atmospheric vigor" of the Bering Sea. Only the Norwegian Sea and the "roaring forties" and "furious fifties" of the Antarctic Ocean have comparable winds. Thus the scientist sees the possibilities for research into the effects on ocean life produced by such extreme conditions—a subject little understood but vital to a determination of resource productivity.[18]

The high productivity of the Bering Sea is known, but not the reasons for it. Why does it support more marine life than other, more temperate seas? Scientists can continue to conjecture; yet it would be more beneficial to mankind if we actually knew the answer. The largest marine mammal populations in the world are found in the Bering Sea, also the largest clam population, the largest bird populations per unit area, the largest eelgrass beds. World records for the greatest number of fish caught per unit area are also held by the Bering Sea.

When all these "firsts" are tallied, we can see the fascination of the Bering Sea for the marine scientists. To most of us the region is just a remote spot on the globe. We know the sea is partially frozen most of the year, cold and foggy even during summer. Yet it has always been a sea of wealth, a sea brimming with life in all seasons, a vastly sustaining sea that man has been exploiting for thousands of years without knowing very much about it. Soon, perhaps, the marine scientists will lift the veil of ignorance that has obscured our knowledge of the region just as surely as its summer fogs have confused navigators.

But in the future the unknown resources of the Bering Sea may be more important than those known. Continental shelves of the world's oceans have been among the richest sources of petroleum, and the shelves of the Bering Sea may prove to be rich producers. Additionally, some of the lands bordering the sea are known to be highly mineralized and have been undeveloped only because of transportation difficulties. Transportation development in the North is underway now on a major scale and is likely to continue.

The Coast Guard began making annual summer voyages to the Bering Sea and Arctic Ocean in 1886. Throughout its long service in the North, the Coast Guard (called the Revenue Marine Division until 1894, and, subsequently the Revenue Cutter Service) compiled a splendid record. Its rugged vessels, the *Bear, Thetis, Corwin*, and others, were familiar to the coastal dwellers along the entire littoral of the Bering Sea. Revenue men struggled to keep the peace in Aleut and Eskimo villages, harassed seal poachers and contraband booze dealers, rescued disabled whaling and exploration ships, and offered the closest thing to a ferry system connecting northeastern Siberia to northwestern Alaska. Those who benefited from this transport included adventurous travelers like Harry DeWindt, scientists, missionaries, school teachers assigned to remote villages of St. Lawrence Island, stranded seamen, and the Eskimos of King Island who migrated to Nome each summer. Without the transport made available by the Revenue Service, the islands and mainland of the Bering Sea would have been virtually inaccessible to scientists during the summer navigation season, and the progress of knowledge would have been considerably slowed.

It is only recently that scientists have become somewhat aware of the winter conditions of the Bering Sea. Thanks to the aid of the U.S. Coast Guard, University of Alaska scientists and others have had a chance to make significant studies of ice and geological conditions and of mammals and wildfowl. Dr. Peter McRoy of the University's Institute of Marine Science headed one such project in 1970. The icebreaker *Northwind* acted as a floating laboratory for the scientific investigations. The *Northwind* left Kodiak on January 28 and reached the ice edge in Bristol Bay three days later, after the usual stormy passage through the Unimak Pass of the Aleutians. Nome was reached on February 17. As the ship cruised north the scientists directed their research activities to the environment of the ice edge. Their studies focused on biology, chemistry, geology, and hydrography. Sightings of birds and mammals were recorded. Led by an Eskimo hunter, the scientists stalked across the sea ice to take four unwary walrus. The carcasses of these mammals, including one weighing almost two tons, were taken to Nome where the meat was joyfully received. The viscerals and contents of the stomachs of the animals were stored for further study. Although the marine scientists hoped to make such a cruise each year, it has not been possible to arrange it since 1970. To the author, who made a portion of the sea ice cruise, it was a curious experience. Such a voyage is fascinating and makes one wonder when the winter secrets of the Bering Sea will be unfolded. It also makes one envy the scientists who will share in the revelations that are made.

WOLVES ARE COMING

The "sea of mystery" is an expression that has been used often to describe many regions and could easily be applied to the Bering Sea. But mystery has to give way to science and also to some rational consideration of particular circumstances. Mysteries are compounded of many factors, not the least of which is ignorance. A striking example of the latter was revealed in a letter received recently by Dr. Donald W. Hood, director of the University of Alaska's Institute of Marine Science from the Smithsonian Institution's Center for Short-Lived Phenomena:

> One of our correspondents recently sent us a United Press International release that appeared in a St. Louis newspaper. The release, datelined Moscow, February 4th, concerns the migration of wolves from Alaska across the Bering Sea to the Chukotka Peninsula in the U.S.S.R. It was also reported that the wolves attacked herds of reindeer and the Soviet government provided a helicopter to aid in elimination of the wolves by hunting parties.
>
> We should very much like to get more information on the migration itself, such as, is it a commonplace occurrence or rare, were large numbers of animals involved, what factors contributed to their movement, is the migration over, has it been investigated by scientists or at least noted, the species of wolf, in short, any available facts concerning the migration.[19]

Short-lived phenomena indeed! It would be edifying to substantiate this report of vicious predators from the United States stalking across the ice to attack the reindeer of Siberia. Can it be that now the Bering Strait gap has been bridged by the cunning wolves of the North? Is this another illustration of what has been seen to have been a recurrent trend—the predation of Siberian resources by Americans? Luckily, the Cold War tensions have eased, and this news story did not get wide exposure in the Soviet Union. Had this invasion been reported in the 1950s, there might have been shoe-banging protests made in the General Assembly of the United Nations. And who could blame the Russians for their outrage at such a blatant, destructive violation of national boundaries?

Of course, the report was nonsense. Alaska's wolves have many fine talents as hunters but are not notable maritime travelers. If Americans sent their polar bears over to Siberia to attack reindeer, that would be another matter. But perhaps even politicians appreciate the notorious internationalism of polar bears.

ATOMIC BLASTS

The Bering Sea events that have provoked most discussion in recent years have been the atomic weapon tests on Amchitka Island of the Aleutian chain. To the United States Atomic Energy Commission the Amchitka site provided all kinds of advantages for underground explosions. There are no people living within hundreds of miles, allowing close monitoring of the results of the test. Yet a vociferous minority has protested each of these explosions and, perhaps, to some effect.

In December 1973 the A.E.C. announced that it will conduct no more tests on Amchitka. Over a million dollars have been expended in an effort to restore the island ecologically to its condition prior to the blasts of 1965, 1969, and 1971. One remaining mark is a new lake formed in 1971 when a bomb, buried 5,875 feet in the ground, was set off. This new feature of the island is 55 feet deep and 1½ miles across. Wildlife is beginning to return to the island, although the Bureau of Sport Fisheries and Wildlife predicts that it will be a long time before the animal population regains its former strength.

FUTURE PROSPECTS

Whatever the future holds for the Bering Sea frontier cannot be foreseen with clarity. A planning commission of the State of Alaska has recommended that a railroad transportation corridor be opened up from Fairbanks to Nome. If a railroad or even a highway was ever to be built to the Seward Peninsula it would certainly foster the development of the most highly mineralized region of Alaska. The current construction of a road to support the Prudhoe Bay-Valdez pipeline suggests that capital investment for such huge building projects can be found when wealth beckons, and it could be that mineral discoveries in northwestern Alaska will attract road builders.

American petroleum companies have been investigating the mineral potential of Bristol Bay for some time, just as the Russians have been exploring the Anadyr basin and other areas of northeastern Siberia. Obviously, the discovery of rich deposits will stimulate economic development of the Bering Sea.

The old dream of a railroad linking Alaska and Siberia by way of the Bering Strait is not dead but has taken new forms. A University of California professor, T. Lin, has long urged the feasibility of a "peace bridge" across the strait, a concrete structure that could serve as a transportation corridor and a means of bringing about better international understanding. Lin stands ready to design the bridge but has not been overwhelmed by the attentions of backers.[20]

Recently there has been some discussion among United States and Russian diplomats of the possibility of creating a "Peace Park" on the Bering Strait. The idea is for both countries to designate their portions of the Bering Strait region as national or international parks in order to carry out joint scientific studies in the region. This would be a pleasant gesture. However, if a historical study were to be made of Bering Strait frontier relations, the result could be embarrassing. Cries against the Yankee predators might possibly be revived once more. This would be unfortunate because, after all, most internatiional boundaries have at times been scenes of tension and conflict.

Whatever the future holds, people of the Bering Sea will be affected. Change is inevitable. Some of it will be good, some bad. But there is no reason to be pessimistic about the future of this little-known region. The history of its people shows the same mixture of grandiose dreams, aggressive economic exploitation, muddled social efforts, bungled warfare, and ignorant administration that has existed elsewhere in the world. It shows that Bering Sea frontiersmen were capable of carving out some form of Western civilization in an unlikely region, regardless of the rigors of the climate and the formidable transportation problems.

ENGINEERING SCHEMES

While Americans' visions of engineering projects in the Bering Strait have always run to bridges, tunnels, and railroads, Russian scientists have proposed even grander schemes. Climate control in order to create better agricultural conditions is a particular point of emphasis, and many suggestions on a means of warming the Arctic Basin have been put forward. The latest, a brainstorm of P. M. Borison, calls for building a Bering Strait dam that would block the entry of Pacific water into the Arctic.[21] Each year 140,000 cubic kilometers of cold water would be pumped over from the Chukchi Sea to the Bering Sea in order to prevent the cooling of Atlantic waters by the Arctic waters and ice. Warm equatorial waters would thus move into the Arctic causing changes in the temperature. Winters would be milder, and Soviet agricultural potential would be vastly increased. Well, this may be so, but Western scientists have strong reservations concerning the practicality of Borison's dream.[22]

Everyone, however, must acknowledge the ambitiousness of the notion. If the Soviets ever did attempt dam construction, there would be a hue and cry raised in other North Pacific countries, where climates could also be drastically altered by the discharge of Arctic waters through the Bering Strait. Japanese and Californians are among those who would prefer that their balmy climate not be tampered with.

THE BRIDGING

Whatever the outcome in the next few years, the discovery and, more importantly, the development of petroleum in the North will have momentous effects in molding the new identity of the Pacific Northwest. Perhaps this new sense of identity will spread across the Bering Strait. Indications already exist that it will, particularly in view of the fact that in the spring of 1970 Alaska Airlines was granted Soviet permission to inaugurate the first tour service in history between Alaska and Siberia. However, the service has since been suspended for lack of sufficient traffic. American and Russian specialists of the North are also exchanging information and holding conferences at an increasing rate. American geophysicists are establishing research stations in Siberia in order to track the movement of the aurora borealis across the entire top of the world, while American and Russian geologists are exchanging data about oil structures in order to better correlate Siberian and American deposits.

In 1973 Soviet and United States ships and planes joined together in making a study of ice conditions of the Bering Sea. "The joint investigation," noted *The New York Times*, "was conducted in a cooperative spirit that would have seemed unlikely only a few years ago." [23]

This man-made movement to bridge the Bering Sea is highly significant. It is a decisive movement and indicative of a new awareness on both sides of the Bering Sea that the peoples of the North have much to give each other and much to gain from giving.

NOTES

PREFACE

1. *The Bering Land Bridge*, edited by David M. Hopkins, is a comprehensive review of the geology, past environments, and migrations of the region. A popular account of the migration story is Dan Cushman's *The Great North Trail*.

CHAPTER 1

1. Waxell, *The American Expedition*, p. 225.
2. *Ibid.*
3. Krasheninnikov, *Explorations of Kamchatka*, p. 86.
4. *Ibid.*
5. *Ibid.*
6. *Ibid.*, p. 203.
7. *Ibid.*, p. 121.
8. *Ibid.*, pp. 203–4.
9. *Ibid.*, p. 234.
10. *Ibid.*, p. 205.
11. *Ibid.*
12. *Ibid.*
13. *Ibid.*
14. Fisher, "Dezhnev's Voyage of 1648," p. 7.
15. Golder, *Russian Expansion on the Pacific*, p. 132.
16. *Ibid.*, p. 143.
17. *Ibid.*, p. 144.
18. *Ibid.*
19. *Ibid.*
20. *Ibid.*, p. 148.
21. *Ibid.*, p. 309.
22. *Ibid.*, p. 305.
23. Waxell, *op. cit.*, p. 100.
24. *Ibid.*, p. 103.

CHAPTER 2

1. Golder, *Bering's Voyages*, Vol. II, pp. 17–18.
2. *Ibid.*, p. 18.
3. *Ibid.*, p. 26.
4. *Ibid.*, p. 27.
5. *Ibid.*, p. 23.
6. *Ibid.*
7. *Ibid.*, p. 33.
8. *Ibid.*, p. 34.
9. *Ibid.*
10. *Ibid.*
11. *Ibid.*, p. 35.
12. *Ibid.*, p. 37.
13. *Ibid.*
14. *Ibid.*, p. 40.
15. *Ibid.*, p. 51.
16. *Ibid.*
17. *Ibid.*, p. 60.
18. *Ibid.*, p. 59.
19. *Ibid.*, p. 52.
20. *Ibid.*, pp. 52–53.
21. *Ibid.*, p. 78.
22. *Ibid.*
23. *Ibid.*, p. 85.
24. *Ibid.*
25. *Ibid.*, p. 95.
26. *Ibid.*
27. *Ibid.*, p. 96.
28. *Ibid.*
29. *Ibid.*, p. 95.
30. *Ibid.*, p. 96.
31. *Ibid.*, p. 116.
32. *Ibid.*, p. 117.
33. *Ibid.*, p. 129.
34. *Ibid.*, p. 133.
35. *Ibid.*, pp. 132–33.
36. *Ibid.*, p. 136.

CHAPTER 3

1. Waxell, *op. cit.*, p. 135.
2. *Ibid.*, p. 134.
3. *Ibid.*
4. *Ibid.*

5. Golder, *Bering's Voyages*, Vol. II, p. 161.
6. *Ibid.*, p. 234.
7. *Ibid.*, p. 233.
8. *Ibid.*, p. 183.
9. *Ibid.*, p. 233.
10. *Ibid.*
11. *Ibid.*
12. Krasheninnikov, *op. cit.*, p. 156.

CHAPTER 4

1. Bancroft's *History of Alaska* and Tompkins's *Alaska* have been followed for this summary of Russian-Aleut clashes.
2. Bancroft, *History of Alaska*, p. 126.
3. Beaglehole, *Journals of Captain James Cook*, Vol. III, pp. 1144–45.
4. Masterson and Brower, *Bering's Successors, 1745–1780: Contribution of Peter Simon Pallas to the History of Russian Exploration Towards Alaska*, p. 43.
5. *Ibid.*, p. 44.
6. *Ibid.*
7. *Ibid.*, p. 57.
8. *Ibid.*
9. Dall, *Alaska and Its Resources*, p. 115.
10. *Ibid.*, p. 232.
11. Masterson and Brower, *op. cit.*, p. 58.
12. *Ibid.*
13. *Ibid.*
14. *Ibid.*
15. *Ibid.*, p. 60.
16. *Ibid.*
17. *Ibid.*, p. 61.
18. *Ibid.*
19. *Ibid.*

CHAPTER 5

1. Benyowsky, *Memoirs*, p. 150.
2. *Ibid.*, p. 153.
3. *Ibid.*
4. *Ibid.*, p. 209.
5. *Ibid.*
6. *Ibid.*
7. *Ibid.*
8. *Ibid.*
9. *Ibid.*
10. *Ibid.*, p. 210.

11. Bancroft, *op. cit.*, p. 181.
12. Benyowsky, *op. cit.*, p. 247.
13. *Ibid.*, p. 262.
14. *Ibid.*, p. 263.
15. *Ibid.*
16. *Ibid.*, p. 264.
17. *Ibid.*
18. *Ibid.*
19. *Ibid.*, p. 280.
20. *Ibid.*, p. 345.
21. Dvoichenko-Markov, "Benjamin Franklin and Count M. A. Benyowski," p. 407.
22. *Ibid.*, p. 408.
23. *Ibid.*
24. Beaglehole, *op. cit.*, Vol. III, p. 393.
25. *Ibid.*
26. *Ibid.*, p. 392.
27. *Ibid.*
28. *Ibid.*, pp. 399–400.
29. *Ibid.*, p. 403.
30. *Ibid.*, pp. 410–11.
31. *Ibid.*, p. 411.
32. *Ibid.*, p. 414.
33. *Ibid.*, p. 456.
34. *Ibid.*
35. *Ibid.*, p. 419.
36. *Ibid.*, p. 420.
37. Ledyard, *Journal of Captain Cook's Last Voyage*, p. 92.
38. Beaglehole, *op. cit.*, p. 451.
39. *Ibid.*, p. 458.
40. *Ibid.*
41. *Ibid.*, p. 459.
42. *Ibid.*
43. *Ibid.*, p. 461.
44. *Ibid.*
45. *Ibid.*
46. *Ibid.*
47. *Ibid.*, p. 1123.
48. *Ibid.*
49. *Ibid.*, p. 1149.
50. *Ibid.*
51. *Ibid.*

CHAPTER 6

1. Sauer, *An Account of a Geographical and Astronomical Expedition to the Northern Parts of Russia, 1785–94*, p. 158.

2. *Ibid.*
3. *Ibid.*, p. 157.
4. *Ibid.*
5. *Ibid.*
6. *Ibid.*
7. *Ibid.*, p. 155.
8. *Ibid.*, p. 160.
9. *Ibid.*
10. *Ibid.*, p. 161.
11. *Ibid.*
12. Sarytschew, *Account of a Voyage of Discovery to the North East of Siberia*, Vol. II, p. 11.
13. *Ibid.*
14. Sauer, *op. cit.*, p. 166.
15. *Ibid.*, p. 55.
16. *Ibid.*
17. *Ibid.*, p. 56.
18. Lesseps, *Travels in Kamtschatka*, Vol. I, p. 157.
19. *Ibid.*
20. *Ibid.*, pp. 157–58.
21. *Ibid.*, p. 158.
22. *Ibid.*
23. *Ibid.*, p. 81.
24. *Ibid.*, p. 97.
25. *Ibid.*, Vol. II, p. 84.
26. *Ibid.*, p. 87.
27. *Ibid.*, p. 33.
28. *Ibid.*
29. Bancroft, *History of Alaska*, and Chevigny, *Russian America*, are standard works on the organization of the Russian American Company.
30. Ricks, *The Earliest History of Alaska*, p. 3.
31. *Ibid.*, p. 5.
32. *Ibid.*
33. *Ibid.*
34. *Ibid.*
35. *Ibid.*, p. 7.
36. Bancroft, *op. cit.*, p. 446.
37. *Ibid.*
38. *Ibid.*
39. *Ibid.*, pp. 447–48.
40. Langsdorff, *Voyages and Travels*, Vol. II, p. 32.
41. Cochrane, *Narrative of a Pedestrian Journey*, p. 149 of the Philadelphia, 1824, edition which is in one volume; where "Philadelphia" is not indicated, reference is to the two-volume London edition.
42. *Ibid.*, p. viii (Philadelphia).

43. *Ibid.*, Vol. I, p. 285.
44. *Ibid.*, p. 176 (Philadelphia).
45. *Ibid.*, Vol. I, p. 308.
46. *Ibid.*, p. 311.
47. *Ibid.*, p. 315.
48. *Ibid.*
49. *Ibid.*, pp. 315–16.
50. Wrangel, *op. cit.*, pp. 111–12.
51. Cochrane, *op. cit.*, Vol. I, pp. 320–21.
52. *Ibid.*, p. 398.
53. *Ibid.*, p. 402.
54. *Ibid.*, pp. 397–98.
55. *Ibid.*, p. 398.
56. *Ibid.*, p. 44.
57. *Ibid.*, p. 68.
58. *Ibid.*, p. 69.
59. *Ibid.*, pp. 45–46.
60. *Ibid.*, p. 64.
61. *Ibid.*
62. *Ibid.*
63. *Ibid.*, p. 72.
64. *Ibid.*
65. *Ibid.*
66. *Ibid.*
67. *Ibid.*, p. 40.
68. *Ibid.*, p. 41.
69. *Ibid.*, p. 42.
70. *Ibid.*

CHAPTER 7

1. Beechey, *Narrative of a Voyage to the Pacific*, Vol. II, p. 249.
2. Gough, *To the Pacific and Arctic with Beechey*, p. 145.
3. Burroughs, *Alaska—Narrative*, p. 93.
4. *Ibid.*, p. 94.
5. Jochelson, *The Koryak*, p. 807.
6. *Ibid.*, pp. 808, 809.
7. Bogoras, *The Chukchee*, pp. 656–57.
8. *Ibid.*, p. 731.
9. *Ibid.*
10. *Ibid.*
11. Zagoskin, *Travels in North America*, p. 100.
12. *Ibid.*, p. 106.
13. *Ibid.*, p. 107.
14. Van Stone, *Nushagak, passim.*

15. Zagoskin, *op. cit.*, pp. 102–3.
16. Tronson, *Personal Narratives of a Voyage*, p. 94.
17. *Ibid.*
18. Whittingham, *Notes on the Late Expedition*, p. vi.
19. *Ibid.*, p. 297.
20. *Ibid.*
21. *Ibid.*, p. 295.
22. Whymper, *Travels and Adventures in Alaska*, p. 126.
23. Guillemard, *Cruise of the Marchesa*, p. 78.
24. *Ibid.*

CHAPTER 8

1. Garner, *The Captain's Best Mate*, p. 249.
2. *Ibid.*
3. Perry, *World of the Walrus*, p. 124.
4. *Ibid.*, p. i.
5. Morgan, *Bridge to Russia*, p. 118.
6. Morison, *Maritime History of Massachusetts*, p. 324.
7. *Ibid.*
8. *Ibid.*
9. Williams, *One Whaling Family*, p. 253.
10. *Ibid.*
11. *Ibid.*
12. Hohman, *American Whaleman*, p. 218.
13. Garner, *op. cit.*, p. 249.
14. Williams, *op. cit.*, p. 231.
15. *Ibid.*, pp. 231–32.
16. *Ibid.*, p. x.
17. Petroff, *Report on the Population, Industries, and Resources of Alaska*, p. 10.
18. Murdoch, *Ninth Annual Report for the Bureau of Ethnology*, p. 53.
19. *Ibid.*
20. *Ibid.*
21. Jackson, *Introduction of Domestic Reindeer into Alaska*, p. 4.
22. *Ibid.*, p. 32.
23. Allen, *Children of the Light*, p. 264.
24. *Ibid.*
25. *Ibid.*
26. *Ibid.*
27. *Ibid.*
28. *Ibid.*, p. 202.
29. *Ibid.*
30. *Ibid.*, p. 203.
31. *Ibid.*
32. *Ibid.*

33. *Ibid.*, p. 200.
34. *Ibid.*
35. *Ibid.*, p. 201.
36. *Ibid.*
37. *Ibid.* Barker and other early visitors to northeastern Siberia could not distinguish Eskimos from Chukchi. Eskimos resided at Indian Point, Plover, and Emma Bays.
38. *Ibid.*, p. 202.
39. *Ibid.*
40. *Ibid.*
41. *Ibid.*
42. *Ibid.*, p. 204.
43. *Ibid.*, p. 205.
44. *Ibid.*
45. *Ibid.*
46. *Ibid.*, p. 261.
47. Garner, *op. cit.*, p. 46.
48. *Ibid.*, p. 103.
49. *Ibid.*, p. xix.
50. *Ibid.*, p. 44.
51. *Ibid.*, p. 33.
52. *Ibid.*, pp. 45–47.
53. Cook, *Pursuing the Whale*, p. 5.
54. *Ibid.*
55. *Ibid.*
56. *Ibid.*
57. *Ibid.*, p. 6.
58. *Ibid.*, p. 7.
59. *Ibid.*, p. 17.
60. *Ibid.*

CHAPTER 9

1. Morgan, *Dixie Raider*, p. 24.
2. *Ibid.*, p. 113.
3. Horan, *C.S.S. Shenandoah*, p. 145.
4. *Ibid.*, p. 158.
5. Hunt, *Shenandoah*, p. 155.
6. Horan, *op. cit.*, p. 167.
7. *Ibid.*, p. 168.
8. Hunt, *op. cit.*, p. 201.
9. *Ibid.*, p. 202.
10. *Ibid.*, p. 204.
11. *Ibid.*, pp. 205–6.
12. Horan, *op. cit.*, p. 175.

13. *Ibid.*, p. 176.
14. Summersell, *Journal of George Townley Fullam*, p. xxii.

CHAPTER 10

1. Collins, *Siberian Journey*, p. 45.
2. *Ibid.*, p. 33.
3. Bush, *Reindeer, Dogs, and Snow-Shoes*, pp. 25–26.
4. *Ibid.*, p. 33.
5. Dall, *op. cit., passim.*
6. Dall to Baird, April 26, 1867, for this and other Dall quotes.
7. Dall, *op. cit.*, p. 66.
8. Dall to Baird, April 26, 1867.
9. *Esquimaux*, October 14, 1866.
10. *Esquimaux*, November 4, 1866.
11. *Ibid.* All quotes in this paragraph.
12. *Esquimaux*, July 7, 1867.
13. Taggart, "Journal of George Russell Adams," p. 293.
14. *Ibid.*, p. 294.
15. *Ibid.*, p. 296.
16. *Ibid.*
17. *Ibid.*, p. 297.
18. *Ibid.*, p. 301.
19. *Ibid.*, p. 302.
20. *Ibid.*, p. 303.
21. *Esquimaux*, August 4, 1867.
22. *Dyea Trail*, January 19, 1898.

CHAPTER 11

1. Bancroft, *History of Alaska*; Fedorova, *Russian Population in Alaska and California*; Okun, *The Russian-American Company*; and Tompkins, *Alaska* are the standard studies of the American colony.
2. "Baron F. P. von Vrangel's Observations on the Eskimos and Indians of Alaska," translated and edited by James W. Van Stone. Wrangel's various scientific studies were collected by Karl E. von Baer, *Beitruge zur Kenntnis der ressischen Reiches und der angrezenden Lander Asiens.*
3. Simpson traveled to Alaska and made some shrewd observations on the Russian traders. Simpson, *An Overland Journey Round the World.*
4. Wrangel, *A Journey's Sketch, from Sitka to St. Petersburg.*
5. A recent, substantial biography is Glyndon Van Deusen, *William Henry Seward* (New York: Oxford University, 1967).
6. Jackson, *Introduction of Domestic Reindeer into Alaska*, p. 6.
7. *Ibid.*, p. 7.

8. *Ibid.*
9. *Ibid.*
10. *Ibid.*, 1893 report, p. 5.
11. *Ibid.*, p. 8.
12. *Ibid.*, p. 9.

CHAPTER 12

1. Libby manuscript.
2. *Ibid.*
3. Harrison, *Nome and Seward Peninsula*, p. 57.
4. Lomen diary, September 12, 1919.
5. *Seattle Star*, October 15, 1928.
6. Vanderlip, *In Search of a Siberian Klondike*, p. 200.
7. *Ibid.*, p. 225.
8. *Ibid.*
9. *Ibid.*, p. 226.
10. *Ibid.*, p. 229.
11. *Ibid.*, p. 310.
12. *Ibid.*, p. 315.

CHAPTER 13

1. *Nome Nugget*, August 20, 1901.
2. Stefansson, *Northwest to Fortune*, p. 298.
3. *Ibid.*
4. *Ibid.*
5. DeWindt, *Through the Gold Fields of Alaska to Bering Straits*, p. 265.
6. *Ibid.*, p. 266.
7. *Ibid.*
8. DeWindt, *My Restless Life*, p. 352.
9. *Ibid.*
10. DeWindt, *Gold Fields*, p. 17.
11. *Nome Nugget*, August 30, 1901.
12. *Ibid.*
13. *Nome Nugget*, February 19, 1902.
14. *Ibid.*
15. *Ibid.*
16. *Ibid.*
17. *Ibid.*
18. *Ibid.*
19. *Ibid.*
20. *Ibid.*
21. *Ibid.*
22. *Ibid.*

23. *Nome Nugget*, February 22, 1902.
24. *Ibid.*, October 21, 1903.
25. *Ibid.*, July 23, 1902.
26. *Ibid.*, August 6, 1902.
27. *Ibid.*, September 24, 1902.
28. *Ibid.*, March 18, 1903.
29. *Ibid.*, August 15, 1903.
30. *Ibid.*, September 16, 1903.
31. *Ibid.*
32. *Ibid.*, May 14, 1904.
33. *Ibid.*, July 16, 1904.
34. *Ibid.*, August 20, 1904.
35. *Ibid.*, June 17, 1905.
36. *Ibid.*
37. *Ibid.*
38. *Ibid.*
39. *Ibid.*, September 6, 1905.
40. *Ibid.*
41. *Ibid.*, December 19, 1905.
42. *Ibid.*, April 7, 1906.
43. *Ibid.*
44. *Ibid.*
45. Clipping from unidentified New York newspaper. Tappan Adney Collection.
46. Advertising brochure. Rosene Collection.
47. Lomen, *Fifty Years in Alaska.*
48. *In Reindeer Realms*, unpaged. Lomen Collection.
49. Santa Claus Book. Lomen Collection.
50. Stefansson to Carl Lomen, May 23, 1940. Lomen Correspondence.
51. Ad copy, Lomen Collection.
52. *Brooklyn Daily Eagle*, April 10, 1927.
53. Lomen, *op. cit.*, p. 302.

CHAPTER 14

1. Jordan, *Report on Conditions of Seal Life*, p. 63.
2. *Ibid.*
3. Martin, *Sea Bears*, p. 96.
4. *Fur Seals and Other Fisheries*, p. xvi.
5. *Ibid.*
6. Jordan, *op. cit.*, p. 24.
7. Anderson, *Alaskan Fur Seals*, pp. 12–13.
8. *Pacific Fishermen*, November 9, 1909. Clipping, University of Alaska Archives.
9. Lewis and Dryden, *Marine History*, p. 429.
10. *Ibid.*
11. Underwood, *Alaska*, p. 264.

12. *Ibid.*
13. *Ibid.*
14. Underwood, *op. cit.*, p. 265.
15. *Ibid.*
16. Lewis and Dryden, *op. cit.*, p. 428.
17. *Ibid.*, p. 429.
18. Evans, *Sailor's Log*, p. 323.
19. *Ibid.*
20. *Ibid.*, p. 325.
21. *Ibid.*
22. *Ibid.*
23. *Ibid.*, p. 325.
24. *Ibid.*, p. 328.
25. *Ibid.*, p. 329.
26. *Ibid.*, p. 330.
27. *Ibid.*
28. *Ibid.*, p. 331.
29. *Ibid.*, p. 334.
30. *Ibid.*, p. 338.
31. *Ibid.*, p. 339.
32. *Ibid.*
33. *Ibid.*
34. *Ibid.*, p. 341.
35. *Ibid.*, p. 355.
36. U.S. Department of State, *Whaling and Sealing Claims*, p. 213.
37. *Ibid.*, p. 103.
38. Evans, *op. cit.*, p. 358.
39. Elliott, *Our Arctic Province*, p. 189.
40. *Alaska Herald*, December 1, 1870.
41. *Ibid.*
42. Hinckley, *Americanization of Alaska, passim.*
43. *Alaska Herald*, June 15, 1868.
44. *Ibid.*
45. *Ibid.*
46. *Ibid.*, September 1, 1868.
47. *Ibid.*, September 15, 1868.
48. *Ibid.*, December 1, 1870.
49. *Ibid.*, January 1, 1871.
50. Bancroft, *op. cit.*, p. 648.
51. *Ibid.*, p. 649.
52. Elliott, *Report on the Seal Islands*, p. 20.
53. *Ibid.*
54. *Ibid.*
55. Martin, *Hunting of the Silver Fleece*, p. 155.
56. *Ibid.*

57. Martin, *Sea Bears*, p. 50.
58. Unidentified newspaper clippings, December 8, 1878, Bancroft scrapbook.
59. Jordan, *Days of a Man*, p. 609.
60. Martin, *Hunting of the Silver Fleece*, p. 235.
61. Wardman to Otis, August 24, 1881. Pribilof Collection.
62. Wentz to Chief, Division of Alaska Fisheries, March 31, 1946. All quotes this paragraph.
63. Physician's Annual Report, March 31, 1942.
64. Kitchener, *Flag Over the North*, p. 70.
65. *Ibid.*, p. 74.

CHAPTER 15

1. London, *Klondike Dream*, p. 126.
2. *Ibid.*
3. Kipling, *Verse*, pp. 113–14.
4. Snow, *In Forbidden Seas*, pp. 263–64. All quotes this paragraph.
5. *Ibid.*, p. 264.
6. *Ibid.*, p. 175.
7. *Ibid.*, p. 270.
8. *Ibid.*, p. 109.
9. *Ibid.*, p. 115.
10. Lomen, *In Reindeer Realms*, p. 203.
11. *Ibid.*
12. *Ibid.*, p. 204.
13. *Ibid.*, p. 205.

CHAPTER 16

1. Swenson, *Northwest of the World*, p. 17.
2. *Ibid.*, p. 68.
3. *Ibid.*, p. 92.
4. *Ibid.*, p. 92.
5. McCracken, *Roughnecks and Gentlemen*, pp. 119, 151.
6. *Nome Nugget*, September 21, 1910.
7. *Ibid.*
8. *Ibid.*, September 22, 1910.
9. *Ibid.*, October 3, 1910.
10. *Ibid.*, October 4, 1910.
11. Clipping from scrapbook. Author's files, 1913.
12. Starokadomskiy, *Five Voyages in the Arctic Ocean*, p. 46.
13. *Ibid.*, p. 49.
14. *Ibid.*, p. 50.
15. *Ibid.*
16. *Ibid.*, p. 51.

17. *Ibid.*
18. *Ibid.*, p. 92.
19. *Ibid.*, p. 94.
20. *Ibid.*
21. *Ibid.*, p. 104.
22. *Ibid.*, p. 156.
23. *Ibid.*
24. *Ibid.*, p. 166.
25. *Ibid.*
26. *Nome Nugget*, July 26, 1916.
27. *Ibid.*, July 12, 1916.
28. *Ibid.*, July 21, 1916.
29. *Nome Nugget*, July 26, 1916.
30. *Ibid.*, August 10, 1916.
31. Starokadomskiy, *op. cit.*, p. 172.
32. *Ibid.*
33. *Ibid.*
34. *Ibid.*, p. 277.
35. Discussion with William Barr, Starokadomskiy's translator.
36. Starokadomskiy, *op. cit.*, p. 300.
37. *Ibid.*, p. 301.
38. *Ibid.*
39. *Ibid.*

CHAPTER 17

1. Beavis, "Trading into Siberia," p. 36.
2. *Ibid.*, p. 37.
3. *Ibid.*
4. "Report on Fur Trade in the Kamchatka Province," Elphick to HBC, December 3, 1921.
5. *Ibid.*
6. *Ibid.*
7. "Itinerary of the HBC's Siberian Fur Trade Venture," Elphick to HBC, December 3, 1921.
8. *Ibid.*
9. Hoogendijk, "HBC's Kamchatka Venture, 1921."
10. *Ibid.*
11. *Ibid.*
12. "Secretary's Memorandum re Kamchatka Venture 1920/25," June 13, 1925.
13. Parry, "Washington B. Vanderlip, the 'Khan of Kamchatka,' " p. 314.
14. Swenson, *op. cit.*, p. 163.
15. *Ibid.*, p. 167.
16. *Ibid.*, p. 171.
17. *Ibid.*, pp. 162–63.

18. Armstrong, *Geographical Journal*, June 1964, p. 277.
19. Swenson, *op. cit.*, p. 267.
20. *Ibid.*
21. *Ibid.*
22. Bergman, *Through Kamchatka*, p. 20.
23. *Ibid.*, p. 34.
24. *Ibid.*, p. 37.
25. *Ibid.*, p. 38.
26. *Ibid.*, p. 36.
27. *Ibid.*
28. *Ibid.*, p. 40.
29. *Ibid.*, p. 244.
30. *Ibid.*
31. *Ibid.*, p. 245.
32. *Ibid.*
33. *Ibid.*, p. 106.
34. *Ibid.*
35. *Ibid.*, p. 107.
36. Masik and Hutchison, *Arctic Nights' Entertainment*, p. 140.
37. *Ibid.*, p. 156.
38. *Ibid.*
39. Burnham, *Rim of Mystery*, p. 15.
40. *Ibid.*, pp. 15–16.
41. *Ibid.*, p. 17.
42. *Ibid.*
43. *Ibid.*, p. 27.
44. *Ibid.*, p. 26.
45. *Ibid.*, p. 43.
46. *Ibid.*
47. *Ibid.*, p. 44.
48. *Ibid.*
49. *Ibid.*, p. 50.
50. Rasmussen, *Fifth Thule Expedition 1921–24: Eskimo Archaelogy and Ethnology*, p. 83.
51. *Ibid.*, pp. 90–91.
52. Slavin, "American Expansion in the Northeast of Russia," p. 2.
53. *Ibid.*, p. 12.
54. *Ibid.*, p. 13.
55. *Ibid.*, p. 14.
56. *Ibid.*, p. 27.

CHAPTER 18

1. Morison, *History of U. S. Naval Operations*, p. 1.
2. *Ibid.*, pp. 3–4.

3. Garfield, *Thousand-Mile War*, p. 71.
4. Morison, *U.S. Naval Operations,* p. 14.
5. *Ibid.,* p. 16.
6. *Ibid.,* p. 18.
7. *Ibid.,* p. 22.
8. *Ibid.,* p. 36.
9. Tatsugghi, "Attu Diary," unpaged.
10. World War II Scrapbook, author's files.
11. Morison, *U.S. Naval Operations*, p. 66.

CHAPTER 19

1. *Tundra Times*, April 11, 1973.
2. *Fairbanks News-Miner*, September 15, 1973.
3. *Ibid.*, July 20, 1973.
4. *Ibid.*
5. Lecture at the University of Alaska, fall 1973.
6. Garrett to Tingle, July 28, 1887. Pribilof collection.
7. Jackson, *Report of the Bureau of Education*, p. 57.
8. *Ibid.,* p. 58.
9. *Ibid.*
10. *Ibid.,* p. 54.
11. *Ibid.,* p. 55.
12. Starokadomskiy, *op. cit.,* p. 51.
13. Darnell, *Education in the North*, pp. 59–74.
14. St. George, *Siberia*, p. 324.
15. *Ibid.,* p. 330.
16. *New York Times*, October 25, 1973.
17. *Fairbanks Daily News-Miner*, February 7, 1974.
18. *National Science Foundation Proposal for International Bering Sea Study*, p. 2.
19. Meselson to Hood, April 10, 1970.
20. Lin, "Intercontinental Peace Bridge," *passim.*
21. Borison, "Global Weather Modification and the Arctic Basin," *passim.*
22. Dunbar, "On the Bering Strait Scheme," *Polar Notes, passim.*
23. *New York Times*, March 7, 1973.

Bibliography
Index

BIBLIOGRAPHY

I. ARCHIVAL SOURCES

British Columbia Provincial Archives
Letter of Dr. J. T. Rothrock and the Edmund Conway Diary concerning Western Union Telegraph Expedition (xerox and microfilm copies in the University of Alaska Archives).

California Historical Society
Minutes of the Alaska Commercial Company Meetings, 1868–1918 (microfilm copy in University of Alaska Archives).

Dartmouth College, Baker Library, Stefansson Collection
Adney Tappan Papers. Correspondence with and biography of John J. Healy.

Hudson's Bay Company Archives
Papers on the Kamchatka venture. Quotations made from these papers with the permission of the Hudson's Bay Company.

Library Association of Portland, Oregon
Bulkley, Charles S. Papers (microfilm copy in University of Alaska Archives).

Smithsonian Institution
Dall, William H. Report relating to the Western Union Telegraph Expedition to S. F. Baird, April 26, 1867.

University of Alaska—Fairbanks, Elmer E. Rasmuson Library—Archives
Alaska Commercial Company Records (Erskine Collection).
Brooks, Alfred H. Newspaper clippings.
Dimond, Anthony. Papers.
Documents Relative to the History of Alaska. Alaska History Research Project, 1936–38.
Fairbanks, Lulu M. Papers.
Lomen, Carl. Diaries.
Lomen Family Collection.
Pribilof Islands Papers.
Tatsugghi, Nebu (Paul N. Tatsuguchi). Attu Diary, May 29, 1943.
Western Union Telegraph Expedition Collection (xerox copies from originals held by Western Union).

363

University of California, Berkeley, Bancroft Library
  Bancroft Scrapbook (xerox copy in University of Alaska Archives).
  Chisholm Papers.
University of Washington Archives
  Western Union Telegraph Expedition Diaries of George R. Adams, Fred M. Smith,
  and J. W. Wanless in Charles S. Hubbell Collection (microfilm copies in University of
  Alaska Archives); J. W. Wanless Collection (xerox copy in possession of the author);
  John Rosene Collection.

II. GOVERNMENT PUBLICATIONS

(Except where another publisher is indicated, all books were published by the Government Printing Office.)

Anderson, Chandler P. *Alaskan Fur Seals.* Washington, 1906.

Annual Report of the Governor of Alaska. Washington, 1885–1940.

Collins, Henry B., Jr., et al. *The Aleutian Islands.* Washington: Smithsonian Institution, 1945.

Elliott, Henry W. *Report on the Seal Islands.* Washington, 1880.

Fur Seals and Other Fisheries of Alaska. Washington, 1889.

Healy, M. A. *Cruise of the Revenue Marine Steamer Corwin in the Arctic Ocean . . . 1884.* Washington, 1889.

Hooper, C. L. *Report of the Cruise of the U.S. Revenue Steamer Thomas Corwin in the Arctic Ocean, 1881.* Washington: Anglim, 1885.

Hrdlicka, Ales. *Anthropological Survey in Alaska.* Washington, 1930.

Jackson, Sheldon. *Introduction of Domestic Reindeer into Alaska, 1890–95.* Washington: 1891.

Jackson, Sheldon. *Report of the Bureau of Education for the Natives of Alaska, 1913–18.* Washington, 1919.

Jordan, David Starr. *Reports on Conditions of Seal Life on the Pribilof Islands . . . 1868 to 1895.* Washington, 1898.

Murdock, John. *Ethnological Results of the Point Barrow Expedition.* Washington, 1892.

Orth, Donald J. *Dictionary of Alaska Place Names.* Washington, 1967.

Petroff, Ivan. *Report on the Population, Industries and Resources of Alaska.* Washington, 1880.

Rosse, Irving C. *Cruise of the Revenue-Steamer Corwin in Alaska . . . 1881.* Washington: Anglim, 1883.

Stejneger, Leonard. *Results of Ornithological Explorations in the Commander Islands and Kamtschatka.* Washington, 1885.

Stejneger, Leonard. *Russian Fur Seal Islands.* Washington, 1896.

United States Department of State. *Whaling and Sealing Claims Against Russia.* Washington, 1902.

United States Navy. *Battle Experience: Assault and Occupation of Attu Island.* May, 1943, Secret Information Bulletin No. 9. Headquarters of the Commander in Chief.

III. NEWSPAPERS

Alaska Appeal, 1879–80.
Alaska Dispatch, 1918–23.
Alaska Herald, 1868–72.
Alaska Tribune, 1873. Scattered file.
Alaska Weekly, 1923–24.
Fairbanks News-Miner, passim.
Nome Chronicle, 1900–1901.
Nome Gold Digger, 1900–1901, 1907.
Nome News, 1899, 1905, 1907.
Nome Nugget, 1901–23.
Nome Pioneer Press, 1907–8.
Sitka Alaskan, 1898–99.
Tundra Times, passim.

IV. BOOKS

Academy of Sciences of the U.S.S.R. *The Pacific: Russian Scientific Investigation.* Leningrad: Academy, 1926.

Aldrich, Herbert L. *Arctic Alaska and Siberia.* Chicago: Rand, McNally, 1889.

Allan, Alexander. *Hunting the Sea Otter.* London: Cox, 1910.

Allen, Edward W. *North Pacific.* New York: Professional & Technical, 1936.

Allen, Everett S. *Children of the Light.* Boston: Little, Brown, 1973.

Andrews, Ralph W., and Kiwan, Harry A. *This Was Seafaring.* Seattle: Superior, 1955.

Armstrong, Terence. *Northern Sea Route.* Cambridge: Cambridge University, 1952.

Armstrong, Terence. *The Russians in the Arctic.* London: Methuen, 1958.

Ashley, Clifford W. *The Yankee Whaler.* London: Hopkinson, 1926.

Ashton, James M. *Ice-Bound: A Trader's Adventure in the Siberian Arctic.* New York: Putnams, 1928.

Bailey, Alfred M. *Field Work of a Museum Naturalist, 1919–22.* Denver: Museum of Natural History, 1971.

Bancroft, Hubert Howe. *History of Alaska, 1730–1885.* New York: Antiquarian, 1960.

Bank Ted, II. *Birthplace of the Winds.* New York: Crowell, 1956.

Barbeau, Marius. *Pathfinders in the North Pacific.* Caldwell, Idaho: Caxton, 1958.

Bartlett, R. A., and Hall, R. T. *Last Voyage of the Karluk.* Boston: Small, Maynard, 1916.

Bauer, Josef Martin. *As Far As My Feet Will Carry Me.* London: Deutsch, 1957.

Beaglehole, J. C. *The Journals of Captain James Cook: Voyage of the Resolution and Discovery, 1776–1780.* Cambridge: Hakluyt Society, 1967.

Beechey, F. W. *Narrative of a Voyage to the Pacific and Beering's Strait.* London: Colburn and Bentley, 1831.

Benyowsky, Count. *Memoirs and Travels of Mauritius Angustus Count De Benyowsky.* London: Fisher, 1893.

Bergman, Sten. *Through Kamchatka by Dog Sled and Skis.* London: Seeley, Service, 1927.

Berkh, Vasily. *Chronological History of the Discovery of the Aleutian Islands.* St. Petersburg,

1823. Trans. Dimitri Krenov. Seattle: W.P.A., 1938.

Birkeland, Knut B. *Whalers of Akutan.* New Haven: Yale University, 1926.

Bixby, William. *Track of the Bear.* New York: McKay, 1956.

Bodfish, Hartson H. *Chasing the Bowhead.* Cambridge, Mass.: Harvard University, 1936.

Bogoras, W. *The Chuckchee.* New York: Johnson Reprint, 1969.

Buck, Eugene H. *Alaska and the Law of the Sea.* Anchorage: University of Alaska, 1973.

Burch, Franklin W. *Alaska's Railroad Frontier: Railroads and Federal Development Policy, 1898–1915.* Washington, D.C.: Catholic University, 1965.

Burnham, John B. *Rim of Mystery.* New York: Putnams, 1929.

Burns, Walter Noble. *Year with a Whaler.* New York: Outing, 1913.

Burroughs, John, et al. *Alaska—Narrative, Glaciers, Natives* (Harriman Expedition). London: Murray, 1902.

Bush, Edwin M. *Alaska Fishing Controversy of Japan and the United States, 1936–38.* Boulder: University of Colorado, 1941.

Bush, Richard J. *Reindeer, Dogs, and Snow-Shoes.* New York: Harper, 1871.

Campbell, Archibald. *The Restless Voyage.* Ed. Stanley D. Porteus. London: Harrop, 1950.

Cappock, Henry Aaron. *Interaction Between Russians and Native Americans in Alaska, 1741–1840.* East Lansing: Michigan State University, 1970.

Capture of Attu. Washington: Infantry Journal, 1944.

Carr, Edward Hallet. *Bolshevik Revolution, 1917–23.* London: Macmillan, 1953.

Chevigny, Hector. *Lord of Alaska.* London: Hale, 1946.

Chevigny, Hector. *Russian America.* London: Cresset, 1965.

Cochrane, Capt. John Dundas. *Narrative of a Pedestrian Journey through Russia and Siberian Tartary.* London: Knight, 1824.

Cole, Allan B., ed. *Yankee Surveyors in the Shogun's Seas.* Princeton: Princeton University Press, 1947.

Collins, Perry McDonough. *Siberian Journey: Down the Amur to the Pacific, 1856–1857.* Ed. Charles Vivier. Madison: University of Wisconsin, 1962.

Cook, John A. *Pursuing the Whale.* London: Murray, 1926.

Coxe, William. *Account of the Russian Discoveries Between Asia and America.* London: Nicholas, 1787.

Cushman, Dan. *The Great North Trail.* New York: McGraw-Hill, 1967.

Czaplicka, M. A. *Aboriginal Siberia—A Study in Social Anthropology.* Oxford: Clarendon, 1969.

Dalby, Milton A. *Sea Saga of Dynamite Johnny O'Brien.* Seattle: Lowman and Hanford, 1933.

Dall, William H. *Alaska and Its Resources.* Boston: Lee and Shepard, 1870.

Darnell, Frank, ed. *Education in the North: The First International Conference on Cross-Cultural Education in the Circumpolar Nations.* Anchorage: University of Alaska and Institute of North America, 1972.

Demidoff, E. *A Shooting Trip to Kamchatka.* London: Ward, 1904.

DeWindt, Harry. *From Paris to New York by Land.* New York: Warne, 1904.

DeWindt, Harry. *My Restless Life.* London: Richards, 1909.

DeWindt, Harry. *Through the Gold Fields of Alaska to Bering Straits.* London: Chatto and Windus, 1899.

Dobell, Peter. *Travel in Kamchatka and Siberia.* London: Colburn and Bentley, 1830.

Dugan, James. *The Great Iron Ship.* New York: Harper, 1953.

Dunmore, John. *French Explorers in the Pacific.* Oxford: Oxford University, 1965.

Durham, Bill. *Canoes and Kayaks of Western America.* Seattle: Copper Canoe, 1960.

D'Wolf, John. *Voyage to the North Pacific.* Fairfield, Conn.: Ye Galleon, 1968.

Efimov, A. V. *Atlas of Geographical Discoveries of the 17th and 18th Centuries.* Moscow: Nauka, 1964.

Elliott, Henry W. *Our Arctic Province, Alaska and the Seal Islands.* London: Sampson, Low, 1886.

Ellsworth, Lyman R. *Guys on Ice.* New York: McKay, 1952.

Evans, Robley D. *A Sailor's Log.* New York: Appleton, 1901.

Evans, Stephen. *United States Coast Guard.* Annapolis: U.S. Naval Institute, 1949.

Fedorova, Svetlana G. *The Russian Population in Alaska and California from the Late 18th Century–1867.* Kingston: Limestone, 1973.

Foote, Donald C. *Exploration and Resource Utilization in Northwest Arctic Alaska Before 1855.* Montreal: McGill University, 1965.

Foote, Donald C.; Fischer, Victor; and Rogers, George W. *St. Paul Community Study.* Fairbanks: University of Alaska, 1968.

Ford, Corey. *Where the Sea Breaks Its Back.* London: Gollancz, 1966.

Ford, John D. *American Cruiser in the East.* New York: Barnes, 1898.

Garner, Stanton. *The Captain's Best Mate: The Journal of Mary Chipman Lawrence on the Whaler Addison, 1856–1860.* Providence: Brown University, 1966.

Gibson, James R. *Feeding the Russian Fur Trade.* Madison: University of Wisconsin, 1969.

Gilman, William. *Our Hidden Front.* New York: Renyal & Hitchcock, 1944.

Godsell, Philip H. *Alaska Highway.* London: Sampson, Low, n.d.

Golder, F. A. *Bering's Voyages.* New York: American Geographic Society, 1922.

Golder, F. A. *Russian Expansion on the Pacific, 1641–1850.* Gloucester: Smith, 1960.

Gough, Barry M. *To the Pacific and Arctic with Beechey: The Journal of Lieutenant George Peard of H.M.S. 'Blossom.'* Cambridge: Hakluyt Society, 1973.

Guillemard, F. H. H. *Cruise of the Marchesa to Kamchatka and New Guinea.* London: Murray, 1886.

Gunther, Erna. *Indian Life in the Northwest Coast of North America.* Chicago: University of Chicago, 1972.

Habersham, A. W. *North Pacific Surveying and Exploring Expedition, Or My Last Cruise.* Philadelphia: Lippincott, 1858.

Handleman, Howard. *Bridge to Victory.* New York: Random House, 1943.

Harrington, J. J. *The Esquimaux.* San Francisco: Turnbull and Smith, 1867.

Harrison, E. S. *Nome and the Seward Peninsula.* Seattle: E. S. Harrison, 1901.

Hegarty, Reginald B. *Birth of a Whaleship.* New Bedford: Free Public Library, 1964.

Hinckley, Theodore C. *Americanization of Alaska.* Palo Alto: Pacific Books, 1972.

Hohman, Elmo Paul. *American Whaleman.* New York: Longmans, Green, 1928.

Holmes, Rev. Lewis. *The Arctic Whaleman; or, Winter in the Arctic Ocean.* Boston: Wentworth, 1857.

Hooper, W. H. *Ten Months Among the Tents of the Tuski.* London: Murray, 1853.

Hopkins, David M., ed. *The Bering Land Bridge.* Palo Alto: Stanford University, 1967.

Horan, James D., ed. *C.S.S. Shenandoah: The Memoirs of Lieutenant Commanding James I. Waddell.* New York: Crown, 1960.

Howay, F. W. *A List of Trading Vessels in the Maritime Fur Trade, 1785–1825.* Ed. Richard A. Pierce. Kingston: Limestone, 1973.

Howe, Lowell John. *History of the Sealing Industry of Alaska.* Berkeley: University of California, 1926.

Hudson, Will E. *Icy Hell.* London: Constable, 1937.

Hunt, Cornelius E. *Shenandoah, or the Last Confederate Cruise.* New York: Carleton, 1868.

Hunt, William R. *Changing Ideas about the Northwest Coast as Reflected in Cartography Between 1708–1780.* Seattle: University of Washington, 1966.

Hunt, William R. *North of 53°.* New York: Macmillan, 1974.

Hutchison, Isobel W. *North to the Rime-Ringed Sun.* London: Blakie, 1935.

Hutchison, Isobel W. *Stepping Stones from Alaska to Asia.* London: Blakie, 1937.

James, James Alton. *First Scientific Exploration of Russian America.* Chicago: Northwestern University, 1942.

Jochelson, Waldemar. *History, Ethnology and Anthropology of the Aleut.* Washington, D.C.: Carnegie Institute, 1933.

Jochelson, Waldemar. *Memoir of the American Museum of Natural History: The Koryak.* New York: Stechert, 1905.

Jochelson, Waldemar. *Peoples of Asiatic Russia.* New York: American Museum of Natural History, 1928.

Johnson, Philip R., and Hartman, Charles W. *Environmental Atlas of Alaska.* College: University of Alaska, 1969.

Jones, W. B. *Argonauts of Siberia.* Philadelphia: Dorrance, 1927.

Jordan, David Starr. *Days of a Man.* New York: World, 1922.

Keim, Charles. *Aghvook, White Eskimo.* College: University of Alaska, 1969.

Kellett, Henry. *Narrative of the Voyage of H.M.S. Herald.* London: Reeve, 1853.

Kennan, George. *Decision to Intervene.* London: Faber and Faber, 1958.

Kennan, George. *E. H. Harriman: A Biography.* Freeport, N.Y.: Books for Libraries, 1969.

Kennan, George. *Tent Life in Siberia.* New York: Putnams, 1910.

Khlebnikov, K. T. *Baranov.* Kingston: Limestone, 1973.

Kipling, Rudyard. *Jungle Book.* London: Macmillan, 1953.

Kipling, Rudyard. *Verse, Definitive Edition.* London: Hodder and Stoughton, 1940.

Kitchener, L. D. *Flag Over the North.* Seattle: Superior, 1954.

Knox, Thomas W. *Overland Through Asia.* Hartford: American, 1870.

Koughan, Helen R. *An Account of the Alaska Salmon Industry Since 1878.* Palo Alto: Stanford University, 1971.

Kovach, Michael G. *Russian Orthodox Church in Russian America.* Pittsburgh: University of Pittsburgh, 1957.

Krasheninnikov, Stepan P. *Explorations of Kamchatka, 1735–1741.* Portland: Oregon Historical Society, 1972.

Langsdorff, George H. *Voyages and Travels in Various Parts of the World.* Amsterdam: Israel, 1968.

Lantzeff, George V., and Pierce, Richard A. *Eastward to Empire.* Montreal: McGill-Queen's University, 1973.

Lazell, J. Arthur. *Alaskan Apostle: Life Story of Sheldon Jackson.* New York: Harper, 1960.

Le Bourdais, D. M. *Northward on the New Frontier.* Ottawa: Graphic, 1931.

Ledyard, John. *Journal of Captain Cook's Last Voyage.* Corvallis: Oregon University, 1963.

Lesseps, M. de. *Travels in Kamschatka During the Years 1787 and 1788.* London: Johnson, 1790.

Levin, M. G., and Potapov, L. P. *Peoples of Siberia.* Chicago: University of Chicago, 1956.

Lewis and Dryden, *Marine History of the Pacific Northwest.* Ed. E. W. Wright. New York: Antiquarian, 1961.

Life and Work of Innocent. San Francisco, 1897.

London, Jack. *Klondike Dream.* Ed. Arthur Calder Marshall. London: Bodley Head, 1966.

London, Jack. *The Sea Wolf.* Ed. Matthew J. Bruccoli. Boston: Houghton Mifflin, 1964.

MacInnes, Tom. *Klengenberg of the Arctic.* London: Cape, 1932.

Madsen, Charles, with John Scott Douglas. *Arctic Trader.* New York: Dodd, Mead, 1957.

Martin, Fredericka. *Hunting of the Silver Fleece.* New York: Greenberg, 1946.

Martin, Fredericka. *Sea Bears.* Philadelphia: Chilton, 1960.

Masik, August, and Hutchison, Isobel W. *Arctic Night's Entertainment.* London: Blakie, 1935.

Masterson, James R., and Brower, Helen. *Bering's Successors, 1745–1780: Contributions of Peter Simon Pallas to History of Russian Exploration Toward Alaska.* Seattle: University of Washington, 1948.

Matthews, Leonard Harrison. *The Whale.* London: Allen and Unwin, 1968.

McCracken, Harold. *God's Frozen Children.* New York: Doubleday, Doran, 1930.

McCracken, Harold. *Hunters of the Stormy Sea.* London: Oldbourne, 1957.

McCracken, Harold. *Roughnecks and Gentlemen.* New York: Doubleday, 1968.

Menager, Francis M., S. J. *Kingdom of the Sea.* Chicago: Loyola University, 1962.

Mikkelsen, Ejnar. *Mirage in the Arctic.* London: Rupert Hart-Davis, 1955.

Morgan, Murray. *Bridge to Russia.* New York: Dutton, 1947.

Morgan, Murray. *Dixie Raider.* New York: Dutton, 1948.

Morison, Samuel Eliot. *History of U.S. Naval Operations in World War II: Aleutians, Gilberts and Marshals, June, 1942–April, 1944.* Boston: Little, Brown, 1962.

Mortimer, George. *Observations and Remarks Made During a Voyage . . . Fox Islands.* Dublin: Bryne, 1791.

Mowatt, Farley. *The Siberians.* Baltimore: Penguin, 1970.

Neatby, L. H. *Discovery in Russian and Siberian Waters.* Athens: Ohio University, 1973.

Nelson, E. W. *The Eskimos about Bering Strait.* New York: Johnson Reprint, 1971.

Niedieck, Paul. *Cruises in the Bering Sea.* London: Ward, 1909.

Noble, Algemon. *Siberian Days.* London: Witherby, 1928.

Nordenskiöld, A. E. *Voyage of the Vega Round Asia and Europe.* London: Macmillan, 1881.

Norton, Henry Kittredge. *Far Eastern Republic of Siberia.* London: Allen and Unwin, 1923.

Okun, S. B. *Russian-American Company.* Cambridge, Mass.: Harvard University, 1951.

Olsen, Dean F. *Alaska Reindeer Herdsmen.* College: University of Alaska, 1969.

Perry, Richard. *Polar Worlds.* Newton Abbot: David and Charles, 1968.

Perry, Richard. *World of the Walrus.* London: Cassel, 1967.

Pierce, Richard A. *Russia's Hawaiian Adventure, 1815–17.* Berkeley: University of California, 1965.

Poncius, Gontran de. *Ghost Voyage.* New York: Doubleday, 1954.

Potter, Jean. *Flying North.* New York: Macmillan, 1947.

Ransom, M. A. *Sea of the Bear.* Annapolis: U.S. Navy Institute, 1964.

Rasmussen, Knud. *Report of the First Thule Expedition 1921–24.* Copenhagen: Glydendalska Boghandels, 1952.

Ray, Dorothy Jean. *Artists of the Tundra and Sea.* Seattle: University of Washington, 1961.

Rydell, Carl. *Adventures of Carl Rydell.* Ed. Elmer Green. London: Arnold, 1924.

Sage, Bryan L. *Alaska and Its Wildlife.* London: Hamly, 1973.

Saint George. *Siberia the New Frontier.* London: Hodder and Stoughton, 1969.

Sarytschew, Gawrile. *Account of a Voyage of Discovery to the North East of Siberia.* London: Phillips, 1806–7.

Sauer, Martin. *An Account of a Geographical and Astronomical Expedition to the Northern Parts of Russia, 1785–94.* London: Cadell, 1802.

Savage Landon, A. H. *Alone with Hairy Ainu or 3800 Miles on a Pack Saddle and a Cruise to the Kurile Islands.* London: Murray, 1893.

Saylor, Guy E. *Bering Sea Arbitration, 1889–1893.* Athens: Ohio University, 1935.

Scammon, Charles M. *Marine Mammals of the Northwestern Coast of North America.* New York: Dover, 1968.

Seemann, Berthold. *Narrative of the Voyage of HMS Herald, 1845–51.* London: Reeve, 1853.

Semushkin, Tikhon. *Children of the Soviet Arctic.* London: Travel Book Club, 1947.

Semyonov, Yuri. *Siberia, Its Conquest and Development.* London: Hollis and Carter, 1963.

Shelikhop, Gregory. *Voyage of . . . a Russian Merchant, from Okhatkian the Eastern Ocean to the Coast of America.* London, 1795.

Sherwood, Morgan. *Exploration of Alaska, 1865–1900.* New Haven: Yale University, 1965.

Simpson, George. *An Overland Journey Round the World . . . 1841–2.* Philadelphia: Lea & Blanchard, 1847.

Snow, H. J. *In Forbidden Seas.* London: Arnold, 1910.

Spears, John R. *Story of New England Whalers.* New York: Macmillan, 1908.

Stefansson, Vilhjalmur. *Adventure of Wrangel Island.* New York: Macmillan, 1925.

Stefansson, Vilhjalmur. *Northwest to Fortune*. New York: Duell, Sloan, and Pearce, 1958.

Stejneger, Leonhard. *George Wilhelm Steller: Pioneer of Alaskan Natural History*. Cambridge, Mass.: Harvard University, 1936.

Stuck, Hudson. *A Winter Circuit of Our Arctic Coast*. New York: Scribners, 1920.

Sukhanov, Y. *From the Urals to the Pacific*. Moscow: Progress, 1972.

Summersell, Charles G. *Journal of George Townley Fallam*. University: University of Alabama, 1973.

Swenson, Olaf. *Northwest of the World*. New York: Dodd, Mead, 1944.

Tarnovecky, Joseph. *Purchase of Alaska: Background and Reactions*. Montreal: McGill University, 1968.

Thornton, Harrison. *Among the Eskimos of Wales, Alaska, 1890–93*. Baltimore: Johns Hopkins University, 1931.

Tikkmenov, P. A. *Historical Review of the Formation of the Russian and American Company*. St. Petersburg, 1861. Trans. D. Krenov. Seattle: W.P.A., 1930.

Tilton, George Fred. *"Cap'n George Fred" Himself*. New York: Doubleday, Doran, 1929.

Tolmachoff, Innokenty P. *Siberian Passage*, New Brunswick: Rutgers University, 1949.

Tompkins, Stuart R. *Alaska, Promyshlennik and Sourdough*. Norman: University of Oklahoma, 1945.

Tronson, R. N. *Personal Narrative of a Voyage to Japan, Kamtschatka, Siberia*. London: Smith, Elder, 1859.

Tupper, Harmon. *To the Great Ocean*. Boston: Little, Brown, 1965.

Tussing, Arlon R., et al., eds. *Alaska Fisheries Policy*. Fairbanks: University of Alaska, 1972.

Underwood, John. *Alaska, an Empire in the Making*. New York: Dodd, Mead, 1913.

Vanderlip, Washington B., and Hulbert, Homer B. *In Search of a Siberian Klondike*. New York: Century, 1903.

Van Stone, James W. *Eskimos of the Nashagak*. Seattle: University of Washington, 1967.

Waxell, Sven. *The American Expedition*. London: William Hodge, 1953.

West, Ellsworth L., and Mayhew, Eleanor R. *Captain's Papers*. Barre, Mass.: Barre, 1965.

Whipple, A. B. C. *Yankee Whalers in the South Sea*. Garden City: Doubleday, 1954.

White, John Albert. *The Siberian Intervention*. Princeton: Princeton University, 1950.

Whittingham, Captain Bernard. *Notes on the Late Expedition against the Russian Settlements in Eastern Siberia*. London: Longman, Brown, 1856.

Whymper, Frederick. *Travels and Adventures in the Territory of Alaska*. New York: Harper, 1869.

William, Glyndwr. *British Search for the Northwest Passage in 18th Century*. London: Longmans, 1962.

Williams, Harold, ed. *One Whaling Family*. London: Gollancz, 1964.

Wrangel, Ferdinand von. *A Journey's Sketch, from Sitka to St. Petersburg*. St. Petersburg: Grechi, 1836.

Wrangel, Ferdinand von. *Narrative of an Expedition to the Polar Sea, 1820–23*. London: Madden, 1844.

V. PERIODICAL ARTICLES

Bank, Theodore P., II. "The Aleuts." *Explorers Journal*, October 1959, pp. 2–11.

Bank, Theodore P., II. "Botanical and Ethnobotanical Studies in the Aleutian Islands." *Michigan Academy of Science, Arts & Letters,* Vol. XXXVII, 1951.

Beavis, L. R. W. "Trading into Siberia HBC Outfit 252." *Beaver*, September 1938, pp. 36–41.

Borison, P. M. "Global Weather Modification and the Arctic Basin." *Northern Engineer*, Fall 1971, pp. 7–9.

Chard, Chester S. "The Kamchadal: A Synthetic Sketch." *Kroeber Anthropological Society Papers*, nos. 8 and 9, 1953.

Dunbar, M. J. "On the Bering Strait Scheme." *Polar Notes*, November 1960, pp. 1–17.

Dviochenko-Markov, Eufrosina. "Benjamin Franklin and Count M. A. Benyowski." *Proceedings of the American Philosophical Society*, December 1955, pp. 405–17.

Fay, Francis H. "Distribution of Waterfowl to St. Lawrence Island, Alaska." *12th Annual Report of the Wildfowl Trust*, 1961.

Fisher, Raymond H. "Dezhnev's voyage of 1648 in the Light of Soviet Scholarship." *Terrae Incognitae*, Vol. V, 1973, pp. 7–26.

Gibson, James R. "Russian America in 1833: Survey of Kirill Khlebnikov." *Pacific Northwest Quarterly*, January 1972, pp. 1–13.

Hinckley, Theodore C., and Hinckley, Caryl. "Ivan Petroff's Journal of a Trip to Alaska in 1878." *Journal of the West*, January 1966, pp. 1–46.

Hunt, William R. "Harry DeWindt." *Alaska Journal*, Summer 1971, pp. 44–46.

Hunt, William R. "To Bridge the Gap." *The Beaver*, Summer 1969, pp. 50–53.

Kenyon, Earl W., and Phillips, Richard E. "Birds From the Pribilof Islands and Vicinity." *AUK*, 18 November 1965, pp. 624–35.

Krog, John. "Notes on the Birds of Amchitka Island, Alaska." *Condor*, November–December 1953, pp. 299–304.

Kuzakov, Kuona. "Aleuts of the Komandorski Islands." *Beaver*, Summer 1963, pp. 38–41.

Lin, T. Y. "Intercontinental Peace Bridge." *Northern Engineer*, Spring 1974, pp. 15–20.

McRoy, C. Peter. "Winter Ice Studies on the Bering Sea." *Northern Engineer*, Spring 1970, p. 18.

Parry, Albert. "Washington B. Vanderlip, the 'Khan of Kamchatka.' " *Pacific Historical Review*, August 1948, pp. 311–30.

Pierce, Richard. "New Light on Ivan Petroff, Historian of Alaska." *Pacific Northwest Quarterly*, January 1968, pp. 1–10.

Quimby, George I. "Aleutian Islanders." *Chicago Natural History Museum*, Anthropology, Leaflet No. 35, 1944.

Ray, Dorothy Jean. "The Omilak Silver Mine." *Alaska Journal*, Summer 1974, pp. 142–48.

Rausch, Robert. "On the Land Mammals of St. Lawrence Island, Alaska." *Murrelet*, Vol. 34, no. 2, pp. 18–26.

Slavin, S. V. "American Expansion in the Northeast of Russia at the Beginning of the Twentieth Century." *Letopis Severa*, 1949, pp. 136–53.

Sokol, Anthony E. "The Cruise of 'Schiff 45.'" *U.S. Naval Institute Proceedings*, May 1951, pp. 477–89.

Taggart, Harold F. "Journal of George Russell Adams." *California Historical Quarterly*, December 1956, pp. 291–307.

Taggart, Harold F. "Journal of William H. Ennis." *California Historical Quarterly*, March 1942, pp. 147–68.

Van Stone, James. "V. S. Khromchenko's Coastal Explorations in Southwestern Alaska, 1822." *Fielding Anthropology*, November 1973, pp. 1–95.

Vdovin, I. S. "Politique Législative, Economique, Sociale et Culturelle de L'U.S.S.R. en Faveur du Developpement des Esquimaux et des Tchouktches." *Inter Nord*, January 1968–March 1969, pp. 113–22.

Vivier, Charles. "The Collins Overland Line and American Continentalism." *Pacific Historical Review*, August 1959, pp. 237–53.

Wrangel, F. P. "Observations on the Eskimos and Indians of Alaska." Ed. James Van Stone. *Arctic Anthropology*, Vol. XVI, no. 2, 1970, pp. 1–20.

VI. OTHER SOURCES

Collins Overland Telegraph. An unpublished sketch of the project provided by Western Union.

Extracts from the Soviet Press on the Soviet North, December 1970–November 1973.

Hood, Donald W. *Proposal for International Bering Sea Study to the National Science Foundation*, July 1972.

Meselson, S., to Hood, D. W. Letter, April 10, 1970.

Starokadomskiy, L. M. *Five Voyages in the Arctic Ocean, 1910–15.* An unpublished translation by William Barr.

INDEX

375